Performance Costume

Performance Costume: New Perspectives and Methods

Edited by
Sofia Pantouvaki and Peter McNeil

BLOOMSBURY VISUAL ARTS
LONDON • NEW YORK • OXFORD • NEW DELHI • SYDNEY

BLOOMSBURY VISUAL ARTS
Bloomsbury Publishing Plc
50 Bedford Square, London, WC1B 3DP, UK
1385 Broadway, New York, NY 10018, USA

BLOOMSBURY, BLOOMSBURY VISUAL ARTS and the Diana logo are
trademarks of Bloomsbury Publishing Plc

First published in Great Britain 2021

Cover design by www.ironicitalics.com
Cover image: 44th Karlovy Vary International Film Festival, Czech Republic, 2009.
Director/choreographer, set and lighting designer: Šimon Caban; costume designer:
Simona Rybáková. (© REUTERS/ David W Cerný)

A catalogue record for this book is available from the British Library.

A catalog record for this book is available from the Library of Congress.

ISBN: HB: 978-1-3500-9879-4
PB: 978-1-3500-9880-0
ePDF: 978-1-3500-9882-4
eBook: 978-1-3500-9881-7

Typeset by Integra Software Services Pvt. Ltd.
Printed and bound in India

To find out more about our authors and books visit www.bloomsbury.com
and sign up for our newsletters.

Table of Contents

Section 3 **Costume Voices, Costume Histories**

Snapshots

Section 4 **Costume and the Body**

Snapshots

Section 5 **Costume and its Collaborative Work**

Snapshots

Section 6 **Costume and Social Impact**

Snapshots

List of Illustrations

Figures

Table

Notes on Contributors

Editors

Sofia Pantouvaki is a scenographer and Professor of Costume Design at Aalto University, Finland. Her credits include over eighty designs for theatre, film, opera and dance productions in Europe and the curation of many international projects. She trained in scenography (PhD, University of the Arts London, UK) and specialized in design for opera at La Scala, Milan, Italy. She was a post-doctoral research fellow with the Greek State Scholarship Foundation. She is a founding editor of the international peer-reviewed journal *Studies in Costume and Performance*, Vice-Head for Research of the OISTAT Performance Design/Costume Sub-commission and Chair of *Critical Costume*. Her research includes practice-based projects and collaborations with archives, museums and collections, and focuses on the critical enquiry of costume design and making, costume curation and clothing in the concentration camps of the Second World War. Pantouvaki was costume curator for World Stage Design 2013; associate curator, *Costume in Action*, co-curator of the Finnish Student exhibit (Gold Medal at Prague Quadrennial 2015) and a jury member for Prague Quadrennial 2019. Her publications include *History of Dress: The Western World and Greece* (2010, with E. Georgitsoyanni), *Yannis Metsis: Athens Experimental Ballet* (2011), *Presence and Absence: The Performing Body* (2014, edited with A. Anderson), *Dress and Politics* (2015, edited with E. Petridou) and *The Tribes: A Walking Exhibition* (2017, with S. Lotker). Her work has been exhibited on three continents, including at World Stage Design 2017. Pantouvaki is founder of the 'Costume in Focus' research group and she also led the research project 'Costume Methodologies (2014–2018)' funded by the Academy of Finland.

Peter McNeil FAHA is an award-winning design historian who works at the University of Technology Sydney (UTS), Australia. He is a fellow of the Australian Academy of the Humanities and section head for 'The Arts'. His interdisciplinary research examines the past, present and future of critical fashion, as well as many other aspects of design with a focus on identities and material culture from the eighteenth century to the present day. For a decade he was Foundation Professor of Fashion Studies at Stockholm University, Sweden, where he worked to establish the dignity of the topic in the European university system. More recently, he was Academy of Finland Distinguished Professor (FiDiPro) at Aalto University, Finland (2014–18). His many publications include the award-winning *The Fashion History Reader: Global Perspectives*, (2010, with G. Riello) and *Fashion: Critical and Primary Sources: Renaissance to the Present Day* (4 Vols, 2009). His monograph *'Pretty Gentlemen': Macaroni Men and the Eighteenth-century Fashion World* was published in 2018. McNeil has written for exhibitions with the Sydney Jewish Museum ('Dressing Sydney') and the Los Angeles County Museum of Art ('Reigning Men'). He was awarded a UTS human rights award in 2018 for his work on visual culture and LGBTQI communities. He currently works with Indigenous Australian collaborators to develop a National Indigenous Fashion Archive with 'Right of Reply'.

Foreword authors

Maija Pekkanen is an internationally renowned Finnish costume designer. With a career spanning over four decades, Pekkanen was the resident costume designer at Helsinki City Theatre for thirty-seven years and taught the first costume module in Finland for almost twenty years, nurturing several generations of professional designers. She is a past president of the International Organization of Scenographers, Theatre Architects and Technicians (OISTAT), the first woman in this role.

Simona Rybáková is an award-winning Czech costume designer who studied at the University of Applied Arts in Prague, the University of Art and Design, Helsinki and at the Rhode Island School of Design (RISD) in Providence, USA. Her work includes designs for a wide range of performance events, film, TV and multimedia. Currently, she is the Chair of the Performance Design Commission/Costume Sub-commission of OISTAT. She curated the 'Extreme Costume' exhibition at Prague Quadrennial 2011. She was awarded the Swarovski Award '96, Prague Quadrennial 1999 Golden Triga, a Gold Award for costume design at World Stage Design 2013 Cardiff and a Bronze Award for costume design at World Stage Design 2017 in Taipei.

Contributors

Donatella Barbieri is the author of *Costume in Performance: Materiality, Culture and the Body* (2017) and a founding editor of *Studies in Costume and Performance*. Her practice-based research includes performances, workshops and installations in the UK and internationally, presented in curated and non-theatrical spaces. Over the last two decades she has pioneered approaches to making performance through costume at the London College of Fashion, University of the Arts London, UK, through her teaching, practice and publishing.

Alexandra Bonds is Professor Emerita of Costume Design at the University of Oregon, USA. An award-winning costume designer and scholar, her research focuses on contemporary theory, aesthetics, conventions and practice for costumes in traditional Beijing opera. She has conducted field research in Beijing, China and at the University of Hawaii, Manoa, USA.

Emily Brayshaw is a research associate at the University of Technology Sydney (UTS), Australia. Her research interests include fashion, textile and costume designs in France and America between 1890 and 1930, including dress and costume during the First World War and the aesthetics of kitsch. Emily also works as a lecturer and tutor at UTS and as a theatre costume designer in Sydney. She actively researches and publishes in all of these fields.

Jessica Bugg is Dean of the School of Media and Communication at the London College of Fashion, University of the Arts London, UK. She has over twenty years of teaching, leadership and research experience in graduate and post-graduate education in the UK and Australia. Her research and practice develops corporeal and embodied methods for clothing design and communication in performative contexts and extends an understanding of the performative dynamic between designers, wearers and viewers.

Vicki Ann Cremona is the Chair of the School of Performing Arts at the University of Malta. She has researched costume and theatre costume in Malta and was a consultant for the first historical costume exhibition in Malta, which traced the evolution of clothing from the seventeenth century to contemporary times. She was the main writer of the *Catalogue Raisonné* for the exhibition and co-edited the volume *Costume in Malta: A History of Fabric, Form and Fashion*. She has published internationally about carnival, Maltese theatre and *commedia dell'arte* and discusses costume in her recent book, *Carnival and Power: Play and Politics in a Crown Colony* (2018).

Sally E. Dean has been an interdisciplinary choreographer, performer, teacher and somatic practitioner for over twenty years across Europe, Asia and the USA. Sally leads the collaborative 'Somatic Movement, Costume & Performance Project' (2011), an on-going artistic research collective that designs 'somatic costumes' to elicit psychophysical awareness in wearers and generate performative experiences. Her work has been supported by the Arts Council England and the British Council and she is a doctoral candidate at Oslo National Academy of the Arts (KHiO), Norway.

Mateja Fajt studied scene design at the Academy of Theatre, Radio, Film and Television, Ljubljana, Slovenia. She is an emerging costume designer, working in the fields of theatre and film costume design, as well as an independent researcher. Her research interest is in the intersection of costume, hierarchies and class.

Jennifer Gall is Acting Curator of Documents and Artefacts at the National Film and Sound Archive of Australia and a visiting fellow at the Australian National University Research School of the Humanities and Arts. Her research focuses on the history of costume design in Australian film. Her recent exhibitions include 'Starstruck: Australian Movie Portraits' (2018–19) and 'The Dressmaker' (2019).

Veronica Isaac is currently a university lecturer and freelance consultant and spent seven years as an assistant curator in the Department of Theatre and Performance, Victoria and Albert Museum (V&A), UK. Her research specialism is historic dress and theatre costume and her recent publications include 'Towards a New Methodology for Working with Historic Theatre Costume: A Biographical Approach focusing on Ellen Terry's "Beetlewing Dress"' for *Studies in Costume and Performance* (2017) and 'Costume' for the *Oxford Handbook of Opera* (2014).

Christina M. Johnson is Associate Curator of the FIDM Museum at the Fashion Institute of Design & Merchandising, Los Angeles, USA. She received her BA in Art History from the University of California, Los Angeles and her MA in Visual Culture: Costume Studies from New York University, USA.

Chrisi Karvonides-Dushenko has more than twenty-five years of experience as a professional costume designer in theatre, film and television. In 2003, she received an Emmy for her costume design work on NBC's *American Dreams*, along with seven Emmy and Costume Designers Guild Award nominations. She has also designed for three feature films, dozens of television series, several theatrical productions in US theatres, including on Broadway, and operas for both American and European opera houses.

Michiko Kitayama Skinner is originally from Tokyo and has designed scenery and costumes for over twenty years. Michiko has worked with prominent designers and directors such as Paul Tazewell, Amon Miyamoto and Nilo Cruz. Her design of *Woyzeck* entered the 2003 Prague Quadrennial. She is currently working on a new piece, a collaboration between Oslo and Miami about immigration. Michiko is an associate professor at the University of Miami, USA and belongs to Local USA 829.

Viveka Kjellmer is a senior lecturer in Art History and Visual Studies at the University of Gothenburg, Sweden. She has written about advertising and the image of scent, fashion exhibitions and visual consumption. Her current research concerns costume, the body and scenography, as well as the relations between olfaction, architecture and space.

Christina Lindgren has designed costume and scenography for performances in all genres. She studied at Oslo National Academy of the Arts (KHiO), Norway, and Universität der Künste Berlin, Germany. She is Professor in Costume Design at the KHiO and a leader of the artistic research project 'Costume Agency' (2018–21).

Keith Lodwick is Curator of Theatre and Screen Arts at the Victoria and Albert Museum, UK. He has contributed to a number of V&A and international publications including *Oliver Messel: In the Theatre of Design* (2011), *Hollywood Costume* (2012), *Alexander McQueen: Savage Beauty* (2015) and *Vivien Leigh: Actress and Icon* (2017). Keith was the V&A curator for the major exhibition 'Hollywood Costume', which examined 100 years of costume design for film.

Margaret Mitchell is Professor of Theatre at the University of the Incarnate Word in San Antonio, Texas, USA. She is a co-author of *Making the Scene: A History of Stage Design and Technology in Europe and the United States*and a general editor of *Theatre Design and Technology*. Margaret has worked as a freelance costume and scenic designer for thirty-one years.

Aoife Monks is a reader in Theatre Studies at Queen Mary, University of London, UK. She is the author of *The Actor in Costume* and co-author (with Ali Maclaurin) of *Costume: Readings in Theatre Practice*. She has recently worked on the exhibition and catalogue 'Costume at the National Theatre' with the costume department at the National Theatre in London.

Alexandra Murray-Leslie is an artist, researcher, performer and co-founder of the international art collective Chicks on Speed. Her artistic research and practice explores designing, fabricating and performing computer-enhanced footwear for a new theatrical, audiovisual expressivity of the feet, underwater, on land and in the air. She undertook her PhD at the Creativity and Cognition Studios, University of Technology Sydney, Australia and is currently guest Professor of Art Science at Trondheim Academy of Fine Arts, the Norwegian University of Science and Technology.

Deborah Nadoolman Landis, Director, UCLA David C. Copley Center for Costume Design, USA, is the costume designer of many iconic films, including *The Blues Brothers* (1980), *Raiders of the Lost Ark* (1981), Michael Jackson's *Thriller* (1983), *Trading Places* (1983) and *Coming to America* (1988) for which she was nominated for an Academy Award. Landis has authored six books including *Hollywood Costume* (2012), the award-winning catalogue for the blockbuster V&A exhibition. She is also the Editor-in-Chief of the *Bloomsbury Encyclopedia of Film and Television Costume Design* (2020).

Suzanne Osmond is a course leader and senior lecturer at the National Institute of Dramatic Art in Sydney, Australia. She has been costume supervisor and coordinator for diverse projects including the Asian Games in Doha, the Sydney Olympics Opening Ceremony, *The Lion King* and *Love Never Dies* in Australia. She is an editor for *Studies in Costume and Performance*. In 2017, she was post-doctoral research fellow within the funded 'Costume Methodologies' research project at Aalto University, Finland.

Delphine Pinasa is an art historian and currently Director of the Centre National de Costume de Scène, France. She has worked for the V&A, the Ministry of Culture and the Opéra national de Paris from 1993 to 2003, including as Head of the Costume Patrimony department beginning in 2001. A specialist in stage costume, Delphine has published and curated many exhibitions in France and abroad. Since 2005, with the exhibition *Rouge* at the Paris Opera Library-Museum, she has collaborated regularly with Christian Lacroix.

Natalie Rewa is Professor of Drama in the Dan School of Drama and Music at Queen's University, Canada. She is the author of *Scenography in Canada: Selected Designers* (2004). She was also co-curator of the Canadian delegation to the Prague Quadrennial 2007, and co-editor of the catalogue *Imprints of Process* (2007–08), editor of *Design and Scenography* (2009) and 'Costumes and Costuming' *Canadian Theatre Review* 152 (2013). Her research has appeared in *Canadian Theatre Review, Theatre Research in Canada, Australasian Studies* and *Scene*.

Drake Stutesman is the Conference Director at the Barrymore Film Center, Fort Lee, USA. She teaches theoretical approaches to film costume at New York University, USA, where she co-organized a biennial film costume conference. She edits the peer-reviewed cinema and media journal *Framework* and has published on costume, literature and other topics. She is the author of *Hat: Origins, Language, Style* (Reaktion Books, 2019) and she is writing biographies of costume designer Clare West and milliner Mr. John. She holds a PhD on the work of experimental writer Susan Howe.

Madeline Taylor is a costume creator and researcher. A lecturer in Fashion at Queensland University of Technology, and a doctoral candidate at the University of Melbourne, Australia, her primary research focus is collaboration during costume design realization. Other research interests include alternative modes of engaging with fashion, performance design history and the interpersonal dynamics of theatre. She contributed to both volumes of *World Scenography*, the second as Australian editor, and has published in *Behind the Scenes* and *Clothing Cultures*.

Melissa Trimingham has a background in professional theatre as a designer and maker, and is a senior lecturer in drama at the University of Kent, UK. Her interests are contemporary performance, puppetry and applied theatre. She is co-investigator on the AHRC project 'PlayingA/Part: Autistic Girls, Identities and Creativity' (2018–2021).

Merja Väisänen is a costume designer and a university lecturer in costume design at the School of Arts, Design and Architecture, Aalto University, Finland. She has been an award-winning costume designer for film and television since 1988. Her artistic research relates to hospital clowns' costumes.

Fausto Viana is a set and costume design professor in the School of Communication and Arts at São Paulo University (USP), Brazil. He gained his doctoral degree in Arts (2004) at USP and an additional doctoral degree in Museology (2010) at the Lusófona University of Humanities and Technologies, Portugal. He has written, among other books, *The Theatrical Costume and the Renovations of the 20th Century* (in Portuguese, 2010).

Helen Margaret Walter completed her PhD in the history of design at the Royal College of Art and the V&A. She teaches at Plymouth University and the University for the Creative Arts, Epsom, UK. Her research explores the intersection between dress, performance and identity in images of late Victorian actor-managers and she has published articles on this subject in *Costume*, *Visual Culture in Britain* and *Studies in Costume and Performance*. She is currently researching the role of theatrical performance in the creation of fashion archives and museum collections.

Joanna Weckman is an independent post-doctoral costume researcher, exhibition curator, lecturer and costume designer from Finland. Her recent publications include 'A Printed Thought: Treatment of Materials in the History of Finnish Stage Costumes' (2019) and '*Toisen näköinen: Roolihahmon etnisyyden rakentaminen maskeerauksen avulla sotien välisen ajan Suomen näyttämöille?*' (Looking like the other: Creating ethnic characters with the help of make-up practices for early Finnish stage performances, 2018).

Clare M. Wilkinson is Associate Professor of Anthropology at Washington State University, USA, after earning her PhD at the University of Pennsylvania, USA. She has been studying art, creativity and culture in India for many years, most recently focusing on how costume production is understood and organized in the Hindi film industry, popularly known as 'Bollywood'. Her book on this research, titled *Fashioning Bollywood: Costume and Culture in the Hindi Film Industry* was published in 2013.

Foreword

Maija Pekkanen

My good friend for decades, the Japanese costume designer Kazue Hatano, gave me a small gift many years ago: a kaleidoscope. When I turn the cylinder, the colourful figure inside changes form. It is always different.

In our everyday work, we – costume designers – face similar situations: we must change our point of view and find new ways to solve problems. The contributors to this book offer us a wide range of models to think about. Thinking, after all, is the most important tool in creative work.

Today, the term 'performance costume' covers all kinds of costume design, from traditional theatre costumes to costumes for carnival or opening ceremonies of sports events, even for the prominent Olympic Games.

Performance Costume: New Perspectives and Methods is a collection of chapters and shorter 'snapshots' or focused reflections highlighting the diversity of costume-related issues that interest costume designers, educators, researchers and curators. Its authors come from twelve countries and even within the pages of this book they constitute a network. This virtual, but also print-based, network therefore aptly replenishes the over twenty-year-old international 'Costume Working Group', known today as the 'Costume Sub-Commission' of Performance Design of OISTAT (International Organization of Scenographers, Theatre Architects and Technicians). The aim of such global dialogue is to cut across national, linguistic and cultural borders, bring about change and new ideas, provoke thinking, generate dialogue and create opportunities to meet face-to-face, in order to share and to learn. Costume design as a profession is certainly a life-long learning process, dynamic and transformative for both practitioners and world cultures in general.

Many costume designers work alongside their professional design practice as tertiary design educators, teaching costume design at universities and colleges, offering the next generation of costume designers the benefit of their instruction and sharing their inherent experience and expertise. Some are also researchers of costume history, or they research costume in many related and adjacent areas including textiles, technologies, crafts, visual culture and ethnography. Research is in fact one of the most important tools that costume designers use in everyday practice. For some, research becomes a passion and develops further to be shared within the larger professional and scholarly community.

To collect and publish a book on the diverse and multi-faceted themes that costume, as a practice and profession, addresses, including practical as well as theoretical and historical approaches, has long been the dream and passion of Dr Sofia Pantouvaki, Professor and Costume Designer at Aalto University, Finland, who has edited the vast material compiled here, together with Distinguished Professor Peter McNeil of the University of Technology Sydney, Australia. This book is the outcome of a four-year project supported by the Academy of Finland.

The work therefore also bears witness to the imagination and rigour of the Finnish higher education system, as well as Aalto University and all of its expert departments and staff – academic and professional – which hosted, supported and encouraged the production of this new collection of knowledge. Now, it is time to share it with the global community.

Helsinki, May 2020

Foreword

Simona Rybáková

Costume design is a complex discipline. The world-renowned stage designer Josef Svoboda (1920–2002) notes in an interview with Jarka Burian:

> You know, it was clear to me in those days already that studying only stage design is not enough. I believe that stage designers should also have studied a classical discipline before – such as painting or architecture. [Designers] must be 'complete persons' who keep on educating themselves, especially in music, literature and all art disciplines in order for them to do theatre. (Příhodová 2014)[1]

Svoboda speaks of the 'complete person', a state towards which every good costume designer should aim.

The book you now hold in your hands is a significant resource and a major contribution to creating and perceiving this very complexity contained in the field of costume design.

In this volume we find diverse, yet complementary, perspectives on costume. It enables costume designers to view and reflect on their own work, place it firmly in the context of current developments in the discipline, gain inspiration and be educated by a wide variety of contemporary studies that address both the theoretical and practical aspects of costume.

Even though I myself have been active in the field of costume design for decades, entering into academia through my practice-based doctoral dissertation on alternative costumes helped me to open new doors and see afresh undiscovered layers of this field. Thanks to international conferences, festivals and other events focused on costume design, including the *Costume Methodologies* FiDiPro research project wherein this book was generated, I had the opportunity to become familiar with the work and research of many of my colleagues – who are also part of this book. The presentations at the Critical Costume conferences in the UK and Finland in 2013, 2015 and 2018 focused on the latest developments in thinking about performance costume in relation to the human body, debated costume as an object within the wider practice of installation and explored the curating and exhibition of costume. They also spoke of new technologies, as well as of the political, cultural and social elements of costume around the world.

The longstanding work of the OISTAT's Costume Design Sub-Commission and the considerable increase of interest in the group's activities and programme in recent years demonstrate that costume design is an essential domain within contemporary artistic production. Its emancipatory efforts have now allowed us to surpass the limitations that were formerly imposed by considering costume as mere applied arts or decoration. We are in a unique stage in theatre and visual arts development wherein costume design has been elevated, significantly expanding its field of possibilities and enabling it now to bear whole new aesthetics.

A costume can not only determine the habitus of actors and their bodies, but also that of an entire play or project, just as it can express an artistic idea or define the theatre's visual identity.

Costume design as a distinctive discipline, unlike the rapidly expanding field of fashion research, has not previously been marked by much publishing that reflects its role within the field of theatre, dance or film. This volume therefore furnishes a significant enrichment for our expert 'library', as well as reaching new readers who work in inter-disciplinary ways.

The dictionary of technical terms in our field is constantly changing and developing and English terms dominate because they better capture the reality of an Anglophone globe. Many other world languages adopt English terms almost automatically. In form and content, this book aims to encourage the dissemination of wider languages, terminologies and thought patterns through its international community of contributors. It is an important addition on these terms alone.

I feel deep gratitude to all who contributed to the making of this book with their practice, scholarly experiences and 'know how': they now share this passion for the field of costume design. Designers, historians, scholars, curators, performers, technicians, educators and makers whose fields overlap into many other disciplines and practices, too, have authored this book. The greatest acknowledgment and thanks belongs to Sofia Pantouvaki, who, in cooperation with Peter McNeil, has constantly and tirelessly demonstrated, as can be seen here, her expert erudition across both theory and praxis, inspiring others to think about these topics and the connections between them.

Prague, May 2020

Note

1 Příhodová, B. (ed.) (2014), *Scénografie mluví: Hovory Jarky Buriana s Josefem Svobodou* (*Scenography Speaks: Conversations of Jarka Burian with Josef Svoboda*), Brno: Nakladatelství Masarykovy univerzity (Masaryk University Press).

Acknowledgements

This volume developed from the research project 'Costume Methodologies: Building Methodological Tools for the Field of Costume Design' funded by the Academy of Finland (2014–18) within the Finland Distinguished Professor (FiDiPro) scheme by Principal Investigator Sofia Pantouvaki and FiDiPro Professor Peter McNeil. The work was based in the Department of Film, Television and Scenography at the School of Arts, Design and Architecture, Aalto University. We would like to express our thanks to the Head of Department, Anna Heiskanen, for her support throughout this work. We would also like to thank our language editor, Bettina Exner Mara and our editorial assistant, Alexandra Ovtchinnikova, for her tireless support in the preparation of this volume, often beyond her formal role.

We express our greatest debt to all the contributing authors who enthusiastically entrusted us with their research; without them, this volume would not have existed. We also extend our thanks to the many individual photographers, designers and institutions who generously granted us permission to use their photographs and artworks gratis.

Finally, we would also like to thank our editorial director at Bloomsbury Visual Arts, Frances Arnold for her wholehearted encouragement and considerate support; Yvonne Thouroude, assistant editor; Deborah Maloney, project manager, and the entire production management team for having helped us so patiently and efficiently throughout the process.

Sofia Pantouvaki and Peter McNeil

Introduction

Activating Costume: A New Approach to Costume for Performance

Sofia Pantouvaki and Peter McNeil

Costume is an active agent for performance-making on stage, screen and beyond. It is a material object that dresses the performing body and embodies ideas shaped through complex networks of collaboration, creativity and artistic work.

Although it has been omnipresent in the practice of performance since antiquity, methods for the analysis of costume on a scholarly level remain tentative. This might seem surprising and it relates in part to the complexity of theatrical performance, which is rarely authored by one individual, a model that came to characterize post-Renaissance art. Performance is also ephemeral; costume was not always valued in aesthetic, dramaturgical or monetary terms (although at times costumes were the main source of portable wealth for a performance troupe). Theatre studies, and in the past century, film studies, have tended to privilege text, space, acting (word and kinesics) and reception, but not costume itself, despite its vital relationship to the performer's body as a contributor to and often a generator of their performance. Costume is often thought of by public and academic audiences alike as the grand gesture, the artistic trace or as an integral part of the *mise en scène*. We remember performances through images of actors or dancers in costumes, but we think much less about how the costume came to be, was worn and activated performance itself.

In recent years, coinciding with the 'material', 'embodied' and other cultural 'turns' that have highlighted new ways of thinking through culture, costume has been re-connected in new and exciting ways to theories of the body and embodiment, wider design practices including process studies, co-design and other forms of collaboration, renewed practical and theoretical studies of artistic creation and developments in teaching and learning in international educational settings. Costume, like fashion and dress, is now viewed as an area of dynamic social significance and not simply as a passive reflector of a pre-conceived social state or practice. Nor is it seen anymore as being 'in service of' performance in a subordinate role, but rather as a central contributor to an often-renewed sense of collective practice, proposing new directions in turn, to the making of performance itself. There, costume becomes a catalyst as well as a subject and object of study.

This volume proposes precisely the above. It sets out an alternative vision for exploring costume across time, place and context. How should knowledge about costume be connected to other domains of knowledge and human experience? How do archives and collections function as much more than simply resources and repositories of and for costume design? What methods and approaches are most appropriate for a twenty-first-century field and how can they be combined in multi-modal ways characteristic of cognate areas of study in the contemporary university or training ground?

As this book attests, costume as a field and disciplinary practice is finding new theoretical tools and investigative frameworks. The volume therefore departs from previous literature in the field, which tended to study the more visual and finalized aspects of costume. Instead, we return to the core of costume – its design practice – highlighting the voice and experience of practitioners, but also place it in dialogue with the many cognate disciplines that inform, illuminate and propel costume forward. These include well-established disciplines such as art history, social history, theatre studies and theatre pedagogy, film studies, performance theory, reception theory, cultural studies, museum studies, anthropology, design studies, haptics and kinesics by a wide range of academics and other cultural workers including those employed in design, theatre and the performing arts, film, television and curation. Our study therefore proposes new perspectives and connections regarding the analysis of costume as a dynamic field, as well as fresh viewpoints on the well-established frames of historical, theoretical, practice-based and archival research into costume for performance on the stage, screen and street. This book offers new insights into existing practices, as well as creating a space of connection between practitioners and researchers from design, the humanities and social sciences. In so doing, it aims to contribute towards a new understanding of how costume actually 'performs' in time and space and how costume shapes cultural and social ideas, even new representations of humanity, including multiplicities and intersections of racial, gendered, post-colonial and sexual identities.

The work draws on the experience of established researchers, as well as emerging voices from across the world. We are proud to bring together voices from four continents. The urge to unite global work in an English-language publication is challenging, as language itself is precise and culturally specific. We thank our multi-lingual writers for agreeing to the stimulating journey the reader now finds resolved here. The book therefore introduces diverse perspectives, intra- and trans-national positions, innovative new research methods and approaches for researching design and the costumed body in performance. Such approaches investigate costume design as both a practice and a means of representation with historical, cultural, social, pedagogical, communicative, political and somatic dimensions.

Divided into six parts, the volume provides readers with a critical and contemporary understanding of costume in a diversity of contexts.

Part One, 'Interpreting and Curating Costume', offers methods for the study of visual and textual sources as well as moving images and takes into consideration cultural variation and historical and social context. The authors here address the materiality and visuality of costume in constructing representations of character and social realities. They also discuss costume as a part of cultural heritage and propose models for reflecting on its ephemerality and network of creation through new curation and exhibition strategies.

Part Two, 'Personalities in Costume' focuses on how costume constructs identities on and off the stage and becomes a carrier of memory. The contributions to this part propose that costume embodies narratives for self-representation and offer methods for this analysis through material culture and cultural studies.

Part Three, 'Costume Voices, Costume Histories' interprets the oral record and brings into discourse the voice and experience of the costume designer. How do professional networks and structures enable or sometimes inhibit the work of the costume designer? The authors here engage explicit and implicit oral narratives and empirical and ethnographic approaches to bring new insights to understanding costume and its inter-linked structures, context and modes of production in numerous national settings, genres and formats.

Part Four, 'Costume and the Body' addresses costume practice as research through the prism of practice-based and practice-led research and phenomenology. This is particularly pertinent to performance-making today in the field of live performance. The authors propose somatic and body-centred approaches to exploring the agency of costume from an experiential, embodied perspective via materiality and the creation of costume-based performance.

Part Five, 'Costume and its Collaborative Work' centres on the collaborative skills and partnerships involved in the creation of costume and transfer of tacit knowledge. How do new conceptualizations of collaboration and co-creation allow new meanings of costume to emerge? The authors here propose models to analyse the communication practices involved in the exchange undertaken within collaborative teams and address the competence required to create a space of collaboration where costume is a central driving force.

Finally, Part Six, 'Costume and Social Impact' approaches costume as a social agent in contemporary societies. What are the cultural politics of costume and its potential for psychological and social benefits? The authors suggest ways in which costume functions as a tool for learning and social integration and how it effects social change in different formats, especially in relation to youth. These contributions provide evidence of how costume can generate ambiguity, going beyond conventional formats of gender and sexuality and becoming in turn, a tool for active participation, emancipation and self-exploration.

This material engages well-established and leading voices from the field of costume for performance on stage, film and television in a new dialogue with the emerging voices of practitioners and scholars from a wide range of other fields. The authors represent numerous international networks related to costume that meet and interact on a regular basis and many of these interactions are captured here in new and fruitful ways. They include the International Organization of Scenographers, Theatre Architects and Technicians (OISTAT) and especially its Performance Design: Costume Sub-Commission, as well as the recently established international platform for costume research 'Critical Costume'. Most contributors to this volume have been founders or members of these associations, or have been invited to join events related to these networks, which was very much the avenue through which the contents of this book were developed. All of this has been activated, enabled, tested and re-framed within the major European international research project 'Costume Methodologies: Building Methodological Tools for the Field of Costume Design', a four-year project (2014–18) funded by the Academy of Finland within the Finland Distinguished Professor (FiDiPro) scheme, hosted by Aalto University. The aim of this scheme is to connect Finnish researchers with 'know how' and expertise found elsewhere, and in this case, a Greek national working in Finland, Sofia Pantouvaki, worked with an Australian citizen, Peter McNeil, within a genuinely global scenario made possible by Finnish research policy. The 'Costume Methodologies' project enabled a series of international events, including the 'Critical Costume 2015' conference and exhibition in Helsinki (25–27 March 2015), the 'Thinking Costume' seminar at World Stage Design 2017 in Taipei (6–7 July 2017) as well as over thirty workshops, seminars and the international travel of both full-time researchers and doctoral candidates alike. Through this research ecology, the vast majority of contributors to this work met, discussed, debated and eventually developed the work presented in this volume, which was based on their current research or on a critical reappraisal of their work in light of new perspectives on costume research.

Ranging across time and place, from the actress on the Victorian stage to design for high-quality contemporary TV, from high-budget film production to experimental performance practice or the street, this book is unusual for its range, which combines historical perspectives with contemporary practice, as well as both practical and theoretical engagement with costume. It is a truly international volume in terms of contributors, content and scope. The book unlocks notions of conceptualization of costume, what costume 'is' and what costume 'does' and therefore how costume can be approached, working towards a deeper understanding of costume and its role, function, agency and potential. It also invites readers, practitioners and researchers in other fields to consider issues of the terminology and articulation of costume for future debate within wider scholarly thought, deliberation and discussion. Such work enables a new awareness and dignity for costume when it is considered in and on its own terms.

Section 1

Interpreting and Curating Costume

1.1 Real or Virtual? Studying Historical Costume Drawings and Sketches

Margaret Mitchell

Introduction

Historical drawings, paintings and engravings depicting historical costume designs pose risks, limitations and benefits to the researcher. These artefacts cannot begin to be understood without written and additional visual materials that give a context to their uses.[1] Even with well-rounded written and visual documentation, the modern researcher is usually left with only a partial story or understanding of the research subject. This chapter will identify various lines of inquiry used to resurrect the possible original life of a historic costume design with a focus on analysing images. It discusses obstacles and assumptions that confront the researcher and offers suggestions for understanding what can be known and what will remain unknown about a particular costume research subject. It also points to the impossibility of a wholly net- or web-based approach to comprehensive research about a costume image or artefact.

The Researcher and the Survivor

Primary-source historic costume drawings offer the modern researcher a physical bridge to the past. Researchers today spend a great deal of time on the internet studying images of archival materials which are immediately accessible in digital formats. Digital images are made of light waves; when it comes to digital images that are digital reproductions of hardcopy images (e.g. costume drawings), they are images made of images, removed by at least two degrees from the viewer. The first degree away from the human eye is the camera lens that captured the digital image. The second degree away from the human eye is the image transmitted on the computer screen. Image resolution in the central focus of the average human eye is greater than the image resolution of a camera or of a typical computer screen (Wright 1989: 53). Because the naked human eye and brain have degrees of resolution, but no pixilation variances to dissect when viewing a physical object, the naked eye has a greater capacity to view an object in person versus viewing an object on a screen or in a reprinted format (Wright 1989: 53). Colour variances on monitors, flicker fusion frequency (Ramamurthy and Lakshminarayanan 2017), screen brightness, environmental illumination and display equipment capacities also provide wide varieties of image distortion. However, on-line research and digital reproductions provide positive features: often the first publication of an image, visual magnification, comparative images in multiple archival collections and rough language translation. However, studying the actual costume drawing allows us to see and regard the design in the same spatial relationship and with the same tool, the human eye, as its original artist. In the presence of the artefact we have no visual separation or distortion caused by digital screens. Even if a researcher cannot physically touch a historical costume drawing, it can still be magnified and scrutinized with lenses and the human eye; both of these are more perceptive than seeing within a digital non-physical format that acts as a mediator. In the presence of an actual costume drawing, we have a sense of scale. We, in the present relate to the object spatially and visually as the artist did in the past.

From the time a costume drawing was made, until the time we open an archival box in a museum or library, the drawing has been handled by multiple people, possibly altered by multiple people, and it has existed through periods of care or neglect or both. The paint, pencil or ink colours and graphite marks are perhaps dulled or damaged by time, but we can engage with the drawing on a human scale and begin to attempt to unpack the story of the costume drawing from the point of least distortion: its current physical reality. The journey through time may affect inquiries of study.

The Study of Visual Images

Authenticating the creation of the image in time and space is the first step to contextual placement. If the artist is known, locating and dating the image is usually somewhat easier than working with a costume drawing of unknown authorship. Works housed in museum archives often, but certainly not always have been accessioned or catalogued (many collections have partial inventories, uncatalogued works, new acquisitions and also mistaken attributions in old hands, etc). Such records record a hierarchy of information, including attempts to identify authorship. If the artist is known, the second contextual issue is the placement of a particular artwork within the artist's total body of work (known as the *oeuvre* in conventional art history). It may be important to understand if the work in question is late, early or climactic in the artist's career. Biographical reference sources for artists living before the nineteenth century are sometimes less detailed depending on the status and the nature of record holding for that particular individual, but even in the Western European eighteenth century the famous 'salons' recorded precise information as to the names of artists and titles of works. Such information is also found in much older Chinese works for example and must be assessed within the frames of convention, the status of art practice, the nature of studios, the prevalence of copying and many other social and cultural factors.

Cross-referencing general source material with more detailed documents such as letters, inventories, bills of sales and public records can aid in dating and locating an artist and a costume drawing. If a work is not signed or stamped with an authentic and original signature or mark, more detective work is in order. Similar works by known artists can be compared, but in some cases, definitive artist identity may remain unknown. In many cases in the past, the costume design drawing was anonymous or carried a sense of authorship that differed from our modern perceptions. Often the person commissioning the work was socially more important than the designer and design decisions were greatly influenced by a patron.[2]

The available technology that was used to create the costume drawing is the essential baseline for generalized identification. The identification of papers, canvas materials, graphite, charcoal, ink and colour media may help the researcher understand ranges of time periods and locations. For example, a costume drawing painted with a mauve aniline dye could not have existed prior to 1856 and likely not prior to the late nineteenth century.[3] Written records in museum archives should be scrutinized to understand media technology used in the drawing. Further complications in assessing media can arise when it is hypothesized that the original drawing has been altered through time. The researcher must determine whether or not all media used is original and at what points in time the drawing may have been altered. Once the physical object is understood, the researcher understands at the very least what the artwork is not.

Art is never purely mimetic, even if a painting or drawing is rendered in the style of 'realism', a much-debated topic itself in the nineteenth century following the development of photography. A costume drawing may have been the wellspring of the designer's original idea or it may have been produced after the performance for publication or presentation. Without photographs or an extant costume for comparative study, researchers must approach a costume design as a highly interpretative work with varying relationships to reality.

Costume researchers also investigate and use historical portraits in their work. Historical portraiture is often used for design inspiration and information as well as for contextualization and corroboration with a specific historical period. Unless a photograph or physical garment in a painting is extant and can be compared to the painting, the modern researcher has no way of knowing whether or not a painter was depicting the subject accurately. Even if a garment exists, it too may have experienced changes over time.[4] The artist employs his or her interpretative style (and perhaps biases) and it is very possible that the person who commissioned the painting also had some control over the painter's decisions. Primary source written documentation describing clothing style and materials may also be used in a comparative study, but such detailed written inventories are more typical among royal, noble, mercantile and other wealthy subjects. Letters, pawn documents, bills of sale of clothing, tailoring services, wills, as well as the sale of human beings if they were wearing clothes are more common sources relating to merchants, artisans, labourers and slaves. For understanding the demotic (everyday) view of performance, historians make use of songs, ditties, broadsheets (early types of prints hung in public) and other forms of popular culture including oral traditions.

A Case Study: A Study of a Costume Design for *Récit de l'Amérique* in *Ballet Royal du Grand Bal de la Drouairière de Billebahaut*

The unsigned costume design for *Récit de l'Amérique* (Story of America) (Figure1.1.1), created in France for two performances in the early seventeenth century and now housed in the Robert L. B. Tobin Theatre Arts Collection at the McNay Art Museum in San Antonio, Texas, is a curious expression of the Native Peoples of the New World/ the Americas. This design was discovered with 187 other costume

Figure 1.1.1 *Costume for* Recit de l'Amerique, *Tobin Archives TL1990.10.1.3, McNay Art Museum. Courtesy of McNay Art Museum.*

designs which were from a larger grouping of approximately 239 designs for entertainments that took place at the French court of King Louis XIII between 1614 and 1634 (McGowan 1986). Of the 188 costume sketches, twenty-seven of them can be attributed to the *Ballet Royal du Grand Bal de la Drouairière de Billebahaut* (Ballet of the Grand Ball of the Dowager of Bilbao), which was performed in Paris in February of 1626. As part of this entertainment, a pageant entitled 'The Four Parts of the World' included *Récit de l'Amerique.* This title is inscribed in the upper-right-hand corner of the sketch. The designer is documented as Daniel Rabel, or an unknown artist from his *atelier* (studio or workshop).

Asking Questions and Identifying the Lens of the Researcher

Upon encountering this image, the following general questions arise:

1 Is this sketch Daniel Rabel's or is it from his *atelier*?

2 Is the sketch a copy of an earlier work?

3 Do the physical properties of the sketch match the dates of the documented performances?
4 Are there multiple documents or sources that can be used to place this sketch in a context?
5 What was the original function of the sketch?

Conducting research is in part a process of curiosity; questions beget more questions and sometimes our prejudices can lead us to assumptions that have little to do with the truth and everything to do with hopeful speculations. Studying a time period or place beyond our lived experience may lead us to imagine in detail what it might have been like to be in that place and time, but a researcher can never really know the truth in totality, of another place and time. To assert absolute certainty based on partial evidence outside of a lived experience is a romantic exercise of interpretation. Awareness of bias (also known as 'subject position') and intellectual circumnavigation of the subject lead to richer and more nuanced interpretations. My biases – or indeed my interests – related to this sketch are as follows:

1 There is a desire to prove the sketch is not a copy.
2 There is a desire to discover the biases of the artist.
3 There is a desire to discover the sources the artist used in order to make design decisions about the costume.
4 The researcher has admired this sketch for many years.
5 The researcher has a contemporary bias regarding current issues around imperialist appropriation of the cultures of Native Peoples.

Biases two and four are particularly leading. Bias two cannot be factually and completely discovered unless a large amount of introspective primary research exists that was generated by the artist. Bias four is completely subjective and although admiration may fuel the motivation to conduct the research, it may also prejudice the researcher during study. Bias five assumes that the artist or his or her audience may have had an imperialist nature and the researcher looks at the work through a modern cultural lens, which may or may not be appropriate or analogous.

The Sources and Context

René Bordier's libretto for the *Ballet Royal du Grand Bal de la Drouairière de Billebahaut* includes songs and speeches as well as descriptions of dances and costumes; however, it is an incomplete document. Primary source materials related to Daniel Rabel's costume work are housed in archives at the Bibliothèque nationale de France and the Louvre in Paris, the Victoria and Albert Museum (V&A) in London, the Morgan Library and Museum and the Metropolitan Museum of Art in New York City, the Getty Research Institute in Los Angeles and the McNay Art Museum in San Antonio. Some Rabel ballet costume designs are owned by private collectors and galleries. Multiple locations of archival materials provide contextual corroboration and possibly complications for the researcher. A major secondary source is Margaret McGowan's 1986 exhibition catalogue, *The Court Ballet of Louis XIII : A Collection of Working Designs, 1615–1633*.

One of the first contextual issues is to discover whether the drawing is an original sketch, or if it is a copy, or the base sketch for other copies. Processional drawings for the pageant for this ballet exist in the *Cabinet des Dessins* of the Louvre and at the Bibliothèque nationale. The Louvre drawings, acquired in 1775 are considered to be the primary work and the ninety-three drawings acquired in 1896 in the Bibliothèque nationale are considered to be the copies of the Louvre material.[5] The Louvre and the Bibliothèque nationale drawings show costumed characters in groups and were likely executed after the performances, probably for commemorative purposes.[6] Neither archive contains the total number of sketches researchers believe existed in 1626. The Metropolitan Museum acquired a drawing in 1960 of *Récit de l'Amerique* depicting two male dancers. In 1985, another set of drawings was discovered in a library in Germany. Professor McGowan argues that these sketches served as working drawings for the ballet and were executed for the workshop personnel:

> Nearly every drawing in the collection is heavily annotated, sometimes by three or four hands, and these indications furnish us with a unique fund of information about some of the practical issues involved in the production of the Court Ballets. (McGowan 1986: 3)

Indeed, these drawings are different from the previously known sets. They are detailed, but they are not tightly finished. Of the six extant total drawings depicting the American portion of the ballet, five of the drawings have a high level of finishing. The drawing in the Tobin archive is coloured with a loose transparent wash and in general it does not have tight detail finishing. The more recently discovered drawings found in Germany contain instructions for construction or for changes to the original design, indicating the designs were used more than once and changed with subsequent uses (McGowan 1986: 5). The Tobin drawing within this group bears the directive 'make in these colours'. This instruction indicates that at some point in time a function of this particular drawing was a roadmap for costume makers, used in the same way as most costume sketches are used today. It is the only drawing in this set depicting a character from the American portion of the ballet. To date, it appears that the Tobin drawing is a one-of-a-kind original and no known copy has come to public attention.

The Physical Artefact

Close examination reveals that the 11 5/16" X 7 ½" sketch is an original drawing and not a hand coloured print.[7] The figure is drawn with pen and ink and in some areas graphite may be beneath the ink. The sketch has two numbers, one in the upper-right-hand corner, which appears to be original and one graphite number in the top centre of the sketch which is consistent with nineteenth-century numbering (McGowan 1986: 3).[8] All notes are in ink and the image is coloured with watercolour and decorated with gold paint or leaf. The figure is drawn on laid paper, which is consistent with its documented date. Laid paper can be identified by examining the pattern of the paper's texture.

There is no watermark. Some paper deterioration is evident with minor foxing. One of the graphite numbers and a word near the number have faded completely. The drawing has a long slanted mark on the left side, which could be damage from years of storage within a book or stack of other papers. The drawing also experienced moisture damage at some point; this could have occurred in an accident, in poor storage conditions or in an attempt to clean or conserve it.[9] There are four regular small holes in each corner, indicating that the paper was once pinned to a surface. When the Tobin design was photographed for McGowan's book, it was apparently mounted on its album binding leaves. Between 1986 and 1990, tears and holes in the laid paper were repaired. Repair is evident by comparing photographs of the drawing taken in 1986 and 1990. The drawing is currently mounted on card. Rectangular discolouration consistent with residue from an acidic mat surrounds the image. It is clear that the four holes in each corner were made before original mounting took place and it was bound on its album leaves. The mounting undoubtedly supported the paper, but the original integrity of the sketch was forever altered and if there were any notes or sketches on the back of the paper, they are lost to researchers until the paper is again severed from its mount.

The Journey of the Artefact

Information about the various locations of this sketch between the seventeenth century and 1985 is unclear. Upon rediscovery in 1985, Professor McGowan studied the drawings, comparing them to the presentation books housed in the Bibliothèque nationale and the Louvre. The sketches were bound in a book with watermarks dating to the 1580s (McGowan 1986: 3), so the original binding pre-dated Rabel's work. McGowan notes that the designs corresponded to performances between 1614 and 1634 and that the sketches probably had some sort of use after the original production(s) because notes reveal changes of character name, dancers and construction. The designs may have been re-used for later ballets.[10] The notes are in different hands and inks. At some time in the nineteenth century, the pages were re-numbered and drawings appear to have been re-cut and re-ordered several times, although the dates of re-ordering are unknown (McGowan 1986: 3). Shortly after their re-discovery in 1985 this set of drawings was exhibited in New York City and sold at auction, disbursing the designs to multiple buyers. Robert Tobin purchased this drawing, along with four other drawings from this set in 1986.[11]

The Artist

The life and work of Daniel Rabel (1578–1637) is not well documented in general encyclopedias and no thorough biographies exist according to international database searches and bibliographical references. Some biographical details are also included in the archives of the Bibliothèque nationale and the Louvre. Robin Thurlow Lacy's book, *A Bibliographical Dictionary of Scenographers: 500 B.C. –1900 A.D.* (first published in 1990), appears to be a central source of information for other later citations. An important reference source for costume, *Theatrical Costume: A Bibliography and*

Iconography, by Sidney Jones and John Cavanagh, contains seven sources in English and French related to Rabel. This Motley Press bibliography (vol. four) published in 2000, is organized like an old-fashioned Reader's Guide. Easy to use and referencing only the subject of costume, finding targeted sources in this volume is faster than conducting sweeping internet searches. Both reference sources listed above are invaluable and should be the costume researcher's first places of inquiry in the English language about particular designers.

Daniel Rabel was the son of the court painter Jean Rabel. The younger Rabel became the Ordinary Engineer to Louis XIII and along with his other artistic duties he was in charge of court spectacles (Thurlow Lacy 1990: 500). Daniel Rabel was approximately forty-eight-years-old when he designed or supervised other artists in his atelier creating the costumes for the *Ballet Royal du Grand Bal de la Drouairière de Billebahaut* in 1625 and 1626. Thurlow Lacy pinpoints his flourish dates between 1619 and 1626; if this is an accurate estimation, Rabel's work on this ballet was at the end of his intense period of theatrical work. He became ill in 1633 (Thurlow Lacy 1990: 500). Rabel was also a printmaker, landscape painter and a botanical painter. Authorship of the design of *Ballet Royal du Grand Bal de la Drouairière de Billebahaut*, attributed to Rabel or the atelier of Rabel can be corroborated through the primary source records of the performances housed in the Bibliothèque nationale. According to these records, Rabel did not design the machines or the pyrotechnics. Rabel was married, but little else is known of his personal life.

The Performance

The *Ballet Royal du Grand Bal de la Drouairière de Billebahaut* was performed at the Louvre in the Great Hall and at the Arsenal later in the day on 24 February 1626. A quick re-organization of the machines was required for setting the second performance and the king ordered that the rooms be configured for banqueting. Musicians performed in each room.[12] The following day, the ballet was performed at the City Hall of Paris to celebrate the signing of a peace agreement between the Protestants and King Louis XIII, which had taken place 5 February 1626. This ballet was the first recorded public performance of a court ballet in Paris.[13] (A section of the ballet, *The Four Parts of the World* was later danced in 1629.) This entertainment consisted of five parts with thirty-four entries. The ballet was commissioned by the Count of Nemours, Henri I of Savoy. The vocal music was composed by Antoine Boësset, with assistance from François Richard and Paul Auget. The machines were designed by Horace Morel, Michel Bourdin and Tomaso Francini.[14]

King Louis XIII danced, as did twelve lords from his court. The majority of the performers were hired professional dancers and there is no evidence that this ballet had female performers. It was customary for female courtiers to participate in entertainments of the serious *ballet de cour*, but according to Roy Strong, the comic burlesque ballets were typically danced by men (Strong et al. 1981: 20). Notes on another design for 'A Lady of the Seraglio' indicate all male names as dancers for that role. Cross-dressing or cross-gender portrayal may have provided additional comedy. Some of the costumes also required athleticism that may have been considered unsuitable for female court performers. The figure in the Tobin sketch appears to be tall and muscular, likely more male than female.

The story of the ballet centres around the ridiculous marriage of an old dowager to a fictional suitor, Fanfan de Sotteville. Most scholars believe that the dowager in question was Marguerite de Valois (1553–1615), Louis XIII's grandmother. According to Bibliothèque nationale documentation, the ballet may have been a satire of 53-year-old Maria de Medici (1573–1642) (Strong et al. 1981: 20), mother of Louis XIII, who was in exile at the time of the performance. The main action of the ballet is a procession of entries by characters from around the world who come to pay homage to the grotesque dowager. The ballet parodies the nobility and exploits themes of war, madness, imperial conquest and disharmony with a final restoration of peace: 'it is a reverse allegory of the world. This ballet is a ballet of disharmony or of the upside down world that goes through the mockery of the "theatre of the world" and the court.'[15] The costume design for this ballet was not romantically Italian in aesthetic. Rabel's atelier did not focus on beauty; the focus was largely comedic and grotesque. Some costume designs depicted courtly inside jokes at the king's expense. For example, a dancer wore a large headless doublet, while another dancer wore a large pair of breeches covering the entire body. This was a joke about the king's allowance to the court. The courtiers complained that he gave them so little money they could not afford an entire outfit (McGowan 1986: 71). Many dancers were masked in grotesque faces; they had exaggeratedly padded body parts or distended, distorted unrealistic costumes based on the fashions of the time. The overall look of much of the ballet appeared to depict the king's courtly and political environment as unpleasant, raucous, comedic and perhaps out of control. The costumes expressed through humorous exaggeration the king's confining personal and political situations.

The Context of the Native Characters

The section of the ballet depicting the Americans was likely a satire of the Spanish conquests of the Americas. The portrayal included the entry of King Atahualpa, the last Incan king of Peru who was ambushed, robbed of the equivalent of a state treasury and then publically executed by Francisco Pizzaro and his men.

The comparison of the costume (Figure1.1.2) and a contemporary image of King Atahualpa (Figure1.1.3) reveal Rabel's comic sense, especially in regard to the oversized head. The other extant costumes in the American portion of the ballet do not employ such exaggeration, rather they are simpler (and perhaps composite interpretations) of drawings and prints of artists attempting to document the New World for a European audience (Figure1.1.4). The entries of Asia, Africa, the Americas and the Peoples of the North included exaggerated costumes, exotic animals (some costumed, some mechanical) parodying ambassadors and diplomatic delegations to amuse the spectators with discord and hyperbole. Ellen Welch argues in her book *A Theatre of Diplomacy*, 'the ballet's structure mocks diplomatic competition for prestige, [and] also satirizes the tradition of praise for the host sovereign' (Welch 2017: 65). When the European characters arrive in the ballet, they too are ridiculous, but the songs and speeches praise Louis XIII, who also danced in the ballet, bringing harmony to discord. The entire event and Rabel's designs worked on two levels: the ballet poked fun

Figure 1.1.2 *Entry of King Atahualpa in* Recit de l'Amerique, *Bibliothèque Nationale de France, Department of Prints.*

at the traditions of the court and, in doing so, satirized Louis XIII's family while simultaneously setting him apart and praising him.

Rabel's sources for visual information were likely Cesare Ripa's *Iconologia*,[16] a catalogue of emblems and symbols collected from ancient literature and translated pictorially for artists, first published in 1593 (Figure1.1.5). The work was frequently re-printed and used by practitioners of nearly all the visual or applied arts as well as painting. This book contains allegorical figures of the four parts of the world, which correspond to the four parts of the world danced in the ballet. Ripa's notes in a 1618 edition describe the Americans: 'Americans go about nude or partially clad, wear feathers and carry the bow and arrows as arms. Many practice cannibalism, particularly on those conquered in battle (the arrow pierced head).'[17]

The Tobin image (Figure 1.1.4) contains the comparable scalloped edges and feather headdress, but there the similarities with Ripa end. Rabel's American holds a guitar and wears a full-length watered silk skirt of European shape, typical of the fashionable silhouette of the period. A feather peplum and feather trim at the neckline and elbow is likely the designer's invention. The rendering of the bodice is vague and may be intended to simulate nudity. The bodice and the skin tone are painted in the same shade of light brown; which could indicate that to depict nudity was the objective. However, the artist's desire is unclear. Some elements of the design could be viewed

Figure 1.1.3 *Portrait of King Atahualpa. The Metropolitan Museum of Art; Gift of David Wagstaff, 1994; 1994.140.1. Bustes de Philosophes et de rois, 1634–1637. After Claude Vignon (French, Tours 1593–1670, Paris), Public Domain.*

simply as customary conventions of the day. For example, the use of feather headdresses commonly signalled a foreign character to the audience in this period. Rabel seemed to be working with a common aesthetic: the conflation of contemporary European fashionable dress with the interpreted descriptions of unknown foreign dress.

The Known and Unknown: Authentication and Function

After conducting research, a partial picture of some possible interpretations emerge about this design. Multiple sources indicate that even though it is unsigned, the drawing is very likely Rabel's or was created under his supervision at his atelier. To date, the sketch appears to be an original

Figure 1.1.4 *Ballet costume from* Recit de l'Amerique *with colours similar to the Tobin image. Bibliothèque Nationale de France, Department of Prints.*

work and not a copy. No other drawings have been discovered which match or relate closely to the garment choices in this drawing; however, it does relate clearly in colour palette and décor to a later drawing for *Récit de l'Amérique*. The physical properties of the sketch coincide with the dates of the performances. There are other documents which can place this sketch in context, primarily the later presentation books and written documentation relating to the ballet and its performances. The original function appears to be that of a working drawing. The primary evidence for this is twofold: the construction note (and other similar notes on other sketches found at the same time) and the four regular holes in the corners of the original page which were clearly present before mounting took place. It seems logical that this sketch was attached to a surface at some point, indicating that it could have been posted as a reference drawing for the makers.

Questions about the sketch (Figure1.1.1) remain. The figure holds a guitar. One could assume that the drawing was for a musician, but we cannot be certain that the guitar was practical. The costume was probably worn by a man but without a detailed cast list, or a reference in a primary source document, there is no proof. Although there are similarities between Ripa's image and this design, certain attribution to Ripa as the source material cannot be proven. Rabel could have used other sources of information and inspiration. The design could simply have been an invention of fantasy.

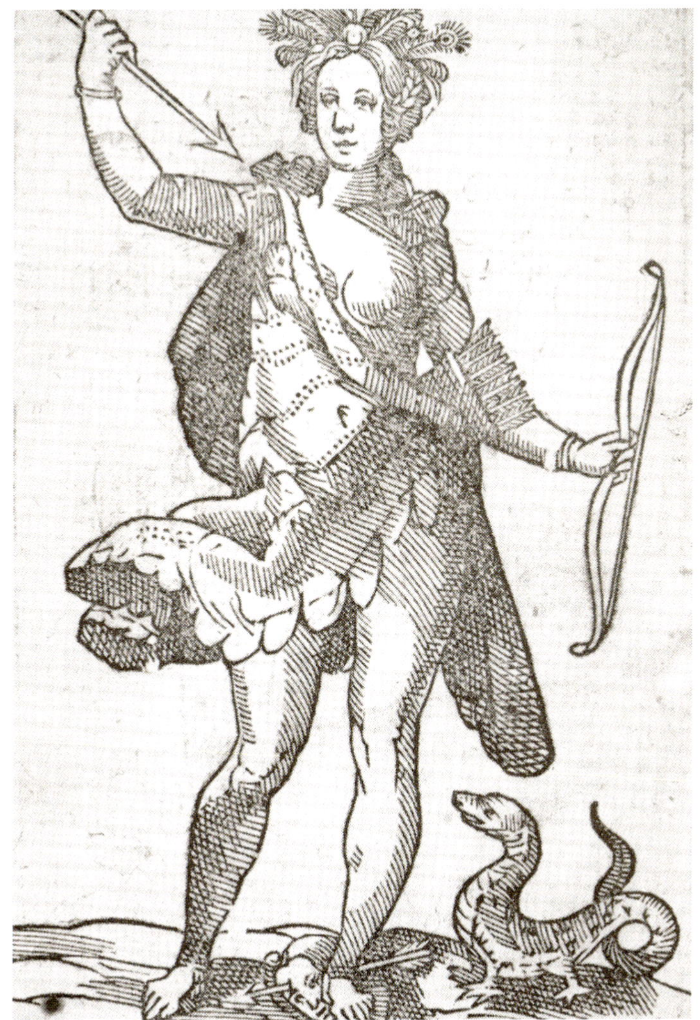

Figure 1.1.5 *Ripa's interpretation of an American,* Iconologia. *The Archive for Research on Archetypical Symbolism, 51562, 5Gv.083a, aras.org., 1603, Public Domain.*

The timeline for the physical locations of this sketch are largely unknown. McGowan believes that the sketches were re-used and if this is the case, they may have been at court ateliers for some time. Rabel died in 1637, but at some point before that he was no longer employed at court. After Louis XIII died in 1643, Cardinal Mazarin hired Giacomo Torelli in 1645 to overtake spectacles. Torelli did not design the costumes. Henri de Beaubrun, then Henri de Gissey designed for the court and after Gissey, Jean Berain who designed costumes for Gaspare Vigarani (who succeeded Torelli) designed both scenery and costumes (Strong et al. 1981: 20). A note signed by de Gissey is on a sketch found in this group, so we can assume that the sketches could have been used practically until 1674 when Berain took over as court designer. Sometime in the nineteenth century, the sketches may have been re-ordered. This assumption is based on the second numbering system consistent with that era. Although the sketches were found in a private library in Germany, the dates of that acquisition are not in the public record. The exact whereabouts of Rabel's working drawings from approximately 1674 to 1985 then, remain a mystery.

Conclusion

McGowan's research on these sketches has been invaluable because she has identified the only known working costume drawings from this place and time. Authentication of this sketch is possible in relationship to other working sketches from the same ballet. It is also related to the later presentation sketches housed in the Bibliothèque nationale and the Louvre. Documentation in these French archives dates to the eighteenth century. Ellen Welch's recent book, *A Theatre of Diplomacy: International Relations and the Performing Arts in Early Modern France*, provides a political and social context for this ballet and sheds even greater light on McGowan's work.

Not all lines of inquiry based on particular cultural viewpoints, ideologies or 'lenses' were adequately investigated in this case study due to a lack of necessary information about the artist or his atelier. Some research questions have, however, been answered. The sketch is not a copy. Physical evidence on the sketch reveals that it was likely first used as a reference sketch in the atelier for the creation of the physical costume. The paper and other archival materials locate the drawing in time and space. It is likely, but not certain, that Ripa's *Iconologia* image was the designer's inspiration. At the point of this publication it is impossible to know exactly how and why Rabel made design decisions and what he thought about the work he was creating. In general, Rabel's costume designs display a high level of fantasy and humour that move beyond the typical beautiful costumes of his predecessors or successors. In order to parody reality and at the same time stay in favour, Rabel likely understood his political and social boundaries within the court and indeed, may have pushed those boundaries as far as he dared. Without further primary source documentation, however, we may never know what he thought about his own work.

The meaning, function and context of this small costume sketch, created for a winter ballet performance in Paris in 1626, required the circumnavigation of multiple archives, the physical, visual scrutiny of the actual sketch, language translation and investigations of cultural performances in the court of Louis XIII of France. It also required the investigation of drawing media and materials, basic fact checking from multiple sources (where possible) and an understanding of researcher biases. A major obstacle in attempting to understand Rabel's intentions or point of view is the lack of biographical or material information on the artist. These blank spaces in the process of inquiry are the stuff of future research on Rabel and the court ballets of Louis XIII.

Notes

1 In cases of pre-history, images must even be interpreted without written sources, but oral or sung traditions might provide some context.

2 Design decisions were often dictated by the patron of the event. For example, King Louis IV of France was dressed as the Sun King when he performed in ballets. This costume choice was a clear propaganda tool, visually centring Louis as the radiant focus of all light and enlightenment.
3 Aniline dye was created in 1856 by Sir William Perkin (1838–1907) and was available commercially in the late nineteenth century. Mauve was the first aniline dye colour. See Brockett, Mitchell and Hardberger, (2010: 215).
4 Costume and dress researchers such as Stella Mary Newton, Aileen Ribeiro and Janet Arnold provide good examples of scholarship dedicated to the comparative study of historical garments and paintings. This tradition developed at the Courtauld Institute, London, in the post-war period. Newton was, in fact, a British costume designer.
5 See Bibliothèque nationale archives, http://catalogue.bnf.fr/ark:/12148/cb45018984n (accessed: 21 March 2019).
6 Ibid.
7 Rabel was also a printmaker.
8 In the nineteenth century, it was customary to number costume drawings in the top centre of the drawing. This re-numbering indicates the sketch was re-used for a production at another time, or it was simply re-numbered for archival purposes.
9 The registrar at the McNay Art Museum speculates that the moisture damage is from an unsuccessful attempt to clean or conserve the drawing.
10 One drawing includes a direct reference to consult with Rabel or, more likely, a descendant or person from his former workshop.
11 As a celebration of Margaret McGowan's work, the Victoria and Albert Museum, in association with Hobhouse Ltd. and Morton and Co. Ltd. published the catalogue of the designs. One-hundred and forty of these court ballet drawings were exhibited in a group by Wheelock Whitney and Co. in November 1986 in New York. At this time the Victoria and Albert Museum, the Getty Research Institute and the Morgan Library all purchased drawings. The Victoria and Albert Museum acquired sixty-nine sketches; thirteen of them are related to the *Ballet Royal du Grand Bal de la Drouairière de Billebahaut*. The Morgan Library acquired eight sketches; two designs are from this ballet. The Getty acquired six drawings; none are from this ballet. In 1986, Robert Tobin purchased five drawings; *Récit de l'Amérique* is the only design from this ballet in the Tobin archives.
12 Bibliothèque nationale, archives http://catalogue.bnf.fr/ark:/12148/cb45018984n.
13 Ibid.
14 Ibid.
15 Leconte, 204, cited in Bibliothèque nationale, http://catalogue.bnf.fr/ark:/12148/cb45018984n.
16 Bibliothèque nationale, http://catalogue.bnf.fr/ark:/12148/cb450143512, *Iconologica*, 1603.
17 Artstor, Archive for Research on Archetypal Symbolism, aras.org.

References

Bibliothèque nationale de France ([1624] 2019), 'Manuscripts', Prints Department of the Bibliothèque nationale de France, Paris, France. Available online: http://data.bnf.fr/en/45009903/gran_bal_de_la_douairiere_de_billebahaut_spectacle_1626 (accessed: 20 March 2019).

Brockett, O. G., M. Mitchell and L. Hardberger (2010), *Making the Scene: A History of Stage Design and Technology in Europe and the United States*. San Antonio: Tobin Theatre Arts Fund.

Cavanagh, J. and S. Jackson Jowers, eds (2000), *Theatrical Costume, Masks, Make-Up and Wigs : A Bibliography and Iconography*. London and New York: Routledge.

Lacy, R. T. (1990), *A Bibliographical Dictionary of Scenographers: 500 B.C. to 1900 A.D.* Connecticut: Greenwood Press.

McGowan, M. (1986), *The Court Ballet of Louis XIII: A Collection of Working Designs for Costumes, 1615–1633*. London: Victoria and Albert Museum in association with Hobhouse Ltd. and Morton Morris & Co Ltd.

Musée du Louvre ([1625] 2019), 'Manuscripts', Cabinet Des Dessins. Available online: https://www.louvre.fr/mediaimages/daniel-rabel-entree-des-%C2%AB-esperlucattes-%C2%BB-six-figures-1625-album-daniel-rabel-fonds-des (accessed: 20 March 2019).

Ramamurthy, M. and V. Lakshminarayanan (2017), 'Human Vision and Perception' in R. Karlicek, C-C. Sun, G. Zissis and R. Ma (eds), *Handbook of Advanced Lighting Technology*, 757–84. Cham: Springer International Publishing. Pre-print available online: https://www.researchgate.net/publication/275891163_Human_Vision_and_Perception (accessed: 30 December 2018).

Ripa, C. (1603), *Iconologia*. Woodcut (Rome). Available online: http://library.artstor.org/asset/AWSS35953_35953_31701292 (accessed: 14 March 2018).

Strong, R., I. Guest, R. Buckle, B. Kay and L. Da Costa (1981), *Designing for the Dancer*. London: Elron Press.

Welch, E. R. (2017), *A Theatre of Diplomacy: International Relations and the Performing Arts in Early Modern France*. Philadelphia: University of Pennsylvania Press.

Wright, R. (1989), 'The Image in Art and Computer Art.' *Leonardo*, Supplemental Issue, 2, 49–53. Available online: https://www.jstor.org/stable/1557944 (accessed: 30 December 2018).

1.2 Cooking: Studying Film Costume Design

Drake Stutesman

to close one's eyes to the peculiar contexts in which [the] … 'deep structure' – of the tale is continually recreated by individual performers is to deny this art form its very life and blood.
OKPEWHO [1975] 1979: XII

The epigraph above is from a study of African oral epics in which the author, Isidore Okpewho, defines a tale that is meant to be spoken or sung as a story that becomes a story only through details such as how it is told, how it is sung, how it is repeated, how it is paced and how it is stressed. These are the 'peculiar contexts' that exist in the moment. The relationship among these contexts is what makes the story, because the relationship is the story's core, a deep structure continually formed and re-formed *ad infinitum*. It is a living thing. Every film and every film costume has much the same kind of deep structure that is made out of peculiar contexts.

Context, in studying film costume, is possibly the most important thing. It provokes countless questions that set up numerous ways of theorizing a film's costumes. When was the film made? When and where is the film set? What is the film's genre or is it a riff on a genre? Is there a star? What age is the star? Who is the audience? What are the audience's expectations? Does the audience change over decades? Do different countries create a different kind of audience or the same? Is the film a B-movie, underground movie, niche movie, re-enactment movie, blockbuster movie, cell phone movie? If the film is avant-garde, is its agenda hard to understand? Is the film foreign and based on cultural modes unknown to a viewer? Is the film affected by censorship? Is it a law or a prejudice? What are the consequences of defying it? Prison? Blacklist? Ridicule? Stature? Is the film set in another century and made twenty years ago? Which of the two periods (that of the film's story or that of the film's making) is more important in an analytical approach? Both? Who is the costume designer? Who is the production designer, the cinematographer, the screenwriter? All of these elements affect the costume designer's ideas. All of these elements affect the scholar's ideas.

The contexts in which these questions arise, in each costume, are arguably singular (or peculiar, to use Okpewho's word) to that costume's role in a film. Using three examples, this chapter looks at ways to approach a specific film costume. One is a macro-approach, situating the costume, in this case a top hat and tails, in its history and showing how the actor appropriates that history in order to play her part. The second is a micro-approach, where the costume, in this case a T-shirt, is minutely re-constructed to create a context that increases the actor's ability to be his character. The third is a broad approach: here, specifically through the art of cooking, it is an approach that comes from outside the subject of costume, but serves as a way to understand the period or periods that the costume reflects. The concept of 'period' affects all these examples.[1] Even last year's film is in the past and knowing how to approach the reality of the everclose past (contemporary film) or ever-far past (historical film) is difficult, but in the surreal displacement of a cinema world that is made up of material culture (food, clothes, structures, lighting, bodies), whatever works to bring that palpable idiosyncratic 'past' closer is valuable.

An interesting, and not exceptional, example of 'peculiar contexts' can be found in Marlene Dietrich's famous cabaret scene in Josef von Sternberg's 1930 film *Morocco*, influenced by the Berlin club culture he'd discovered when he arrived there in 1929.[2] *Morocco* was Dietrich's introduction to American viewers. Having starred in the German film *The Blue Angel* the year before, also directed by von Sternberg, Dietrich had 'all Europe … at her feet' (von Sternberg 1965: 252). But *Morocco* brought her a wider audience and international fame. The film opens in Mogador, Morocco (filmed in California) with Foreign Legion soldiers marching into the dusty sunlit town. Special attention is focused on Dietrich's love interest, played by Gary Cooper, portraying him as on the make (as he flippantly negotiates with prostitutes) and derisive of authority. In the next scene, Dietrich is standing on the crowded deck of a ship at night, about to dock at the Moroccan port. The scene is so darkly lit that it is hard to tell what she is wearing, but it seems to be a thin, dark coat and black cloche with a half-veil. She has a brief conversation with a wealthy man, who is interested in her, but whom she blows off. When he asks a ship officer about her, the officer speculates that she is probably 'a vaudeville actress' and dismisses her as one of his 'suicide passengers – one way tickets. They never return', considering her a *persona non grata* at the end of her rope, like others he sees 'every day' (von Sternberg 1973: 13). Her costume suggests that she is not well-off, but is perhaps straightforward, as she is dressed plainly and her attitude shows her to be unconcerned and independent. That her dress is so obscured puts more emphasis on the brightly lit cabaret costume she wears in the scene that follows and perhaps makes viewers all the more curious to look closely at her to discover Dietrich's character. The respective introductory scenes of the two leads link them together as similar. Both are indifferent to those with power and both are accustomed to sexual encounters, but each seems disaffected to the point of tedium: the man is on the make as a habit and the woman shrugs off such men. The third scene is in the theatre, smoky and somewhat tattered which is crammed with an impatient mixed audience of soldiers and rich and poor Arab and European men and women. Dietrich appears backstage dressed for her act in a man's black evening tails and trousers, white shirt, white vest and white bow tie (Figure 1.2.1). Smoking a cigarette, she puts on her black top hat and strolls on stage where she is met with boos and hisses. She begins to sing in sultry French over the jeers and Cooper, who has seen her for the first time, then stands and demands quiet. Dietrich walks slowly through the audience, touching her top hat forward and back on her head with a memorized insouciance, a manner described in the script as 'bland, casual' (von Sternberg 1973: 18). She stops and has a sip of champagne at a table and kisses a woman on the mouth after she agrees to Dietrich's request for her flower.[3] Dietrich later throws the flower to Cooper who puts it behind his ear.[4] The crowd wildly applauds the whole display. The two leads meet after the second show (once Dietrich

Figure 1.2.1 *Marlene Dietrich in her costume for* Morocco*, 1930. Courtesy of Photofest.*

gives Cooper her apartment key) and begin an obsessive attraction based on their feeling (which they never declare) that they are soulmates.[5] The two never consummate, (which could have been scripted as the film was pre-code) or even kiss, but only run to and from each other, fervent with love.[6] The end is ambiguous and has been interpreted as either a successful union or a destroyed one.

In the 1920s, Dietrich was already wearing men's clothes. Von Sternberg saw Dietrich in 1929 at a noisy Berlin party wearing the 'full dress regalia of a man, high hat and all' and he deliberately costumed her for *Morocco* exactly as he had seen her (von Sternberg 1965: 246–7). Dietrich in trousers caused contention with Paramount's studio heads, but von Sternberg refused to back down and he and Dietrich proved to be presciently on the fashion cusp. By the early 1930s, partly because of Dietrich's style, women in trousers became high fashion, though women publicly wearing men's clothing already had a complex, long history.[7] The image of Dietrich in the cabaret in her tails and top hat costume has been and continues to be much reproduced. It promotes Dietrich as the beautiful woman, the star, the icon in men's power clothes and her 1930 appearance in this costume has been discussed as an act of defiance. But is that why her restless, demanding audience jeers at her? Looking at the costume in the context of the late 1920s, it is obvious that Dietrich's costume was not daring at the time and not meant to be daring. By 1930, the sight of a woman on stage in male trappings such as hers was old-fashioned. A cabaret audience in a colonized North African port town probably would have thought that Dietrich was about to play a much-performed British music hall and American vaudeville act of a woman dressed as a rich man about town, usually in top hat and tails, singing a song about the rich man's exploits. These stage acts, billed as 'male impersonations' and popular in the late nineteenth century and early twentieth, were world famous, played by women like Vesta Tilley, Hettie King, Ella Wesner and many others. The ship officer had already identified Dietrich as 'vaudeville' and this makes it plausible that the reason the crowd initially disliked her was that they didn't want to be bored by an old hat routine and this is what they thought she was going to do, dressed as she was. The audience had paid to be excited and that's what they ended up getting, but their thrill was induced by the context of the costume as much as by Dietrich's sensual manner. Dietrich, in walking through the crowd, in bringing an overt queerness into the scene with her lesbian kiss and her exchange of the woman's flower for a likely liaison with Cooper was an exciting combination, but what she (and von Sternberg) brought to the 1930 film was not just Dietrich's act, but also a subversion of the 1910s 'male impersonation' act. The music hall/vaudeville impersonators never overtly intended their show to be salacious, but to be one of imposture.[8] Dietrich's intransigence was not in wearing the male clothing, but in the way she sexualized the old rote act. In so doing, she sexualized its key feature – the costume *as* a costume. Dietrich's way of performing suggests that Cooper's attraction to her was coloured less by how she handled the crowd without fear (something common to women who worked rough clubs) than by how she approached the old-style male impersonation. The costume plays a critical part in this turning point of the two leads' attraction. In subverting the Vesta Tilley type of show, Dietrich, previously dismissed as a vaudevillian nobody shows herself as iconoclastic. Her costume references the old male impersonation stage act, and hence theatre history and it allows Dietrich to eroticize the act as both homosexual and heterosexual and hence point to present and future public displays of sexuality.

Travis Banton, head of costume at Paramount, designed Dietrich's costumes. He ensured that she was not actually wearing a man's regular suit, (as the impersonation act did and on which it depended) but instead was dressed in Banton's version of the suit, subtly altered to feminize it. Keeping the suit roomy to punctuate that it was men's wear, Banton modified the clothes just enough to hint at Dietrich's body. He cut the vest slightly to fit her breasts, heightened the waistline and tightened it to glimpse her figure and tapered the trousers to suggest the hips and thighs. The vaudeville impersonation depended on the act being recognized not as a woman dressed as a man, but a woman disguised as a man. By Dietrich's sexualization of it, the old act itself was revised, making her version of the act about a woman in a costume that referenced male attire. But it was the impermeability of the *costume* of the top hat and tails that allowed the Dietrich character in *Morocco* to be distinctive. The tails and top hat costume was stable. It was a platform not of 'men's clothes', but of the 'costume of men's clothes.' Without that context, the meaning of Dietrich's performance would have been different. Dietrich was radical not for wearing the costume, but in how she used it to re-make the context of a woman on stage in such gear. With that revision, the era of the act's attraction (1890s, 1910s) was appropriated to represent a new era of attraction (1920s, 1930s). In this way, von Sternberg and Dietrich placed the film into a context that was tinged with modernity, looking beyond 1930 towards the future.

Modernity is linked to fashion through fashion's tendency to change, but the study of costume as an indicator of the modern because it tends not to change, holds many possibilities. An approach to understanding the effect of that stability can be made through ideas that are used creatively in other mediums. The description of the uncanny by Carl Dreyer, the Danish film director revered for his ability to convey the supernatural as if it is an ordinary part of life can throw light on what 'peculiar contexts' can do:

> Imagine that we are sitting in a very ordinary room. Suddenly we are told that there is a corpse behind the door. Instantly, the room we are sitting in has taken on another look. The light, the atmosphere have changed, though they are physically the same. This is because we have changed and the objects are as we conceive them. This is the effect I wanted to produce in *Vampyr*. (Dreyer 1973: 53)

Dreyer's example shows that a single detail can transform the entire scene. The 'past' can be that detail in a film and its costume. A film, even if it is only a few years old is still a 'period' film because its contemporary moment is over. The past lives in the imagination and its memory (if the viewer lived through the period) or its projection (if the viewer is too young to know that era) shapes its renditions. In Dreyer's story, it is the concept of a corpse and not the corpse itself that actually enters the room. His point is that a certain detail (implied corpse) oddly directs the perception away from the real detail (literal dead body) and instead it transforms everything else. The way the past is perceived is similar.

The two opening sentences of L.P. Hartley's novel, *The Go Between* – '[t]he past is another country. They do things differently there' ([1953] 2012: 1) – underscores that the past is unreachable. The past has disappeared. Its existence has had a milieu, a felt world which is lost in time. William Faulkner stressed the power of this unknowable past by approaching it from the present when he wrote that the 'past is never dead. It's not even past' (Faulkner [1951] 2012: 233). Between the two perspectives, a realistic version of the past emerges. It is a living organic world 'not even past' and also an untouchable reality where 'they do things differently.' Roland Barthes, in his exploration of fashion, identified the oddity of trying to handle 'history' by situating any aspect of the past as always slippery. He adamantly wondered - '[w]hen does an item of clothes *really* change? When is there *really* history?' (Barthes 2006: 4). These questions declare that there is a frame through which to see time. That frame is this statement: 'I don't know.' With his suspicious – When is there really history? – Barthes poses the idea that not only is the past ever present and ever different, it is also ever non-existent. It can't be found.[9]

'When does an item of clothes *really* change?' Barthes' more specific point is the more specific focus of this chapter. In studying a film's costumes, this sense of material history, of movement in fashion, marketing, invention, technology and commerce to name only a few currents that affect clothing, becomes a sideline to what a 'costume' is. A costume is different from other clothing because it is constructed to make the viewer feel a targeted emotion.[10] The costume reveals these meanings by riffing on the meaning that cultures assign to clothes. For example, the sight of big shoes might make a person laugh, but the sight of a tight waistline might make a person feel. In the first instance, the shoe, in a Western cultural context, is pre-determined to be seen as funny, (such as a clown's shoe that is too long) but these contextual 'givens' can fade away and be forgotten. Interviews with people who were alive during the film's period can reveal details about the past that is 'ever different' in ways that archival research at times cannot. The odd, difficult to fathom subtleties or 'givens' of every period almost always need clarification. They can easily be missed unless one is told to look for them. In the second instance, the tight waistline, the viewer (or the scholar) may respond not just from a trope, but from a bodily sensation because s/he had worn clothes with tight waists or wanted to, or refused to. This personal peculiar context needs to be plumbed by the viewer and analysing what that means has fascinating ties to the kind of iconicity that 'costume' has in culture.

The place where costume and clothing separate is almost indeterminable, but the two categories are also kept apart. In one sense, costume is viewed as a pejorative version of clothing, simply artificial and relevant only to a 'show.' In another, costume is given a stability that places it beyond clothing and is regarded as able to coordinate a person's crucial interactions with the world. Patrizia Calefato argued the latter when she conflated clothing and costume, at one level by theorizing that as it is through personal choices that a person builds a wardrobe, a sense of self is built with it. She posited that as such, clothing was perceived by the wearer as a performance, in a sense a costume, one through which the wearer became self-aware (Calefato 2004: 2). Once a person considered their own clothes to be an individual style, that style/costume transformed clothes from mere objects into a means to objectify (and thus make visible) the subjective self.[11] In *The Actor in Costume,* Aoife Monks viewed costume as a 'hinge', emphasizing that the costume on the body is layered with meaning for the viewer representing both personal and historical attachments and that the costume worn by the actor is used by the viewer as a means to sort through the many emotions that the viewer feels when watching an actor acting (Monks 2010: 25). The costume becomes more than a theatrical covering, but rather is made into a structure stable enough to help a person address inner chaos. Monks' idea places costume in a role as culturally central and as deeply personal as the one that Calefato recognizes.

The creativity that makes the costume itself is the micro-world where the actor's and the narrative's peculiar contexts are made. A film costume's nuances are almost always precise and an interview with the costume designer regarding their work can reveal a scope of labour that is almost unimaginable, as well as offering answers to specific questions on choices.[12] Maren Reese, in costuming the 2010 American film *Night Catches Us*, which was set in 1976 in a residential neighbourhood in Philadelphia and directed by Tanya Hamilton, cited that the reason her characters' costumes were slightly looser than a typical '70s tight fit was to show that they didn't have the money for new clothes and wore the same ones for years. Reese built her costumes by keeping in mind this one small detail that, though almost negligible to the eye, revealed vital backstory information.[13] Carol Oditz, costume designer for the 1997 American Ang Lee film *The Ice Storm*, also set in the seventies, entered the film's world through her own experience of the era. She decided that vintage or imitation '70s clothes would not work for the film:

> Fashion designers go back to the early 70s again & again for inspiration. I didn't use any new clothes, on the market, which are 'in the style of the '70s,' because to my eye the differences are too extreme. Particularly the fabrics being used now are quite different from the originals. So I designed practically everything and found fabrics or had pieces knit and crocheted that were more truthful to the period. (Oditz, 1998 [DVD])

This re-fashioning of various kinds, is necessary in most film costuming. Costume designer Jeffrey Kurland underscored that costume parts have to be adjusted:

> I've never just bought an item and then put it on screen. With the character being created by a team – the writer, the actor, and the costume designer – one can't just go 'find' some clothing and expect it to be right. Everything is filtered through a creative process. So even if an item is purchased, in the end, it too must be created, just as the writer creates the screenplay and the actor creates the character. (Nandoolman Landis 2003: 69)

An illustration of that process appears in one of cinema's most iconic costumes – the T-shirt worn by Marlon Brando in Elia Kazan's 1951 film adaptation of Tennessee Williams' play *A Streetcar Named Desire,* an image much reproduced. The film's story hangs on the sexuality of the character played by Brando. He is a young stud, magnetic, volatile, self-assured and unsophisticated and his personality drives the narrative. Though he is technically white collar (a travelling car parts salesman), he is also identified as a labourer and his costumes promote this, in part to sexualize him further.[14] In key scenes, Brando wears a fitting T-shirt that, along with his plain belted trousers, watch, ring and signet bracelet, identifies him as an upwardly mobile working-class man of the fifties. The costume designer Lucinda Ballard situated Brando exactly in his contemporary time but nevertheless, as Kurland stated, Ballard needed to mould the costume into the character that Brando played. To do so, she utilized tiny details typically used to make a woman desirable, such as the cut of the collar, sleeve and waistline. Brando was a virile actor who exuded a much commented-on charismatic eroticism and he was chosen to play the role in part because his kind of manliness suited it. It is hard to think of Brando as being made to appear sexier in 1951 as he was exploding onto the scene, but Ballard worked on costume subtleties that eroticized his masculinity in part through softening him. At a casual glance (see Figure 1.2.2), his T-shirt seems as if it is off the rack, but Ballard was careful to augment Brando's seductiveness, especially through his shirt, through highly contrived but almost imperceptible modifications. The late forties/early fifties T-shirt was principally worn as an undershirt, modelled on one in the Second World War military uniform. It was made of dense white cotton and cut in a T-shaped box with four-inch-long square sleeves that covered the top half of the upper arm and had a crew-neck collar which fit snugly to the base of the neck. Ballard's T-shirt was, conversely, a thin cotton jersey, which clung to the skin and which she dyed a shaded colour.[15] Ballard cut the collar into a shape known as a 'low round', a female tailoring style and atypical for males at the time. It was an inch wider than a crew, so that the curve where Brando's neck met his shoulder was revealed, showing more skin and making the line less tight. This suggested voluptuousness, and also suited the character's allure. Ballard eliminated the square, four-inch short sleeves and made cap sleeves which hug the muscle and are short and tight. This is a flattering, sexy cut that accents the bow of the flesh, also typically found in fifties' female clothing and not in men's. On a man, it shows how firm and solid his muscles are and how fit he is. The seam of a regular T-shirt, where the sleeve joins, typically sits just off the shoulder and this placement loses the sensuality of the shoulder's slope. Ballard placed Brando's T-shirt sleeve seam closer to the neckline. By shortening the distance, the curve was visible. Ballard also added small creases to the armpits. The lines, made to look like a consequence of hard physical work, visually placed Brando's character as a man focused on his body, even as a labourer, which intensified the cliché of the

Figure 1.2.2 *Marlon Brando dressed in his highly designed T-shirt in* A Streetcar Named Desire, *1951. Courtesy of Photofest.*

stud. The curve of his chest between the pectoral muscles was soaked in water to show sweat, emphasizing physical labour and the male shape. Ballard placed less sweat under the arms as the shading would break the line of Brando's lean look. To ensure that the line showed, Ballard cut the film costume T-shirt to taper so that the lightweight cotton that clung closely to his body made long folds across his torso and around his waist, underscoring his beauty and, when tucked in, drawing the viewer's eye to the front of his pants.

The third and last example of 'peculiar contexts' is perhaps the most elusive – the context of material culture. This is where the past is dominated by how 'they do things differently there' and is the one distinction of history which is always like the present. The present (like the past) is filled with millions of contradictions and impossible-to-discern reasons for why or how something happens in an atmosphere ever-changing, ever-the same, which is grouped around experiences that always relate to a tactile zeitgeist and are counted in details as tiny as how something tastes or the weight of an object. The 'peculiar contexts' of lived life are impossible to quantify, even while living them, and they are the hardest to understand. They are often the missing piece crucial to understanding a moment in time. Some palpable grasp of the past can make it come alive. Though foods today may have been cooked differently forty years ago, or made from another version of the same ingredients (such as a grain or herb), they can be a way into a film's period milieu, be it a medieval setting or the 1920s. Find a cookbook from the time, cook one of the recipes and eat the food (Figure 1.2.3). The food can act like a sudden physical presence, representing another elusive presence as Dreyer noted, that transforms 'everything else'. Though the food itself can't be part of the film, its reality as a meal, its taste, its texture, the kind of ingredients it uses, the places where the ingredients were bought and the knives or spoons and bowls that were used to prepare it and the way it was cooked, can change a perception of the period considerably.

Figure 1.2.3 *Cooking a pie can bring the past to life. Courtesy of the author.*

Notes

1. The film's time scale is a factor that a costume designer always has in mind. Even if a film is set during the time it is made, the costume designer has to think of the future. If the contemporary costume mimics clothes of the time of its production, the year of its release, or usually at least six to twelve months later, the style will seem dated. If a film has a historical setting, the designer must consider not just the accuracy of the costumes, (if required) but also possible modifications to what is true to the period. Some true dress details won't be acceptable to modern audiences or won't suit the film.
2. See von Sternberg (1965), 228–9, 246–7.
3. See von Sternberg (1965), 247. Von Sternberg devised the scene to, as he described it, 'touch lightly on a Lesbian accent'.
4. A man about town placing a girl's flower behind his ear had some fashion currency in the late 1920s.
5. In her second act, Dietrich, dressed in a one-piece belted bathing suit as the more obvious girly display, sang and sold apples while walking through the audience.
6. *Morocco*'s narrative is built only on the miscommunicated affair between them, where they deliberately part and re-engage. Dietrich follows Cooper wherever he goes and he constantly gives her up while pining for her and even changes his attitude towards life, declaring, 'I've become decent'. Neither shares any of these sentiments with the other. The erotic tension wrought in Dietrich's control and casualness and the shared world-weariness between them is the implied attraction.
7. The complicated history in the Western hemisphere of women and girls wearing male clothing reveals that they were variously received into and in some cases became an accepted, mainstream part of the culture. For in depth research on this topic see: Horak (2016); Berg (2011); Garber (1992); Maitland(1986).
8. See Maitland, (1986: 28, 34, 72–6). Vesta Tilley was one of the first music hall performers to deliberately aim for middle-class acceptance, which meant, in part, a separation from music hall's bawdiness. Her act was straight send up. Maitland notes that the sexual content of acts did not often translate between cultures. Blue innuendo in a British act, such as Marie Lloyd's, was lost on an American vaudeville audience. This makes it more difficult to specify what was 'sexual' in these stage shows, but the Vesta Tilley kind of impersonation was not geared to be blue and the costume was to disguise the female body. The audience must, however, have felt some kind of frisson in this use of cross-dress that muddied gender and class lines.
9. This study uses the general American/Eurocentric approach of consciousness of time, but any knowledge or in-depth study of temporal understanding in Asian, African or First Nations cultures and others can apply the same approach.
10. Uniforms and the like aim for the same effect but, in this sense, can also be construed as costumes.
11. This is a Western version of the concept of 'self' and is not necessarily how other cultures construe it.
12. Costume designers approach their work with the same clarity and teamwork as the writer, art director, cinematographer or any other crewmember. The costume designer also deals

with numerous factors that do not always effect the crew, such as the actor's body type, the character's motives and the actor's psychology, budget issues, collaborations with production designers and the lighting and cameraperson, the close up and the need to evaluate whether a costume detail is better rendered realistically, or if it must be adapted.

13 Maren Reese in an interview with the author, 12 March 2018.

14 In one scene, he is seen with his tight clothes greased by oil from working on his car. This labourer's look deliberately centralizes his key power – his sexual attraction – and in this scene he is also triumphant over the other characters.

15 The film was in black and white.

References

Barthes, R. (2006), *The Language of Fashion*. London: Bloomsbury Academic.

Berg, P. (2011), *Re-Dressing America's Frontier Past*. Berkeley: University of California Press.

Calefato, P. (2004), *The Clothed Body*, trans. Lisa Adams. Oxford: Berg.

Dreyer, C. (1973), *Dreyer in Double Reflection: Carl Dreyer's Writings on Film*, ed. D. Skollar. New York: Da Capo Press.

Faulkner, W. ([1951] 2012), *Requiem for a Nun*. New York: Vintage International.

Garber, M. (1992), *Vested Interests: Crossing Dressing and Cultural Anxiety*. New York: Routledge.

Hartley, L.P. ([1953] 2012), *The Go-Between*. New York: New York Review of Books Classics.

Horak, L. (2016), *Girls Will Be Boys: Cross-Dressed Women, Lesbians, and American Cinema, 1908–1934*. New Brunswick: Rutgers University Press.

Maitland, S. (1986), *Vesta Tilley*. London: Virago Pioneers.

Monks, A. (2010), *The Actor in Costume*. Basingstoke: Palgrave Macmillan.

Nandoolman Landis, D. (2003), *Screencraft: Costume Design*. Burlington: Focal Press.

Oditz, C. *Carol Oditz for the Ice Storm Criterion Collection*, (1998), [DVD].

Okpewho, I. ([1975] 1979), *The Epic in Africa: Toward a Poetics of the Oral Performance*. New York: Columbia University Press.

von Sternberg, J. (1965), *Fun in a Chinese Laundry*. San Francisco: Mercury House.

von Sternberg, J. (1973), *Classic Film Scripts :* Morocco *and* Shanghai Express. New York: Simon and Schuster.

1.3 Displaying Stage Costumes: Exhibitions at the National Centre for Stage Costume, France

Delphine Pinasa

Stage costumes, a key element of performance and an important part of France's cultural heritage, were until recently dispersed in very diverse collections, in different collecting institutions and preserved in a fragmentary manner.

Considered for many years an object of use, like the stage set rather than a work of art, costume has never been the subject of a systematic policy of collection, preservation and conservation in France, despite the fact that it represents a major expense for theatres.

The National Centre for Stage Costume (Centre National du Costume de Scène, known by its French acronym CNCS) is a museum founded with the mission to create, preserve and continuously enrich the national collection of stage costumes emanating from theatres, opera houses, dance companies and individual artists. The relatively recent establishment of this museum (2006) offers a unique opportunity for the study and research of stage costume in many fields of live performance in both contemporary and historical France.

A Place Dedicated to Performance Costume

The creation of the CNCS testifies to the recognition of stage costume as a 'patrimonial' object (denoting inter-generational cultural heritage), the conservation and valorization of which are of relevance to the general public and professionals alike. Unique and unparalleled in France and abroad, the CNCS is the first museum to be entirely dedicated to the material heritage of theatre with a focus on costumes and stage sets. The CNCS places stage costume at the centre of its mission, both as a textile art-object and as a material witness to live performance. The museum's mission is to build, enrich and preserve a national collection whose interest is both 'scientific' (to be offered as a resource for future study and evaluation) as well as being part of a wider cultural heritage. The museum is also responsible for making the collection known to a bigger audience through regular exhibitions and attractive publications.

The National Centre for Stage Costume (Figure 1.3.1) is located in Moulins, Allier, France, a region north of Auvergne, two and a half hours south of Paris. It opened in July 2006 at the initiative of

Figure 1.3.1 *The National Centre for Stage Costume, Moulins, France. © CNCS / Moulins Communauté.*

the French Ministry of Culture. The centre is located in the Quartier Villars, a military headquarters constructed in the late eighteenth century to house cavalry battalions. By the early 1980s it had been abandoned and partially demolished. In 1984, it was rescued thanks to its classification as one of the national monuments of France. The Ministry of Culture, owner of the site, renovated and re-habilitated the structure and built storage spaces with the assistance of the architect Jean-Michel Wilmotte. The aim of this new institution was to ensure the preservation and inclusion of the material theatrical heritage that stage costumes represent within French cultural heritage. At the beginning of the project, three national and iconic institutions, namely the National Library of France (Bibliothèque nationale de France (BNF), the Comédie-Française and the Paris Opera (Opéra national de Paris), were heavily involved, re-locating their costume resources to help create the newly integrated collection at the museum.

A Unique Collection of Stage Costumes

The original aim of collecting stage costumes and disseminating their value as tangible cultural heritage has seen the institution broaden its collecting brief to all forms of live performance, defined by the following criteria: 'given on stage, in the presence of an audience and as part of a professional production'. Since its founding, the CNCS has been approached by many interlocutors anxious to preserve their heritage. These include dance companies (e.g. Bagouet, BARC, Buirge, Duboc, Larrieu, Europa Danse), theatres (L'Illustre théâtre, La Maison de la Culture of Nantes) and opera companies (Opéra de Marseille), artists or legatees (Régine Crespin, Jacqueline François, Noureev [Nureyev] Foundation) and costume designers (Christian Lacroix, Franck Sorbier). Given that it is not always possible or relevant to accept such donations in their entirety, the CNCS – like all museums – is forced to make a selection via various secondary criteria. It preserves and maintains significant memories through exemplary items, yet not in an exhaustive or encylopedic manner. Before selecting specific items to enrich the collection, the CNCS takes into consideration their patrimonial, artistic, technical and historical value (Figure 1.3.2). This decision is taken in consultation with the founding institutions – the Paris Opera (Opéra national de Paris) and Comédie-Française with regard to new acquisitions – or with donors. Since 2009, when the CNCS was recognized as a 'museum of France' each donation has been validated by the CNCS Scientific Steering Committee and the inter-regional commission of museums.

The costumes in the CNCS collections come from theatre, opera, ballet or contemporary dance productions that have ceased to be part of the performance repertory of theatres. They were

Figure 1.3.2 *Costume for Lady Macbeth in Shakespeare's* Macbeth, *costumes by Thierry Mugler, Comédie-Française, 1985. © CNCS / Pascal François.*

selected to become part of the CNCS collections and due to their cultural significance are preserved in the appropriate conditions. The south wing of the museum, newly built during the renovation, is dedicated to the preservation of the costumes: the furniture, room temperature and humidity guarantee optimum conservation conditions. The CNCS preserves more than 10,000 stage costumes, comprising approximately 23,000 articles. Although most of them are from the period spanning the second quarter of the nineteenth century to the present day, some date back to the eighteenth century. The first large deposit was 8,500 costumes from the Comédie-Française and the Paris Opera – the two major national theatres of France – as well as from the National Library of France which collects costumes from French companies or theatres within its 'Performing Arts' department. The CNCS was thus endowed from the outset with unique and exceptional collections, representative of many years of French stage creation.

In 2008 the Nureyev Foundation donated the Rudolf Nureyev Collection to the CNCS. To honour the Russian ballet dancer's last wishes, the Nureyev Foundation had looked for a space dedicated to his memory in order for the collection to be shown to the public. It was first presented at the CNCS during a temporary exhibition in 2009, then in St Petersburg in 2010 and in San Francisco in 2012. The Nureyev Collection is now part of CNCS's permanent collection: it includes stage costumes, personal garments, pictures, engravings, furniture and other personal items that illustrate the career of this iconic twentieth-century ballet dancer. Ezio Frigerio, a great Italian scenographer and one of Rudolf Nureyev's collaborators and best friends, designed a 350 m^2 space to display his collection (Figure 1.3.3).

Rare and exceptional collections such as these confer upon the museum a unique and unusual position within the cultural heritage of the performing arts. Unlike the majority of theatre archives, whose collections often consist of archival materials and documents and more rarely of three-dimensional objects, the CNCS places costume artefacts themselves at the heart of its collections, particularly for in-house exhibitions.

The Exhibitions at the National Centre for Stage Costume

The CNCS's mission is to promote and disseminate its collections through public presentations. The fragility of the costumes and the constraints of their conservation – an issue faced by all fashion and textile museums – mean that these exhibitions are time limited and temporary. Focused exhibitions on various themes are the result.

The CNCS organizes two temporary exhibitions per year. In the past twelve years, more than twenty-five exhibitions have been presented under various themes relating to historical, artistic or technological perspectives. The programme is established by the management of the museum and then validated by the scientific and cultural orientation council, as well as by the institution's board of directors. Since its opening, the CNCS has raised questions about how to display performing arts costumes. This raises another general question: how to display stage costumes outside their scenic context? What themes do these objects represent beyond their immediate materiality? How do you interpret the role played by stage costumes and their significance in the history of theatre? How

Figure 1.3.3 *Costume for Prince Siegfried in* Swan Lake, *choreography by Rudolf Nureyev based on that by Marius Petipa and Lev Ivanov, costumes by Nicholas Georgiadis, Vienna Opera, 1964. © CNCS / Pascal François.*

do you expose them in the museum space without the bodies of those who wore them? What is the target audience for such exhibitions? These observations prompted the CNCS to embark on a strategic reflection that helped structure the future organization of its exhibitions. It was decided to take into account the following factors: firstly, the need to develop original curatorial concepts in relation to the collections to discover this new and unique heritage. Secondly, to create a frame for study and research around these collections that considered the archives and documentary resources, as well as the oral testimony and memory of the creators. Thirdly, the desire to reach the widest possible audience, especially in the cultural milieu where the museum is located. Thus, various approaches and methodologies have been put in place, some of which are discussed below.

Each temporary exhibition at the CNCS is defined by its theme and supported by research co-ordinated by the exhibition's curator. The preparation of an exhibition takes into account information and documentation from the programmes of related performances, specialist press clippings and other theatrical archives. The exhibition team organizes meetings and conducts interviews with the costume designers, the costumers, the artisans and the artists who have worn the costumes. This background information about a production and the artistic team that designed the show and costume-making process informs the exhibition. The iconography related to the costumes, including the technical sketches and drawings that preceded the production, the archives and the stage photographs bring indispensable complementary information from the conception of a design to its representation on stage. Finally, audio-visual materials from the productions for which the costumes were originally created offer valuable insights.

Numerous areas of research are addressed in the preparation of a costume exhibition at the CNCS:

- artistic creation through the work of costume designers studied alongside the specific process of stage production;
- the trades and the technical expertise of manufacturers and craftsmen working for the stage (Figure 1.3.4);
- aesthetic characteristics/features specific to the scenography of the shows;
- the history of theatres and companies; and
- the conservation and restoration of the pieces in the collection.

The exhibition topics are based on multiple criteria related to the wide variety and richness of CNCS collections and the diversity of domains and styles in the performing arts, companies, theatres or institutions, costume designers, manufacturing workshops and contemporary creation in general. Special commemorative events, in relation to the three founding institutions include the 450th anniversary of Shakespeare's birth (celebrated in 2014) and the 300th anniversary of the Opéra Comique (which was founded in December 1714 and celebrated its tricentennial in 2015). For each of these a dedicated exhibition was presented at the CNCS, 'Shakespeare: The Material of the World' (2014) and 'The Opéra Comique and its Treasures' (2015).

Figure 1.3.4 *Showcase from the exhibition 'Artisans and Craftsmen of the Performing Arts' (2017). © CNCS / Florent Giffard.*

Presenting opera, theatre and dance costumes relating to the same topic in a single exhibition triggers a 'conversation' between these three artistic forms, yielding a specific resonance for each of the disciplinary practices. Such an approach, embracing different fields of live performance was applied to the following CNCS exhibitions: military costumes ('I Love Soldiers!', 2007), oriental costumes ('The Thousand and One Nights Costumes', 2009) and signs of power ('The Costuming of Power, Opera and Cinema', 2013). Some exhibitions have focused on the complex techniques used in the making of stage costumes: hand-made decorative painting, embroidery and appliqué techniques ('Garden Scenes: Threaded With Flowers', 2009) or unusual fabrics and materials ('The Unusual: Forms and Materials', 2011). In 2012, the exhibition entitled 'La Source: Christian Lacroix and the Paris Opera Ballet' followed each stage of the production from the drawing board to the workshops through to the backstage and on to the opening night. Other exhibitions paid tribute to scenographers and major theatrical institutions such as the Comédie-Française and the Opéra Comique, whose costume workshops are masters in the art of making stage costumes. Further themes included several other celebrated dance companies (such as Diaghilev and Russian operas in the exhibition 'Russian Operas: At the Dawn of the Ballets Russes', 2009–10); musical ensembles (William Christie and the Arts Florissants in 'Barockissimo! Les Arts Florissants on Stage', 2016); even the personal bond that divas have with their stage costumes ('Divas' Dressing Rooms', 2010).

Some examples are striking for their illustration of these themes. For its inauguration in 2006, the CNCS, eager to attract a large number of visitors, chose a multi-public and family theme. Entitled 'Bêtes de scène' ('Stage Beasts') (Figure 1.3.5) this exhibition featured a range of animal stage costumes representing emblematic or secondary roles, such as the well-known 'Papageno' and 'Coq d'or' accompanied by an exciting catalogue. Beyond the discovery of historical and artistic interpretations of these works, this exhibition was above all a real aesthetic shock for visitors, many of whom saw these stage costumes for the first time in a new context. The objects of the exhibition had not only been chosen for their heritage interest, but also for their visual impact. Plunged into an atmosphere that was both poetic and imaginary, the overall display astonished and delighted visitors and contributed to the success of this particular exhibition.

Figure 1.3.5 *Showcase from the exhibition 'Bêtes de scène' (2006). © CNCS / Pascal François.*

A year later, the CNCS paid tribute to Christian Lacroix, its honorary president. The year 2007 marked the twentieth anniversary of Lacroix's haute couture atelier; the exhibition 'Christian Lacroix: Costumier' (Christian Lacroix: Costume Designer), encompassed many of the couturier's creations, both for the French and international fashion scenes. The art direction and the display conceptualized by Christian Lacroix himself, transformed the rooms of the exhibition space into magnificent, enlarged jewellery cases. Each of them revealed sumptuous opera, ballet and theatre costumes reflecting the rich imagination and artistic talent of this great French fashion designer renowned for his new take on craftsmanship, luxury and feminine beauty which characterized 1980s high fashion.

The CNCS is equally interested in contemporary topics. It has investigated other performing arts such as the circus ('Into the Ring! The Most Beautiful Circus Costumes', 2013–14) and pop and French songs ('Undress Me! Pop and Song Costumes', 2016–17). These topics attracted many visitors, including new demographics and many newcomers. The museum has also dedicated exhibitions to two contemporary choreographers who personify the world of modern dance, namely Régine Chopinot and Angelin Preljocaj ('Jean-Paul Gaultier-Régine Chopinot: The Fashion Parade', 2007–08; and 'Angelin Preljocaj: Dance Costumes', 2015–16). By expanding into current events and artistic spaces, the CNCS was able to broaden its audience by attracting diverse visitors and in particular, young adults generally less interested in historical or heritage exhibitions. The media reported widely on these popular and topical exhibitions.

Creating Context for the CNCS Exhibitions: Costumes, Iconographic and Audiovisual Documents

Costumes are scenic objects with a powerful visual presence; even when their magic is striking, their size is excessive, their fabric is ostentatious and their patina is a sign of craftsmanship and the quality of materials. Despite the fact that costumes are on display without the performer's body, the CNCS aims at keeping their scenic and visual impact alive.

The CNCS space is able to showcase an average of 100 costumes (the number ranges from 90 to 140, depending on the selected theme and designer of the exhibition). Most of them are part of the CNCS collections while others are lent by operas, theatres, museums, workshops, costume designers and private collectors. Some exhibitions, 'Angelin Preljocaj: Dance Costumes' and 'Undress Me! Pop and Song Costumes', for example have been organized through loans, which are often complex and time consuming. By giving the CNCS the opportunity to reach out to and collaborate with French and international institutions, these exchanges served as a means to promote the museum within the world of the performing arts. Dealing with theatres and companies well trained in the shipping of stage costumes is important. A majority of costumes are collected in France; others come from England, Italy, Spain, Switzerland, Germany or the United States. Such exchanges also allow the CNCS to expand its collections, since some of the items borrowed for specific exhibitions have subsequently been donated.

Original iconographic materials and documents, as well as high-quality copies, complement the presentation of the costumes. These are mostly pictures, drawings, posters, stage snapshots and set or costume models, yet rarely paintings. In the eyes of the public, the items providing the most insight are fabric samples and sketches annotated by the costume designers because they constitute the intermediary links between the concept and the final product. None of the written documents on display belong to the CNCS; these are usually borrowed from the National Library of France, the Comédie-Française or from costume designers' personal archives.

In 2010, screens were added next to the windows, featuring excerpts of performances in which artists wear the stage costumes on display. Thanks to a partnership with the National Audiovisual Institute, visitors are able to see the costumes in motion. In the auditorium, more lengthy documentaries and interviews with artists, designers or heads of workshops run during the exhibition. Here, copyright remains a challenge. This combination of stage costumes, documents and audiovisual materials offer a diverse and complete experience. By focusing on the practice of costume design, the accompanying materials amplify the creative process and its numerous stages until opening night. They also emphasize the reasons for including costume in our cultural and artistic heritage.

The Art of Displaying Stage Costumes: *Mannequinage* and Scenography

It is particularly hard to showcase stage costumes since they are now deprived of the body that they once dressed. Costumes on display are taken out of context, estranged from their original stage environment and also lack the interactions between setting and characters. The materials of which they are made of (textiles, etc.) often transform them into complex entities: they are often voluminous, yet fragile objects whose sense of the incomplete (lacking the performer, the space and the environment) means that they take on a particular vulnerability.

Yet, the attempt to master exhibiting stage costumes at the same time transcends them: if visitors look at costumes in storage rooms they will not have the same feeling towards them as when they are displayed on human figures or mannequins. Placing the costumes on mannequins – by taking them from storage to the exhibition – 'enhances' them and they take on a new 'cast'. This implies a process of giving costumes their identity back and making their meaning understandable. That is why CNCS aims to reshape, or, at the very least, to evoke the costumes' original context and intent. To this end, the museum relies on two particular techniques, *mannequinage* and set design.

Mannequinage is a technical term that refers to the formulation of a tailored structure based on the body that once inhabited a costume. Standardized mannequins purchased in retail stores never fit perfectly. Thus, costumes are the subject of particular attention before being put on display. Whatever their structure, it should match the silhouette of the artist for whom the costume was designed. Stuffing and substitutes for underskirts (baskets and the likes) may also be used to return to the costume its three-dimensionality. This indispensable work is both delicate and meticulous, intricate and lengthy (Figure 1.3.6). While allowing a good 'reading' of the costume, *mannequinage* is an excellent preventative device since it re-inforces the costume's most fragile parts and gives it a support that strengthens its form. As a result, the costume will not be altered during the exhibition.

Figure 1.3.6 *Various stages of* mannequinage. *© CNCS / Pascaline Noack.*

Mannequinage is a technique that requires specific sewing skills and knowledge of the history of costumes, as well as an understanding of design and form. It understands the structure of a piece and anticipates its final appearance, as well as taking into account any material deficiencies that may even prevent its display. Given the variety of the CNCS exhibitions, the teams responsible for *mannequinage* always consider it a point of honour to meet the curator and set designer. In doing so, they learn about their specific vision and get to know their objectives and the manner in which the costumes will be presented.

Even though mannequins are usually given a neutral or inert attitude, they can sometimes look special. 'Shakespeare: The Stuff of the World', our 2014 celebration of the 450th anniversary of the British playwright's birth is an apt example. Curators Catherine Treilhou-Balaudé and Anne Verdier wished to translate the character of the protagonists through their costumes. The next question was which postures the mannequins should adopt. In the window dedicated to performances staged by Ariane Mnouchkine at the Théâtre du Soleil, some mannequins mimicked the actors' body language. The heavy stage make-up and hairstyles were also faithfully rendered (Figures 1.3.7 and 1.3.8). The final result was successful, but such re-constructions are somehow too real; they read more like motionless 'duplicates' of the performance. For that very reason, they do not really 'belong' to a museum approach; they would probably fit better into the kind of display on show in wax museums. CNCS exhibits do not aim at a veristic reconstruction of performance, but rather at a medium through which the public can see costumes which were once on stage; in doing so, they can re-imagine the performance.

'La Source: Christian Lacroix and the Paris Opera Ballet' was another case in point. For this 2012 exhibition, Lacroix hoped to bring forth the idea of dance and movement via the use of costume. Some mannequins were fashioned after the body of dancers who struck a pose for hours. This particular experience was notable as it went beyond using the traditional mannequins made for fashion display or tailoring. It was instead a specific approach to create movement in the exhibition

Figure 1.3.7 *Showcase from the exhibition 'Shakespeare : The Stuff of the World' (2014). © CNCS / Pascal François.*

and bring closer together the realms of stage and exhibition. It was however, not repeated due to extra delays and financial costs occasioned by these 'tailored' mannequins.

One of the most essential characteristics of the museum is working in conjunction with professionals well-versed and experienced in the performing arts. To assist the CNCS curator or guest curator, the museum calls upon a set designer to create an artistic environment, the 'scenography' of the exhibition and contextualize the costumes. Moreover, the CNCS strongly supports scenographers, costume and set designers whose strength lies in conveying a theatrical vision.

The decoration of the thirteen CNCS exhibition spaces was decided on when the museum was still a project. After much debate concerning the advantages and disadvantages of vitrines (window-like cases) it was decided that eight rooms would be furnished with 25m^2 vitrines designed like small-scale theatre stages by the museum's architect Wilmotte. The absence of windows in the other five rooms offers unlimited possibilities to the set designer for each exhibition, especially in the penultimate space which has a length, width and height equivalent to those of a real theatre stage.

The set designer's mission is to envision and conceive scenography for the exhibit in each room. The set designer supervises the making of the spatial elements and the installation of the visuals, graphics and lighting, including the support elements or frames used to present the costumes. Set designers and curators consult each other here. The display and wall captions and signs, as well as the spaces regulating the flow of the public are also integrated into the setting. This unified approach encourages the visitors to immerse themselves in an aesthetic environment that reinforces the curatorial theme. Some examples follow.

The CNCS 2011 exhibition 'The Art of the Costume at the Comédie-Française' showcased a large variety of costumes manufactured in the workshops of this celebrated theatre house. To 'stage'

Figure 1.3.8 *Showcase from the exhibition 'The Opéra Comique and its Treasures' (2015). © CNCS / Pascal François.*

those historical and contemporary creations, the set designer Roberto Platé played on the notion of theatre décor. Thanks to mirrors placed carefully against the background of the windows, the visitors could admire the costumes as if they were part of the audience and at the same time as if they were standing backstage. The illusion created by this multi-faceted rendering took another dimension in the stage-like room, the larger exhibition room of the museum. There, the costumes were hung above a pool and therefore mirrored in the water. This technical strategy was a great success with the public.

In 2008 the stage setting for 'Garden Scenes: Threaded with Flowers' was grandiose as well. The purpose of this exhibit was to display a selection of costumes ornamented with botanical sources. From window-to-window, the public enjoyed seeing the sophisticated techniques – embroidery, lace, *appliqués*, painting and serigraphy – through which an infinite number of flowers for stage costumes were shaped. The set consisted of miniature stage-décor gardens of various periods designed by Bernard Connan. Each one was a story in itself, leading the visitor into a special world directly related to the costumes on display: The King's Garden, The Winter Garden, The French Garden – these were spaces re-created with special decorations (giant fruits, artificial snow, etc.) to stimulate spectators' imaginations.

To sum up, each exhibition is a new journey within a universe made of colours, atmospheres and stories that our keen visitors look forward to discovering and taking on board. The stage setting is one of the key elements that best stimulate the desire to come to the museum, discover the costumes and grasp the selected themes proposed there. Via scenographic elements, such as wall backdrops, specific lighting, carpets or other floors designs, accessories and furniture the visitor is introduced into an atmosphere that contributes to heir experiencing a range of emotions. The exhibition design becomes a direct route into a fantasy.

While stage costume studies have often benefited from a supporting framework of contextual documents and archives – registers of inventories, accounting registers, staging books, models and drawings, press, iconography, recordings and films – the object of the costume itself was not generally accessible to researchers. Today, thanks to the CNCS collections, it is possible to fill this gap by offering the actual costume for research. This development opens up a whole field of knowledge at the crossroads of many scientific disciplines that are essential for art historians, ethnologists and performance historians, as well as practitioners including directors, costumer designers and performers. Exhibiting costume on its own terms and in new ways thus becomes a field that brings together – in distinct ways – professional, artistic, creative, scientific and heritage worlds.

Snapshots

1.4 Cross-Cultural Costume Research: Beijing Opera Costumes

Alexandra B. Bonds

In 1990–91, I received a Fulbright appointment to teach costume courses at the National Institute for the Arts (now Taipei National University for the Arts) in Taipei, Taiwan. During my year immersed in that culture, I became drawn to the performance of Chinese opera, in particular the actor's complete transformation through costume and makeup. When I enquired about these costumes, a colleague replied 'the goal of the costumes is to communicate the roles to the audience'. As a costume designer, this statement resonated with my own approach to the design process. I was intrigued to learn more about how this simple commonality translated between the costumes of Chinese traditional *Jingju* (capital drama), known in the West as Peking/Beijing opera, and the Euro-American theatrical conventions of my training. I recognized my viewpoint as a costume designer and researcher would always be that of a passionate outside observer of Chinese culture. Yet, through my process of discovery I could bring observations to this art form that might illuminate it in a unique way, while seeking to preserve cultural understanding and sensitivity. In immersing myself in the history, culture and aesthetics of China and the performance of *Jingju*, I learned as much about the research process as the topic of inquiry and have described my observations below.

Definition of Terms

Over 300 forms of indigenous theatre entertainment incorporating music and song, commonly translated as Chinese opera, have evolved in China. *Jingju* is based in Beijing and is the most widespread and influential of the theatre forms, presented today in three types: traditional, newly written historical and contemporary. My research, conducted between 1991 and 2002, focused on the costumes used in traditional *Jingju* as it has been performed in the late twentieth and early twenty-first centuries and resulted in the publication of my findings in *Beijing Opera Costumes: The Visual Communication of Character and Culture* (2008).

Every character in every *Jingju* play is assigned to a role type relating to the character's important personality traits and the circumstances of the play. The four major role types are *sheng* (male characters), *dan* (female characters), *jing* (painted-face characters) and *chou* (lit. 'ugly', clown characters). The role types also contain subdivisions for age and performance skills and each role

Figure 1.4.1 *In the Ming dynasty (1368–1644), the practice of face painting with multiple colours and decorative patterns for the bold* jing *characters emerged. This character is wearing a* kao *(armour) based in part on historical armour with theatrical modifications, such as the broad, padded waist piece in the front and the four flags.* The Ruse of the Bamboo Forest (Zhulin ji) (excerpt). *Character: Yu Hong, actor: Zhang Chengli. National Academy for Chinese Theatre Arts, Beijing, China. 31 May, 2002. Photo by the author.*

projects an ideal through distinct techniques of movement and vocal quality, as well as specific criteria for their representation through hair, makeup and dress. There are four major costume garments: *mang* (court robe), *pi* (formal robe), *kao* (armour; Figure 1.4.1) and *xuezi* (informal robe). While each of these costume categories shares the same basic form, they can be infinitely varied and specific for each of the role types through the selection of fabric colour and embroidery patterns when they are constructed. Each troupe acquires a collection of these conventionalized costumes, which are prepared for the performances of all the plays by trained dressers.

Cultural Choices in the Research Approach

In studying the performance style from another culture, I acknowledge the importance of learning the language in order to be able to conduct in-depth research. After studying Mandarin for one year I realized that I could either write a book or learn the language, yet I could not accomplish both while working and designing full time. Committed to making this information available to others, I made the choice to mould my research to my capabilities by focusing on contemporary costumes and practice accessible through field research, interviews and performance attendance. I depended upon the support of translators for the interviews and engaged the assistance of Fan Yiqi, a Beijing resident and student of *Jingju* and the University of Oregon who became my personal Rosetta Stone. As a local expert, Fan identified the characters, role types and actors in my performance slides, adding a critical factor to my findings. As it would be a lifelong challenge to learn everything about Chinese culture and *Jingju*, I sought supplementary information from American experts in the field: Dr Elizabeth Wichmann-Walczak (University of Hawai'i Manoa) for performance questions and Dr David Rolston (University of Michigan) for questions about the dramatic literature and proper use of pinyin for transliteration of the language. To encounter this subject in the field, I arranged to have tutorials in theory and practice at the Zhongguo Xiqu Xueyan (National Academy for Chinese Theatre Arts) in Beijing, China in 1996, 2000, 2001 and 2002. I attended over sixty performances and with the lenient attitude towards copyright then was allowed to take photographs.

Early in my process, in trying to find a place to land in the complexity of *Jingju* costumes and their context, I thought I had made a brilliant discovery of a link between Chinese and Western theatre. The role types mentioned above became a measure of how not to proceed with my research. Having studied European theatre history, I was familiar with the stock characters of *commedia dell'arte* and how each performer learns to play a fixed type of character. The stock characters in *commedia* are intended to be stereotypes and are limited in their personality range. The role types of *Jingju*, however, do not imply this narrow focus, for they are defined by what the characters in each category have in common, while also accommodating a variety of dispositions. The evolution of the two performance styles are unrelated, as is the execution of these characters in performance. This critical lesson led me to exercise caution when constructing the remainder of my study. Sensitivity to cultural uniqueness was required to build my understanding of this performance style, rather than seeking a relation to something with which I was already familiar.

Framing the information acquired involved developing a suitable translation for expressing the nature of costume within this traditional performance form. While the system of costumes is based on patterns of dress from the Chinese imperial and theatrical past, there is a balance between the historical method and the theatrical execution, with fluidity and flexibility playing a part in the process. I learned to shape my descriptions to allow for mutability of choice, preference and variable circumstances in the company, story and characters. Rather than absolute statements of fact, my descriptors were regularly tempered with qualifiers such as 'generally', 'typically', 'sometimes', 'usually', 'often', 'tend to' and so on. The issue of gender also was a factor in describing the clothing differences among the role types. The gender of the performer is not always the same as the gender of the character and it is important to point out the differences in costumes for the male and female role types. I endeavoured to link the gender of the costume to the roles or the characters consistently by writing about male characters or female roles.

Design and Technology in the Research Approach

My research efforts began with locating the books on *Jingju* costumes available in the English language. Credit must be given to A.C. Scott, who pioneered the study of Chinese theatre starting in the mid-twentieth century. *An Introduction to the Chinese Theatre* (1962) and *Chinese Costume in Transition* (1960) contained information about performances of *Jingju*, translations of scripts, descriptions of the role types and their costumes and makeup. I also found books in English that originated in Chinese-speaking countries which contained similar explanations of the basic elements of costume. The more resources I uncovered, the more I realized that each one contained similar introductory-level information about the costumes, focusing on the role types and their four major garments, the use of colour to express the character and the range of costumes used onstage that were sourced from different periods. The books rarely progressed beyond a beginner's level of appreciation for the costumes. I recognized that as a costume designer, I could bring a new perspective to this subject. Most other writers had been focused on the overall performance, whereas I would be able to answer specific questions that designers may have. The typical steps of inquiry for designing costumes for a production in a Euro-American environment include conducting research into the time and place of the script, exploring both the aesthetic and cultural context and re-imagining these findings through elements of design in a theatrical construct. These fields served as the outline for my book. My research also incorporated the study of making the costumes and the actor's preparation for performance to provide an all-inclusive exploration of analysis and practice.

Time and Place

I widened my research efforts to include studies of dress throughout the history of China, particularly the writings of John E. Vollmer of Canada on imperial dress of the Qing dynasty (1644–1911) such as *Decoding Dragons* (1983) and *Five Colours of the Universe: Symbolism in Clothes and Fabrics of the Ch'ing Dynasty (1644–1911)* (1980). Vollmer's books served as a basis for analysing reflections of and deviations from historical dress onstage. Schuyler Cammann, in his book *China's Dragon Robes* (1952) observed:

> Before 1950 in China, one's Chinese friends invariably said, 'If you are interested in Chinese costume, you must go often to the Chinese theatre'. Such advice is worse than useless. As China has no tradition of theatrical research, both actors and their managers lack any true conception of what the costumes and furniture and weapons were like at earlier periods. Anachronisms are countless and often very ridiculous, even in plays about the last dynasty. (Cammann 1952: 130–1)

During my study of historical dress in China, I learned that throughout the history of imperial China the rule of the Han majority alternated with that of non-Han invaders. Cross-cultural influences in clothing existed in the intervening periods, when invaders took over the rule of the country and established their own form of clothing. For example, the last era of Han rule was the Ming dynasty (1368–1644). Their robes for court were voluminous with wide sleeves. In the subsequent Qing dynasty (1644–1911) under Manchu rule, official clothing was regulated and all in attendance at court were required to dress in the Manchu court robe style with narrow torsos and the fitted sleeves of the Manchu rulers, regardless of their ethnicity. Dress at home was not under court edict and the majority of Han people continued to wear their own style of fuller clothing for private functions. In addition to dress from these two ethnicities and eras being worn simultaneously, hybrid clothing developed from the country's interplay of cultures. The real-life environment of dress that mixed ethnic models contributed to the current interpretation of clothing on the traditional *Jingju* stage. Rather than being discordant by combining costumes of different times and places, the *Jingju* costumed image may be considered a logical theatrical interpretation of the larger Chinese cultural context. The *Jingju* wardrobe today is made up of approximately one-third Han-based costumes and one-third Manchu-based costumes. The other one-third are theatrically derived costumes, which were developed by actors to support specific actions, situations or characters (Figure 1.4.2).

Imperial dress was imbued with significant messages communicated by the symbolism of the images on the surface. For example, the robes of court officials were decorated with a terrestrial composition of waves, mountains and clouds with dragons floating above. The number of claws on the dragons was an indication of official's rank. The five-clawed dragon (*long*) represented the highest achievement and ranked above the four-clawed dragon *(mang)*. As actors had not earned the right to wear the *long*, their court robes initially had dragons with fewer claws. The name for the court robe onstage is *mang*, in reference to these lesser dragons. The number of dragon claws is now, however, all but ignored in theatrical dress. Among existing robes from the late Qing dynasty are examples with dragon claws added later, indicating that more of the higher officials were gaining the right to wear the five-clawed version, making the five-toed dragons less exclusive (Cammann 1952: 32). Furthermore, with the end of the dynastic era in 1911, there was no longer any pressure to subscribe to imperial regulations of dress. Now most dragons on traditional *Jingju* costumes have the full complement of five claws per foot. Dragons, along with other imperial symbols applied to Jingju costumes, are utilized to continue the tradition of symbolic ornamentation, though the language of the precise meaning is flexible today.

Aesthetic and Cultural Context

Another valuable discovery came from my examination of the related arts in China, when I ascertained how painting and embroidery merged during the Song dynasty (960–1279). Embroiderers in search of innovative subject matter began stitching duplicates of famous paintings including admired floral compositions. Rather than depicting an entire bush, the painter created a branch with several blossoms to represent the whole. The flowers were stylized into the essence of the blossom, rather than realistically rendered. Individual petals were beautifully evoked by blending two or three shades of colour on each petal to enhance the contours, yet the flowers cast no shadow. While every painted or embroidered flower is unique, all of the flowers are represented with this same idealized appearance. Pieces of embroidered textiles from the Song dynasty verify the clear links between that era's aesthetics and contemporary embroidery on *Jingju* costumes, which, still to this day, carry the characteristics of flowers painted in that era. Though the stylization of the flowers has been retained, the flowers' cultural messages are no longer implied as with the court costumes.

Figure 1.4.2 *The character on the left is dressed in the* qimang *(Manchu robe), a full-length narrow robe derived from the dress of Manchu women in the Qing dynasty, (1644–1911) because she is a princess of a foreign northern dynasty while the figure on the right, as the wife of a Tang dynasty (618–907) prime minister, wears a* nümang *(woman's court robe) reflecting her Han heritage.* The Red-Maned Fiery Steed (Hongzong liema). *Character, left: Daizhan gongzhu, actor: unidentified. Character, right: Madam Wang, actor: Zhai Mo. Beijing Jingju Company, Beijing, China, 6 October 2001. Photo by the author.*

Elements of Design

A key moment in my discovery process was recognizing that the elements of design in *Jingju* costumes have parallels with the elements of design in Western art training: line, form, colour and texture. The Chinese use a system of 'outer' and 'inner' elements to describe the visual impact. The 'outer' describes the overall image, primarily the silhouette which is rather simple and geometric and corresponds to line and form. Visual clues from the 'outer' can identify the character by their given circumstances: status, gender, wealth, nationality, age and whether they are military or civilian. The 'inner' image is created on the surface of the costume with colour and texture, which reveals further information about the specific character, their personality and relationship to others. The 'outer' and 'inner' characteristics work together to communicate notions of the character to the audience.

Practice

In addition to understanding these costumes on a theoretical level in terms of background and design, costume practitioners also want to know how to make and use these costumes. Therefore, in my research, I chose to address the technology of the costumes on equal terms with their historical, contextual and visual analysis. My tutorials encompassed lessons in how to dress actors, including the layers of costumes typically worn, how to tie knots in the sashes and lash the flags for the characters wearing armour. Another course examined the application of makeup and the configuration of the hairstyles. In addition, I arranged a field trip to a factory where the costumes were made to witness the embroidery process and observe the stages of costume construction. I also drafted scaled and gridded patterns of twenty-two of the frequently worn costumes. This grouping of technical studies had not been provided in previous writings about *Jingju* costumes and formed a significant part of my original research, contributing to the study of *Jingju* costumes with a technological perspective.

Absence of a Designer and the Dresser's Role

Often, the aspect of traditional *Jingju* costumes that surprises most in the field of costume is the absence of a single designer to conceive and create the stage picture for every performance. As a traditional performance style, the costumes have developed with a conventional pattern of use and imagery. The wardrobe personnel maintain a stock of these standardized costumes with a selection of garments suitable to dress each character in every performance in the troupe's repertoire. They learn the costume plots and lists of characters for every play, as well as the patterns of costumes designated for the role types in given circumstances. To illustrate this approach I sourced a book with a written record of costume plots for several frequently performed plays. Working with a translation of one of the plots, I then compared it to the costumes I observed and recorded in two different performances of the same play, *The Phoenix Returns to Its Nest* (*Feng huan chao*) (Beijing Jingju Company, 9 July 2000, and National Jingju Company, 3 October 2001). By showing the written descriptions, along with the photographs of two dressers' interpretations of each character, I was able to establish the fundamental concept of conventionalized dress, as well as demonstrate how to assemble the costumes for a performance without a designer in the room (Bonds 2019: 263–75).

Recognizing the Similarities and Honouring the Distinctions

From this brief overview, it is apparent that the approach to costuming in *Jingju* shares some similarities with the Euro-American method of costuming yet also has unique qualities. Both forms tend to include a theatrical interpretation of the past and draw from elements of design within culturally based definitions. *Jingju* costumes have developed within living cultural traditions over long periods of time without the benefit of a dedicated costume designer. The costumes have been conventionalized to allow them to be used for all plays, while contemporary Western performances generally have a costume designer who designs specific costumes for each production. Both forms, through very distinct processes, share a goal to communicate the role to the audience through costume. From my perspective as an outsider to Chinese traditional *Jingju*, I have been able to convey these insights and fresh connections to the conversation about collected knowledge of *Jingju* costumes while also preserving the art form at this moment in time. My awareness of the techniques of expressing the roles in *Jingju* costumes now also informs my costume design and teaching and provides a more inclusive worldview of the theory and practice of imaging the body onstage.

References

Bonds, A. B. (2008), *Beijing Opera Costumes: The Visual Communication of Character and Culture*. Honolulu: University of Hawai'i Press.

Bonds, A. B. (2019), *Beijing Opera Costumes: The Visual Communication of Character and Culture*. New York and London: Routledge.

Cammann, S. (1952), *China's Dragon Robes*. New York: The Ronald Press Company.

Scott, A. C. (1957), *The Classical Theatre of China*. New York: The Macmillan Company.

Scott, A. C. (1960), *Chinese Costume in Transition*. New York: Theatre Arts Books.

Scott, A. C. (1962), *An Introduction to the Chinese Theatre*. New York: Theatre Arts Books.

Vollmer, J. E. (1977), *In the Presence of the Dragon Throne: Ch'ing Dynasty Costume in the Royal Ontario Museum*. Toronto: Royal Ontario Museum.

Vollmer, J. E. (1980), *Five Colours of the Universe: Symbolism in Clothes and Fabrics of the Ch'ing Dynasty (1644–1911)*. Edmonton: Edmonton Art Gallery.

Vollmer, J. E. (1983), *Decoding Dragons*. Oregon: University of Oregon.

Glossary

Chou	lit. 'ugly', used for clown roles, foolish magistrates, nagging women and servants
commedia dell'arte	a sixteenth-century form of theatre based in Italy and characterized by masked character types
dan	female roles
jing	painted-face roles; men of great strength with formidable physical or mental powers
Jingju	capital drama, the Beijing style of performance combining music, speech, song, pantomime, dance and acrobatics in a single unified presentation. Name used after mid-twentieth century
kao	stage armour for generals and high-ranking military roles
long	dragon with five claws. Also historical garments with this dragon embroidered on the surface
mang	dragon with four claws. Also court robe costume for the emperor and highest-ranking courtiers and generals with embroidery of dragons and waves
nümang	court robe for Han women
pi	formal robe with symmetrical opening, worn by *sheng and dan* for domestic scenes
qimang	Manchu court robe for non-Han women
sheng	standard male roles with intrinsic dignity
xuezi	informal robe with asymmetrical opening for men

1.5 Reading Maltese Carnival Costumes

Vicki Ann Cremona

A carnival costume is charged with possibilities – what the wearer chooses to wear or to omit indicates whether s/he wants to reveal or hide her/his identity. Does the costumed figure wear a mask? A wig? A hat or a head covering? Do wearers deform their bodies through the costume? What operations do the costumes perform regarding the individual's social status?

Carnival in Malta under British rule in the nineteenth and early twentieth centuries took place in the street, in private ballrooms and later at public balls. All social classes mixed in the street and in this context, ostentation or dissimulation of identity was also linked to social background. People from poorer backgrounds used basic elements to complicate their identity, the most common being sheets covering the whole person, especially their faces and sometimes exaggerating their natural figure by making it appear taller by means of poles or brooms held aloft under the sheets. Persons from wealthier backgrounds wore 'dominos', long, loose cloaks associated for centuries with Venetian carnival, often dark in colour, but sometimes adorned with bows and ribbons, generally with a hood that covered the head; the face was often covered with a mask. In 1891, the press commented that dominos accounted for five-sixths of the Carnival disguises that year stating that they were comfortable (*comodi*) and cheap (*poco costosi*) (*Malta* 1891: 2).

A wide variety of costumes were characteristically worn including the peasant costumes that were usually attributed to a couple who featured in popular farces, Żeppi and his wife Grezz:

Grez u Zeppi, Domino ed Arlecchini	Grez and Zeppi, dominos and harlequins
Pagliacci, Turchi, Maghe e Saltarelli	Clowns, Turks, witches and dancers
Diavoli, mascolini e femminini,	Devils, male and female
Divertivan con cento giocarelli	Provided amusement with hundreds of games
(*L'Asino* 1894: 2)	

Poor-looking clothing was also used to hide the perpetrators of bad behaviour. Members of the '*jeunesse dorée*' (gilded youth or the fashionable young) were glimpsed wearing tatty clothes (*alla peggio*) and with strange coverings on their heads (*Malta* 1895: 2). In certain cases, dissimulation of class and identity using a shabby appearance was exploited to molest humble women. Poorer people from the countryside, wearing rags and dirty clothes as disguises were criticized for entering the capital city of Valletta and behaving rudely and disrespectfully there (*Il-Berka* 1932: 2). A poem in a satirical newspaper emphasized that social status was turned upside down through costume:

Tilmah fkir bla habba f'butu	One can note a poor man without a penny in his pocket
Icun liebes bhal sinjur	Dressed as a gentleman
Cull min f'butu ghandu il-liri	Whoever has pounds in his pocket
Bl'ghar ilbies johrog idur.	Goes out wearing the worst clothing.
(*Dr. Brombos* 1934: 15).	

Group identity in the streets was characteristic of all social classes, but during Carnival it was manifested differently. Bands of poorer young boys created a common identity through blackened faces as well as through the noise they produced by beating on tins. More privileged youth wore thematic and often sophisticated costumes. In 1902, they included 'Music', 'Daisies' and 'Chinese', the latter being described as 'original and very elegant' (*GM* 1902: 2). Although such costumes provided a group identity, it is probable that the wearers were showing off their individual identities as well,

Figure 1.5.1 *The Carnival Ball at the Governor's Palace in Malta.* The Minuet Dancers Saluting the Throne. *Published in* The Graphic, *18 March 1899. Courtesy of the author.*

not simply hiding behind a mask. Expensive costumes attracted attention, identifying their wearers as belonging to the bourgeoisie or more privileged classes.

Private balls were a different affair; entrance was reserved for people from the upper echelons of society. Being present at such a ball meant the social recognition of one's rank; while people bowed and smiled to each other, they acknowledged each other's importance and the fact that they belonged to the same social elite. This mutual appreciation prolonged itself beyond the confines of a carnival ball and not only impacted upon business relations but could also result in advantageous marriages. Therefore, in these contexts, carnival costume not only had to appeal through beauty or originality but attract attention to the wearer themselves, especially if they were considered a good match (Cremona 2018: 102). Costumes could be either rented or especially made. Shops advertised various costumes, often linked to operas or operettas for rent in newspapers before Carnival. As well as showing the inter-relationship and popularity of those two genres, it also revealed that theatre costume makers could earn extra money during Carnival. One such advertisement stated that a particular shop had 'historical, dramatic, burlesque and fancy costumes – for sale or hire' made by 'first class opera tailors' (*DMC* 1898: 9). Another, appearing the next day advertised the availability of silks and satins, indicating the quality of the costumes, as well as the fact that fabrics which caught the light were favoured (electricity had already been introduced into private houses and was installed in the streets from 1894). The lists of costumes worn by persons in fancy dress at the Governor's Ball were published in newspapers; they showed a huge variety of costumes, some of which certainly displayed great lavishness and detail. In 1878, the gentlemen's costumes included Florentine nobles, a khan, a grand vizier, knights, a Figaro but also a lollipop man, fishermen and huntsmen. The ladies wore costumes ranging from that of Marie Antoinette, to queens – of night, of May, of Tartary and more – and a Venetian lady and her page, but they also included peasants of different nationalities, probably creating much colour and variety, as well as a milkmaid, a shepherdess and a fishwife (*The Enterprise* 1878: 1). Since clothing covers – or reveals – the body, it is affected by the norms and rules of how the body is expected to appear in society. Carnival, which is often described as a liberatory moment also had limits regarding appearance that were socially imposed. A singer competing for the best costume in a public ball was disqualified in 1912 because her costume was too revealing (*troppo a nudo*) (*Malta* 1912: 2).

In the 1920s, the rise of organized competitions at public balls and in the street brought new costume developments. Much originality was generated by the participation of artists who designed both costumes and carnival floats, creating fantastical figures and original costumes. Yet costumes of this period must also be read against the new social habits and customs that had developed including the introduction of cinema. Costumes such as 'Harold Lloyd' (whose career stretched from 1913 to the 1920s), *Coster Bill* (a British film dating from 1912) or Mickey and Minnie Mouse produced new Carnival appearances (*Il-Berka* 1934: 6). Politics was also satirized through costume, especially when the Maltese began to claim more autonomy in their domestic affairs. As Maltese politicians rose to the fore, claiming self-government, contesting elections or protesting against imperial repression, rival politics became choice subjects for satire. Using masks in papier-mâché that caricatured the faces of eminent politicians, transforming their bodies to look like theirs and wearing the type of suits they would wear, members of rival political parties – or people paid by them – used Carnival to pour criticism on political adversaries. People also poked fun at dignitaries:

> The League of Nations was also represented by Mr. Pio Muscat Azzopardi complete with decorations which included the Star of Kiwi Boot Polish and the Order of the Bar, which in this case proved to be a miniature bottle of Johnnie Walker. (*ToM* 1936: 7)

This particular costume had subversive racist connotations, as Kiwi boot polish was a brand of shoe black common in the British colonies, a Kiwi being a New Zealander and boot polish being black.

Costume cannot be divorced from the circumstances in which it is worn, even if these appear to be totally immersed in fun. Carnival costumes can also be read through the lens of the social and political realities of a society. Although they link past to present and reality to imagination, they are firmly entrenched in the contemporaneity that produces them.

References

Cremona, V. A. (2018), *Carnival and Power: Play and Politics in a Crown Colony*. London: Palgrave Macmillan.

The Daily Malta Chronicle and Garrison Gazette (*DMC*) (1898), 16 February, 9.

The Enterprise (1878), 18 March, 1.

'F'Jem l'Iblah' (1934), *Dr. Brombos*, 3 February,15.

Il-Berka, 26 January, 1934, 6.

'Il Carnival u'l Piazzez ta Sda. Rjali' (1932), *Il-Berka*, 8 February, 2.

La Gazzetta di Malta (*GM*) (1902), 12 February, 2.

'Le Maschere' (1894), *L'Asino*, 3 February, 2.

Malta (1891), 11 February, 2.

Malta (1912), 28 February, 2.

Times of Malta (*ToM*) (1936), 25 February, 7.

1.6 Curating Costume: Reflection

Aoife Monks

Costumes on display in an exhibition seem to want to tell us about their stage lives but, like Samuel Beckett's voices of the dead, they often feel insufficient (Beckett 1954/1982). Exhibitions of costumes are often disappointing. Somehow, the display of a tutu, or a cloak, or a man's suit in a glass case does little to communicate these artefacts' previous lives onstage, even if framed by words or other objects, or even photographic or video recordings. They withhold their secrets from us and fail to communicate their extraordinary stage lives.

It is tempting to conclude from this problem that ultimately the issue lies in the ephemerality of performance. According to scholars such as Peggy Phelan (1993) or Herbert Blau (1982), performance's incapacity to ever repeat itself exactly (a failure that is seen by these writers as key to its radical potential) means that the material residues of theatre can only point to the essential absence that they represent. The performance is gone, is no more and cannot be re-captured. The costume on display only reminds us that an exhibition comprises an essentially unsatisfactory attempt to reclaim the lost theatre experience through its material afterlives.

Additionally, as Elizabeth Wilson reminds us, unworn clothes may prompt the discomforts of the uncanny. As she puts it: 'Clothes are so much part of our living, moving selves that, frozen on display in the mausoleums of culture, they hint at something only half understood, sinister, threatening' (Wilson 1985/2003: 2). Although Wilson generally writes about fashion, her comments can also be applied to costume. Her claim that exhibitions only serve to remind us of the porous boundaries between the body and dress, with empty clothing discomfiting us with its uncanny status as an 'almost-body', has relevance for theatre costume too. There, the apparently autonomous body of the performer turns out to have been partly made of 'stuff' all along, produced by other theatre-workers, an object remaining long after the performer has gone but failing to communicate the powers and pleasures that it once produced in performance.

Certainly this argument of insufficiency, incompleteness and ephemerality should become part of the picture in understanding why theatre costume is so challenging to curate. But I wonder if there might be a question of the idea of the 'picture' itself being part of the problem? This question is prompted by Rebecca Schneider's querying of 'the ways in which performance remains, but remains differently [. . .] The ways, that is, that performance resists a cultural thrall to the ocular – a thrall that would delimit performance as that which cannot remain to be seen' (Schneider 2001: 101). Schneider's query rests on the proposition that scholars attached to the notion of theatre's 'disappearance' proceed from the assumption that theatre is primarily a visual art form. However, as she puts it '[this] predominant art historical attitude toward performance might overlook different ways of accessing history offered by performance' (Schneider 2001: 101). Schneider's investigation of the alternative models of theatrical remains which sidestep the ocular ones, means that she insists on the value of oral and performed memory particularly historical re-enactment. She is invested in the idea that it is in the bodies of performers that the memories and meanings of performance might 'remain'. This work maps onto the material and embodied 'turns' that are currently being pursued in other fields and disciplines from dress history to experimental archaeology.

I would like to take her up on her challenge regarding the thesis of ephemerality in another vein, by returning to an aspect of theatrical remains that is usually presented as 'to be looked at' by asking what would happen if we refused to curate costume as a *visual* form. What would it mean to sidestep the 'ocular' as a model for the display of costume in the museum? What would an exhibition on costume become if audiences weren't asked to 'look' but rather to 'attend to' the other non-visual functions of theatrical dress in a museum of costume?

In asking this, costume's other sorts of theatrical lives and the people who work with costume might come to light. Costume, after all can be understood as (sometimes literally) coating the 'surface' of an actor's body onstage, but it can also be framed as the glue that holds a series of working relationships together backstage at the theatre. Costume does more than simply constitute a border for the actor's body, as Wilson suggests it also comprises a series of intersections between the work of actor and tailor, designer and maker, performer and dresser, tailor and dyer, director and designer, designer and photographer, actor and role and so on. My expression of this network of relations here fails to take into account the complicated web it comprises suggesting only a binary form, whereas in practice it constitutes a shifting, always dynamic interplay between a wide range of theatre workers. Costume, then, can be seen as the intermediary that facilitates these workers and their cultures and practices backstage at the theatre.

If this is the case, then costume shifts from being a visual object to be understood through looking, to becoming a far more complicated set of practices and processes that are multi-sensory. How might a costume exhibition offer a visitor the familiar smell of sweat, cloth, mustiness and bodies that hits you when walking into the costume store or hire shop, or the smell of detergent that wafts through the halls by the wardrobe rooms or the odour of chemicals in the dye shop? What about the sensation of the insides of a corset for the performer or the play of silk against the tailor's hands as she irons out its seams? What of the rustle of taffeta or the clattering of tap shoes or the clanking of armour or the tinkling of sequins in a row of costumes hanging on a rail? How might the taste of thread or pins in the maker's mouth or the leather licked by an actor onstage (tasting no doubt their predecessor's residues within a re-used costume) be made available to a visitor? What about the parts of the costume that the audience *can't* see – the perfectly rendered button holes, the beautiful seams, the work done by makers for the pride of it all rather than in any service to the theatrical illusion? What of the feelings engendered in an actor while being adjusted by a dresser that they know well from other performances or the affects produced by wearing a costume previously inhabited by a famous ancestor? Or how might the systems of taxonomy employed by buyers and administrators for the ordering of costumes and their materials or the mess of the workrooms and the dye shop in the midst of a set of urgent performance deadlines be represented? How might an exhibition of costume take account of these experiences and what would costume end up 'looking' like if it did?

Curation, after all, shares an etymological root with the concept of 'care'. Curating costume, then, should not only involve caring for the clothes themselves but also for the experiences of those who worked with them. In this way, the skills, ethos, labour, time, creativity, techniques, affects and investments that comprise theatre-work might come to light. Curating costume then could become an act of representation – not only of the experiences of past performances but also of the values that undergird the performance of making and wearing, the sociability of theatre workers and the various cultures and hierarchies backstage at the theatre.

While discussions of theatre have often centred on the work of writers, designers, directors and actors, an exhibition of costume has the potential to remind us that it is not only the materials of costume that remain after a show is over. So too do the people who made them and worked with them, who carry on to the next production shifting their ethos of excellence and commitment over to the job at hand with the ruthless pragmatism demanded by the on-going work of the theatre. Curating *their* experience may well be the true work of caring for costume.

Note

I wrote this piece at the beginning of a project to produce a book and exhibition on the work of the costume department at the National Theatre in London. My argument here forms the basis of my approach to curation and editing, and in it, I aim to emphasize the non-object status of theatre costumes in favour of representing the cultures of work that produce them. The exhibition opened on 4 October 2019 with its original run scheduled until 27 June 2020.

References

Beckett, S. (1954/1982), *Waiting For Godot*. New York: Grove Press.

Blau, H. (1982), *Take Up the Bodies: Theater at the Vanishing Point*. Urbana, IL: University of Illinois Press.

Phelan, P. (1993), *Unmarked: The Politics of Performance*. New York: Routledge.

Schneider, R. (2001), 'Performance Remains', *Performance Research* 6 (2), 100–08.

Wilson, E. (1985/2003), *Adorned in Dreams: Fashion and Modernity*. New Brunswick, NJ: Rutgers University Press.

Section 2

Personalities in Costume

2.1 Costume Centre Stage: Re-membering Ellen Terry (1847–1928)

Veronica Isaac

Resurrecting the Dead

There is something uncanny about a costume on display: though inanimate, it is a garment which insists on the absent body. Indeed, the mannequin and its 'shroud' are consciously employed to resurrect the absent or deceased performer(s) who once inhabited it. To suggest that curators are engaged in resurrecting the dead, risks conjuring up images of body snatching, séances and melodrama. Whilst this evokes an atmosphere of dramatic spectacle appropriate to a discussion of theatre costume in the late nineteenth century, the spirits under consideration in this chapter have no malicious intent. To summon these benevolent spirits, costumes, rather than Ouija boards, are required: these are, after all, garments which carry 'magic' in their fibres.

Sybil Thorndike felt a particular reverence for costumes worn by her fellow actress Ellen Terry declaring that:

> Ellen's stage clothes became such a part of her that some magic seemed to belong to them. I know her daughter Edith Craig never liked them being cleaned, she said it spoilt them and the magic went out of them.[1]

Thorndike's description of the 'magic' which was an intrinsic part of Terry's costumes resonates with what Susan Pearce has described as 'the power of the "actual object"' (Pearce 1994: 25). Stage costumes, unlike many examples of historic dress derive this perceived power directly from the close connection they develop with their original wearer(s). This connection transforms them from a simple garment into a carrier of their 'identity' with the ability to take on the role of the 'effigy' perpetuating the 'memory' of the lost production and literally, 're-membering', the absent performer (Roach 1996: 36).

This chapter illuminates the important function that stage costumes can have in what Marvin Carlson termed 'ghosting' (Carlson 2003). Having established the role of costumes as 'carriers of identity' and 'memory' it considers why and how performers might deliberately reference their own past roles by re-creating or alluding to costumes which reference a previous performance or a specific aspect of their celebrity. Through the close analysis of specific examples from the wardrobe of celebrated Victorian actress Dame Ellen Terry (1847–1928), it will highlight the degree to which costumes are haunted by 'ghosts' of 'performers' and 'performances' both during the lifetime of their original wearer(s) and after their death.

'Haunted by the Absent Body' (Hodgdon 2006: 143)

Recalling a visit to the Royal Shakespeare Company Collection (hereafter RSC Collection), Barbara Hodgdon offered an evocative description of '[…] the thrill of touching a costume's fabric, feeling its weight and drape in one's hand' (Hodgdon 2006: 140). Hodgdon's observations capture the excitement of direct engagement with surviving costumes. It is only by examining a costume at first hand that one can fully appreciate and document material evidence of the body or bodies, which once inhabited it. These traces of past performers and performances are significant, because whilst certain costumes are preserved, the majority are re-used, re-cycled and ultimately discarded. Costumes which survive often do so because of their association with the celebrated performers who once wore them. In such cases, the original wearer shapes not only the physical form of the costume but also its historical identity. These are garments which are 'indelibly imprinted' with both the physical and spiritual 'ghosts' of their wearers (Hodgdon 2006: 141).

It is arguably the perceived presence of these 'ghosts' which enable costumes to take on what Hodgdon terms a 'talismanic function', offering a tangible connection between performers past and present. Terry's respect for the 'memories' carried by costumes is apparent in the large collection of costumes and related ephemera she assembled in the collection now housed at her former home, Smallhythe Place in Kent. There were also occasions on which relics of past performers provided inspiration for her own performances. For instance, when taking on the role of Lady Macbeth in 1888, Terry kept a pair of shoes, reputedly worn by Sarah Siddons in the same part, in her dressing room at the Lyceum Theatre.[2]

For Terry, these precious shoes were 'not to wear, but to keep with [her]'.[3] When performers move beyond looking and touching to wearing surviving costumes, however, this 'talismanic function' is intensified. Indeed, Thorndike's description of her experience when wearing Terry's 'Beetlewing Dress' (co-incidentally also from *Macbeth*) suggests that actors can become temporary 'hosts' of the 'ghosts' preserved within certain costumes:

> The moment I put on Ellen's dress, something happened, not a tremor, not a quake, I waltzed through the play on air. When it came to the banquet scene, the fine American star lost himself, his nerve went. But the beetlewing dress came to the rescue. I wasn't a very hefty girl in those days but something pushed me from behind and I took hold of that huge man and I hurled him across the stage, whispering his words in his ear […] that was Ellen Terry's dress, she pushed me on. That's what Ellen did to her dresses.[4]

Evidence that this 'ghosting' is an established part of theatrical practice can be found in Hodgdon's analysis of the fate of a 'rat coloured cardigan with pockets' within the RSC Collection. The 'power' attributed to this 'everyday sort of garment' stemmed from its connection with actress Peggy Ashcroft

(1907–91) who wore it when playing the Countess of Rossillion in the 1982 Royal Shakespeare Company production of *All's Well that Ends Well* (her last Shakespearean role). Returned to the theatre's wardrobe after the final performance, by 1999 the cardigan had a name, 'The Peggy', and was part of 'material memory system' in which performers resurrected and wore the garment, simultaneously referencing the previous wearers and productions and adding to its history (Hodgdon 2006: 160–1).[5]

Simon Sladen (2017) has drawn attention to the important role that deliberate 'ghosting' plays within contemporary pantomime. Through an examination of pantomime dame Chris Hayward's tribute to star performer and female impersonator Danny La Rue (1927–2009), Sladen highlighted the part that costume can play in what he describes as the 'hosting' process. As he demonstrated, this was a performance in which both Hayward's body and his 'borrowed' costume worked to 're-member' the lost performer, resulting in a performance 'ghosted' by the memories of La Rue's former triumphs which took full advantage of the 'halo' effect this produces.

Terry's recognition of the 'meanings' and 'memories' costumes carry for both the performer and the audience will be made apparent in the case studies which follow. Before considering how Terry sought to exploit the power of 'ghosting', however, it is first necessary to establish why the actresses felt she needed the protection afforded by the 'halo effect' (Carlson 2003: 58–9).

'They Love Me, you Know, Not for What I Am, but for What They Imagine I Am'[6]

The second child of two strolling players, both Ellen Terry and her elder sibling Kate were trained for the stage from an early age. Terry made her first stage appearance aged eight, performing the role of Mamillius in *The Winter's Tale* opposite the actor/manager Charles Kean (1811–68) as Leontes. She remained with the Keans' company at the Princess Theatre, London until the Keans departed for America in 1860. Having completed this useful apprenticeship, Terry began a more nomadic existence, moving in pursuit of new engagements, and between 1860 and 1863 she performed in London, toured 'the provinces' and worked with a stock company in Bristol.[7]

Between 1864 and 1874, Terry's career was then punctuated by what she termed two 'vacations' from the stage (Terry 1908: 76). The first, to marry the painter George Frederick Watts (1817–1904) in 1864. The second, between 1868 and 1874, when distressed by the failure of her first marriage and the pressure to re-kindle her stage career, Terry eloped with the architect and designer, Edward Godwin (1833–86). As Terry acknowledged, both men had a lasting impact on her approach to dress and design, training her to make careful judgements 'about colours, clothing and lighting' (Terry 1908: 150). The relationships provided an opportunity to learn not only from the work of Watts and Godwin, but also to gather ideas from the other artists they both brought her into contact with.

Terry spent six years living with Godwin. They never married, but did have two children together: Edith Craig (1869–1947) and Edward Gordon Craig (1872–1966).[8] In 1874, however, financial necessity coupled with the gradual collapse of her relationship with Godwin compelled Terry to return to the stage. Over the next four years she gradually re-built her professional career and by 1878 had become established as a 'general favourite' with 'aesthetic credentials, and a following alert to decorative elegance' (Meisel 1983: 403). This success brought Terry to the attention of Sir Henry Irving (1838–1905) who invited her to become the leading lady of the Lyceum Company (Terry 1908: 147).

This invitation marked the commencement of a partnership which endured over twenty years and established both Irving and Terry at the pinnacle of their profession. The seven tours of America which the Lyceum Company undertook between 1883 and 1902 brought them international celebrity and by the late 1880s Terry was one of the most popular and celebrated actresses of her generation and amongst the 'best paid women in England' (Powell 1997: 7).

From 1889 onwards however, tensions began to develop between the two performers. The success of Terry's partnership with Irving was founded upon her ability to perform the role and 'roles' of a 'leading lady'. This made it impossible for her career to follow the traditional path from leading lady towards 'heavy business' in secondary and more mature female roles (graduating in Shakespeare's *Othello* from Desdemona to Emilia and in *Hamlet* from Ophelia to Gertrude) (Davis 1991: 22). Instead Terry, now approaching her fifties, remained confined to 'young parts' (Terry 1908: 313). There were fleeting moments of brilliance, with Terry's performance as Imogen in *Cymbeline* in 1896 'accounted one of her greatest triumphs' and the fifty-year-old actress was described as 'radiant' and 'full of girlish spirits' (A.B. Walkley quoted in Richards 2005: 44). Yet in Terry's view, this production represented her 'only inspired performance of these later years' and sustaining the illusion of 'eternal youth' was becoming an increasingly oppressive burden for the actress (Terry 1908: 316).[9]

By 1902, she was conscious that 'the Lyceum reign was dying' and understood the pragmatic motivation that prompted Irving to revive 'his biggest "money-maker"' *Faust*. She was nevertheless determined that 'it was [now] impossible that [she] could play Margaret' (Terry 1908: 313):

> There are some young parts that the actress can still play when she is no longer young: Beatrice, Portia, and many others come to mind. But I think that when the character is that of a young girl the betrayal of whose innocence is the main theme of the play, no amount of skill on the part of the actress can make up for the loss of youth. (Terry 1908: 313)

Gail Marshall attaches specific importance to the emphasis reviewers placed on Terry's 'eternal youth'. She argues that when faced with the pressure to continue performing young roles, the 'only way in which [Terry] might remain on stage was through the turning back of the theatrical and social clock, which the illusion of an ever-youthful Terry enabled' (Marshall 2009: 157). Building on this point, Marshall suggests that:

> [Terry's] perpetual charm is precisely that, a perpetuation of her audiences' initial enamoured response. That stasis begins to explain why it is not only possible, but necessary, for Terry to play the parts of much younger characters, or to reprise some of her earlier successes in later life: it […] reminds her audiences of why they have adored her, and enables them to keep on loving her, and watching her play. (Marshall 2009: 155)

Marshall's observations resonate with Carlson's descriptions of the extent to which an audience's 'reception of each new performance is conditioned by inevitable memories of this actor playing similar roles in the past' (Carlson 2003: 58). Engaging with Joseph Roach, Carlson observes that the 'power of performance' is such that the 'theatrical body' (unlike the physical body) cannot be 'invalidated by age or decrepitude' (Carlson 2003: 58).

I extend Carlson's idea, arguing that the garments in which this 'theatrical body' is clothed have the potential to play an integral part in evoking 'the ghost or ghosts of previous roles' (Carlson 2003: 11). Focusing specifically on two connected pairs of costumes from Terry's wardrobe, I argue that the actress consciously sought to harness the 'memories' carried by these garments, ensuring that her later performances would be 'haunted' and 'protected' by the 'ghosts' of her youthful successes.

'A Dream of Beauty': Tragic Heroines

From the commencement of her professional partnership with Irving, Terry played an active role in the design and creation of her costume and was granted an unusually high level of control over this process (Isaac 2018). Between 1878 and 1887, the primary designer of Terry's costumes was Patience Harris (1857–1901). As the surviving costumes and images attest, Harris generally created elaborate gowns, made from stiff and heavy silk damasks and silk velvets.[10] From *c.*1882 onwards, however, Terry also engaged Alice Comyns-Carr (1850–1927) to assist with the design of her costumes. A known advocate and wearer of aesthetic dress, Comyns-Carr's taste in dress and approach to costume design were in much closer accord with the flowing, lightweight dresses that Terry favoured for her personal wardrobe.[11] Comyns-Carr worked alongside Harris for nearly five years, but the collaboration was not a success and Harris 'had but little use for the simple designs [she] suggested' (Comyns-Carr 1926: 79).

In her *Reminiscences*, Comyns-Carr attributes Terry's decision to dismiss Harris to a disagreement over the design of her costumes for the 1887 production of *The Amber Heart*. Admiring a 'simple, unstarched muslin frock' Comyns-Carr was wearing, Terry determined that it was 'just the thing' she wanted for the role of Ellaline and demanded to be told how the designer had achieved the 'crinkly effect'. Undeterred by Comyns-Carr's confession that she 'twisted the stuff up into a ball and boiled it in a potato steamer to get the crinkles', she commanded Comyns-Carr to explain the process to Harris, declaring: 'I don't care whether Pattie likes it or not … if a potato steamer is necessary to make a frock look like that, then I am going to have a lot of my dresses "steamed"' (Comyns-Carr 1926: 79). A few days later, Harris left Terry's service and Comyns-Carr was invited 'to undertake the designing of all her stage clothes' (Comyns-Carr 1926: 79).

The Amber Heart (1887)

The Amber Heart by Alfred Calmour (fl.1887–1900) was the first production for which Comyns-Carr had sole responsibility for the design of Terry's costumes. It was an important milestone in the careers of both women, as this was also the moment that Terry made her first appearance on the Lyceum stage without Irving.

Irving took advantage of the opportunity the initial matinee production offered to watch Terry's whole performance from the auditorium. Though he had been sceptical about the play, he was so impressed by her performance that he bought the rights and wrote to Terry, declaring: 'I wish I could tell you of the dream of beauty that you realized' (Terry 1908: 249–50). The production, which achieved success in both Britain and America, remained in the company repertoire until Terry's departure in 1902 (Terry 1908).

The role of Ellaline, (a beautiful woman whose heart is broken when she puts aside the amulet which has previously granted her immunity from the pain of love) fitted securely within Terry's established repertoire of tragic heroines.[12] Terry's 'fantastic, graceful, Ellaline' certainly appealed to critics who felt that 'the one actress of our time [had] secured perhaps the surest acting triumph of her long career'[13]

A key element of the production, for both actress and costume designer were the costumes in which Terry performed the role. Only one costume from the production is captured in the surviving black and white photographs (Figure 2.1.1). These images show Terry wearing a floor length, softly

Figure 2.1.1 *Window & Grove, photograph of Ellen Terry as Ellaline in* The Amber Heart, *1887. © Victoria & Albert Museum, London.*

pleated tunic with a round neck and wide, hanging sleeves. The gown fits loosely to the figure, extending into a slight train at the rear and is largely plain, the only decoration focused in a narrow band at the neckline. A costume which strongly resembles the dress depicted in surviving photographs and believed to have been worn in *The Amber Heart* is preserved in the collection at Smallhythe Place.[14] When examining this costume alongside surviving photographs of Terry, however, strong similarities between this garment and a gown worn by the actress in the 1893 production of *Becket* became apparent (Figure 2.1.2).

The surviving dress is made from very fine translucent silk through which the inner tunic, made from a pale yellow silk and fitting slightly closer to the body than the loose outer dress, is visible. Decoration, including metallic braid, spangles and circular cut-glass discs has been added at the 'V' shaped neckline, around the cuffs of the wide-hanging sleeves and at the hem. Much of the stitching has been carried out by hand and whilst the construction of the garment is based around a comparatively simple T-shape, weights added at the centre front bodice and at the interior hem of the inner tunic have been used to control the garment's fall.

No direct match could be identified between images from either the 1887 production of *The Amber Heart* or *Becket* in 1893. The colour palette fits with the amber tones suggested by the former, yet the decoration at the neckline, sleeve cuffs and hem fits more closely with the design of Terry's costume in *Becket* than that worn for *The Amber Heart*, where only the neckline was embellished. However, the cut glass discs used to decorate the centre front neckline of the extant costume are not visible in surviving photographs of either production.

Given the fragility of the surviving costume (which is torn in several places), together with Terry's reputation for dashing on to the stage with moments to spare – damaging her costumes in the process – it is almost certain that the actress would have required replacement costumes during the fifteen years that *The Amber Heart* was staged (Comyns–Carr 1926: 209–10). It is very likely therefore that this surviving costume is a re-make of Terry's original dress from the play. Rather than create a direct replacement, however, this new costume has evolved to incorporate the decorative elements seen on the gown used for *Becket*. It is therefore a costume which carries the 'ghosts' of both productions.

Whichever production the surviving dress was worn for, the strong similarities between the style of the gown that Terry wore in both 1887 and 1893 reveal that this was a costume she deemed successful enough to return to and re-work six years after it was originally devised. The question that remains to be answered, however, is why Terry selected to revive this specific costume for the 1893 production of *Becket*.

Becket (1893)

In 1887, Terry was arguably at the peak of her career: yet to play Lady Macbeth and only just turned forty, she still felt youthful enough to take on 'young parts' like Rosalind.[15] Six years later, however, her confidence in her ability to sustain the eternal youth required to take on roles such as 'Fair Rosamund' in *Becket* was faltering.

Figure 2.1.2 *Photographer Unknown. Photograph of Ellen Terry as Fair Rosamund in* Becket, *1893. © Smallhythe Place, National Trust.*

The play's original text had been provided by Sir Alfred, Lord Tennyson (1809–92); and with his approval, Irving made significant alterations to the script, changing the order and re-working characters and speeches to create a drama which would suit the talents of the Lyceum Company and its lead performers (Richards 2006: 342). Rosamund, mistress of the king, rival of Queen Eleanor and protected by Becket, was technically a fallen woman but a character whom, as Jeffrey Richards suggests, 'the play is keen to show redeemed' (Richards 2006: 346). Her presence provides a useful counter to the queen and gave Irving as Becket the chance to display compassion, but it was a role which offered little scope for Terry's talents and left her frustrated, unable to escape her enduring characterization as a 'charming actress'.[16]

The 1893 production of *Becket* proved a triumph for Irving, but not for Terry, whose part was felt by one critic to have 'been dragged in by the hair' (Melville 1987: 145). Terry shared their misgivings, confessing to W.G. Robertson that she did not know what to do with the role: 'She is not there. She does not exist. I don't think that Tennyson ever knew very much about women, and now he is old and has forgotten the little that he knew. She is not a woman at all' (Robertson 1931: 153).

Given the doubts that Terry had about her role, her decision to seek the protection offered by the 'halo effect' becomes more understandable. As Carlson has observed 'any physical element' of a past production can carry 'certain memories of their previous usage even in a quite different play' (Carlson 2003: 119). The 'reception advantages' Carlson attributes to this 'recycling', specifically the 'powerful accumulation of meaning and emotion' built up in 'the audience's mind' offers further insight into the rationale behind Terry's choices of costume (Carlson 2003: 129). Although Terry was not wearing an exact replica of the earlier costume, the resemblance to the dress she wore in *The Amber Heart* would have been immediately apparent, enabling her to re-capture and revive memories of this past success, both within her own mind and that of her audience (Carlson 2003: 58–9).

From 'Macbethshire' to Camelot: Warrior Queens

Reflecting on her time with the Lyceum Company, Terry observed: 'My mental division of the years at the Lyceum is *before* "Macbeth" and *after*' (Terry 1908: 191). This statement suggests that the 1888 production of *Macbeth* marked, in Terry's mind at least, the pinnacle of her achievements with the company. This mindset offers important insights into the instances of visual references to earlier roles that are identifiable in Terry's costumes during her last decade with the company. Direct evidence of the specific importance that Terry attached to her performance in *Macbeth* can be found in her decision to resurrect the costume for her appearance in *King Arthur* seven years later.

It was a close examination of the surviving garments, rather than any striking similarities visible in production photographs, which brought to light the relationship between a costume worn by Terry as Guinevere in 1895 (Figure 2.1.4) and the 'Beetlewing Dress' now synonymous with the 1888 production of *Macbeth* (Figure 2.1.3).[17] A direct comparison of these costumes revealed parallels in their fit, construction and external appearance which are much harder to identify in two-dimensional sepia photographs and sketches.[18]

Figure 2.1.3 *Photographer Unknown. Ellen Terry as Lady Macbeth in* Macbeth, *1888. © Smallhythe Place, National Trust.*

Figure 2.1.4 *Window & Grove, photograph of Ellen Terry as Guinevere in* King Arthur, *1895. © Victoria & Albert Museum.*

Terry admired not only the visual effect, but also the fit of the iridescent green and silver/blue gown covered with beetle-wing cases she wore as Lady Macbeth. The external gown which fits closely to the body from shoulder to hip is supported on an internal knitted silk jersey bodice. This knitted structure helps to sculpt the body of the wearer and the addition of a hanging weight at the centre front hem controls the fall of the bodice, making it possible to create a costume that did not rely upon internal boning or a stiff corset to achieve the desired silhouette. It was a design ideally suited to an actress who did not like to wear corsets on or off the stage and, as Terry enthusiastically informed an interviewer in 1888, made it easy for her to move gracefully on the stage (Terry 1911: 88).[19]

Whilst this internal bodice was not directly replicated in Terry's costume for *King Arthur,* the flattering dropped waistline and hanging belt detail at the waist – a design which lengthened Terry's torso and defined her waist and hips – does appear in both garments. Similarities can also be traced between the colour palettes of the two dresses. Both costumes are based around varying tones of green, with the *Macbeth* costume tending towards the bluer end of the spectrum, whilst *King Arthur* is more yellow. The most striking parallel, however, lies in the crocheted structure used for the bodices and skirts of both gowns. As both Comyns-Carr and Terry would have been aware, the strands of metal thread running through this crochet work meant that both dresses looked magnificent in the ethereal glow of the Lyceum Theatre's gaslights. Whilst great importance was attached to creating costumes which were visually appealing and suited Terry's maturing body, the garments she wore in both productions were also carefully designed to anticipate and manipulate the 'public reception' of her performance.

Macbeth (1888)

The announcement in 1888 that Terry was to play Lady Macbeth had provoked immediate controversy. Terry's costumes therefore had a particularly important part to play in placating critics who declared that she was 'too good, too gentle, too feminine for the part' ('Macbeth at the Lyceum', 1888). They also needed to appease others who argued that, to 'suppose that Lady Macbeth was other than diabolical and fiendish is impossible; and these are qualities to represent which is beyond the wide scope of Miss Terry's genius, great as it unquestionably is' ('The Real Macbeth', 1888).

The actress's personal papers and published writings testify to her conviction that Lady Macbeth was 'A woman (all over a woman)' who 'was *not* a fiend, and *did* love her husband.'[20] Despite the criticism provoked by her interpretation, Terry resolved 'not [to] budge an inch in the reading of it, for that I know is right'. She was therefore prepared to 'what is vulgarly called "sweat at it," each night' in order to counter any critics who claimed she wanted to 'make [Lady Macbeth] a "gentle, lovable woman"' for 'She was nothing of the sort' (Terry 1908: 307).

Portraying Lady Macbeth as a woman whose actions were motivated by passionate love for her husband, enabled Terry to emphasize and exploit the feminine qualities within the character. This 'new Lady Macbeth', was an 'exquisite creature' who was both 'passionate [...] sensuous and finely strung'. Her 'femininity' was a source of strength, rather than weakness: a device she employed to manipulate her male counterparts and satisfy her craving for absolute power ('Macbeth at the Lyceum', 1888).

Terry's costumes were designed to help communicate and support her portrayal of Lady Macbeth and the spectacular 'Beetlewing' dress in which she made her first appearance provided an immediate statement of her reading of the character. The crochet ground of this costume sought to reproduce the effect of 'chain mail', an impression heightened by the serpentine gleam of the blue green beetle-wing cases and strands of metal 'tinsel' which covered its surface (Comyns–Carr 1926: 211–12). Encasing Terry within this 'armour' enabled her to convey Lady Macbeth's majesty and power and yet retain sufficient femininity and beauty to placate even the harshest of critics. As one reviewer concluded:

> Is this Lady Macbeth? Who shall decide? That it is not the Lady Macbeth of Mrs. Siddons we know. It is scarcely a Lady Macbeth we realise. It is perhaps, one of which we have dreamed. [...] This is Miss Terry's Lady Macbeth. ('Lyceum Theatre' 1888)

In spite of the criticism that Terry's Lady Macbeth received, the production remained a popular part of the Lyceum Company canon until her departure in 1902. Its popularity was certainly boosted by the visual impact of her costumes. Contemporary reviews remarked upon 'the marvellous costumes designed by Mrs. Comyns-Carr' and declared Terry's performance to be 'a continual feast to the eye' (*Pall Mall Gazette* 1888: 4). The 'beauty' and 'picturesque' qualities of the scenery and costumes led some reviewers to soften their criticism of Terry's performance, leading one critic to argue:

> difficult to deal with is the Lady Macbeth of Miss Ellen Terry. That it is convincing few will maintain. It is, however, divinely beautiful. The woman who, in a quaint and indescribably beautiful costume, read by the light of the fire the letter of her husband [...] might have stood in the Court at Camelot, and gained the wondering homage and obeisance of Sir Galahad, as well as Sir Lancelot. (*Morning Post* 1888)

King Arthur (1895)

Audiences would have to wait another seven years before Camelot came to the Lyceum Theatre. Clement Scott's analysis of *King Arthur* (eventually staged in 1895) makes apparent the excitement surrounding the play and the long-standing desire for a Lyceum production that addressed the Arthurian legends. 'At last', he declared, 'Ellen Terry is to be the Queen Guinevere we have pictured in our imaginations these countless years' (Scott 1897: 373).

The high expectations of both critics and audiences heightened the pressure on Irving and Terry, who were expected to deliver a spectacular production and mesmerizing performances. For the script, Irving relied upon the husband of Terry's costume designer, Joseph Comyns-Carr (1849–1916) (an established writer and connoisseur of the arts). Comyns-Carr's blank-verse drama, though not charming all critics, was deemed 'very effective and interesting' and made respectful allusions to the Arthurian traditions established by both Thomas Malory (*c.*1415–71) and Tennyson (Scott 1897: 374).

The production's chief attraction, however, was the involvement of an artist from amongst the 'aristocracy of English art': Edward Burne-Jones (1833–97) (Shaw 1895: 93–5). Extolled by George Bernard Shaw (1856–1950) as 'the greatest among English decorative painters,' Burne-Jones had agreed to design both the scenery and the costumes 'stipulating only that he should not be required to superintend the carrying out of his designs in detail' (Comyns-Carr 1926: 205). The spectacle of the resulting production drew together figures from across the arts and cemented the Lyceum Theatre's status as 'a Temple of Art [and] a theatre of Beauty' (Meisel 1983: 402).

The production did not achieve universal praise, however, and whilst acknowledging the splendour of the picture that Irving had presented, Shaw dismissed the production as a 'picture-opera' and criticized many elements of the direction, script and acting. His chief frustration lay in the limited scope that both text and narrative provided for the performers – Terry in particular (Shaw 1895: 93–5):

> As to Miss Ellen Terry, it was the old story, a born actress of real women's parts condemned to figure as a mere artist's model in costume plays [...] It is pathetic to see Miss Terry snatching at some

fleeting touch of nature in her part, and playing it not only to perfection, but often with a parting caress [...] What a theatre for a woman of genius to be attached to! (Shaw 1895: 94)

Shaw's remarks highlight many of the constraints – not least in terms of the roles she was offered and Irving's 'pictorial' approach to design – that were an inescapable part of Terry's position at the Lyceum. Although Guinevere offered a brief escape from the role of a young and innocent heroine, Terry was still called upon to perform a part praised for being 'very loveable in its true womanliness' (Archer quoted in Richards 2006: 29). Contemporary reviews re-inforce Terry's imprisonment within this 'womanly' role. William Archer, for instance, observed that 'Miss Ellen Terry is an ideal Guinevere to the eye [...] and her performance is altogether charming' (Archer quoted in Richards 2006: 29), whilst another reviewer praised Terry's embodiment of the 'true nature' of 'the representative woman – a nature that rests not upon mind but upon emotions' (quoted in Richards 2006: 27).

Whilst Terry regretted the frequency with which she was obliged to play 'second-fiddle' parts, she was conscious that 'for one thing [she] did not like doing at the Lyceum, there would probably be a hundred things [she] should dislike doing in another theatre' (Terry 1908: 164).[21] Nevertheless, she remained determined to demonstrate that there was 'there [was] something more in [her] acting than *charm*' (Terry with St. John 1932: 13).

Resurrecting 'Lady Macbeth'

Although Burne-Jones had been commissioned to design the scenery and the costumes for *King Arthur*, it was Alice Comyns-Carr who was entrusted with transforming the 'coloured sketches' he produced into workable designs for Terry's costumes (Comyns-Carr 1926: 206). Comyns-Carr was given a relatively 'free hand' by the artist who, recognizing the value of her experience, approved the substitutions the designer made with regard to the colour and fabric selected for the actress's costumes (Comyns-Carr 1926: 206). As was the case with *Macbeth* in 1888, Ada Nettleship (1856–1932) was asked to create the garments Comyns-Carr had designed. Terry was therefore collaborating with two women who understood her stage wardrobe and its history and together they could create costumes carrying the required 'ghosts'.[22]

Returning to a costume associated with the ruthless and powerful figure of Lady Macbeth – and a role in which she had actively rebelled against her 'womanly' persona – provided Terry with a means through which to resurrect the 'memories' and 'spirits' associated with this previous performance. This strategy – reliant on visual effect – was also particularly well suited to a production in which she was required to provide 'a beautiful living picture'.[23]

The dresses that Terry wore in *King Arthur* were 'far more elaborate than those [Comyns-Carr] had previously designed for her' (Comyns-Carr 1926: 206). Indeed, over £150 (equivalent to £18,750 today) was spent on one dress, 'twilled by [Nettleship's] girls entirely of gold thread' for the actress to wear as Guinevere (*New Zealand Herald* 1900: 2). The immense sums invested in the creation of Terry's costumes were soon justified, however, not least by the significant part they played in securing positive responses to her performance. Reviewers were entranced by the 'marvellous witchery' of Terry's first appearance as 'the very Guinevere of fact or legend' (quoted in Richards 2006: 27). Critics remarked specifically on her 'lustrous and flowing robe', (Review of J. Comyns-Carr's *King Arthur* 1895: 95) its 'sheen rippling like water to her feet' (quoted in Richards 2006: 27). As Scott observed: 'The entrance of Miss Ellen Terry – glorious in priceless costume – as the Queen Guinevere, intensifies the attention. Now the romance is about to begin and the interest starts in real earnest' (Scott 1897: 376).

A comparison of the surviving costume with contemporary reviews, and the illustrations that Bernard Partridge (1861–1945) produced for the souvenir programme, confirmed that this was the costume worn by Terry in Act 1 of the production and therefore the dress in which she first appeared on stage. This information brings added significance to the parallels between this surviving costume and Terry's 'Beetlewing dress'. Both costumes were worn by Terry to make her first entrance on the stage. These were therefore the garments which conditioned audiences' impressions of her performances from the start. Terry's decision to make her first entrance in a costume which echoed the 'Beetlewing dress' so closely ensured that her long-anticipated appearance as Queen Guinevere would be forever 'haunted' by the 'ghost' of Lady Macbeth.

Conclusion: Re-membering Ellen Terry

Employing her costumes as a means of rebellion enabled Terry to control the character she communicated to her audience and to manipulate the public reception of her performances. The level of agency Terry was able to exercise over her costume design was unusual and she took full advantage of the opportunity her costumes provided to ensure that she remained an active, rather than passive, 'artist's model'. Together, Terry and Comyns-Carr recognized and sought to harness the power of 'ghosting' by creating garments which were 're-incarnations' of costumes worn earlier in Terry's career. This approach to costume design enabled Terry to invoke the 'ghosts' associated with her past triumphs, encircling her performances securely within the 'halo' which, as Carlson has observed, masks failings and directs the minds of audiences away from the present performance, towards 'previous high achievement' (Carlson 2003: 58–9).

This analysis has focused on one specific form of 'ghosting' and its role within the career of a single actress. It is, however, an area of theatre history and costume design which merits far wider investigation and discussion, particularly given the part it continues to play within current theatre practice.[24] Close examination of Terry's costuming strategies, together with a consideration of the afterlives of her stage dress, has, for instance, brought to light at least four types of 'ghosting' which these costumes can facilitate. These are: self-ghosting (in which an actor deliberately wears a costume which carries or summons memories of their own past performances); protection (in which 'haunted' costumes are regarded as 'talismanic objects which carry the benevolent spirits of their past wearers'); possession (in which a performer deliberately summons the 'ghost(s)' of the previous wearer(s) of a costume and allows themselves and their performance to become 'possessed' by these spirits) and resurrection (in which the inanimate costume is displayed, rather than worn, and is used to 're-member' the body of the absent performer).

As this examination of her costumes has demonstrated, 'self-ghosting' played a crucial part in Terry's costuming strategies. Terry also appreciated that costumes could offer 'protection', drawing inspiration from the 'ghost' carried by Sarah Siddons' shoes when performing *Macbeth* in 1888. During Terry's lifetime and after her death, her costumes were loaned to other performers. These new wearers of Terry's costumes became 'hosts' for the spirit of the actress and were able to deliver performances enhanced by this temporary 'possession.' Today, Terry's costumes have entered the final stage of their 'afterlives', one which she and her daughter Edith Craig anticipated when they sought to establish a long-term home for her collection at Smallhythe Place.[25] The costumes which Terry and Craig preserved continue to play a crucial part in sustaining her legacy. These 'talismanic garments' have now taken on the role of 'effigies', with the power to 'resurrect' the lost performer. In doing so, they enable new audiences to 're-member' the famous actress whose 'ghost' they carry in their fibres.[26]

Notes

1. Sybil Thorndike, Transcript of audio recording, Smallhythe Place, 1960.
2. An interview conducted with Terry at the time of the original production confirms that the actress kept the shoes in her dressing room. A copy of this interview, entitled 'How I sketched Mrs. Siddon's Shoes: A visit to Miss Ellen Terry's Dressing Room' is bound within Terry's copy of *Macbeth,* National Trust Inventory Number 3119105.
3. Terry made this remark in a letter sent to the critic Clement Scott (1841–1904) in 1888. (Auerbach 1987: 259).
4. Thorndike, audio recording. For further discussion of the performance history of this costume, see Isaac (2017).
5. Though, as Hodgdon notes, the cardigan may have had 'an interim resurrection', she found definite evidence that it was worn by Estelle Kohler as Paulina in the 1999 production of *The Winter's Tale* and again by Alexandra Gilbreath (who played Hermione in the 1999 *Winter's Tale*) as Katherina in *The Taming of the Shrew* in 2003.
6. Terry, letter from Ellen Terry to George Bernard Shaw (1856–1950), 23 September1896. Letter, published in St. John (1931: 70).
7. For a full outline of Terry's early career see both biographies of the actress and the first two chapters of Terry (1908).
8. Both of Terry's children went on to have significant stage careers. Gordon Craig's work as a theatre director and designer has been well documented and continues to receive widespread recognition. Edith Craig's equally important career as both a theatrical costumier and director has, however, only recently achieved recognition, largely through the work of Katharine Cockin (2017), who examines Craig's important contribution to the stage and the suffrage movement.
9. For further discussion on this theme see also Jenny Bloodworth (2011: 49–64).
10. One notable exception to this pattern were the dresses which Edward Godwin designed for Terry to wear in the 1881 production of *The Cup*. The diaphanous fabrics and loose cut of these costumes alluded both to the Roman period in which the play was set and the revival of classically inspired dress promoted by Godwin and other leading members of the aesthetic movement.

11 Comyns-Carr discusses her own dress and her working partnership with Terry in her *Reminiscences* (Comyns-Carr 1926: 26, 79).

12 Since 1878 these tragic roles had included: Ophelia in *Hamlet* (1878); Desdemona in *Othello* (1881); Juliet in *Romeo and Juliet* (1882) and Marguerite in *Faust* (1885).

13 n.a. 'Lyceum Theatre,' handwritten annotation: *'The Amber Heart, June 7th 1887.'* Press clipping, Ruth Canton Album, Volume 2: 1884–1892. Garrick Collection, London.

14 This costume forms part of the Ellen Terry Collection at Smallhythe Place, Inventory Number NT 1118885.

15 Sadly, and much to Terry's disappointment, this was one of the few Shakespearean roles which she never had the opportunity to perform (Terry 1908: 302). Looking back upon her career, Terry confessed that this sacrifice ranked amongst 'the greatest disappointments of her life.' Ellen Terry and Christopher St. John (1932: 97).

16 n.a, 'The Laureates play at the Lyceum', press clipping, Ruth Canton Album, Volume 1: 1892–1898. Garrick Collection, London.

17 These parallels were first brought to my attention by the conservator who has treated both garments, Zenzie Tinker, in 2010. Personal communication with the author, 14 July 2010. Zenzie Tinker's Conservation Studio, Brighton.

18 The surviving costumes worn by Ellen Terry as Lady Macbeth and held at Smallhythe are: SMA. TC/COST.115a, 1118840.1; SMA.TC.115b, 1118843; NT/SMA/TC/114a, 1118839.1 and NT/SMA/ TC/114b,1118839.2. For *King Arthur* only one costume survives: SMA/TC/118, 1118843.

19 The actress actually inserted a copy of this interview entitled 'How I Sketched Mrs. Siddons Shoes: A visit to Miss Ellen Terry's Dressing Room' into the final page of a copy of the script for this production. The name of the author and title of the publication are not recorded. See Terry's copy of *Macbeth*, National Trust Inventory Number 3119105.

20 Terry, handwritten annotation on her copy of Joseph Comyns-Carr's *Macbeth and Lady Macbeth: An Essay* (1889: 28); Terry (1908: 307).

21 See also Ellen Terry with Christopher St. John (1932: 96).

22 For further discussion of this working relationship see Isaac (2018: 74–96).

23 George Bernard Shaw quotes here a review from *Saturday Review of Politics: Literature and Art*, 17 July 1897 in his volume, *Our Theatres in the Nineties* (Shaw 1932: 193).

24 As demonstrated by Sladen (2017).

25 Joy Melville has explored Craig's role in preserving Terry's legacy in her joint biography of the mother and daughter. See, in particular, Melville (1987: 250–1).

26 For further consideration of this form of 'ghosting' see: Isaac (2017).

References

Auerbach, N. (1987), *Ellen Terry: Player in our Time*. London: Dent & Sons.

Barbieri, D. (2013), 'Performativity and the Historical Body: Detecting Performance through the Archived Costume,' *Studies in Theatre and Performance* 33 (3), 281–301.

Bloodworth, J. (2011), 'The Burden of Eternal Youth: Ellen Terry and The Mistress of the Robes', in K. Cockin (ed.), *Ellen Terry: Spheres of Influence*, 49–64. London: Pickering & Chatto.

Bratton, J. (2011), *The Making of the West End Stage: Marriage, Management and the Mapping of Gender in London, 1830–1870*. Cambridge: Cambridge University Press.

Carlson, M. A. (2003), *The Haunted Stage: The Theatre As Memory Machine*. Ann Arbor: University of Michigan Press.

Cockin, K., ed. (2011), *Ellen Terry: Spheres of Influence*. London: Pickering & Chatto.

Cockin, K. (2017), *Edith Craig and the Theatres of Art*. London: Bloomsbury Academic.

Comyns-Carr, A. (1926), *Mrs. J. Comyns-Carr's Reminiscences*. London: Hutchinson & Co.

Davis, T. C. (1991), *Actresses As Working Women: Their Social Identity in Victorian Culture*. London: Routledge.

Hodgdon, B. (2006), 'Shopping in the Archives: Material Memories', in P. Holland (ed.) *Shakespeare, Memory and Performance*. Cambridge: Cambridge University Press.

Isaac, V. (2017), 'Towards a Methodology for Analysing Historic Theatre Costume', *Studies in Costume and Performance*, 2 (2): 115–35.

Isaac, V. (2018), 'A Well-Dressed Actress': Exploring the Theatrical Wardrobe of Ellen Terry (1847–1928)', *Costume* 52 (1), 74–96.

Marshall, G. (2009), *Shakespeare and Victorian Women*. Cambridge: Cambridge University Press.

Meisel, M. (1983), *Realizations: Narrative, Pictorial, and Theatrical Arts in Nineteenth-Century England*. Princeton, NJ: Princeton University Press.

Melville, J. (1987), *Ellen and Edy: A Biography of Ellen Terry and her Daughter Edith Craig, 1847–1947*. London: Pandora.

Pearce, S. (1994), 'Objects as Meaning: Or Narrating the Past', in S. Pearce (ed.), *Interpreting Objects and Collections*. London: Routledge.

Powell, K. (1997), *Women and Victorian Theatre*. Cambridge: Cambridge University Press.

'Review of J. Comyns-Carr's *King Arthur*' (1895), *The Athenaeum*, 19 January, 95.

Richards, J. (2006), *Sir Henry Irving: A Victorian Actor and His World*. London: Hambledon Continuum.

Roach, J. (1996), *Cities of the Dead*. New York: Columbia University Press.

Robertson, W. G. (1931), *Time Was: The Reminiscences of W. Graham Robertson*. London: Hamish Hamilton.

Scott, C. (1897), *From* The Bells *to* King Arthur*: A Critical Record of the First Night Productions at the Lyceum Theatre from 1871–1895*. London: John Macqueen.

Shaw, G. B. (1895), 'Review of J. Comyns-Carr's King Arthur,' *Saturday Review*, 19 January, 93-5.

Shaw, G. B. (1932), *Our Theatres in the Nineties, Volume 3*. London: Constable and Company Ltd.

Sladen, S. (2017), 'From Mother Goose to Master: Training Networks and Knowledge Transfer in Contemporary British Pantomime', *Theatre, Dance and Performance Training* 8 (2), 206–24.

St. John, C. (ed.) (1931), *Ellen Terry and Bernard Shaw: A Correspondence*. London: Reinhardt & Evans Ltd.

Terry, E. (1908), *The Story of My Life*. London: Hutchinson.

Terry, E. (1911), 'Stage Decoration.' *The Windsor Magazine*. (Copyright by S.S.McClure Company in the United States of America): 71–90.

Terry, E. (1932), *Four Lectures on Shakespeare*, (edited and with an introduction by C. St. John). London: Martin Hopkinson Ltd.

'Untitled Article' (1900), *New Zealand Herald*, 25 August, 2. Available online: http://paperspast.natlib.govt.nz/cgi-in/paperspast?a=d&d=NZH19000825.2.57.31(accessed: 20 August 2014).

Primary Sources

Acting Copies of Playtexts

Calmour, A. C. (1887), *The Amber Heart*. Acting Copy. Previously owned and used by Ellen Terry. Garrick Collection, London.

Shakespeare, W. *Macbeth*. Acting copy. Previously owned and used by Ellen Terry. Smallhythe Place, National Trust Inventory Number 3119105.

Press Cuttings

'Lyceum Theatre' (1888), 31 December, press cutting. Mounted in Percy Fitzgerald Album, Volume V: 331, Garrick Club, London.

'Macbeth at the Lyceum' (1888), *The Standard*, December, press cutting. Mounted in Percy Fitzgerald Albums, Volume V: 333, Garrick Collection, London.

Morning Post (1888), December 31, Press cutting (publication unidentified), Lyceum Theatre, Production Box, Macbeth, 1888, Victoria and Albert Museum, London.

Pall Mall Gazette (1888), December 31: 4. Press cutting mounted in Percy Fitzgerald Album, Volume V: 330, Garrick Club, London.

Percy Fitzgerald Albums, Vols. 1-22. Garrick Collection, London. [assembled by the painter and sculptor, Percy Hetherington Fitzgerald (1834–1925)].

Ruth Canton Albums, *Chronicles of the Lyceum Company*, Volume 1: 1892–1898 and Volume 2: 1884–1892. Garrick Collection, London. [assembled by an artist, Susan Ruth Canton (1849–1932) and contain press cuttings and articles relating to Lyceum Productions together with many of Canton's own painted illustrations of productions she had seen.]

'The Laureates play at the Lyceum', press cutting, Ruth Canton Album, Volume 1: 1892–1898. Garrick Collection, London.

'The Real Macbeth' (1888), press cutting, *Unidentified periodical*, December. Mounted in Percy Fitzgerald Albums, Volume V: 311, Garrick Collection, London.

Other

Personal Conversation with Zenzie Tinker (conservator), Zenzie Tinker Conservation Ltd., Brighton.

Thorndike, Sybil. Typed transcript of audio recording from a talk in the Barn Theatre, Smallhythe Place, 1960.

2.2 'On and Off the Stage': Costume, Dress and Locating the Actor-Manager's Identity, 1870–1900

Helen Margaret Walter

In the context of official narratives about theatre in the late nineteenth century in Britain, the figures of the actor-managers that controlled the theatres in London's West End loom large. Starting their careers as leading actors, they transitioned to the position of 'actor-manager' by taking on the license of a theatre and acting in essence as producer and director, as well as star of that theatre's productions. This is a role that historian Jeffrey Richards has likened to that of the twentieth-century cinematic *auteur*, with the added complication that as licensees of the theatres they were financially as well as artistically invested in the success or failure of productions (Richards 2005). As Tracy Davis and Jacky Bratton have argued, the reality of theatrical management was undoubtedly more nuanced than these narratives would suggest, with a network of men and women involved in everyday decisions, commercial and even artistic transactions that bypassed the actor-manager's control (Davis [2000] 2007; Bratton 2011). Yet in the perception of theatregoers, and particularly critics, whose narratives form a large part of the official histories of this theatrical epoch, London's actor-managers were the public face of legitimate Victorian theatre. They were also the focus of a singular public fascination and nascent celebrity culture, which ensured their prominence in the visual and verbal record of this period. While it is important not to take these narratives entirely at face value, it is worth interrogating these figures to see how and why such identities were established. As those who tried to capture these individuals for posterity, including the actor-managers themselves, would discover, the identity of the actor-manager was multi-valent and was made more complicated, both by their chosen artistic profession and by their position as representatives of the theatre not only on the stage but also off it. Rather than looking at specific productions and theatrical costumes in some detail, this chapter looks at the role of dress and appearance in debates about the identity of the actor-manager in this period and suggests that breaking down the barrier between onstage and offstage bodies is a useful addition to the study of the history of both theatrical costume and the theatrical personalities who wore it.

Figure 2.2.1 *Window & Grove,* On and Off the Stage, *1873. Photographic reproductions.*

On and Off the Stage

In 1885 husband and wife Squire and Marie ('Effie') Bancroft (née Wilton), who had made their names as actors and then managers at the Prince of Wales and Haymarket theatres in London's West End in the 1870s and early 1880s, jointly recorded their life experiences in a memoir entitled *The Bancrofts On and Off the Stage: Written by Themselves* (Bancroft and Wilton 1891). As the title implies, this volume was notable for skating through all aspects of the Bancrofts' lives, with descriptions of memorable productions and tales of performances juxtaposed alongside stories of personal holiday adventures and accounts of social occasions, dinners given in honour of foreign visitors and sporting events, like the Epsom Derby (Bancroft and Wilton 1891: 121–2, 132–3, 155–6, 158–9). The work's framing by both its title and content, as a narrative of life within and outside of the theatre demonstrates the authors' awareness of a public interest in actors' private lives as well as their desire to see them on the stage and the Bancrofts' consciousness of their own place in a burgeoning celebrity industry. This was vindicated by the auto biography's popularity and the printing of at least eight editions of the work in its first six years of publication (1885–91), and it was perhaps this popularity and a further twenty years of intermittent stage appearances that led to the publication of another memoir in

1909 called *Recollections of Sixty Years.*[1] Providing a similarly eclectic account of the Bancrofts' lives, this second autobiographical text was also notable for containing thirty-four illustrations of a variety of subjects from both their theatrical and everyday lives. Figure 2.2.1 appears in this work. A plate of two photographs of Squire Bancroft taken in 1873 by the Window & Grove photographic studio 'on the same day', it illustrates the transformation of Bancroft from a thirty-two-year-old fashionable gentleman, with a snugly fitting double-breasted frock coat, elaborately tied cravat and the actor's signature monocle into the somewhat older, more sombrely attired Dr Speedwell, a character in Wilkie Collins' *Man and Wife*, produced by the Bancrofts at the Prince of Wales Theatre in 1873. In these images, Bancroft's dress and appearance is ineluctably tied to his identity, signalling his transformation from actor to character and they indicate the transformative nature of costume and make up in the process of theatrical characterization.

The images may have been placed side-by-side, but the use of the terminology 'on' and 'off' the stage in both the biography and image caption suggests that they represented two separate aspects of Bancroft's life, with his everyday offstage activity and appearance juxtaposed with, but contrasted to the performance of his theatrical characters. The image and the accompanying text suggests that this can be analogized to a contrast between the genuine man and the constructed and illusory theatrical characters he played. As an illustration within a biographical text, Figure 2.2.1 is also particularly interesting because it mimics a trend, remarked upon in Julie Codell's work on Victorian artists' biographies, for the inclusion in such works of photographs of artists next to their paintings, with the added complication that in the case of the actor, the artist and the work of art are sited in the same body (Codell 2003). In a period where some of London's leading actor-managers, including Squire Bancroft himself, were trying to establish acting as an art form and rehabilitate it as a socially acceptable profession, it is unsurprising that there was a palpable anxiety about the elision of the actor as an artistic and professional figure and the characters he played on the stage. This anxiety was expressed by Edmund Gosse when he attempted to posthumously memorialize the figure of actor-manager Herbert Beerbohm Tree, who trained with arguably the most prominent actor-manager of the late nineteenth century, Henry Irving at the Lyceum Theatre, and then succeeded the Bancrofts at the Haymarket, which he managed successfully for ten years from 1887 to 1897 before moving to Her Majesty's Theatre which he had re-built to his own specifications. Asked by Tree's half-brother, Max Beerbohm, to 'send him a sketch from memory of his brother Herbert as I remember him', a seemingly simple task, the writer quickly realized that his recollections of Tree were not so straightforward and any attempt to memorialize the man as a 'real person' with 'genuine characteristics' would be made necessarily more complex by the nature of his profession as an actor and Gosse's memories of his body in performance (Gosse 1920: 203). His 'sketch' therefore begins with the following disclaimer:

> While the recollection of what a man of some other class looked like may be simple and direct, that of what an actor was is bound to be complex, and confused with his manifold impersonations on the stage. Of most actors whom I have slightly known I should instantly refuse to make any portrait whatever, because I lose their reality in their assumed parts. Is there any real person at all, any bundle of genuine characteristics left, one asks one's self, under the Protean disguises? (Gosse 1920: 203)

In explaining this conundrum, Gosse's text not only problematized the separation of the actor-manager's real self from that of his parts, but also revealed that from the perspective of memorialization, capturing the actor's real nature was bound up with remembering his appearance and finding a memory of his real body which contrasted with that of his 'manifold impersonations on the stage'. This appearance was obviously intrinsically connected in Gosse's memory with the identity of Tree, because, as the author went on to say, he was able to eventually produce a portrait as a result of the fact that 'in spite of all the costumes and all the attitudes, an unusually hard core of personality did survive, and even actively protrude, in him' (Gosse 1920: 203).

Gosse may have encountered difficulties with remembering Tree's offstage persona, but he obviously thought that it was important to do so, crucial that there be a 'reality' distinct from the actor's 'assumed parts'. This may have partly been a reflection of a particularly Victorian preoccupation with realism and authenticity in the capturing of figures for posterity, and a desire to locate and connect with the 'real' self of the celebrity was certainly not limited to actor-managers in this period.[2] Anne-Marie Millim has described the way in which Alfred Lord Tennyson was hounded at Farringford, his Isle of Wight retreat, by autograph hunters (Boyce, Finnerty and Millim 2013) and Chris Rojek ([2001] 2010) posits the distinction between the 'staged [public] self' and the 'veridical [private] self' as central to the construction of celebrity culture more generally. Gosse's writing suggests, however, that his problem was not just about the memorialization of Tree as a public figure but was also the result of a very real and specific anxiety about the identity of actors as opposed to any other celebrities; by posing the question 'Is there any real person at all, any bundle of genuine characteristics left [...] under the Protean disguises?' Gosse pre-supposed that in some cases the answer would be no (Gosse 1920: 203). What Gosse appears to have been proposing as a site of anxiety was that, for the actor, the construction of self and particularly the framing of the body as a manifestation of character was specifically informed by the nature of his profession and the juxtaposition between real and imagined bodies which characterized both his working method and the visual expression of his lives. Gosse's concern was not therefore necessarily about the literal reconstruction of the actor's appearance, but rather a fear that the theatrical nature of his profession rendered even Tree's real body imagined and that therefore it could not be trusted. Later in his sketch, he wrote 'It seems to me that the complicated aspect of the actor [...] affected him externally' (Gosse 1920: 203). As in the photographs of Bancroft, whose portraits 'on and off the stage' are largely distinguished by dress, it is interesting that in his verbal portrait, Gosse defines the manifestations of character as 'all the costumes and all the attitudes', siting the confusion of identity once again in the body.

Performance as Metaphor

It is now almost a truism of theories about identity that all public manifestations of self are, to some extent, constructed or performed and that this performance of identity is partially conveyed through the body. In addition, as sociologist Joanne Entwistle has pointed out, the body in question is almost always a dressed one and, as a signalling medium, dress provides one of the most immediate ways to construct an identity. Discussing the link between the dressed body and social interaction she describes the relationship as one of 'situated practice [...] a means by which individuals orientate themselves to the social world' (Entwistle 2000: 39). Similar assertions have been made by a number of other fashion theorists and historians, including Jennifer Craik, who saw fashion as 'an elaborated body technique through which a range of personal and social statements can be articulated' (Craik 1994: 16). Elizabeth Wilson and Amy de la Haye, introduced their collection of essays on dress as 'Object, Meaning, and Identity' with the idea that 'the body is now explicitly understood not as a biological, but as a social construct producing multiple meanings. Dress is clearly a part of that meaning' (Wilson and de la Haye 1999: 3). In Erving Goffman's influential work on *The Presentation of Self in Everyday Life,* he referred to this crafting of identity through physical attributes as the creation of a 'personal front' divided into stimuli of 'appearance' and 'manner', both of which were defined through the construction and presentation of the body (Goffman [1959] 1990: 34–5). Whilst some physical elements of appearance could be considered fixed, many of them can be physically manipulated in the process of dressing to create a particular effect for an audience and in this respect the body functions as a conscious rather than reflexive feature of self-presentation and should not be separated from its outward trappings.

When considering the problem of the actor's body, Goffman's work is particularly notable for his adoption of theatrical terminology, not only seeing the presentation of self as a 'performance' but talking explicitly of sets, costumes and scenes, at one point stating that 'sometimes an individual who dominates the show in this way and is, in a sense, the director of it, plays an actual part in the performance he directs' (Goffman [1959] 1990: 60), which could well be a description of the role of the Victorian actor-manager. As an explicit response to Goffman and other social theorists writing on performance, theorist Bert O. States' 1996 article 'Performance as Metaphor' picked up on Richard Schechner's ideas of 'insider' and 'outsider' writings on performance to address the problem of the 'semantic impossibility' of defining performance and the way that its linguistic meaning drifts when it is removed from the theatrical context and applied to the issue of identity in everyday life. States' work is particularly interesting because it reflects not only a historical, but also a historiographical need to separate the performance of identity inside and outside the bounds of the theatre that appear time and again, not only in histories of acting but also those of theatrical costume. Obviously, there is a referential difference between the dressed body of the actor in the theatrical paradigm, where an audience is conscious of the act of construction and performance and the body in everyday life or an offstage portrait, where that consciousness is often (although not always) deliberately repressed. Anne Hollander summed up this opinion by stating that theatre costume should be considered differently because 'the frame around the [theatrical] events invites intensified attention to what is being worn; we know it is there intentionally even though it represents something worn casually' (Hollander [1975] 1993: 239). The implication of both States' and Hollander's approach is that eliding these boundaries is dangerous, because applying the metaphor of performance to everyday life takes away from the clarity of defining performance within the theatrical context. The legacy of this approach however is sometimes a reluctance to apply more theoretical models of fashionability to theatrical costume, or to consider the actor's everyday dress as an extension of his theatrical costumes and disregard the fact that theatre costume and everyday dress are inseparably linked through the body and the experiences of dressing undertaken by the actor who wears them.

Figure 2.2.2 *Anon., Mr. Hare's Dressing Room, and Mr. Hare's Inner Room, 1891.*

Studying up a Character

> I take about a month to study up a character. I always wear the clothes I am going to play in for some time previously, so as to get them to my figure. The longest time I ever bestowed on a make-up was in *The Profligate*. I took half an hour over it.' ('Actors' Dressing Rooms' 1891: 183)

In the second issue of the monthly periodical *The Strand Magazine*, founded by editor George Newnes in 1891 as a site for the meeting of 'the best British writers' and 'eminent artists' of the late nineteenth century, an unattributed article entitled 'Actors' Dressing Rooms' presented for the magazine's readership an analysis of the 'robing apartments' of five of London's leading actor-managers: Henry Irving at the Lyceum, John Lawrence Toole at his eponymous Toole's Theatre, Herbert Beerbohm Tree at the Haymarket, John Hare at the Garrick Theatre and Charles Wyndham at the Criterion (Newnes 1891: 3;'Actors' Dressing Rooms' 1891: 178). Aside from a lengthy description of each of these rooms, the article also contained illustrations of the spaces in question and in a couple of instances short interviews with the actor-managers themselves. In the case of John Hare, who, by his own admission, had been acting primarily on the London stage, the interviewer asked him what his favourite role was and immediately after confessing that it was the one he was currently playing in *A Pair of Spectacles*, the actor offered the couple of sentences quoted above on his way of 'studying up a character' and making himself up for his parts ('Actors' Dressing Rooms' 1891: 182). These brief sentences indicated two things: firstly, that creating his characters' appearance and fitting their clothes 'to my figure' was an important part of Hare's preparation for any role and secondly, that the elaborate construction of his appearance on the night of the play was a work which took some time and skill.

Following on from this short interview was a description of Hare's rooms at the Garrick, accompanied by two illustrations, of 'Mr. Hare's Dressing Room' and of 'Mr. Hare's Inner Room' (Figure 2.2.2). These two rooms, both in their visual manifestations and the written descriptions that accompanied them, were seen by the author as representing the two sides of Hare's business, as manager and actor respectively, with his 'Dressing Room' being described as an 'office', with speaking tubes which communicated with the stage door, prompter, box-office and acting manager. By contrast, the smaller, 'Inner' room was described as follows:

> There, hanging up, is the light suit worn as *Benjamin Goldfinch*, with the long black coat which flaps about so marvellously – the actor finds plenty of 'character' even in a coat – and the shepherd's plaid trousers.
>
> The looking-glass is of walnut, with electric lights on either side shaded with metal leaves. In front of this he sits, amidst a hundred little oddments. ('Actors' Dressing Rooms' 1891: 183)

Whilst not all of the actors described in the article had two separate rooms dedicated to the pursuit of their profession, the article was careful to include in all cases, spaces which were considered the personal territory of the Actor-Manager. These could be used either for the pursuit of leisure, such as J. L. Toole's 'cosy parlour' or as in the case of Hare as more of an office, but all of the Actor-Managers described had spaces within the dressing rooms, even if they were not partitioned off which were dedicated to physical transformation and which were always described in terms of work ('Actors' Dressing Rooms' 1891: 180, 183). In the case of Herbert Beerbohm Tree for example, the author is careful to say that the whole room 'is regarded rather as a workshop than a lounging-room, and it certainly possesses that appearance' ('Actors' Dressing Rooms' 1891: 181).

While Hare's two rooms seem to perpetuate a distinction between the offstage business of the Actor-Manager and his performance identities, the inclusion of these different types of spaces within the article all under the remit of 'Actors' Dressing Rooms' and particularly spaces such as Toole's parlour and the apartment, 'in which Mr. Wyndham entertains his friends … capable of seating some twenty or twenty-five persons' demonstrates the fluid line between the work of the actor and his social life. In the case of Wyndham, even 'whilst the actor paints his face, he can see many an invitation to dinner negligently thrust in the edges of the gilt frame', suggesting that his offstage life intrudes even into the process of his transformation into character in his Dressing Room, a space Aoife Monks has described as 'a third space between stage and life' (Monks 2010: 13). She claims that images of actors in their dressing rooms are, in general doomed to be disappointing, because whilst promising to reveal the secrets of the acting profession and the '"real" actor' they cannot ultimately convey the magic of theatre, focusing instead on the 'everyday routine labour of the actor' (2010: 17) and that therefore 'acting remains unknowable: hermetically sealed from prying eyes' (2010: 33). This legacy of the search for the 'real' actor's identity is interesting because in concentrating on the mystification of the process of bodily transformation, Monks seems to be ignoring the fact that the 'everyday routine labour of the actor' is a constituent part of his identity and one in which clothing and the act of dressing played a key role.

Many of the spaces described in the article contained mirrors, makeup and often elements of costume and whilst Benjamin Goldfinch's coat and plaid trousers, described above and illustrated hanging off the hooks in Figure 2.2.2, referred to Hare's current role in *A Pair of Spectacles*, some of the other costumes present in the actor-managers' rooms were not from current roles, but elements of dress from previous productions or even ones that had been used several times in different roles. In the case of Henry Irving for example, 'That old beaver hat was worn in *Charles I* and *The Dead Heart* – now it is the characteristic head-gear of *The Master of Ravenswood*' ('Actors' Dressing Rooms' 1891: 179). The transition of clothing from one production to another, particularly peripheral items of dress and accessories, suggests that an actor-manager's corpus of theatre costume or wardrobe should be considered concurrently with the construction of individual characters and thus brings it into line with narratives of fashionable wardrobes and clothing choices. Writing of the connection between fashion accessories and identity, Cristina Giorcelli analogizes the accessory with the *pargergon*, a framing device which fills in gaps in ensembles (*ergon*) of clothing, so that it 'is almost indispensable, particularly to any investigation of identity through dress' (Giorcielli 2011: 4). As Christopher Breward and Laura Ugolini have both touched upon, it was through the customization of menswear and close attention to details such as dress accessories that masculine sartorial identities were established in the late nineteenth century (Breward 1999; Ugolini 2007). The idea that the beaver hat which had acted as a frame for Irving's royal Charles I and religious Abbe Latour could then also function as an accessory for the young Edgar Ravenswood connects the identity of these three individual characters, but also to some measure elides them, subordinating their identity to that of the actor who made the sartorial choice to wear them and to whom the hat belonged. Speaking of Irving again, the author makes the further claim that 'Mr. Irving clings to an old coat so long as it will cling to him. He makes his clothes old – wears them during the day' ('Actors' Dressing Rooms' 1891: 179), a sentiment echoing Hare's statement that he always wears his clothes 'for some time previously, so as to get them to my figure' ('Actors' Dressing Rooms' 1891: 183). If in this article the boundaries between onstage and offstage spaces were blurred by the actor-managers' apartments within the theatres they managed, the fact that these costumes were obviously worn outside the performance moment while the actor-manager was present in an 'offstage' capacity suggests that the costumed body of the actor-manager also transgressed these boundaries and that theatrical costume should not necessarily be separated from the actor-manager's everyday embodied experience of dress and fashion.

Multi-Valent Identities in Everyday Life

If we accept that the barrier between theatrical costume and everyday life was more permeable than fixed, there is an argument to be made that there is also a literal truth in Gosse's assertion that the actor-manager's training in performance may have intrinsically affected the way he interacted with his own character, identity and bodily construction outside the theatre (Gosse 1920). In Philip

Zarrilli's 2004 essay on the actor's 'embodied modes of experience', he suggested that one of the fundamental differences between an actor's relationship with his body and that of other men is what he terms the development of 'extra-daily' experiences of the body as the result of 'long-term, in-depth engagement in certain psychophysical practices or training regimes [...] forms of embodied practice which engage the physical body and attention (mind) in cultivating and attuning both to subtle levels of experience or awareness' (Zarrilli 2004: 661). While he is focused on training regimes in contemporary theatrical practice rather than historical acting methodologies, Zarrilli has written elsewhere of the need to develop meta-theoretical constructs of acting that can be applied across a range of performance traditions, both historical and geographical and this 'extra-daily' experience is one such model. It is in fact, an approach that is clearly reflected in the writings of nineteenth-century actor-managers themselves, including Herbert Beerbohm Tree, whose 1893 lecture to the Royal Institution, entitled 'The Imaginative Faculty' focused on the way in which an actor trained his mind to inhabit the part he was playing, so that eventually the actor's inhabitation of the character's mental landscape affected his physicality: 'By aid of his imagination he becomes the man, and behaves unconsciously as the man would or should behave [...] Even the physical man will appear transformed' (Tree 1913: 112). Similarly, in 'The Art of Acting', an address to the students of Harvard University (1885), Henry Irving focused on the constant mental and physical practice required to successfully inhabit and embody theatrical characters.

Given the acculturation of actors in this period to techniques of embodiment, rather than separating out the onstage and offstage bodies, there is ultimately, in the case of such figures an argument for creating a separate category for self presentation in everyday life that is explicitly theatrical. This allows for a reading of the offstage dress of the actor-manager as part of a systematic rather than a haphazard programme of identity formation and also permits the application of modes of theatrical performance to both of the images of Squire Bancroft shown in Figure 2.2.1. I have written elsewhere on the importance of photographic portraits to the memorialization of the actor-manager and of their active involvement in these images' production and dissemination (Walter 2015), but establishing the offstage image of the actor-manager as explicitly theatrical, in conception if not always in motif is important because it imbues these images and particularly their choice of attire, with the quality of intentionality. As proxies for identity, portraits and biographical narratives share many common features, but as Shearer West has discussed in her survey of the history of portraiture, they differ in the sense of 'occasionality', the reality of the portrait as the encapsulation of one moment in a person's life that, whilst it may attempt to capture a person's character 'is at odds with the sprawling and developed aspects of character and action that comprise biographical narratives' (West 2004: 50–1). In representing the subject at a point in time, rather than over the span of his lifetime, the portrait is ostensibly at a disadvantage compared to the biographical narrative, but, it is also arguably more flexible, allowing for concurrent and non-contiguous narratives of identity to be presented through differentiated images. Richard Brilliant noted that this can be a problem for choosing images which encapsulated a subject for the process of memorialization as 'such an abundant repertoire of images may also present the viewer with a confusing range of options, destabilizing the characterization of the person portrayed and obscuring the mental image of the subject' (Brilliant [1991] 2013: 132).

This turn of phrase, used by Brilliant to refer to portraiture and memorialization more generally, echoes Gosse's anxieties about the recollection of the actor-manager and when he finally managed to reconcile himself to the task of describing Herbert Beerbohm, it appears that while he overcame the destabilizing force of Tree's theatrical characters he encountered the same problem of a multi-faceted recollection of the actor's offstage identity:

> I find it hard to bring into accord two visions of him, the one of a certain dandified elegance, the other sturdy, four-square, and a little Batavian. In youth – for he was still young when I met him first – he had not arrived at that impressiveness which he achieved at last. He was then, in fact – with his red hair, his pale complexion and faint eyes – the reverse of impressive off the stage, and I think he may have adopted what I call his 'elegance' of manner in order to remove this deficiency. At all events, as years went by, his increased solidity of form and authoritative case of address made him more and more a 'figure' in social intercourse. (Gosse 1920: 203)

It is clearly important to note the body's centrality to Gosse's recollection of Tree and that he saw it as a reflection of his internal character with an 'increased solidity of form' accompanying an increased social authority. However, instead of, as Brilliant suggested choosing one aspect of Tree's body as representative of the actor-manager, he has attempted to reconcile two presentations by characterizing Tree's style as a linear progression, with the framing of his body altering as a result of his changing social status. The result of this, according to Gosse was that he achieved a transition from 'dandified elegance' to an 'increased solidity of form' once his social prominence had been achieved.

These two aspects of Tree's self-presentation, of youthful 'dandified elegance' and older 'solidity' are shown respectively in Figures 2.2.3 and 2.2.4 (Gosse 1920: 203). In line with Gosse's narrative, a half-plate glass negative from the Alexander Bassano archive, taken in 1884 and now in the collection of the National Portrait Gallery (NPG), shows Tree elegantly dressed in a formal morning coat and posed in a manner reminiscent of Napoleon Sarony's famous 1882 portraits of Oscar Wilde in Aesthetic dress. By contrast, Figure 2.2.4 shows the actor-manager transformed into the 'sturdy, four-square' figure of his later life, an 'At Home' image of Tree used by Ogden's as a cigarette card and which was also widely reproduced and distributed in postcard format in the early twentieth century; three additional copies of this postcard are present in the Victoria and Albert Museum (V&A) collections. The inclusion in the background of this image of a portrait of Tree in character suggests that it was intended, as with other narratives of celebrity in this period, to remind the viewer of his accomplishments as well as his personality and it also shows the continued awareness of the costumed body in the actor-manager's everyday life.[3]

Looked at in isolation, these images seem to confirm Gosse's narrative of a progressive development from an elegant, fashionable figure with a hint of dandyism in his self-fashioning to a more conventional social figure associated with the high end of theatrical and social practice. Figure 2.2.5, Another photograph in the same series of Bassano portraits from 1884 belies Gosse's liner narrative however and suggests instead that Tree was engaged in the concurrent presentation of himself in both a dandified and conservative manner even relatively early on in his career. Figure 2.2.5 shows Tree in exactly the same morning attire, morning coat, collar and tie and dark trousers,

Figure 2.2.3 *Alexander Bassano,* Herbert Beerbohm Tree, *1884. London: National Portrait Gallery.*

Figure 2.2.4 Sir Herbert Beerbohm Tree, *c.1894–1907. London: National Portrait Gallery.*

as in Figure 2.2.3 and is almost certainly from the same sitting, Tree's pose and manner and his face-on engagement with the camera create a far more formal and less 'aesthetic' image of the actor-manager. It is a cogent reminder of the constructed and fixed nature of memorializing narratives against the fluid nature of identity as expressed in everyday life and is also an illustration of the dangers in selectively viewing images and portraits of anyone and particularly celebrities in isolation. Finally, it demonstrates the flexibility of one (material) body in the construction of identity, which can be designed and shaped, as Goffman ([1959] 1990) articulated, through a synthesis of appearance and manner rather than by one of these alone and which is further mediated by the translation of that body into a visual narrative. Interestingly, in contrast to the glass negative of Figure 2.2.3, Figure 2.2.5 is the only one of Bassano's images of Tree from this sitting for which there are any printed copies and it therefore suggests the possibility that Tree preferred this manner of self-presentation to that of the dandified body.

There is evidence therefore, of the longevity of a conservative self-expression within the range of Tree's photographic portraiture, but as Figure 2.2.6 indicates there is also evidence for the persistence of his fashionable, mannered body in the public eye. Taken by Herbert Rose Barraud a number of years after Bassano's more conventional portrait of the actor-manager, this cabinet card shows Tree fashionably dressed in a single-breasted and square-lapelled lounge jacket, accompanied by striped trousers that were used to introduce individuality into the otherwise uniform lounge suit.[4] Whilst his dress is constructed with an eye for fashionability, with its embrace of the modern lounge suit and

Figure 2.2.5 *Alexander Bassano,* Herbert Beerbohm Tree, *1884. London: National Portrait Gallery.*

Figure 2.2.6 *Herbert Rose Barraud,* Herbert Beerbohm Tree, *1890. London: National Portrait Gallery.*

the doing-up of only the top button of the jacket seems to have been designed to create an air of informality that may have been used to establish the sitter's creative or artistic identity. As with Figure 2.2.3, this air of creative informality is mirrored in his pose, sitting across his chair, although situating this image within the range of Barraud's portraiture reveals this pose was not exclusive to those in artistic professions.[5] As a signed photograph, it was obviously distributed directly by the actor-manager to his public and is thus an image that functioned as a link between the actor-manager and his audiences, a type of interaction that Rojek identified as a 'para-social' experience of celebrity identities (Rojek [2001] 2010). Although the inscription dates this particular cabinet card to 1890, at least four copies of this image exist in the theatre collections at the V&A, one of which is in a smaller, mounted format similar to that of the *carte-de-visite* and two of which are engravings of the image by the Direct Photo Engraving Co. which suggests a relatively widespread dissemination for this identifying image of Tree over a number of years.

In both Figures 2.2.5 and 2.2.6, the bodies presented by the actor-manager could be described as fashionable, but they are divided in terms of both physical appearance and manner into the categories of the slightly unconventional, or what might be called the creative body and a more normative or conservative expression of masculine identity. This duality may have seemed counter-intuitive to Gosse in his efforts to memorialize and fix Tree's identity for posterity, but in terms of the conception of an actor's everyday identity, it was a fluid model that could be adapted for different purposes and audiences and is therefore easily analogous to the actor-manager's work on the stage. As Fred Inglis recognized in his *Short History of Celebrity,* however, this duality was actually intrinsic to the nineteenth-century construction of the artistic individual, caught up as he stated between two competing narratives of celebrity, one of which held them up as unconventional, distinctive individuals with a talent for artistry and the other, which presented them as exemplary figures worthy of emulation. Inglis characterized this construction of celebrity as requiring a multi-faceted approach to self-expression, saying 'The oscillation between outlaw and legislator, creator and critic, checking out and joining in, finds its social and expressive form in the tense familiarity of avant-garde and bourgeoisie' (Inglis 2010: 78) in essence suggesting that by marrying creative and conservative identities, most artistic celebrities engaged in an everyday construction of self that could be considered as a performance.

Conclusion

While this chapter has considered the work of a small group of elite, male, actor-managers in a particular time period and even more specifically the problem faced by one author in capturing the identity of one actor-manager, Herbert Beerbohm Tree, the problem of locating the performer's identity can be found in any number of studies of those involved in the acting profession. In Mary Corbett's work on actresses' autobiographies, she also poses the question 'where does performance-as-identity-construction leave off and performance-as-theatrical-work begin?' (Corbett [2004] 2005: 109) by looking at the theatrical performances of Elizabeth Robins as performative acts that helped to constitute her gendered identity off the stage. Yet, the term 'performative' suggests a self-reflexive rather than a conscious mode of identity formation and I would argue that in the case of the theatrical personality, their offstage identities were as carefully crafted as their onstage characters and in both onstage and offstage presentations of self, the dressed body was key to the conveying of identity. In the words of Charles Wyndham, actor-manager of the Criterion Theatre, when embodying a character:

> [The actor] has first to study diligently the spirit and intention of his author's words, and then conveys them onto an ideal canvas, which is represented by the conception of the part, by the dress of the character, and by the make-up of the man. (Wyndham cited Pemberton 1904: 244–5)

Notes

1. Squire Bancroft actually claimed in his preface to their second autobiographical narrative, *Recollections of Sixty Years* (Bancroft and Wilton 1909: vii) that *On and Off the Stage* had run to seven editions, but there is definitely evidence for the publication of an eighth edition in 1891.
2. In their work on the biographies of exemplary figures, Cubitt and Warren (2000) have spoken about the perceived importance of accuracy and detail in these narratives as characteristic of the Victorian era.

3 In her recollections of his career, his wife Maude discussed the success of Tree's original production of *Hamlet* and his subsequent revivals and touring appearances in the piece between 1892 and 1906 (Tree 1920: 72–5, 84, 92, 124, 134, 137).

4 For the fashionability of this attire in the 1890s, as expressed through illustrations in *The Tailor and Cutter*, cf. Breward (1999: 39–41).

5 Similar poses can be found in Barraud's portraits of poet Robert Browning, musician Charles Halle, author Arthur Conan Doyle and playwrights J. M. Barrie and W. S. Gibert in the same period, but also in images of explorer Thomas Heazle Park, attorney-general Charles Arthur Russell and financier Sir John Lubbock, although in the last, their appearances are characterized by a far more formal dress style.

References

Bancroft, S. and M. Wilton (1891), *Mr. & Mrs. Bancroft On and Off the Stage: Written By Themselves*, 8th ed. London: Bentley.

Bancroft, S. and M. Wilton (1909), *The Bancrofts: Recollections of Sixty Years*. London: Murray.

Beerbohm Tree, H. (1913), 'The Imaginative Faculty: Being an Address Delivered at the Royal Institution' in *Thoughts and After-Thoughts*, 91–121. London: Cassell.

Boyce, C., P. Finnerty, and A-M. Millim (2013), *Victorian Celebrity Culture and Tennyson's Circle*. Basingstoke: Palgrave Macmillan.

Bratton, J. (2011), *The Making of the West End Stage: Marriage, Management and the Mapping of Gender in London, 1830–1870*. Cambridge: Cambridge University Press.

Breward, C. (1999), *The Hidden Consumer: Masculinities, Fashion and City Life,1860–1914*. Manchester: Manchester University Press.

Brilliant, R. ([1991] 2013), *Portraiture*. London: Reaktion Books.

Codell, J. F. (2003),*The Victorian Artist: Artists' Lifewritings in Britain, ca. 1870–1910*. Cambridge: Cambridge University Press.

Corbett, M. ([2004] 2005), 'Performing Identities: Actresses and Autobiography' in Kerry Powell (ed.), *The Cambridge Companion to Victorian and Edwardian Theatre*, 109–26. Cambridge: Cambridge University Press.

Craik, J. (1994), *The Face of Fashion: Cultural Studies in Fashion*. London: Routledge.

Cubitt, G. and Warren Allen, eds. (2000), *Heroic Reputations and Exemplary Lives*. Manchester: Manchester University Press.

Davis, T. C. ([2000] 2007), *The Economics of the British Stage, 1800–1914*. Cambridge: Cambridge University Press.

De la Haye, A. and E. Wilson (1999), 'Introduction', in A. de la Haye and E. Wilson (eds), *Defining Dress: Dress as Object, Meaning and Identity*. Smallhythe Place, Manchester: Manchester University Press.

Entwistle, J. (2000), *The Fashioned Body*. Cambridge: Polity Press.

Giorcielli, C. (2011), 'Accessorizing the Modern(ist) Body', in C. Giorcelli and P. Rabinowitz (eds), *Accessorizing the Body: Habits of Being Vol. I*, 1–6. London: University of Minnesota Press.

Goffman, E. ([1959] 1990), *The Presentation of Self in Everyday Life*. London: Penguin Books.

Gosse, E. (1920?), 'A Sketch' in Max Beerbohm (ed.), *Herbert Beerbohm Tree: Some Memories of Him and His Art*, 2nd ed., 203–05. London: Hutchinson.

Hollander, A. ([1975] 1993), *Seeing Through Clothes*. Berkeley: University of California Press.
Inglis, F. (2010), *A Short History of Celebrity*. Princeton: Princeton University Press.
Irving, H. (1885), *Address to the Students of Harvard University*. London: Chiswick Press.
Monks, A. (2010), 'Dressing Rooms: The Actor's Body and Costume', in A. Monks, *The Actor in Costume*, 13–33. Basingstoke: Palgrave Macmillan.
Newnes, G. (1891), 'Introduction', *The Strand Magazine*, January, 1 (3).
Pemberton, T. E. (1904), *Sir Charles Wyndham: A Biography*. London: Hutchinson.
Richards, J. (2005), 'The Actor-Manager as Auteur', *Nineteenth Century Theatre and Film* 32 (2), November: 20–35.
Rojek, C. ([2001] 2010), *Celebrity*. London: Reaktion Books.
States, B. O. (1996), 'Performance as Metaphor',*Theatre Journal*, 48:1–26.
Tree, M. (1920?), 'Herbert and I', in Max Beerbohm (ed.), *Herbert Beerbohm Tree: Some Memories of Him and His Art*, 2nd ed., 1–171. London: Hutchinson.
Ugolini, L. (2007), *Men and Menswear: Sartorial Consumption in Britain,1880–1939*. Aldershot: Ashgate Publishing.
Walter, H. M. (2015), 'Artist, Professional, Gentleman: The Actor's Offstage Portrait (1875–95)', *Visual Culture in Britain* 16 (3): 267–84.
West, S. (2004), *Portraiture*. Oxford: Oxford University Press.
Zarrilli, P. B. (2004), 'Towards a Phenomenological Model of the Actor's Embodied Modes of Experience', in Harry J. Elam, Jr. (ed.), 'Theorizing the Performer', *Theatre Journal* 56: 653–66.

2.3 Extravagance, Expense and Notoriety in Costume: Gaby Deslys and Parisian Modernity on the American Stage, 1911–14

Emily Brayshaw

Introduction

The early twentieth century saw the major theatres of London, Paris and New York develop strong commercial and aesthetic links with the global fashion industry and department stores, which shaped transatlantic tastes and economic and cultural exchanges. As Kaplan and Stowell (1994), Schweitzer (2009) and Evans (2013) have documented, this nexus was influenced by the rise of the socially and economically independent 'New Woman', whose voracious appetite for fashion and amusements meant that theatres on both sides of the Atlantic became sites of consumer spectacle where *haute couture* performance costumes attracted paying audiences. The internationally famous French music hall star of the *Belle Époque* and quintessential Parisian New Woman, Gaby Deslys (1881–1920, born Marie-Elise Gabrielle Caire), was largely forgotten by the mid-twentieth century, but had an indelible influence on performance costumes and worldwide fashions during her lifetime. This chapter situates the Parisian-made performance costumes that Deslys wore in America between 1911 and 1914 within the intersecting and complex domain of the intercontinental theatre and fashion industries that also included fashion retailing and women's imaginations.

It also examines theatre and media ephemera, photographs, cartoons and popular songs through the lens of methods and approaches including costume and fashion theory, art, theatre, social, fashion and urban histories, as well as musicology. It argues for the particular significance of Deslys' choices of wearing Parisian haute couture and extravagantly plumed millinery on stage for her American tours between 1911 and 1914. It shows how this enabled a series of deliberate and inter-related strategies: to attract female audiences, demonstrate support for the French fashion industry and communicate her personality as a self-made 'New Woman' for the new century. The influence of the European avant-garde on Parisian fashions from late 1912 manifested in a dramatic shift in the aesthetics and symbolisms of Deslys' performance costumes from her Belle Epoque creations, which by the end of 1913 were among the first displays of European modern fashion aesthetics on the commercial American stage. The methodology employed here, therefore, also demonstrates how and why Deslys' stage ensembles from late 1913 alienated American audiences, despite giving them a Parisian perspective on how costume and fashion could shape experiences of gender and modernity.

Seeing the Actress in America: 1890–1911

American social and cultural expectations around how successful actresses should be seen were established in the 1880s and developed between 1900 and 1920. This was a period when New York's 'theatre managers aggressively pursued the imagination and presence of female theatregoers by transforming the stage into a glorious site of consumer spectacle' (Schweitzer 2009: 4). Between 1895 and 1908, for example, the impresario Florenz Ziegfeld, Jr. (1869–1932), positioned the Parisian actress Anna Held (1872–1918) as the pinnacle of beauty and fashion by dressing her on and off the stage in expensive French haute couture to attract wealthy female audiences (Brayshaw 2014). Female theatregoers of that era included the figure of the socially and economically independent New Woman whose spending power and influence was courted by the 'large-scale promotional efforts of couturiers in London and Paris' (Schweitzer 2009: 4). The New Woman emerged in the social and sexual upheavals of the 1890s in London and Paris and contributed to the increasing intersection of fashion, retail and entertainment environments (Kaplan and Stowell 1994). In America, the New Woman's appetites for amusements and fashion also strongly contributed to collaborations between Broadway theatres, department stores, the nascent mass media and the Parisian fashion industry (Schweitzer 2009 and Evans 2013).

The New Woman's increasingly voracious appetites and desire to be seen were predicted by the aesthete Oscar Wilde (1854–1900) in his one-act French play, *Salomé* (1891). Wilde, who was at the peak of his popularity in the Parisian literary scene in 1891, re-told the Biblical story of the notorious Salomé, the *femme fatale* stepdaughter of the tetrarch Herod Antipas who derived pleasure from being looked at and requested the head of Jokanaan (John the Baptist) on a silver platter for performing the dance of the seven veils. *Salomé* became a global phenomenon from its Parisian opening in 1896. It inspired the 1905 opera by Richard Strauss (1864–1949) and so-called 'Salomania' took America by storm around the same time. Productions starring a 'Salomé' ran at venues from the New York Metropolitan Opera to Broadway theatres and large vaudeville houses (Glenn 2002). This included the production of *Salomé* (1906–10) that the Canadian dancer Maud Allan (1873–1956) made famous through her opulent, Orientalist-style costumes and bodily display.

Wilde used disidentification in *Salomé* to destabilize gender differences between men and women. This had the effect of accommodating contradictory interpretations of Salomé's sexuality as 'the liberating power of the New Woman' and her seemingly transgressive desires (Im 2011: 370). The themes of 'seeing' women and destabilizing female sexuality were also evident in many of the era's risqué musical farces, including the 1907 London production of Franz Lehár's operetta *The Merry*

Widow (1905). It starred the actress Lily Elsie (1886–1962) and featured costumes made in Paris by the English couturier, 'Lucile', Lady Duff Gordon (1863–1935). It also included the so-called 'Merry Widow' hat, which was crowned by costly black bird of paradise plumes and made by the Paris branch of London's largest millinery house, Maison Lewis (Bigham 2012: 129). Broadway also had a production of *The Merry Widow* in 1907 which starred the American actress Ethel Jackson (1877–1957) and although her costumes were not Lucile designs, they were copied faithfully enough. Compared with Wilde's Salomé, however, who is ultimately decapitated for her desire to be seen, the merry widow marries her true love and keeps her fortune, while actresses like Elsie and Jackson dominated their audiences' attentions. It was into this social and cultural milieu that Deslys came to America in 1911 to perform and to be 'seen'.

Gaby Deslys: Notoriety, Fashion and Extravagance Personified

Deslys commenced her Parisian career around 1902 and gained a reputation in the music halls of London and Paris as a pretty, hard-working reliable actress. Her early stage contemporaries included the leading courtesans of *fin de siècle* Paris, Caroline (*La Belle*) Otéro (1868–1965), Liane de Pougy (1869–1950) and Emilienne d'Alençon (1869–1946) (Gardiner 1986: 12). These notorious women captivated the public with their extravagant displays of expensive fashions and jewels and exploits with rich, powerful lovers which 'helped create … popular perceptions of the female entertainer as femme fatale and gold-digger' (Gundle 2008: 136). Courtesans were considered 'among the leaders of fashion … because they were much less constrained than most women by the fear of looking immodest or conspicuous' (Steele 2010: 284). By 1910 Deslys, whose body seemed to echo the courtesans' fluid lines and large *poitrines*, similarly attracted scandal in the popular, tabloid, theatre and fashion presses with her rich lovers, displays of expensive pearls and costly, risqué fashions.

Deslys' links to several high-profile men, including her well-publicized tryst in 1910 with King Manuel II, the king of Portugal (1889–1932) fascinated the public. The international tabloids for example, blamed Deslys for the collapse of the Portuguese monarchy, despite the complex factors that caused the Portuguese revolution in October 1910. Deslys' notoriety was echoed in the bold fashions that she appeared to favour for publicity photographs and stage costumes, which were designed and made by the Parisian couture houses of Doucet, Callot Soeurs and Maison Paquin (Gardiner 1986: 40). Maison Paquin and Callot Soeurs had deliberately cultivated an openly theatrical glamour in their heavily ornate styles since the 1890s, presenting 'the first real challenge' to the House of Worth's monopoly of on and off stage fashion in Paris and London (Kaplan and Stowell 1994: 10). Deslys, from the start of her career, also augmented the air of theatricality in her performance costumes by complementing them with costly, expansively plumed hats.

Deslys teamed up with Maison Lewis in 1910 and had the pick of their range in return for publicizing their hats (Gardiner 1986: 33). Her sartorial style, which oscillated between performance costume and fashion is evident in an image published in April 1911 in *Comœdia Illustré*, the illustrated weekly supplement of the Parisian daily newspaper *Comœdia*. The photograph shows Deslys wearing a costume from her show at the exclusive Théâtre des Capucines in Paris, simply entitled *La Revue*

Figure 2.3.1 *'Armand Berthez, Gaby Deslys and Irène Bordoni in "Midi bouge" by Michel Carré et André Barde'. Sketch by Yves Marevéry, c. 1911. Image courtesy of the Bibliothèque nationale de France.*

(1911), which included a heavily beaded gown by Callot Soeurs, her valuable pearls and a hat from which protrudes a large quantity of aigrette feathers. The costume's visual impact was highlighted in a sketch by the illustrator and caricaturist Yves Marevéry (1888–1914) who omitted the ornate details of her gown, but drew Deslys' feathered hat, pearls and *poitrine*, thereby re-inforcing her ties to the *fin de siècle*'s courtesans within the Parisian public imagination.

Deslys' notorious entanglement with King Manuel II also made headlines in America in 1911, thus fuelling a desire among New York audiences to see the actress who had captured the heart of a king. The American press described Deslys as a 'freak', a term that referred to, 'people who appear upon the stage, propelled there by the quantity of publicity or notoriety received in the daily newspapers'.[1] The influential American theatre impresarios, brothers Lee (1871–1953) and J. J. (1879–1963) Shubert capitalized on the scandal and hired Deslys in the autumn of 1911 to star in their New York productions *The Revue of Revues* (1911) and *Vera Violetta* (1911). She received a salary of four thousand dollars a week for the latter production.[2] Deslys catered to American demands to see the latest Parisian fashions and wore her own couture gowns, plumes and jewels in both productions.

These were exaggerations of the latest styles, but were nonetheless praised by the New York theatre and fashion press. *Variety*, for example, wrote:

> [e]ven the show girls, dressed at the height of managerial extravagance, couldn't outshine Gaby. A silver gown lined in emerald was a marvel but later when a coral colored [*sic*] gown completely covered in a bead fringe was worn, Gaby made every one sit up. ... I noticed many of the dresses were slit [up the right side to the knee], while Gaby's were slit up the front about twelve inches.[3]

In November 1911, the New York magazine *The Theatre* published a dressing-room interview with Deslys from the Winter Garden Theatre.[4] It praised her beauty, fashions and jewels, noting that Deslys had 'slipped out of the splendour of the green brocade velvet cloak she had worn on the stage into the apparent simplicity of a white lace negligée' and sat at a dressing table covered with solid gold toilet articles.[5] The article featured a photograph of Deslys seated before a mirror at her dressing table wearing her negligée, famous pearls and makeup. The image of the mirror, as Monks explains, signalled Americans' 'desire to see behind the theatrical mask' and allowed them the 'slightly sordid pleasure of peeking backstage unnoticed' (2010: 17). This let readers imagine what King Manuel II might have seen and pointed to how Deslys used the dressing room hierarchy to signal her star persona in America; instead of dressing backstage with the chorus girls, she had a luxurious private space. Deslys' press coverage and expensive costumes in 1911, therefore, confirmed American social and cultural expectations of how a successful actress should be seen.

'The Gaby Glide': Costume, Choreography and Conveying a Fashionable Modernity

The American desire to see the latest French styles on stage was so strong that many criticized Deslys' decision to re-use some of her gowns from *The Revue of Revues* in *Vera Violetta*. *Variety* claimed that they looked 'tired', but reported that a dance called 'the Gaby Glide' was a big hit, which highlighted audience expectations that a musical production should be a blend of fashion and entertainment.[6] 'The Gaby Glide' reflected the global dance craze of the early 1910s when fashion designers and choreographers began to 'cross boundaries' to study the intersection between movement and dress (Evans 2013: 50). These designers included Lucile and Paquin, 'who insisted upon the persuasiveness of fabric in motion' to sell their fashions (Kaplan and Stowell 1994: 117). The 1911 sheet music cover for 'The Gaby Glide' shows a photograph of Deslys and her dancing partner, Harry Pilcer (1885–1961), doing the 'Glide'.[7] Deslys wears a white gown with a slit running higher than the knee in the manner described by *Variety*, pointing to the notoriety that she expressed through fearlessness in dress. The gown's designer is not credited, but in April 1911 all of the leading French designers produced a hybrid gown with an asymmetrical knee-high split that 'only showed when the wearer moved, and the gown was favourably reviewed in the U.S.A. where it was rapidly copied' (Evans 2013: 207). Even Deslys' feathered hat in the photograph is smaller than usual, indicating the importance of movement in this instance, as a trimming of larger plumes would have proved cumbersome.

The importance of movement in fashion was also demonstrated in the choreography, music and lyrics of 'The Gaby Glide'. The choreography placed Deslys in front of Pilcer with her back slightly offset to create the look of gliding. The melody of the song's chorus contains held minims as a counterpoint to dotted, syncopated quavers, which gives the musical effect of a series of quick steps accompanied by a glide. Deslys' ability to dance to the fast ragtime tune demonstrated to American audiences that she moved and dressed in wholly contemporary ways. The choreography, music and lyrics to 'The Gaby Glide' also linked Deslys to the mechanized, idealized movements of haute couture models known as the 'mannequin glide', as Evans states (2013: 29). Fashion mannequins would often 'incorporate the walking elements of popular dance performances such as "The Gaby Glide", as women often imitated others whom they deemed were successful and desirable' (Evans 2013: 224). It is entirely possible however, that Deslys similarly absorbed the movements of fashion models at Lucile, Maison Paquin and Callot Soeurs in Paris, where she bought her clothes. 'The Gaby Glide' was, as the song states, 'just a real Parisian slide'.

The Armory Show: European Art and Fashion in America in 1913

Deslys and her extravagant fashions were not the only notorious amusements imported from Paris in 1911. Modernist aesthetic movements, including Cubism and Futurism were 'introduced as "freakish" European imports in *The New York Times* from August 1911' and the paper published updates of European modernist exhibitions throughout 1912 (Carlson 2014: 4). It was not, however, until 1913 with the *International Exhibition of Modern Art* that ran from 17 February to 15 March in New York, that the styles of Cubism and Futurism became widely known in America.[8] The exhibition comprised 1,300 pieces, including works by Picasso, Duchamp and Braque and was known as the 'Armory Show' because of its location at New York's 69th Regiment Armory on Lexington Avenue.[9] The Armory Show works were not generally understood by the broader American public and were satirized in the New York press, including in a series of cartoons entitled 'Seeing New York with a Cubist' by the artist J. F. Griswold. The series ran in March 1913 in *The Evening Sun* a successful, politically-conservative newspaper aimed at the mass market.

On 13 March 1913, the American department store magnate, John Wanamaker (1838–1922), also used the language and the logo of the Armory Show in the press. Instead of lampooning Cubism however, Wanamaker brought Modernist art into communication with the consumption of fashion and ran a full-page advertisement in the New York newspaper, *The Evening Mail* to promote a fashion show at his Broadway store.[10] Prior to 1910 there was 'little distinction between *couture*, clothing made to measure, and *confection*, ready-made clothing. In 1910, the two activities were clearly divided and the nomenclature *la haute couture* was strictly reserved for salons that produced collections for private clients' (Palmer 2010: 393–6). Designers often give their imaginations free rein to produce highly theatrical designs for their haute couture collections which are then adapted as department store confections. The 1913 haute couture of many leading Parisian fashion houses underscored the interplay of the aesthetic modernism of European avant-garde movements, which derived from easel painting and sculpture, but moved across all of the applied arts, literature and music. Wanamaker's advertisement promoted the 1913 confections of Callot Soeurs, Doucet, Lanvin, Paquin and Poiret, but underscored their avant-garde influences by stating:

> The gowns are inspired by the paintings. … Those who have gone to the International Exhibition of Modern Art … have seen the new movement in painting and sculpture … At last the modern spirit is developing in the realm of women's dress. … The Paris couturiers have been working hand in hand with the artists of the new schools and have embodied in the Spring Fashions the best of the new principles.[11]

From 1909, the Futurist avant-garde had 'aimed at "reconstructing the universe," not only through the design of … objects and spaces, but also by exploiting the mass media and public spectacle' (Braun 1995: 34). The Italian Futurists stressed the technological values of speed, dynamism and constant innovation. Although they were not represented at the Armory Show however, the terms Cubism and Futurism were, 'used interchangeably in the marketing of the new fashion [in America], the former becoming a catchall term for the European avant-garde' (Carlson 2014: 3). Wanamaker's advertisement promised that his stores would present the, 'straight lines of the Cubists and the color [*sic*] combinations of the Futurists … in the new Paris Fashions' for the first time in America. It underscored the gowns' connections to the Armory Show by presenting mannequins as living works of art, posing inside frames. Not all Americans, however, were impressed by the modernist fashions. The cartoonist Harvey Peake (1866–1958), for example, lampooned the styles in the highly influential daily newspaper *New York World* on 16 March 1913, despite the paper's more liberal leanings. Peake's cartoon, 'Why Not Let the Cubists and Futurists Design the Spring Fashions?' included a female figure wearing a triangular-shaped hat, a dress made from a series of triangles and a string of smaller pink triangles that resembled a feather boa.

The 1913 fashions' connections with the European avant-garde meant that the American press soon 'associated the commercial gowns with radical feminism' which included calls for women's suffrage, access to tertiary education and the right to work in male-dominated professions (Carlson 2014: 3, 4). This association was influenced by the Futurist belief that 'the tyranny of tradition could only be overcome by a constant assault on *passéiste* institutions, social mores, and even gender roles' (Braun 1995: 34). These ideas further contributed to the derision of the fashions in the conservative press where Griswold for example, published a cartoon in *The Evening Sun* on 19 March 1913 entitled 'A Spring Day on Fifth Avenue'. It shows rectangular women promenading along New York's fashionable Fifth Avenue wearing geometric clothing and hats that allude to Cubism and to the Futurist spring collections. If the broader American public in 1913 associated Parisian modernist confections with radical ideologies, then there was a real risk that the haute couture collections and their New Woman wearers like Deslys would be similarly linked to American cultural anxieties around female emancipation.

In February 1913 Deslys starred at the Winter Garden Theatre in the Shuberts' production *The Honeymoon Express* and toured America with the production in spring 1913. *The Honeymoon Express* was a scenographic spectacle reflecting Futurist ideals of speed, technology, fashion and youth, albeit a Futurism co-opted and repackaged to meet American mass-entertainment tastes by the commercially savvy Shuberts. The production featured an express train racing with a car in its staging and 'with the switch on stage set as a blinder, the auto and the engine with their headlights appear[ed] to be coming right into the audience.'[12] These cutting-edge special effects were a combination of film, stage-lighting and scenography and made the production a huge financial success. One show made $8,400 alone at the box office as audiences flocked to see the effects and Deslys' costumes which contributed to the spectacle and almost upstaged her.[13] *Variety* stated that the show would be a hit not because of Deslys, but because of her '$50,000 worth' of Parisian 'dresses and hats'.[14] Deslys' costume changes also highlighted the frenetic pace of *The Honeymoon Express*, with the press noting:

> This little old earth has a new wonder to add to its collection of seven — the wonderful gowns of Mlle Gaby Deslys and her mile-a-minute speed of changing them. ... On the right side of the ... stage is a little green screen-coop, with a mirror ... where Gaby makes her lightning changes and [two] maids help. ... "The Honeymoon Express" was slow compared to Gaby's speed between her dressing room and the footlights.[15]

In addition, a reviewer known as 'Sime' stated that in front of a police presence during one performance, 'Pilcer tore Gaby's skirt off ... in the bedchamber undressing scene ... It was a very vulgar bit'.[16] The scene may have been risqué, with Pilcer's eagerness to remove the garment adding to the production's frenzied pace, but part of its appeal was likely that Pilcer tore an expensive garment with no regard for cost, or for censorship. Deslys' costumes and how she interacted with them on stage therefore emphasized her destabilizing sexuality and underscored her notoriety, while *Variety*'s granting them agency demonstrated their commercial value as extravagant curiosities that attracted audiences. Deslys' performance, costume changes and her haute couture garments themselves in *The Honeymoon Express* consequently explored dialogues in America on the relations between commercialized Modernist art, a public affinity for extravagance and the stage. As 1913 progressed, however, Desly's modernist haute couture costumes remained costly and extravagant, but their aesthetics differed markedly from what American audiences wanted to see.

Deslys Frees Herself From Fashion

Deslys returned to Paris in April 1913, where she played a version of *The Honeymoon Express.* After a brief rest, she starred in the London production *A la Carte* in the summer and early autumn of 1913. It is clear that by this point, Deslys deliberately wore extreme examples of haute couture on stage compared with her offstage ensembles. On 15 July 1913, for example, Deslys appeared at the Longchamp races wearing a Callot Soeurs gown that combined, 'white chiffon with "Callot-blue" taffeta. ... [I]t was little wonder that fashionable women as well as manikins cast most envious glances at [her]'.[17] In contrast, Deslys' costumes for *A la Carte* were made at Maison Paquin in Paris to her own designs and those of the French fashion illustrator, Etienne Drian (1885–1961) and the French costumier, M. Landolff, who made the costumes for the Ballets Russes' production *The Blue God* (1912). Maison Lewis made the headdresses.

In the 1910s, 'ninety percent of the coverage in Paquin's press albums consisted of theatre reviews, showing how important the stage press was in fashion dissemination' (Evans 2013: 58). This volume of reportage, however, demonstrates the importance of Deslys to Maison Paquin. In an article that played on Paquin's own 1913 acceptance of the prestigious Legion d'Honneur to recognize her economic contributions to France, the Parisian fortnightly satirical magazine *Fantasio*, wrote:

> Madame Paquin made Miss Gaby Deslys a Knight of the Legion of Honor [for commissioning] sixty-three ensembles … each more bold, frightening and unheard of than the other, for Miss Gaby Deslys considers herself the great leader of Parisian fashion around the world. … And, in the … calm provinces, the good bourgeois admire, not without astonishment, her excess of tiger skins, her omnipresent ostrich plumes, her Mohawks of aigrette [plumes] and her vanishing skirts.[18]

Figure 2.3.2 *Deslys in the white tulle gown with ostrich feather trim by Drian for Paquin and headdress by Maison Lewis. Image from the author's collection.*

Evans has demonstrated how, despite Maison Paquin's art-nouveau aesthetic, the house's choreography, scenography and staging of its fashion shows were grounded in Modernism (2013: 54). In 1913, this extended to Deslys' stage costume designs which included one ensemble 'made of a leopard skin laid crosswise, so that the center of the animal's back rests on the center of the back of Gaby Deslys. … The mantle is finished off by a collar in silver fox falling to the waist. Another ensemble was made entirely of white tulle in flounces edged with ostrich feathers.'[19]

Deslys' Paquin ensembles received glowing reviews in the French fashion press, with the illustrated women's magazine *La Vie Heureuse*, noting that Deslys had worked with Drian in order to free herself from fashion after being its leader for so long.[20] London also fêted Deslys in 1913, where she became 'the darling of a new society' eager to remove the restrictive shackles of Victorianism (Gardiner 1986: 84). The increasingly conservative social environment of pre-World War I America however, meant that many women shunned the modernist styles of 1913 despite merchandisers' attempts to, 'manipulate the cultural significance of the style after the Armory Show to make it distinctly American and progressive' (Carlson 2014: 27). The American press linked the fashions to the New Woman from the outset including 'radical suffragists and young, fashionable celebrities' even though American feminists generally eschewed the styles (Carlson 2014: 21, 22). On 6 April 1913, for example the *Chicago Sunday Tribune* featured a cartoon that included Deslys, the dancer Alla Nazimova (1879–1945), who starred as Salomé on Broadway and the prominent suffragist Carrie Chapman Catt (1859–1947). The cartoon mocked women's suffrage, was drawn in a Cubist style and lampooned the women as attention-seekers like Griswold's Fifth Avenue fashionistas. It depicted Deslys holding a teddy bear-shaped muff, perhaps as a reference to Pilcer, who had worn a bright yellow suit and carried a teddy bear upon his arrival in New York in November 1912 (Gardiner 1986: 72). The cartoon also claimed there were two little slits cut in the brim of Deslys' hat, 'which enable her to see without being seen' pointing to the New Woman's relationship with celebrity, fashion and the stage.

The American press continued to paint Deslys as a New Woman throughout 1913, although the coverage was not always positive. In April, the Los Angeles press printed an interview in which Deslys stressed the importance of women's financial independence.[21] In September, a comic flow chart appeared that outlined the categories of staff that Deslys claimed were necessary for a woman to be successful. Almost half of the forty-one categories were related to 'being seen' and included a coiffure maker, modiste, milliner, tailor, furrier, corsetiere, boot and glove makers, jeweller, costumer, wardrobe mistress, wardrobe maids and make-up maids.[22] The article included a sketch of twelve identical personal maids lined up like chorus girls, which also likely re-inforced connections between the New Woman and the actress in the public mind. Another series of cartoons likened Deslys to a highly paid escort: one stated that she charged five hundred dollars to, 'make you the envy of all other diners'; another stated that she charged two-hundred-and fifty dollars 'to be pointed out as your companion on Fifth Avenue'.[23] In contrast with other stars of the era, including the American ballroom dancing star Mrs Irene Castle (1887–1969) whom Lucile dressed for the stage from November 1913, the American press painted the unmarried, financially independent Deslys as a gold-digging courtesan.

It is within this context that Deslys and her collection of Paquin ensembles returned to America in November 1913 to tour in two Shubert productions, *The Little Parisienne* (1913–14) and *The Belle of*

Bond Street (1914).[24] Her costumes, which included two hundred thousand dollars worth of jewels and almost two hundred thousand dollars worth of 'Paris hats' did not however garner favourable reviews outside New York.[25] One American press report from early 1914 declared the gowns, 'meaningless. They were designed … to shriek aloud, "I am Gaby. I am the most startling thing in three continents. I am bizarre. I am different. I am stunning"'.[26] Elin Diamond writes that the materiality of costume re-inforces ideologies that remain long after a theatrical event has finished including 'political and cultural pressures that are consciously and unconsciously acknowledged' (2006: 13). The colours of Deslys' gowns, particularly one pale green Paquin creation that was paired with a purple cloak likely connected her with the women's suffrage movement in the public's mind, as purple, green and white were the colours the suffragettes used for their campaign, although Deslys had not discussed the issue in America. The same article also alluded to American retailers' attempts to popularize modernist fashions in its summation of Deslys' leopard-skin ensemble noting, 'the effect may have been sensational, but it was not a dress. It was a futurist advertisement'.[27]

Even American *Vogue*, which had praised Deslys' attire at Longchamp, panned the ensembles and undermined her agency in costume choice, stating that her 'beauty is diminished by the extravagant and preposterous costumes which she is forced to wear'.[28] It appears therefore, that Deslys had

Figure 2.3.3 *Gaby Deslys (Marie-Elise Gabrielle Caire), by Talbot, c. 1913. Image courtesy of the National Portrait Gallery, London.*

difficulty 'selling' her European modernist haute couture and ideologies of women's emancipation to American audiences in 1913 for similar reasons that American department stores had trouble selling the Parisian modernist confections.

Conclusion

This chapter has discussed the expensive haute couture performance costumes that Deslys wore on her American tours between 1911 and 1914 with a focus on the images and discussions of her stage ensembles that were disseminated by the mass media in American and France. It has also shown, by using a purposeful survey of archival resources and theatre ephemera, musicology, costume theory, art and American and French theatre and fashion history, how Deslys used her costumes to attract audiences, underscore her extravagance and notoriety and to signal her status as a self-made New Woman. This chapter, therefore, also invites costume scholars and practitioners to consider how they might use similar methodological approaches to support their own work on costume and performance.

Deslys, however, deliberately changed her style of costuming in mid-1913, moving from the popular styles of couturiers like Lucile to displays of haute couture ensembles by Drian and Landolff for Paquin and Maison Lewis and her own designs. Her new look, which impressed fashionable European audiences in late 1913 and early 1914, did not appeal to conservative American audiences who had anticipated how she should dress for the stage based on the costumes of her 1911 and 1912 tours and their associated press coverage. Furthermore, the aesthetic departure of Modernist art and fashion in 1913 from the popular American commercial tastes of the previous decade was marked and extreme. Deslys' costumes in the *The Little Parisienne* (1913–14) associated her in the American public's mind with the radical ideologies of the European avant-garde, especially when viewed within the context of her destabilizing, confident sexuality and public statements about women's financial independence. It is evident, therefore, that Deslys may have freed herself from fashion in 1913, but like a modernist Salomé had pushed American audiences too far in her desire to be seen and was punished for her perceived sexual and sartorial transgressions through ridicule in the press.

Notes

I would like to thank Randy Bryan Bigham for sharing his encyclopaedic knowledge and primary resources concerning Deslys' involvement with Lucile around 1912. This project is situated within 'Imagining Fashion Futures Lab', led by Peter McNeil at the University of Technology Sydney (UTS), Australia.

1 '"Freak Acts" – In and Out', *Variety*, Vol. XXX. No. 3, 23 December 1911, 41, 117.
2 'Straight Vaudeville Show Winter Garden's Policy', *Variety*, Vol. XXIV. No. 10, 11 November 1911, 11.
3 '"The Skirt" Says: Speaking of Woman, Mostly', *Variety*, Vol. XXIV, No. 12, 25 November 1911, 17.
4 'Gabrielle of the Lilies On and Off the Stage', *The Theatre*, Vol. XIV, No. 129, November 1911, 156.

5 Ibid.
6 'Vera Violetta', *Variety*, Vol. XXIV, No. 12, 25 November 1911, 21.
7 'The Gaby Glide' was written by Tin Pan Alley composer Louis A. Hirsch (1887–1924), with lyrics and choreography by Pilcer. It was published by the Shapiro Music Publishing Company, New York.
8 The Armory Show also ran in Chicago after its New York display.
9 International Exhibition of Modern Art, http://xroads.virginia.edu/~museum/armory/entrance.html (accessed: 19 December 2018).
10 This intersection of modern art, theatre and advertising is explored in Chapter 8, 'Modern Art Meets Modern Marketing: The Armory Show' (Bradley 2009: 117–35).
11 'The John Wanamaker Store Presents for the First Time in America Color Combinations of the Futurists, Cubist Influence in Fashions in the new Paris Models for Spring', *The Evening Mail*, 13 , 1913 11.
12 'The Honeymoon Express', *Variety,* Vol XXIX, No. XI, 14 February 1913, 18.
13 'Gaby May Leave', *Variety,* Vol XXIX, No. XXII, 21 February 1913, 10.
14 'The Honeymoon Express', *Variety,* Vol XXIX, No. XI, 14 February 1913, 18.
15 'One Maid Removes Gaby's Coat While Another Puts on Her Slippers and Fastens Her Petties and on to the Stage She Springs, Only to Return and Repeat', publication unknown, 1913.
16 Sime, 'Winter Garden', *Variety,* Vol XXIX, No. XIII, 28 February 1913, 26.
17 E. G., 'La Belle Dame De La Merci', *Vogue*, 15 July 1913, 22, 23, 24.
18 'Recorde du monde du nombre de robes', *Fantasio*, September 1913, 169.
19 'Fashions of To-day', *The Theatre*, Vol XXVIII, No. 153, November 1913, xx.
20 'A fashionable artist dressed by a fashion artist', *La Vie Heureuse,* 1913 (month unknown).
21 Gaby Deslys, 'A Lesson in Thrift by the Witty French Artiste who Explains the Folly of Giving Away Anything You May Need and the Wisdom of Holding on to Everything You Have', *Los Angeles Examiner*, 6 April, 1913.
22 'Gaby Deslys's Efficiency Chart, Showing the Number of Persons Necessary in Making a "Woman a Successful Business", Why the New Gospel of Efficiency Must Be Applied to Herself by Every Woman Who Wants to Succeed – and How', *Louisville Herald*, 21 September, 1913.
23 The details of the newspaper in which the cartoons appeared were not recorded, but the clippings were viewed at the Billy Rose Theatre Collection at the New York Public Library.
24 'Recorde du monde du nombre de robes', *Fantasio*, 1913, 169 (month unknown).
25 'Amazing Variety Worn by Her on Stage', publication unknown, 18 December, 1913.
26 'Gaby's Show is Flesh and Fringe', *The Spokesman-Review,* 15 January 1914.
27 Ibid.
28 C. Hamilton, 'Theater: Seen on the Stage'. *Vogue,* Vol. 43, Iss. 12, 1914, 53, 54, 84.

References

Bigham, R. B. (2012), *Lucile: Her Life by Design*. San Francisco: MacEvie Press Group.
Bradley, P. (2009), 'Modern Art Meets Modern Marketing: The Armory Show' in *Making American Culture: A Social History, 1900–1920*, 117–35. New York: Palgrave Macmillan.
Braun, E. (1995), 'Futurist Fashion: Three Manifestos', *Art Journal* 54 (1): 34–41.

Brayshaw, E. (2014), 'Embodying a Modern Luxury: The White Peacock, Distinction and Desire on the Early-twentieth-century Broadway Stage', *Luxury* 1 (1): 155–84.
Carlson, E. (2014), 'Cubist Fashion: Mainstreaming Modernism after the Armory', *Winterthur Portfolio* 48 (1): 1–28.
Diamond, E. (2006), *Performance and Cultural Politics*. New York: Routledge.
Evans, C. (2013), *The Mechanical Smile: Modernism and the First Fashion Shows in France and America, 1900–1929*. New Haven: Yale University Press.
Gardiner, J. (1986), *Gaby Deslys: A Fatal Attraction*. London: Sidgwick & Jackson Limited.
Glenn, S. A. (2002), *Female Spectacle: The Theatrical Roots of Modern Feminism*. Cambridge, MA: Harvard University Press.
Gundle, S. (2008), *Glamour : A History*. Oxford: Oxford University Press.
Im, Y. (2011), 'Oscar Wilde's *Salomé*: Disorienting Orientalism', *Comparative Drama* 45(4): 361–80.
Kaplan, J. H. and S. Stowell (1994), *Theater and Fashion: Oscar Wilde to the Suffragettes*. Cambridge: Cambridge University Press.
Monks, A. (2010), *The Actor in Costume*. London: Palgrave Macmillan.
Palmer, A. (2010), 'Haute Couture', in V. Steele (ed.), *The Berg Companion to Fashion*, 393–6. Oxford: Bloomsbury Academic.
Schweitzer, M. (2009), *When Broadway was the Runway: Theatre, Fashion, and American Culture*. Philadelphia: University of Pennsylvania Press.
Steele, V. (2010), 'Artificial Beauty, or the Morality of Dress and Adornment', in G. Riello and P. McNeil (eds). *The Fashion History Reader: Global Perspectives*, 275–97. Oxon: Routledge.

Snapshots

2.4 *A Foreign Affair* On and Off Screen

Christina M. Johnson

Analysis of film wardrobe always includes its pictorial depiction on the big screen. It is only through material culture analysis, (Prown 1982)[1] supplemented by archival research, however, that the most comprehensive understanding of these objects and their characters/wearers can be determined. This case study focuses on an evening gown worn by Marlene Dietrich (1901–92) as Erika von Schlütow in *A Foreign Affair* (Paramount Pictures, 1948), set in Allied-occupied, post-Second World War Germany (Figure 2.4.1). Originally donated to The Hollywood Museum Associates, an organization that went bankrupt a few years after its founding in the 1960s, the costume is now held by the FIDM (Fashion Institute of Design and Merchandising) Museum in Los Angeles and is part of a group of clothing and accessories assembled by the famed actress to represent her personal and professional life.[2] It is one of the most in-demand objects in the FIDM Museum's collection based on the high number of institutional loan requests received for it.[3] Thousands of people have seen this famous gown; her fans originally beheld it through performance and today it continues to be exhibited. Yet very few individuals have been close enough to discern its indelible wear patterns or interior construction — those were secrets meant only for Dietrich's eyes and those of her privileged intimates. These are also the very details that reveal Dietrich's dedication to embodying character and yielding to the demands placed upon her by adoring audiences. They divulge a seamless merging of her private and professional personas and a personal wish to preserve her legacy.

The strapless, floor-length gown is labelled 'Irene Bullock's Wilshire' and is made of printed silk with a supplemental silver metallic weft, causing it to shimmer when handled. The textile is patterned with large polychrome paisleys and has been methodically pieced together to create the asymmetrical motifs at the bustline and a mirroring effect at the lower front bodice; the floral buds are highlighted in glass bugle beads. The gown is form-fitted to the waist, slightly flared at the hips and tapers into a pegged silhouette.[4] Fastenings include a durable centre back metal zipper that is entirely covered over by a scalloped self-fabric panel affixed with multiple hooks and eyes. The fabric exhibits overall wear and abrasions, especially at the neckline, underarms and sides of the torso where the metal float filaments are kinked and broken. The hem is heavily abraded at either side of the centre back and has been darned due to repeated wear. The gown's inner bodice is sewn from cream silk – now shattered and torn –mended with at least four different threads (not including conservation stitches). It is fully boned with nine long casings descending from the bodice edge to below the waist (Figure 2.4.2).

A figure-enhancing design, complex construction resulting in a perfect fit, exceedingly high-quality textile and dazzling embroidery create the ideal costume for the onscreen character of

Figure 2.4.1 *Film still from* A Foreign Affair, *1948.*

Erika von Schlütow – a glamorous cabaret singer. The graphic quality of the paisleys set against the negative space of the cream silk background is strikingly rendered by the black and white film. The fabric's underside is surprisingly smooth with raw edges overcast or bound in silk; we can deduce the garment's interior was supple against the actress' skin. But why would there be such heavy wear if the gown was only worn in one scene and not a particularly physically active scene at that? The answer is found through archival research. In 1944, *Vogue* reported that Dietrich (who although born in Germany had become an American citizen in 1939)[5] was travelling for extensive overseas USO[6] tours entertaining the troops. Her packing was described in detail and included this 'strapless brocade affair' as part of her government-allotted fifty-five pounds of luggage[7] (Figure 2.4.3). Multiple photographs from the tour record her wearing the gown that would later appear on screen in *A Foreign Affair*.[8] Dietrich travelled throughout war-torn Europe and North Africa entertaining the Allied

Figure 2.4.2 *Interior bodice of gown worn by Marlene Dietrich, FIDM Museum.*

troops between 1943 and 1946 with this gown ever in tow while singing, dancing — even playing the musical saw — at many shows (Naudet et al. 2001: 237). Dietrich roughed it at each base camp, wearing military fatigues, sleeping in canvas tents and travelling in jeeps. The bodice's heavy wear could have derived from strenuous exertion on stage, excessive wear, packing and unpacking and the need to condense the contents of suitcases for transport on military cargo planes. One area of mending might attest to her repeated use of the gown during these years: the back tapered hem is methodically darned at the precise points where her high-heeled shoes repeatedly kicked against it. The fix was likely done using military-grade regulation thread, as it is khaki-coloured and quite thick, very different than the fine cream silk floss used in the gown's original construction.

But even before packing the gown for its around-the-world USO tour and then donning it on film, Dietrich had worn it privately. In 1941 she was photographed in it during an evening at Ciro's nightclub in Hollywood alongside her then lover Jean Gabin (Figure 2.4.4). Dietrich had many paramours during her long marriage to Rudolf Sieber from 1923 to 1976. Her daughter Maria Riva writes of her mother's intense relationship with Gabin: 'Their love affair was to be one of the most enduring, most passionate, and most painful of both their lives' (Riva 1993: 509). Note that the gown is not beaded in the photograph. Determining when this glittering embellishment was applied is

Figure 2.4.3 *Photograph of Marlene Dietrich performing in Anzio, Italy.*

challenging, as it is impossible to discern any detail in the grainy photographs taken at wartime performances. It would make sense if the credited costume designer of *A Foreign Affair,* Edith Head had embellished the gown for filming, as Dietrich is seen primarily from the waist up and the studio's intense lighting units showcased the dazzling beading to full advantage on set. Flowers and leaves were also added for screen wear, carefully tucked into the neckline. In addition to adding visual beauty, these choices certainly covered the gown's abraded neckline and shredded underarms.

Why did Dietrich take a previously worn gown with her on the USO tour when commissioning an entire wardrobe of new stage attire from any leading designer was possible? One speculates it was a conscious choice. Supporting Allied forces and defeating the Nazis was a deeply held concern for both her and Gabin; they were forced to spend time apart as he ultimately became a leader of the Free French Forces. Even with their hefty wartime responsibilities and the serious danger faced at the Front, the lovers did manage to meet during her tour (Dietrich 1987: 139). Did she bring this gown along with her on the trip that she hoped would bring them together, knowing they shared precious memories of her wearing it? Additional research at archival repositories containing correspondence between them may hold answers. And why did she decide to immortalize the gown — albeit newly embroidered and gussied up with flowers — as a film costume? Dietrich had a history of being

Figure 2.4.4 *Photograph of Marlene Dietrich and Jean Gabin at Ciro's nightclub, Los Angeles, 1941.*

heavily involved with her film wardrobes. She re-used not one, but three[9] of her Irene-designed (Riva 1993: 539) USO gowns for *A Foreign Affair*. Re-wearing wardrobe in which she had viscerally experienced the Second World War to portray a complex screen character who had also lived through the tumultuous war infused the actress' performance with direct personal experience and a tangible reality that could not have been accomplished with a brand new costume.

Complicating and illuminating the analysis of this gown is the heavy wear and repair it has incurred by institutional use after her donation, caused both by people unversed in conservation techniques and by over-display. Discerning the difference between the old and more recent damage is difficult. Upon close examination, the silk inner bodice is thought to have been replaced in some areas; the textile does not match the quality of the original, which exists in small patches along the upper interior bodice and at the underside of the centre back panel closure. Was this replacement created for re-purposing as a film costume, or by its later caretakers? The harried stitches rendered in multiple threads used to mend the inner bodice could also have been done on set for a time-pressed filming schedule, or even post-donation for the numerous exhibitions it was a part of from the mid-1960s to the 1990s.[10] Further analysis is required to determine the exact timeline and purpose of the alterations. The overall fading of the gown likely dates to its last fifty years of display. More recently, conservation treatments have stabilized the interior of the garment but a comprehensive intervention will be needed for future display.

Marlene Dietrich created a highly publicized persona of glamour and intrigue both on and off screen through scrupulous attention to her appearance, a sultry demeanour and a long list of famous affairs. Her gown's heavy internal wear and subsequent repairs attest to a famous personality perpetually in demand by audiences around the world. It also embodies the impressive work ethic of an actress with the immense physical drive to live up to her self-created ideal. Ultimately, only she truly knew the private reasons for its re-use and preservation. A desire to remember and be remembered informed her ultimate decision to donate this gown to the original Hollywood Museum, acknowledged by the institution's flattering correspondence with her:

> Certainly, an important collection like this deserves a prominent place in our archives where it will be preserved for all time and can be shared with fellow artists, craftsmen and the millions of visitors who will be coming to the Museum and to whom the name of Marlene Dietrich spells 'Magic.'[11]

Notes

1. This methodology consists of applying three stages of analysis to the object under study: description, deduction and speculation. Its basic framework is utilized for this study.
2. L.88.1.235, Permanent Loan by the Department of Recreation and Parks, City of Los Angeles; The group consists of designs by Irene, Cashin, Grès, Dessès and Dior among others, including: approximately thirty daywear ensembles; fifteen evening ensembles; thirty pairs of custom Vivier and Delman shoes and film costumes. Dietrich donated these pieces to The Hollywood Museum Associates between 1964 and 1966. The planned museum went bankrupt shortly thereafter and its assets were transferred to the City of Los Angeles. The collection was then deposited at the FIDM Museum in 1988. See FIDM Museum institutional files pertaining to this donation. For information regarding The Hollywood Museum, see Trope (2011).
3. In the last fifteen years, the gown has been loaned to: The Museum at FIT (Fashion Institute of Technology, New York City), 'Glamour: Fashion, Film, Fantasy', 2005; Oklahoma City Museum of Art, 'Sketch to Screen: The Art of Hollywood Costume Design', 2010; Skirball Cultural Center (Los Angeles), 'Light and Noir: Émigrés and Exiles in Hollywood, 1933–1950', 2015–16 with additional travelling venues; Imperial War Museum (London), 'Real to Reel: A Century of War Movies', 2017. Although the gown has undergone professional stabilization for these recent displays, it will not undergo future exhibition without extensive conservation treatment.
4. It is likely that the gown originally dates to 1939–41, as 'Peg-top skirts, so much in vogue just before and during the early days of the war, will be once again in high fashion.' Press release draft, unknown date. Irene Scrapbook 2, 1939–1941. Margaret Herrick Library, Academy of Motion Picture Arts and Sciences.
5. 'Marlene Dietrich Becomes Citizen', *The Washington Post*, 10 June 1939, 14.
6. USO: United Service Organizations, a non-profit organization founded in 1941 that provides services to United States service members and families. See: https://www.uso.org/about, accessed: 7 January 2019

7 'Fashion: GI Siren for USO Camp Shows,' *Vogue,* 1 May 1944, 109.

8 For photo of Dietrich in gown, see: 'Welcome, Marlene', *Vogue,* 15 August 1944, 155.

9 The two additional evening gowns worn by Marlene Dietrich in *A Foreign Affair* include a matte sequin illusion gown and an iridescent sequin illusion gown. She is photographed in them multiple times during the tour and they are described as 'two long sequin gowns, slit to the knees, and guaranteed whistle-bait'. See: 'Fashion: GI Siren for USO Camp Shows' *Vogue,* 1 May 1944, 109.

10 Note the narrow red looped ribbon sewn to the inner bodice next to her left breast. Could this be a private denotation of her treasured Chevalier de la Légion d'Honneur award, received in 1950? Recipients were privy to wearing a discreet red ribbon on the left exterior side of their attire. https://www.deutsche-kinemathek.de/en/collections-archives/digital-collection/marlene-dietrich-collection-berlin, accessed: 7 January 2019.

11 Letter to Marlene Dietrich, 13 November 1964 from Mrs Helen Seitz, Registrar, The Hollywood Museum. Copy in FIDM Museum institutional files.

References

Dietrich, M. (1987), *Marlene*. New York: Grove Press.

Naudet, J. J. with M. Riva and W. Sudendorf (2001), *Marlene Dietrich: Photographs and Memories*. London: Thames &Hudson.

Prown, J. D. (1982), 'Mind in Matter: An Introduction to Material Culture Theory and Method,' *Winterthur Portfolio* 17 (1) 1–19.

Riva, M. (1993), *Marlene Dietrich*. New York: Alfred A. Knopf.

Trope, A. (2011), *Stardust Monuments: The Saving and Selling of Hollywood*. New Hampshire: Dartmouth College Press.

2.5 Recording Costume Design in the Theatre and Performance Collections at the V&A: Vivien Leigh and Oliver Messel

Keith Lodwick

The Theatre and Performance Collections at the Victoria and Albert (V&A) Museum in London have grown significantly since their inception in 1924. The focus of the collection, as founded by Gabrielle Enthoven OBE was to 'provide a comprehensive theatrical section in an existing museum to comprise specimens of all the different branches necessary to the working of a play, from the construction of the theatre, to the designing of scenery and costumes' (The Theatre Museum 1987: 6). This contribution will draw on the Oliver Messel and Vivien Leigh archives, where and how these collections intersect and complement each other. It will also examine the creative partnership between designer and performer through written testimony and the costume design process.

The creation of a national museum collection for the performing arts in the UK was a long-held ambition of Gabrielle Enthoven OBE, a writer, amateur actress, suffragette, collector and archivist. The V&A accepted Enthoven's collection in 1924 and she made acquiring, housing and cataloguing her gift to the museum her life's work. Her mission was to establish a centre for theatre research in Britain (she turned down several offers from the United States to sell her collection): 'My object is not to collect curiosities but to make a collection which will be of value in affording reliable material for the art of the theatre and for theatrical history. I am continuing the collection of modern playbills, programmes and photographs' (The Theatre Museum 1987: 6). Today, Enthoven's vision continues through research and interpretation at one of the world's most comprehensive performing arts collections.

The museum continues to acquire major collections of significant directors, writers, designers, performers and theatre companies. These materials often complement each other and allow curators to understand more about the creative process. Theatre is an ephemeral art, so documents, designs and photographs enable researchers to build a larger picture of the jigsaw puzzle which creates the total theatre experience. In some cases, these objects are the only 'material remains' of a production once it is finished.

The V&A acquired Oliver Messel's design collection in 2005. The archive has around ten thousand individual components consisting of works of art on paper, models, masks, technical drawings and costumes. It represents his life's work as a designer for theatre, opera, musicals, film and interior design, along with architecture and buildings in the latter part of his life. From the 1930s until the mid-1960s, Messel was the UK's premier stage designer and one of the first to work on an international stage. The enormity of the collection displays Messel's meticulous work ethic and his goal to create 'perfection' on the stage. Since the acquisition, the V&A has created a touring exhibition, a book and other supporting activities to engage visitor accessibility.

When the museum acquired Vivien Leigh's archive in 2013, it attracted global media interest. That year marked the centenary of Leigh's birth and the goal was to re-position her as one of the most significant performers of the mid-twentieth century. The cataloguing of this archive has enabled a new generation of writers and historians to interpret Leigh's creative output. One of these initiatives was the touring exhibition 'Vivien Leigh: Public Faces, Private Lives', which was the first collaboration between the V&A and the National Trust.

Oliver Messel and Vivien Leigh met in London in the mid-1930s when both of their careers were in the ascendant and they became life-long friends. Messel was establishing himself as one of the most creative designers of the era and he moved with ease between artistic media. Leigh understood early in her career the importance of a good costume designer and their role in the creation of character (Figure 2.5.1).

Figure 2.5.1 *Vivien Leigh researching her script for* Caesar and Cleopatra, *1943. Victoria and Albert Museum, London.*

In 1937, as Leigh and Messel embarked on their first collaboration – *A Midsummer Night's Dream* – Messel had just returned from Hollywood, where he had co-designed the costumes (with Gilbert Adrian) for MGM's lavish production of *Romeo and Juliet*. Leigh's ambition to be part of the Old Vic Theatre Company, regarded as the unofficial 'National Theatre' of the UK was fulfilled when she appeared as Ophelia to Laurence Olivier's Hamlet, performed at Elsinore Castle in 1936. Director Tyrone Guthrie had directed Leigh in *Hamlet* and immediately engaged her for the role of Titania.

The production was set to open on Boxing Day 1937 and be a major highlight of the theatrical winter season. Guthrie wrote a programme note to explain his staging: 'The style of this production is early Victorian. It is one more attempt to make a union between the words of Shakespeare, the music of Mendelssohn and the architecture of the Old Vic'[1] (Figure 2.5.2).

Engaged to design the production, Messel devised gauze drop curtains painted with huge flowers, which seemed to shrink the fairies to diminutive size. Robert Helpmann's Oberon was designed to resemble a stag beetle. Messel's exquisite taste and expert knowledge of fabric was hugely appealing to Leigh and his reputation for creating character-driven and beautifully constructed costumes was widely known in the theatrical circles of the mid-1930s. Actress Evelyn Laye commented on how

Figure 2.5.2 *Robert Helpmann and Vivien Leigh in* A Midsummer Night's Dream, *1937. Victoria and Albert Museum, London.*

Messel's costumes aided her performance when she appeared as Helen of Troy in *Helen!* (1932): 'Oliver made a white dress for me with a blue sash worn like a halter, which he made from a wonderful material called lisse. It's finer than organza. This was the costume I wore when I represented the face that launched a thousand ships. He made me look like a million dollars' (Castle 1986: 58).

For Leigh's Titania, Messel designed a series of costumes using another of his favourite materials: organza. The fabric was not only lightweight for a performer to wear, but it moved with ease on stage, catching the light in the process and offering audiences an ethereal and whimsical experience. Photographs in Messel's archive display Leigh in a variety of poses, using costume to interpret her performance.

Messel created two headdresses for Leigh, both now in the collection of the V&A. One, a small beaded creation, incorporated flowers of silver paper, rhinestones and imitation pearls and features in photographs of Titania's scenes in the wood near Athens. The other is a crown, (Figure 2.5.3) worn when the fairies bless the triple marriage in the final scene. Messel was an ingenious designer, conscious of the Old Vic's small budget. The crown is formed of a wire circlet, to which are attached flowers of velvet and ribbon, organdie leaves, gold cord and cellophane bows, all dotted with silver beads and sequins to catch the light. Artificial pearls on wire alternate with taller spikes of cellophane to create 'points' (Figure 2.5.4).

Figure 2.5.3 *Headdress now in the collection of the V&A Museum, London. Victoria and Albert Museum, London.*

Figure 2.5.4 *Vivien Leigh in* A Midsummer Night's Dream, *1937. Victoria and Albert Museum, London.*

Margaret Furse was one of Messel's design assistants until establishing herself as a costume designer in her own right. Furse created the costumes from Messel's designs, although interpreting Messel's freehand style was not an easy task. She laboured over the individual flowers and foliage which were hand-sewn onto the costumes.

The success of *A Midsummer Night's Dream* was credited to Messel's interpretation of the play and the show was revived again in 1938, this time without Leigh as she prepared to make the transatlantic trip to Los Angeles to be screen-tested for *Gone with the Wind*.

Leigh and Messel's wartime collaboration was in the much anticipated screen version of George Bernard Shaw's play *Caesar and Cleopatra* (1945). Whilst preparing for the role, Leigh wrote to Messel telling him: 'I told Pascal [the director] that nobody in the world must do the costumes except you'[2] (Figures 2.5.5 & 2.5.6).

Messel was on war duty designing camouflage, but the promise of a high-profile film in Technicolor was too tempting. Leigh wanted to keep her familiar theatre coterie around her and asked Messel to hire designer Margaret Furse to assist him with the huge task of costuming the

Figure 2.5.5 *Costume designs by Oliver Messel for* Caesar and Cleopatra, *1945. Victoria and Albert Museum, London.*

Figure 2.5.6 *Costume designs by Oliver Messel for* Caesar and Cleopatra, *1945. Victoria and Albert Museum, London.*

Figure 2.5.7 *Headdress worn by Vivien Leigh in* Caesar and Cleopatra, *1945. Victoria and Albert Museum, London.*

lavish production (Roger and Margaret Furse had just completed the epic version of *Henry V*, directed by and starring Olivier). The film had struck a chord with wartime audiences and was a critical and commercial success.

In 1944, Britain was fatigued by five years of war. Hence, creating an Egyptian court for *Caesar and Cleopatra* with hundreds of extras was a Herculean task for Messel. Clothing and material were still under strict rationing and the usual costume-making staff were re-deployed on war service. So, Messel drew on the stores of theatrical costumiers Berman's, Nathan's and B. J. Simmonds to create a working wardrobe. He then sourced and acquired Indian saris from Liberty & Co., and used the fabric to create shimmering, lightweight, diaphanous costumes. Messel designed nine costumes for Leigh's Cleopatra, mapping the character's journey from the inexperienced, juvenile Queen hiding from Caesar's army in the paws of the Sphinx, to her encrusted and elaborate state robes.

Relishing the opportunity to work on a colour film (which was scarce during the Second World War), he used shades of white, blue, purple and gold chiffon decorated with ornate jewels and lotus flowers. One again, Messel's understanding of and skill with fabric enabled him to create a luxurious wardrobe for Leigh.

Figure 2.5.8 *Headdress worn by Vivien Leigh in* Caesar and Cleopatra, *1945. Victoria and Albert Museum, London.*

Hugh Skillan, a former actor turned prop maker made Leigh's headdresses, skilfully interpreting Messel's designs from papier-mâché, glass and cellophane (Figures 2.5.7 & 2.5.8). Beatrice Dawson, a former school friend of Leigh's created all the jewellery for the film. Dawson was managing a 'make-do-and-mend' shop on London's Oxford Street and thus came to the project well equipped to turn everyday objects into accessories for the Egyptian setting.

A visual feast, *Caesar and Cleopatra* is a testament to Messel's resourcefulness under challenging creative circumstances. The costumes and headdresses radiate splendour and their filmic reach extends far beyond their humble origins. Messel was able to keep many of the costume accessories, now in the collection of the V&A where they can be studied, interpreted and displayed (Figure 2.5.9).

The acquisition of these two major archives continues to allow curators, researchers and the public to understand the creative development between designer and performer. Gabrielle Enthoven's vision of a space for the study of the performing arts, enhanced by recent V&A exhibitions on theatre and performance, continues to inspire new generations of students and practitioners.

Figure 2.5.9 *Vivien Leigh and Claude Rains in* Caesar and Cleopatra, *1945. Victoria and Albert Museum, London.*

Notes

1 Programme for *A Midsummer Night's Dream*, Old Vic Theatre (1937), Old Vic production file, Theatre and Performance Collections, V&A Museum, London.
2 Letter from Vivien Leigh to Oliver Messel, Oliver Messel Archive, Bristol Theatre Collections.

References

Castle, Charles (1986), *Oliver Messel: A Biography*. London: Thames & Hudson.
The Theatre Museum (1987), *Catalogue to The Theatre Museum, London*. London: Scala Books.

Section 3

Costume Voices, Costume Histories

3.1 The First Premiere and Other Stories: Towards a History of the Costume Design Profession in Finland

Joanna Weckman

Introduction

Oral histories are important sources for the under-studied history of costume design. While interviewing certainly *appears* to provide an excellent way of gathering first-hand information about costume designers, their work and life experiences, there are some necessary additional qualifications to be considered. It is not sufficient to merely regard interview material as an authentic preamble to the course of events, or to use oral histories on their own merits to explore certain pre-determined themes of interest. It is, rather, equally important to observe how, why and what information is shared, how the past is re-imagined and how certain topics and foci are brought to the foreground. Dialogical approaches to interviewing that are open-ended enough to allow for the activation of memories, as well as the use of historical material that can unearth and prompt narratives are, when accompanied by careful and reflective analysis, vital methods for developing the means for oral histories to play their part in enriching the scope of historical research.

My focus here is the methodology I used in examining the career of a Finnish costume designer and actress, Liisi Tandefelt, over the most active period of her working life as a costume designer from 1958 to 1992 (Weckman 2015a). From the very beginning of this study, it was clear that Tandefelt held an exceptional position in her field. In the early days of her career she had very few professional colleagues. No other costume designer in Finland who began their career in the late 1950s achieved such a long and versatile working life and simultaneously participated in the development of the costume profession. This body of work not only represents the history of Liisi Tandefelt's career, but also outlines the history of the costume design profession in Finland from the early twentieth century onwards. In addition, my analysis of the content and structure of Tandefelt's explicit and implicit narratives (Weckman 2015a) enable suggestions for new and productive ways of approaching the history of costume design and designers, as well as methodologies and practices of researching costume from a scholarly perspective utilizing oral histories.

Earlier Studies and Publications using Oral Histories when Researching Costume History in Finland

For a long time, both the costume design profession and costume research were considered to be marginal phenomena. Consequently, the costume design research tradition in Finland is fairly young. The first few theoretical master's theses on this topic were completed at the end of the 1980s by Marjatta Nyrhilä (1987) and Leena Lyyra (1988) at the University of Helsinki. Since then, examining contemporary costume design has been far more popular than exploring the history of costume and related work (Weckman 2009: 174, 176). When prompted by an interest in the history of the field however, interviewing people about their personal experiences has been regularly employed as a primary means of building an understanding of the history of Finnish costume work. From the 1970s onwards, the first newspaper articles to briefly discuss what was assumed to be the short-lived history of the Finnish costume design profession were primarily based on interviews with, or the writings of Liisi Tandefelt, one of the first well-established costume designers in Finland (Weckman 2015a: 200, 206–07). In the 1980s and early 1990s, the Theatre Museum in Helsinki began to develop an interest in the history of costume design. This interest resulted in the first two publications (Reitala 1986; Nikula and Helavuori 1991) to utilize the oral histories of costume designers and actors when presenting the history of Finnish costume. Simultaneously, a few costume exhibitions with exhibition catalogues[1] based on the same oral-history sources were curated. In addition, a number of autobiographies – first by actors and directors and later by costume designers and scenographers – briefly discussed earlier costume practices in the twentieth century (see Laine 1967; Saarikoski 1980; Rinne 1985; Forsström and Kalha 1999; Helavuori 2008). These publications were based on the oral histories of personal experiences rather than studies by academic researchers and have been the central source in forming a historical perspective on Finnish costume design (Weckman 2015a: 205–06).

The MA thesis by Leena Jaatinen (Helsinki University 1998) was the first academic study to specifically focus on the history of costume in Finland. Using interviews and extant costumes as source materials, and with an interest in the processes of both designing and making costumes, Jaatinen's study discussed the Finnish National Opera's 1970 production of *The Cunning Little Vixen*. For her thesis, Jaatinen interviewed the production's costume designer, as well as the head of the National Opera costume department. Since then, several research articles, publications and theses have concentrated on the history of costume in Finland by means of interview material. For her 2004 BA dissertation, Heli Koivikko-Heikkinen interviewed several former employees of Helsinki City Theatre's costume workshop, focusing on costume practices from the 1960s onwards. For the book celebrating the fiftieth anniversary of the Finnish Scenographers' Union, the theatre historian Heta Reitala (2005) wrote an article on the work of costume designer Liisi Tandefelt spanning the period from the 1960s to the 1980s and based on interviews Reitala conducted in the early 1990s. In 2010, a doctoral thesis by Leena Juntunen based on interviews with costume designer Maija

Pekkanen discussed Pekkanen's costume design work from the late 1960s and the early 1970s. Over the past few years, scenographer Minna Santakari and researcher Riikka Pennanen (2015) have explored the film costume styles representing Finnish youth in the 1950s, publishing an article for which they interviewed several actors from that era. In addition, for her MA thesis Liisa Niskanen (2017) interviewed several film costume designers about the recent history of their work in the early 2000s.

I myself have completed several studies using interviews as source material for costume history in Finland, (Weckman 1997, 2005, 2006, 2014, 2015a) as well as conducting several interviews for other research purposes. For example, the first of these studies (1997) was based on interviews with the costume designer Ritva Karpio, who gave me the names of other costume designers from the first decades of the twentieth century. This information was particularly significant because it had been assumed that there were no professional costume designers in Finland prior to the early 1960s. In 2005, I tracked down and interviewed Anita Litonius, who had been a film costume sketch artist in the mid-1940s for her husband Bure Litonius, who designed film costumes for most of the major Finnish period films from 1938 to 1962. Seven interviews with Liisi Tandefelt were used as sources for research articles (2006 and 2014) as well as for my doctoral thesis (2015a). Several other interviews provided me with important information when curating costume exhibitions for the Theatre Museum in Helsinki.[2] All of these experiences led me to reflect on the role of interviews as sources for constructing the history of costume in Finland.

My doctoral thesis, 'When you do something, do it to perfection': Liisi Tandefelt as a costume designer 1958–1992' (*Kun jonkun asian tekee, se pitää tehdä täydellisesti':Liisi Tandefelt pukusuunnittelijana 1958–1992*) investigated the conditions – the practices, values and ideals – that have shaped the costume designer's work in recent Finnish history. This study explored the career of actor-costume designer Liisi Tandefelt with a specific focus on fifteen selected theatre productions using oral history as the main source of its data as well as the object of its study. The thesis examined how Tandefelt experienced the circumstances influencing her work, such as staff versus freelance work, her double profession as an actress and a costume designer, her family situation as a working, single mother, her artistic skills and political views. It looked at the ways in which these conditions manifested themselves throughout her career, as well as the strategies she adopted for coping with these conditions. The study offers a closer look at the use of power and the significance of gender in the costume design profession – manifested in relations between Tandefelt and theatre managers, directors, actors and costume workshop staff – as well as the ideals and values Tandefelt brought to her work as a costume designer during the period studied. Furthermore, the dissertation provides an analysis of Tandefelt's narration, its structure and themes and her stories about her work as a costume designer. Tandefelt's narration is approached as a narrative constructing and conveying the history, stories, perceptions and values within the costume design profession, related by an older, more experienced woman to a younger woman, the researcher pursuing the same profession.

Can the Use of Oral History add Value to Costume History Research?

Elaine Aston and George Savona, who viewed the theatre as a signal system, refer to the transition that took place in the twentieth century. They suggest that the question of 'what' is done has shifted to the question of 'how' it is done; for example, by attempting to understand the structures of the language of art (Aston and Savona 1991: 3). Since the scale of stage and film costume research is still limited in Finland however, I believe it remains necessary to discuss both questions in order to develop the research field. My original research objective was to interview Tandefelt with a view to collecting rare, first-hand information about the recent history of and working conditions in the field of costume design. Yet the entire study was driven by the interest sparked while I was researching the interview material itself. The ways in which Tandefelt discussed her costume design work and positioned herself as a costume designer, as well as her views on working in costume design and its practices in general, shed new light on the process of studying and presenting the history of costume (Weckman 2015a: 28).

Finnish historians Jorma Kalela (2006: 74–6, 83) and Taina Ukkonen (2006: 186) claim that in the established field of historical research it has been very important to identify distortions of knowledge. Memory-based information, therefore, has often been deemed unreliable, altered by hindsight or the embellishment of past events. Trying to take both the linguistic, narrative turn which widely shaped the perspectives of humanistic research and the historiographic approach of positivist and post-positivist or post-modern history research into account (e.g. McConachie 1985: 18; Kalela 2002: 17; Assmann and Czaplicka 1995: 125), it became necessary to consider whether it was possible to combine two different epistemiological approaches to the interview material. Could I, on the one hand, examine Tandefelt's narrative itself, seen with its own, intrinsic value and on the other hand survey the memories as historical evidence and highlight the interview material's instrumental informative value?

Even though these two perspectives have sometimes been seen as opposite, or even mutually exclusive, from my point of view they formed a dialogic complementary relationship. So, I was delighted to discover that within post-positivist history studies, one can draw on both approaches to the source material, provided that the narrator's way of remembering and explaining is taken as the basic premise; and this is actually considered an essential idea of oral history research. According to historian Jorma Kalela (2006: 74–7), the researcher must first determine the narrator's understanding of reality and his/her habits of speaking according to that perception. Kalela (2010: 52) also refers to sociologist Isabelle Bertaux-Wiame according to whom 'The forms of life stories are [...] as important as the facts contained therein.' It was this attention to both the form and the content of Tandefelt's narration that I wanted to develop in my study.

This study of Liisi Tandefelt is essentially a research project on Finnish theatre history itself, owing to Tandefelt's long and versatile career spanning five decades as both a costume designer and an actress. History is not, however, only approached based on extensive archival materials, but also in principle, by virtue of Tandefelt's narrative which interprets and dissects this history. My approach draws on the so-called *new histories* with the common endeavour to 'make visible what has been hidden in the past', that is to explore the ways of thinking and the strategies that affect people (Immonen 2001: 19–20). To support this work, I have employed various research methodologies, including oral history research, biography, gender studies, cultural history and micro-history. These fields of study combine interest in issues hidden, forgotten, overlooked or just too commonplace and a concept of knowledge which also takes into account experiential and tacit knowledge. They share goals such as the researcher's own positioning, awareness of the researcher's subjectivity and understanding of the responsibility for the interpretations one makes (Fingerroos and Peltonen 2006: 11–12, 13, 17, 20, 35–6; Immonen 2001: 19; Kalela 2006: 79). Because of my interest in the passing on of professional tradition and the ways in which narration can be supported during interviews with the help of visual material, the museological discussion about cultural memory, the choices concerning its transfer and the importance of objects as storytellers and mediators were significant for my study (e.g. Knell 2005; Kinanen 2007; Turpeinen 2005; Vilkuna 2010).

I approached the interview material in terms of Tandefelt's interpretations of the work, practices and values related to the costume design profession. These interpretations were employed to arrange the memories related to the professional practices, as well as to study further the recent history of these practices with the aid of archival sources. Simultaneously, these different themes – such as 'starting points for a design', 'costume sketches and their realization', 'costume implementation', 'working with an artistic group', 'evaluation of one's own workmanship as a costume designer' and 'topics related to professional values and ideals' – gave rise to new and interesting questions. Therefore, clues and hints from the research material itself were used – as in a micro-historical approach – to navigate deeper into the research material, as well as to search for complementary and more detailed additional sources.[3]

As in this case, it is fairly common to describe the qualitative research process as a hermeneutic spiral in which new research material offers novel perspectives on the already collected material, opening up fresh paths and questioning prior assumptions. This method of research sets its own requirements both during the data analysis and at the writing phase of the study. For example, when describing the interview material used in this study it was important to depict the process of interviewing and the preliminary analysis because in the later phase they influenced the formation of the subsequent material (Weckman 2015a: 18).

In autobiographies, reminiscence may seem like a very straightforward process. The person reading an autobiography is put in a position in which it is assumed that they can see the writer's memories by virtue of their intensity.[4] Historian Katja-Maria Miettunen, however, emphasizes the difference between remembering and reminiscing: 'A person remembers what she/he remembers, but recalls what she/he wants to recall' (Miettunen 2009: 18). Reminiscence is therefore a controlled activity (Miettunen 2009). According to oral historian Taina Ukkonen (2000: 11), it is a question of restoring, interpreting and at the same time re-organizing and even modifying the memories that the narrator selects. In an autobiographical narrative, the person chooses to memorize significant memories worth re-membering, telling and preserving (Ukkonen 2006: 188; Ukkonen 2000: 39; Houni 2000: 66). People best remember the turning points in their lives and the moments that have changed the course of their lives (Purhonen, Hoikkala and Roos 2008: 36). Memories may also be crystallized, perhaps already told several times in great detail to many audiences. Historian Natalie Zemon Davis (1996: 17) defines events of this kind, worthy of celebration or complaint as biographical thematic structures. I sought out such turning points in Tandefelt's life[5] and looked for thematic structures,[6] since I assumed that this would make it possible to arrive at the essential topics, events and perceptions related to a costume designer's work from Tandefelt's perspective.

According to Katja Miettunen (2009: 18), combining different personal narratives generates a story about the past. This is one of the key ways to build so-called 'images of history', perceptions which have been found to be starting points for the work of historians and reviewed and evaluated in studies. By focusing on the narrative and stories told by Liisi Tandefelt, I was able to assess her contribution to the history of costume design in Finland and discuss the transferrence of professional tradition and how a certain individual's experiences and actions become more significant and visible than others' as part of the cultural memory[7] of a profession. In this study, I defined the working conditions and boundaries of costume designers based on Tandefelt's experience, as she is often considered by many as 'a pioneer of her profession' (Weckman 2015a: 17–18).

Presenting Tandefelt's Narrative

The key source of data for my work on costume designer Liisi Tandefelt consisted of seven interviews conducted between 2000 and 2002. The first four are biographical life-story interviews, while the final three focus on costume design productions. In the last three production interviews, visual material such as costume sketches, production drawings and photographs were used to trigger memories.

Interviews were thematic and predominantly chronological. In biographical interviews, a period of ten years was usually discussed during each session of approximately two hours. In practice, however, the interviews shifted back and forth from the time before Tandefelt was born until the moment of the interview. In part, this may have been the result of the interview method. I decided to conduct the interviews using an open method, allowing the interviewee to speak as freely as possible in response to each question. This is related to 'self-directed speech' and Haruna Okumiya's biographical interview method, as introduced by theatre scholar Pia Houni (2000). Okumiya found that open questions trigger both the interviewer and the interviewee in a positive way (Houni 2000: 23). Right after the interview, I experienced 'associative wandering' due to my temporary 'weakness' and felt I had been unable to 'steer' the interview. Yet, my confidence in the interview method strengthened during the transcription phase, when I noted important observations. These connections might have been absent had I intervened more and attempted to control the narrative (Weckman 2015a: 37–8). For example, Tandefelt associated a difficult professional and personal time from the early 1980s with the period of the interviews in 2000 to 2002, when she found the workload to be equally overwhelming. This associated similarity produced a rich description of the earlier difficulties of her life in the theatre (Weckman 2015a: 176).

After the four biographical interviews, fifteen productions out of a total of over 120 were selected for closer scrutiny.[8] This selection was based on Tandefelt's mentioning these fifteen productions in her stories as either pleasant or unpleasant experiences. It included eleven productions repeatedly mentioned during the first four interviews as being especially valued or important, as well as four productions related to unpleasant memories. All of the selected productions turned out to be stage productions, either plays or operettas, even though Tandefelt had also worked as a costume designer for the cinema and television. Her narratives – including all clearly delineated stories and anecdotes – of each production were analysed separately and all individual themes therein were identified. In addition to the production-related conversation, I identified all narratives discussing the costume design profession in general, its values and ideals marked by phrases such as 'typical', 'in those times', 'usually', 'always', 'must' or 'should' (Weckman 2015a: 43–6).

The data collected during the series of oral history interviews was analysed with respect to content and narrative structure. Content analysis served to track various themes that had emerged during Tandefelt's narration. Structural analysis revealed the proportion of narrative related to each theme and made it possible to draw conclusions regarding the influence of the visual material on the interview process (Weckman 2015a: 43, 46, 313). For example, analysis showed thirty different narrative themes in all seven interviews. In each production however, there was narration on approximately two to seventeen themes and on average, between ten and fourteen themes for one and the same production. Thus, even if during the interviews it was felt we had discussed the topics quite equally, the analysis demonstrated that this was a misconception. Nonetheless, the content analysis showed eleven themes repeated in each production interview, such as 'the work process', 'the premises for costume design', 'costume sketches', 'materials and colours', as well as the 'co-operation with different members of the production team' (Weckman 2015a: 314).

To determine the amount of narrative related to various themes I employed a method I call narrative structure analysis, counting all the subjects belonging to one theme and how many lines of transcribed interview material every theme included. For example, the five themes with the most extensive amount of narrative were firstly, 'the work process', for which more than four and a half times the amount of the next theme was produced. The subjects of the work process theme included accounts of the production, the team and the process in general, the time, circumstances, atmosphere and general assesment of the process. The second broadest theme was 'the premises of design work', while 'costume sketches and their making' came in third, followed by 'choosing and aquiring the materials and colours' and then 'the costume making process' (Weckman 2015a: 313–14).

Arranging interview material according to themes is not a straightforward process and the lines of transcribed material are not always identical. However, counting the lines provided a more accurate overview of how much narration every production generated, as well as the amount of narration various themes produced. After comparing the amounts of narration, it was possible to recognize the productions that were discussed in particular as well as the amount, width and themes connected to the various productions. These results would have been impossible to achieve if based only on a careful reading of the transcribed interview material (Weckman 2015a: 313). The amount of narration and the importance of a theme do not necessarily correlate, but in any case a large quantity of narration on a certain topic demonstrates which subjects raised enthusiasm or felt important to discuss, even repeatedly. It should be pointed out though, that even when the amount of some of the thematic narration was scant, its significance was also disclosed by virtue of the emphasis of the content. However, my analysis showed that Tandefelt told me significantly more about the productions she singled out as 'dear' or 'important', whereas the productions linked to unpleasant memories produced a below-average amount of narration (Weckman 2015a: 313–14).

A comparison of the amounts of narration in the biographical and production interviews showed a considerable increase. It was possible that during the first biographical interviews a certain production was only mentioned briefly and most of the production-related narration was produced in the later interviews. Compared with the first biographical interviews, concentrating on significant productions could produce even thirteen times more narration. It was not surprising that the amount of narration concerning each production grew in the later interviews when it was possible to concentrate on fifteen productions instead of going through a period of forty years. The *amount* of increase in the narration was however, surprising. These findings suggest that when a researcher is interested in certain subjects and themes in costume design work and plans or conducts interviews to gather material, they should be aware that focusing either on the life story or the assorted productions may generate very different outcomes with different emphasis on the significance of the same themes (Weckman 2015a: 314–15).[9]

What kind of memories and stories did Tandefelt tell? The topics were personal experiences, experiences of people close to her – especially of costume mistresses and professional colleagues – and experiences identified as historic, which touched many people and Tandefelt's professional communities. Events with a wider impact were presented passively as general knowledge related to, for example, changes linked to actors' work and the principles, work practices and aesthetics of costume design, costume making and scenography, as well as the impact of her left-wing political activity in the theatre (Weckman 2015a: 218).

The memories and stories chosen by Tandefelt often dealt with a variety of powerful emotions, such as pride, joy, shame, sorrow and humiliation. During the interviews, certain stories were repeated and she returned to the same memories several times. Some of the stories told repeatedly in the interviews had already been told several times in the past in different situations – such as the story of 'The First Premiere' about the premiere of her first costume design project *Kuningas Kvantti III* for the Helsinki Student Theatre in 1958; or her insecurity and the great surprise at the positive media feedback, which in her opinion helped her to secure her first job at the Tampere Workers' Theatre, one of the major theatres in Finland. Such so-called 'crystallized' interpretations presented to many audiences can be regarded as communal despite the narrator's personal point of view (Weckman 2015a: 218–19).

Memories and stories told by Tandefelt were also related to topics which over time became more personal. Even a 'crystallized story' (Davis 1996: 17) which had been told several times before can live and change. One such topic for example, is ageing (Weckman 2015a: 221). Tandefelt had already told the story of *Luojan pienet kusiaiset*, which premiered at the Tampere Workers' Theatre in 1964, but during the interviews she repeated it on three separate occasions and did so again ten years later when discussing the research. This story described a chain of events during which Tandefelt unintentionally offended the elderly costume mistress Saimi Vuolle. With this story, Tandefelt simultaneously discussed her own ageing and how she would like to relate to it: the need to let go before becoming angry or aggrieved because someone younger is continuing one's work. As Tandefelt herself grew older, the focus of her story changed from the young, carefree girl's point of view to understanding the older woman's feelings of loss and irrelevance (Weckman 2015a: 71–2).

Using Visual Material as Supplementary Material for Interviews

The visual material that accompanied the interviews proved to be more versatile and productive than originally assumed. In the early stages of the study approximately 250 costume sketches with additional work drawings and only a few photographs served as sources and clues to reconstruct Tandefelt's career, as well as to achieve an understanding of the total amount and quality of the preserved material. After selecting the fifteen productions to be examined in more detail, costume sketches and work drawings as well as some photographs were employed to detect the size, visual character, the workload and the casting of certain productions. For the third time, costume sketches and drawings were explored during the analysis and interpretation phase. Attention was paid to the number of sketches and drawings, the materials and the implementation techniques used, but

Figure 3.1.1 *'Zinaida' by Liisi Tandefelt (1977). Photograph: Ville Holmstedt / Theatre Museum, Finland. Reproduced with the permission of Liisi Tandefelt.*

especially to the notes written on them. The detailed study of visual material clarified the picture of Tandefelt's working processes and practices and it illustrated the phases of design work and preparing the production, as well as their mutual connection (Weckman 2015a: 315–16).

The relationship between reminiscence and visual material proved to be extremely fertile. Visual material – mainly costume sketches – achieved a prominent part in the three production interviews, where we focused on the close examination of the fifteen productions, which were either particularly important to Tandefelt or related to unpleasant memories. Production interviews generally consisted of discussing costume sketches, i.e. looking, commenting on and touching them, one production at a time and in chronological order. Particularly interesting content- and narrative-structure analyses of this interview material indicate that in the context of production interviews, (implemented while simultaneously viewing visual materials) Tandefelt discussed considerably more themes, more broadly and with more versatility than in biographical interviews (Weckman 2015a: 316–17).

The analysis also indicates that in the production interviews, during the reviewing of visual material relating to Tandefelt's particularly significant productions – such as *The Tempest*, *Life of Galileo* and *My Fair Lady* – she produced richer, more explicit narratives related to the ideals and values of the designer (Weckman 2015a: 317). I also noticed that the amount of visual material did not necessarily need to be extensive for it to trigger a narrative. A complete lack of visual material, however, affected both the interviewee and the interviewer. After the basic story of the production was re-counted and discussed there seemed to be not much more to say about the production in an interview situation, as was the case with the operetta *Gräfin Mariza* (Weckman 2015a: 317).

The visual material – especially photographs – created reminiscences *questioning* the previous, possibly crystallized interpretations, or even generating completely new interpretations of different themes. For example, when analysing the narrative structure, I noticed that Tandefelt recurrently evaluated her costume designs, especially the women's costumes for *Kohti maailman sydäntä* performed at the Finnish National Theatre in 1977. The narrative of this production also relates to a well-known and highly regarded reviewer for a major Finnish newspaper who criticized the women's costumes. While looking at the costume sketches, Tandefelt pointed out once again that she could have designed the women's costumes differently in a less stylized way. Looking at the photographs of the final costumes though, she stated that on second thoughts, she felt that they actually looked rather nice and that in fact there was nothing wrong with them. With the help of visual material, it was possible for Tandefelt to verify or question her prior conceptions and even open up a new, more positive interpretation of her designs and their relationship to the play. Viewing photographs of the actors provided more narration about working with them and their connection to their costumes. Viewing the costume sketches, however, provided more and increasingly concrete narration linked to the sketches and the actual making of the costumes, resulting in discussions of shoes, hats and the practical organization of costume work (Weckman 2015a: 317).

Moreover, visual material was an important source of inspiration for me as an interviewer, leading to more detailed questions. Exploring the visual materials in advance and viewing them during the interviews provided me with a better understanding of the play text, the performance structure and the narration related to costumes belonging to a particular production, as well as understanding

Figure 3.1.2 *'Eliza, Ascot scene' by Liisi Tandefelt (1985). Reproduced with the permission of Liisi Tandefelt.*

Tandefelt's more general remarks related to her ideas on costumes and design work. Some costume sketches – often considered to be mere practical tools for costume design work – even proved to possess independent artistic value for Tandefelt. They were especially succesful and because of that, worthy of recollection (*inter alia* the costume sketches for *Kohti maailman sydäntä* (1977) and *My Fair Lady* (1985).)[10]

Outcomes

The conclusion of my study is that the established history of the Finnish costume design profession as we knew it, was the result of an implicit prolonged legitimation process, based on repeated stories and dialogical structures between the narrator and the interviewer. In this study, the process was made explicit by analysing the narrative of costume designer and actress Liisi Tandefelt, who enjoys influental status in the hierarchy of professional costume designers in Finland. The study showed that Tandefelt played a major role in defining the profession, while representing it on a national level in many instances and contexts. During this study, costume design history was not merely narrated, but was actually *created* in a lengthy dialogue between two women sharing the same profession during a certain period of their lives, despite their being different ages and enjoying different positions in

Figure 3.1.3 *Ascot scene from the musical* My Fair Lady *(1985). From the left, Mrs. Higgins (Sylvi Salonen), Freddy Eynsford-Hill (Ilmari Saarelainen), Mrs Eynsford-Hill (Helinä Viitanen), Henry Higgins (Antti Seppä), Eliza (Marita Koskinen), Colonel Pickering (Erkki Thiel), Lady Boxington (Maria Aro) and Lord Boxington (Reijo Lahtinen). Photograph: Petri Nuutinen. Reproduced with the permission of the Theatre Museum, Finland.*

the professional hierarchy. In fact, one major outcome was to observe the impact of our common profession on the way we communicated, because it was always present and tangible thanks to our choice of words and phrases emphasizing the common understanding of the key elements of our work. Based on these findings, it is clear that the creation of costume history knowledge is significantly affected by the interviewer's background, which underlines the importance of various perspectives on the same subject.

This study demonstrates that oral histories – narration in general, as well as stories and anecdotes – can act as flexible and critical sources of data for costume design research. In addition, the process of conducting oral history interviews can be empowering for narrator and researcher alike. The decision to bring supplementary visual material into the interviews proved successful, especially when aiming at a deeper knowledge, or even new information about topics the interviewee had already discussed numerous times throughout her life. The visual material extended the duration of Tandefelt's narration and expanded the breadth of themes that she discussed. It inspired explicit discourse on her personal values and ideals as a costume designer. Costume sketches, work drawings and photographs provoked memories that had been forgotten or were otherwise inactive. The type of visual material had an impact on the subject and emphasis of the narratives elicited: costume sketches sparked memories about the design and creation process and working with the costume department staff, while photographs of actors on stage brought forth memories of the costume designer's co-operation with actors.

Content analysis of the interview material shows that the diverse ideals, practices and structures that appeared both explicitly and implicitly in the narrative had a strong influence on Liisi Tandefelt's work as a costume designer during her years in the field. But they also affected the entire course of her life – not only her motivation for the job, but equally her personal life – and the ways in which she discussed her work as a costume designer ten years after her active career came to an end. A transition between two identities – costume designer and actress – further defined the content and structure of her narrative.

This study shows that Liisi Tandefelt's elevated status in the professional hierarchy was constructed around many intertwining facets: uncompromising artistic work as a costume designer and actress, extensive teaching activities, participation in the designers' union, contributing to costume exhibitions, winning national and international awards and substantial publicity. Experiences related and views expressed by Tandefelt have influenced the image of the history of costume design, they have formed the values and ideals associated with the profession and have represented it not only in the fields of theatre and research, but also in broader contexts. Liisi Tandefelt has in many ways acted as a bearer of cultural memory. Investigating the information gathered by interviewing a prominent professional in the field and analysing not only its narrative content, but also its structure broadened the perspective of the ways in which we consider the history and formation of the profession of costume design in Finland and elsewhere.

Notes

The author would like to thank Donna Roberts, PhD, for her support in editing the language in the first phase of this text.

1 Näyttelyluettelot TeaMA 1310. Costume exhibitions: *Historiallinen teatteripuku* (Historical Theatre Costume), 1990 was curated and the exhibition catalogue written by museum curator Päivi Halonen; *Tähtitaivaan taustajoukot* (On the Backgound of Stars), 1994 was curated by the Finnish Scenographers Union and the exhibition catalogue was written by scenographer Samppa Lahdenperä and theatre historian Heta Reitala; *Historiallinen teatteripuku* (Historical Theatre Costume) 1994–5 and *Déjà vu, Teatteripukuja* (Déjà vu, Theatre Costumes) 1995 were both curated and the exhibition catalogues written by the museum director Hanna-Leena Helavuori with short texts by other writers including Ritva Sarlund, Maiju Veijalainen, Samppa Lahdenperä and Maija Pekkanen. See the archive of the Theatre Museum in Helsinki.

2 In 2009, the touring exhibition *Silkkiä, samettia: Oopperan pukuaarteita* (Silk and Velvet: The Costume Treasures of the Finnish National Opera); in 2010, the costume section for the permanent exhibition *Backstage*; and in 2015, the touring exhibition *e Unelmien kuteita: Eepookkipukujen historiaa Suomessa* (Made of Dreams: Period Costumes for the Finnish Stage). For these exhibitions, I interviewed costume designers Erika Turunen (2009), Anna Kontek (2009) and Sari Suominen (2009), as well as former heads of opera and theatre costume workshops Ritva Kokkonen (2009) and Terttu Pykälä (2014). See also the exhibition publication *Made of Dreams*, Weckman 2015b.

3 See Weckman (2015a: 30); on the micro-historical approach Peltonen (1996: 22) and Ginzburg (1996: 37–76).
4 This is exemplified in the biography of the well-known Finnish theatre director and Tandefelt's contemporary and collaborator in the theatre field, Ralf Långbacka (2011:195).
5 It turned out that there were several turning points in Tandefelt's life, such as her decision in 1959, to apply to the Finnish Theatre School against the will of her parents and fiance or in 1972, her decision to leave a permanent job at Helsinki City Theatre in order to study costume design instead of working as a costume designer with no official education (Weckman 2015: 56, 94). In addition, analysing the stories told by Tandefelt showed that many of them take place in these situations, which appear as turning points in biographical interviews. At such times there was a wealth of events that were in many ways stormy or otherwise significant, e.g., the first or last of their kind or arrivals and departures (Weckman 2015a: 210).
6 For example, the study revealed four major biographical thematic structures which ran through the Tandefelt narrative such as, first, the constant feeling of uncertainty about her own professional skills, second, the importance of the work community, third, issues of justice including experiences of unfair treatment and efforts to change prevailing practices and fourth, the struggle between old and new including discussions of artistic generations, aesthetic and material premises and ageing (Weckman 2015a: 218).
7 For example, Pertti Grönholm (2010: 82) refers to the theory, by Jan and Aleida Assmann, of cultural memory as a reserve of information and symbols and to the ways in which modification and utlilization of this reserve can help the community to unify and express itself. See also Assmann and Czaplicka (1995: 130–3).
8 These included internationally renowned plays and operettas such as *Macbeth* (1964), *The Tempest* (1972), *Life of Galileo* (1973), *Le avventure della villeggiatura* (1975), *Gräfin Mariza* (1976), *Danton´s Death* (1977) and *My Fair Lady* (1985), as well as Finnish plays such as *Luojan pienet kusiaiset* (1964), *Meripoikia* (1971) and *Kohti maailman sydäntä* (1977) (Weckman 2015a: 43–4).
9 During the analysis phase, I located interesting narratives addressing general values, ideals and practices related to the work of costume design, as well as to Tandefelt herself as a costume designer in material that didn't relate to the chosen fifteen productions. Altogether, approximately fifty different stories and anecdotes referring to costumes or costume design work were found. Approximately half of these were connected to the productions selected for a more detailed study (Weckman 2015a: 218).
10 Tandefelt was awarded the Gold Medal for the latter design at the Prague Quadriennal in 1987 (Weckman 2015a: 317–18).

References

Assmann, J. and J. Czaplicka (1995), 'Collective Memory and Cultural Identity', *New German Critique* 65, Cultural History/Cultural Studies: 125–33. http://www.jstor.org/stable/488538 (accessed: 14 June 2018).

Aston, E. and G. Savona (1991), *Theatre as Sign-system: A Semiotics of Text and Performance*. Abingdon: Routledge.

Davis, N. Z. (1996), 'Sosiaalihistorian haasteet' (The Challenges of Social History) in M. Rahikainen (ed.) *Matkoja moderniin. Lähikuvia suomalaisten elämästä* (Trips to the Modern: Close-ups of Finnish Life), 9–17, trans. J. Kokkonen and M. Rahikainen. Helsinki: Hakapaino Oy.

Fingerroos, O. (2010), 'Muisti, kertomus ja oral history -liike'(Memory, Narration and the Oral History movement) in P. Grönholm and A. Sivula (eds), *Medeiasta pronssisoturiin. Kuka tekee menneestä historiaa?* (From Medea to the Bronze Warrior: Who makes Past to History?), 60–81. Turku: Turku Historical Association.

Fingerroos, O. and U-M. Peltonen (2006), 'Muistitieto ja tutkimus' (Oral History and Research), in R. Haanpää, A. Heimo and U-M Peltonen (eds), *Muistitietotutkimus. Metodologisia kysymyksiä* (Oral History: Methodological Questions), 7–24. Helsinki: Finnish Literary Society.

Forsström, R. and H. Kalha (1999), *Ralf Forsström scenografi 1963–1998* (Ralf Forsström: Scenography 1963–1998), Helsinki: Otava.

Ginzburg, Carlo (1996), *Johtolankoja. Kirjoituksia mikrohistoriasta ja historiallisesta metodista* (Clues: Writings on Micro-History and Historical Method), trans. A. Vuola. Helsinki: Gaudeamus, Helsinki University Press.

Grönholm, P. (2010), 'Muistomerkkejä ja kolaroivia kertomuksia. Vuoden 2007 pronssisoturikiista ja yhteisöjen kulttuuriset työkalut' (Monuments and Crashing Stories, 2007: Bronze Warrior Dispute and Cultural Tools for Communities) in P. Grönholm and A. Sivula (eds), *Medeiasta pronssisoturiin. Kuka tekee menneestä historiaa?* (From Medea to the Bronze Warrior: Who Makes Past to History?), 82–109. Turku: Turku Historical Association.

Halonen, P. (1990), *Historiallinen teatteripuku* (Historical Theatre Costume) exhibition catalogue 6.4.–14.10.1990. Helsinki: Theatre Museum.

Helavuori, H.-L. (1995), *Déjà vu, Teatteripukuja* (Déjà vu, Theatre Costumes), exhibition catalogue. 15.6.–15.10.1995.Helsinki: Theatre Museum.

Helavuori, H.-L. (1995), *Historiallinen teatteripuku* (Historical Theatre Costume),Theatre Museum together with Tampere House, exhibition catalogue 24.11.1994–22.1.1995. Helsinki: Theatre Museum.

Helavuori, H- L. (2008), 'Konkretiaa – Sari Salmelan haastattelu' (Concreteness: Interview with Sari Salmela) in H-L. Helavuori and K. Korhonen (eds), *Kiihottavasti totta*, 122–6. Helsinki: Like.

Houni, P. (2000), *Näyttelijäidentiteetti. Tulkintoja omaelämäkerrallisita puhenäkökulmista* (The Identity of an Actor: Interpretation of Autobiographical Discursive Perspectives). Doctoral thesis. Helsinki: Gaudeamus, Helsinki University Press.

Immonen, K. (2001), 'Uusi kulttuurihistoria' (New Cultural History) in K. Immonen and M. Leskelä-Kärki (eds), *Kulttuurihistoria. Johdatus tutkimukseen* (Cultural History: Introduction to Research),11–25. Helsinki: Finnish Literary Society.

Jaatinen, L. (1998), *Ovela kettu -oopperan eläinroolihahmojen puvut: miten illuusio eläimestä on luotu* (The Costumes of the Animal Characters in the *Cunning Little Vixen*: How the Illusion of the Animal has been Created). MA diss., Helsinki University, Helsinki.

Juntunen, L. (2010), *Pukusuunnittelijan ammatti Suomessa vuosina 1960–1975 / Maija Pekkasen tarina*. (Costume Designer's Profession in Finland in the years 1960–1975: The Story about Maija Pekkanen). Doctoral thesis. Helsinki: School of Arts, Design and Architecture.

Kalela, J. (2002), *Historiantutkimus ja historia* (Historical Research and History), Tampere: Gaudeamus.

Kalela, J. (2006), 'Muistitiedon näkökulma historiaan' (Oral History Perspective on the History) in O. Fingerroos, R. Haanpää, A. Heimo and U-M. Peltonen (eds), *Muistitietotutkimus: Metodologisia kysymyksiä* (Oral History: Methodological Questions), 67–92. Helsinki: Finnish Literary Society.

Kalela, J. (2010), 'Historian rakentamisen mieli ja tutkijan valinnat' (The Mind of Creating History and the Choices of the Researcher) in P. Grönholm and A. Sivula (eds), *Medeiasta pronssisoturiin. Kuka tekee menneestä historiaa?* (From Medea to the Bronze Warrior: Who Makes Past to History?), 40–69. Turku: Turku Historical Association.

Kinanen, P. ed. (2007), *Museologia tänään* (Museology Today) Helsinki: Finnish Museum Association.

Knell, S. J. ed. (2005), *Museums and the Future of Collecting*. Farnham: Ashgate.

Koivikko-Heikkinen, H. (2004), *Helsingin kaupunginteatterin puvusto – toimintojen kehittyminen 1960-luvulta lähtien* (Helsinki City Theatre Costume Workshop: The Development of the Functions since the 1960s) BA diss., Häme Polytechnic, Degree Programme in Design, Hämeenlinna.

Lahdenperä, S. and H. Reitala, *Tähtitaivaan taustajoukot: Suomen Lavastustaiteilijain Liiton 50-vuotisjuhlanäyttely*, (The Background Forces for the Shining Stars: 50th Anniversary Exhibition of the Finnish Scenographers Association), exhibition catalogue 8.10.1993–2.1.1994. Helsinki: Theatre Museum.

Laine, E. (1967), *Pitkä päivä paistetta ja pilviä Muistelmia* (Long Day of Sunshine and Clouds: Memoirs). Helsinki: Tammi.

Långbacka, R. (2011), *Taiteellista teatteria etsimässä* (In Search of Artistic Theatre). Helsinki: Kustannusosakeyhtiö Siltala.

Lyyra, L. (1988), *Balettitanssijan tanssivaatteen suunnitteluun liittyvien tekijöiden tarkastelu funktioanalyysin avulla* (Examining the Factors Related to the Design of a Ballet Dancer's Dance Clothing through Functional Analysis), MA diss., Craft Teacher's Training Course. Helsinki University.

McConachie, B. M. (1985), 'Kohti positivismin jälkeistä teatterihistoriaa' (Towards a Postpositive Theatre History) in P. Koski (ed.), *Teatterin ja historian tutkiminen*, 14–52, trans. J. Savolainen, Helsinki: Like.

Miettunen, K-M, (2009), *Menneisyys ja historiankuva. Suomalainen kuusikymmentäluku muistelijoiden rakentamana ajanjaksona*, (The Past and the Image of the Past: The Finnish Sixties as an Epoch Constructed by Reminiscences). Doctoral thesis, Saarijärvi: Finnish Literary Society.

Nikula, K. and H-L Helavuori, eds (1991), *Teatteripuku* (Theatre Costume). Helsinki: Theatre Museum.

Niskanen, L. (2017), *Taistelua aikaa vastaan: Tutkimus pukusuunnittelijoiden työskentelykäytännöistä elokuvan ennakkosuunnitteluvaiheessa*, (Countermeasures: The Working Practices of Costume Designers in the Pre-design Phase of a Film), MA diss., Department of Film and Scenography, Aalto University, Helsinki.

Nyrhilä, M. (1987), *Julian roolipuvut Shakespearen näytelmässä "Romeo ja Julia" Suomen teattereissa vuosina 1881–1985. Julian roolipuku esitysajan muodin, teatterin eri osatekijöiden ja tyylisuuntien näkökulmasta tarkasteltuna*. (Julian's Costumes in Shakespeare's play *Romeo and Juliet* in Finnish Theaters in 1881–1898: Julian's Costume from the Point of View of Fashion of the Time of the Performance, Different Elements of the Theater and Style Trends), MA diss., Department of Education, Craft Studies, University of Helsinki.

Peltonen, M. (1996), 'Carlo Ginzburg ja mikrohistorian ajatus' (Carlo Ginzburg and the Idea of Micro-History) in C. Ginzburg (ed.), *Johtolankoja. Kirjoituksia mikrohistoriasta ja historiallisesta metodista* (Clues: Writings on Micro-History and Historical Method), trans. A. Vuola. 7–34. Helsinki: Gaudeamus, Helsinki University Press.

Purhonen, S., and T. Hoikkala, J. P. Roos, eds. (2008), *Kenen sukupolveen kuulut? Suurten ikäluokkien tarina* (Whose Generation do you Belong To? The story of Baby Boomers). Helsinki: Gaudeamus, Helsinki University Press.

Reitala, H. ed. (1986), *Suomalaista skenografiaa; lähtökohtia tallennukseen, tutkimukseen ja historiaan* (Finnish Scenography: Starting Points for Recording, Research and History). Helsinki: University of Art and Design.

Reitala, H. (2005), 'Taideteollisia linjoja. Liisi Tandefelt ja teatteripuvun murros 1960 ja 70-luvulla' (Art and Industrial Lines: Liisi Tandefelt and the Transformation of Theatre Costumes in the 1960s and 70s) in Reitala (ed.), *Harha on totta. Näkökulmia suomalaiseen lavastustaiteeseen ja pukusuunnitteluun 1900-luvun alusta nykypäivään* (The Illusion is True: Perspectives on Finnish Stage Art and Costume Design from the Beginning of the 20th century to the Present Day), 86–97. Jyväskylä: Atena Kustannus oy.

Rinne, J. (1985), *Muistelija* (Reminiscers), Helsinki: Otava.

Saarikoski, T. (1980), *Tähtiaika. Ansa Ikonen* (Star Time: Ansa Ikonen). Mikkeli: Weilin & Göös.

Salmela, S. and T. Vanhatalo (2004), *Näyttämöpukuja* (Stage Costumes). Helsinki: Like.

Santakari, M. and R. Pennanen (2015), 'Lättähatut ja piukkapöksyt valkokankaalla' (Finnish Youth of the 1950s on the Big Screen) Available online: http://www.elonet.fi/fi/kansallisfilmografia/suomalaisen-elokuvan-vuosikymmenet/1950-1959/lattahatut-ja-piukkapoksyt-valkokankaalla (accessed: 24 February 2019).

Turpeinen, O. (2005), *Merkityksellinen museoesine. Kriittinen visuaalisuus kulttuurihistoriallisen museon näyttelysuunnittelussa* (A Meaningful Museum Object: Critical Visuality in Cutural Museum Exhibitions), doctoral thesis, University of Art and Design, Helsinki.

Ukkonen, T. (2000), *Menneisyyden tulkinta kertomalla. Muistelupuhe oman historian ja kokemuskertomusten tuottamisprosessina*, (Reminiscence Talk as a Way of Interpreting the Past and as a Research Subject), doctoral thesis, Helsinki: Finnish Literary Society.

Ukkonen, T. (2006), '*Yhteistyö, vuorovaikutus ja narratiivisuus muistitietotutkimuksessa*' (Collaboration, Interaction and Narrativity in Oral History Research) in O. Fingerroos, R. Haanpää, A. Heimo and U-M. Peltonen (eds.), *Muistitietotutkimus. Metodologisia kysymyksiä* (Oral history: Methodological Questions), 175-98. Helsinki: Finnish Literary Society.

Vilkuna, J. (2010), 'Museologia ja Suomen museot' (Museology and the Finnish Museums) in S. Pettersson and P. Kinanen (eds), *Suomen museohistoria* (Finnish Museum History), 332–46. Helsinki: Finnish Literary Society.

Weckman, J. (1997), *Taiteilijaksi. Tutkielma pukusuunnittelija Ritva Karpiosta*, (Study of Costume Designer Ritva Karpio), Department of Fashion and Textile Arts, University of Art and Design. Helsinki.

Weckman, J. (2005), 'Pukusuunnittelun pioneereja' (Pioneers of Costume Design) in P. Houni et al. (eds), *Esitys katsoo meitä*, (The Performance Looks at Us), 209–41. Helsinki: Theatre Research Society. Available online: http://teats.fi/category/julkaisut/page/2/(accessed: 18 March 2019).

Weckman, J. (2006), '"Kummallinen, onnistunut erehdys": Liisi Tandefelt pukusuunnittelijana' (A Curious, Succesful Mistake: Liisi Tandefelt as a Costume Designer) in P. Houni (ed.) *Liisi Tandefelt: monessa roolissa* (Liisi Tandefelt: In Many Roles), 51–82. Helsinki: Theatre Museum/Like.

Weckman, J. (2009), 'Puku ja tutkimus' (Costume and Research) in P. Gröndahl, P. Paavolainen and A. Thuring (eds), *Näkyvää ja näkymätöntä* (Visible and Invisible), 172–99. Helsinki: Theatre Research Society. Available online: http://teats.fi/category/julkaisut/page/2/(accessed: 18 March 2019).

Weckman, J. (2014), '"Kun sai hyvät kritiikit niin … sen muisti aina": Näyttämöpuku, pukusuunnittelija ja teatterikritiikki', (When you Had Good Critiques … You Always Remember It: The Interrelationship of Stage Costumes, Costume Designer and Theatre critique) in M. Häti-Korkeila,

H. Järvinen, J. Kortti and R. Roihankorpi (eds), *Teatteri ja media(t)* (Theatre and Media(s)), 37–71. Helsinki: Theatre Research Society. Available online: http://teats.fi/category/julkaisut/(accessed: 18 March 2019).

Weckman, J. (2015a), *"Kun jonkun asian tekee, se pitää tehdä täydellisesti" : Liisi Tandefelt pukusuunnittelijana 1958–1992* (When you Do Something, Do it to Perfection : Liisi Tandefelt as a Costume Designer), doctoral thesis, Department of Art and Design. Aalto University, Helsinki: Aalto ARTS Books. Available online:https://shop.aalto.fi/p/498-kun-jonkun-asian-tekee-se-pitaa-tehda-taydellisesti/(accessed: 24 February 2019)

Weckman, J. (2015b), *Unelmien kuteita: epookkipukujen historiaa Suomessa* (Made of Dreams: The History of Period Costumes in Finland). Helsinki: Theatre Museum Publication Series. Available online: https://www.teatterimuseo.fi/fi/Unelmien-kuteita (accessed: 24 February 2019).

3.2 Spinning Yarns: Locating, Learning and Listening in the Social World of Popular Hindi Film Costume Production

Clare M. Wilkinson

Why Anthropology?

My concern in this chapter is to describe some key ways in which the anthropological approach and the methods it endorses contribute to the larger field of costume studies. The anthropological study of clothing and the body explores diachronic and cross-cultural variation in the meaning and execution of body decoration and dress. At issue are everything from markets to construction techniques and materials, the body as canvas, everyday and ceremonial dress, and of most relevance for costume, forms of dress used in ritual and performance (Eicher 2000; Hansen 2004). Anthropology is relatively unique in its concern to understand human behaviour and expression in small-scale settings and much of its interest in film, television and now social media has arisen from noting the growing influence of these cultural phenomena on the populations to which anthropologists have traditionally been drawn (e.g. Abu-Lughod 2008). Scholarly work on indigenous media production and audience studies is significant, but studies of theatrical, television or film production are much fewer. Perhaps because they constitute an unconventional form of 'community', mass and electronic media makers have not attracted much attention in anthropology.

These facts notwithstanding, anthropology is very well placed to introduce complex layers into the study of costume as a facet of media production, precisely because of its concern with the quotidian and the minute, its repeated circling back to social relationships in the construction of culture, as well as its long-standing interest in the situationally and historically specific elicitation of meaning. By this, I mean that anthropologists are interested in the details of how interactions — between people and between people and materials – accumulate and interweave into cultural artefacts. Costume as the focus of study need be no different in this respect from other phenomena of interest to anthropologists.

Well-established habits of anthropological practice are specifically intended to direct the anthropologist's attention to the unexpected and the overlooked. In my own work, I had always wanted to train my sights not just on to what costumes mean as images or even on to the people responsible for their design, but on to everyone and everything that contributed to the costume as it went on to the actor and as it acquired its 'afterlife' as the film and film paratexts encountered a succession of audiences. Methodological holism at its best yields a sensitivity to context that allows those activities and people that are structurally marginalized to come into view. Taking the filmed image and sequence of images as a starting point of sorts, this investigation exploded into an inquiry about a multitude of social actors, institutions and conventions that together made these visual moments possible.

Some Theoretical and Thematic Precedents

Formally classified as sociological, some key texts and theories have had a marked impact in anthropology. These include Howard Becker's work on art-worlds (Becker 1982; Becker, Faulkner and Kirshenblatt-Gimblett 2006) and Pierre Bourdieu's concept of the cultural field (Bourdieu 1993). The art-world forces attention on the personnel, institutions and conventions without which art could not happen. The cultural field, emerging out of explicitly structuralist precedents, sees the 'field' of social relationships and practices as minutely calibrated, so that change in any one area has implications for all other positions in the field explaining both why change may be resisted by some, as well as sought after by others. Articulating an incisive critique of the distribution of cultural capital – in short, power – in the field, and the extent to which differential ownership of that capital is naturalized, Bourdieu helps us understand why normative descriptions of artistic production are apt to have omissions, with certain personnel not mentioned and practices neglected. Lacking the leverage to convert labour and time into forms of either monetary or intangible capital, the knowledge and capacities these jobs require are largely overlooked. To return to Becker (1982: x), it is not that anthropology (or sociology, in this case) discovers things that no-one knows; 'rather … [it] produces a deeper understanding' of what people do know, both those whose knowledge is already in public circulation and those whose is not.

Within the purview of media studies, a turn towards 'production studies' has opened up a parallel vantage point on the work roles and relationships of what are known as 'above- and below-the-line-workers' (Caldwell 2006; Hesmondhalgh and Baker 2011; Mayer, Banks and Caldwell 2009). Most work in this vein is focused on production in the USA and Europe while the key anthropological contributions to the study of the social and cultural character of media production have been based on ethnography in Asia and Africa (Ganti 2012; Grimaud 2003; Hardy 2015; Martin 2012; Pandian 2015). Costume analysis in anthropology has lingered behind ventures like these (Wilkinson-Weber 2014), but its greatest potential lies in how it can reveal the structure of relationships and relative prestige within the fields of dress and cultural performance. In the sections to follow, I draw on my own efforts, culminating in a monograph titled *Fashioning Bollywood* (Wilkinson-Weber 2014), to make an anthropological investigation into costume in Hindi film which contends that the description of its specifics has broader implications for the study of costume elsewhere.

Finding Costume within Hindi Film Production

Before one has any idea of the composition of the art world or field, one must find it. As a cultural phenomenon, film is intimately wound into the identity of Mumbai. Films feature Mumbai as a setting, as a character even. Most of its most powerful figures live in the city and many of its historic facilities, including iconic studios such as Mehboob, Filmalaya and the vast back-lot Film City are in active use. No less important is the simple fact that filmmaking draws on the labour and resources of a vast number of people in the city, many of them with a known and enduring relationship to the industry, but just as many, if not more, without.

Labour associations and professional societies circumscribe some areas of operation in the industry. For costume, the Cine Costume, Make-Up Artistes and Hairdressers Association groups together 'dressmen' (on-set costumers) with other practitioners involved in some capacity in the production of 'look' (Wilkinson-Weber 2012). Working on a film set is forbidden without possession of an association card and cards are issued along lines of gender. The right of women to obtain make-up artiste cards was granted by India's Supreme Court in 2014 (*The Hindu* 2014). Less noted is that it is still the case that only men can be dressmen, and only women can be hairdressers. Costume designers, concerned to establish a better negotiating position for themselves with respect to producers, joined art directors in 2013 in the subsequently renamed Cine and Television Art Directors and Costume Designers Association (Bains and Wilkinson 2015). The measure was arguably as much a statement about the newly professional self-conception of designers, many of whom in the industry's history had been regarded as little more than part of star actors' retinues.

The attachment of designers to stars has caused and is caused in turn by the absence of any identifiable costume 'department'. It is only very recently that single designers have been given responsibility for a film's costume design; prior to that, responsibility for costume was divided among a variety of personal designers and stylists, dance-dress designers and dressmen (on-set costumers). The title and job description of a 'costume designer' (or dress designer in the conventional parlance of the Hindi industry) did not in fact emerge until several decades after Indian filmmaking began in the early twentieth century. Male stars provided their own clothing from menswear shops and heroines might have their own ladies' tailors to hand to do any tailoring their garments needed. Some men's tailoring establishments laid claim to a *filmi* calling, (like Jaggi Tailor and Super Tailor) but designers from Bhanu Athaiya (the first overtly credited costume designer) onwards had their vision trained on film work specifically, although the stars they designed for were often focused on staking a claim to relevance in both the film and fashion worlds. Athaiya, perhaps because of her early association with esteemed directors like Raj Kapoor and Guru Dutt, and because she worked film-wise and not star-wise, was always a singularity. Other designers drew around them a succession of stars, mostly heroines to start with but later heroes too, for whom they professed to offer a more sophisticated approach to design from that offered by a tailor. For some, this meant a better 'eye' for what looked good and literally 'fitting'; for others it was a better fashion sensibility, and a more intuitive sense of what the director and actor wanted.

These facts notwithstanding, even the most hierarchically organized costume departments involve many more people than it is practically possible to encompass. This is first because the production of costume necessarily reaches into non-industry occupations, like fashion retail, launderers and dry cleaners, fabric merchants, street markets, knock-off retailers and major fashion centres like Bangkok and Dubai in the global flow of apparel. Second, making costume, unlike building a set or actually shooting scenes is not confined to more easily scrutinized studios or locations. The collective activities that produce costume defy simultaneous, straightforward observation and one is constantly concerned as to how one can possibly sketch the great variety of elements at work. As a qualitative social scientist, I did not seek to grapple with the complexities of the situation by using surveys as my quantitatively inclined colleagues might have done, although I still faced a problem of sampling. How, for example to balance the necessary descriptive detail that anthropology demands – an approach Marcus and Fischer (1999: 16) call bringing a 'jeweller's eye' – to bear on the fact that costume is 'done' in a multiple of different places and spaces by a great many people. Acknowledging this dispersal and distribution cannot and should not be omitted, since it is part and parcel of bringing to light what may otherwise be overlooked. One answer is to emphasize the links between persons and places, or the ways in which film practices intersect not just with each other, but with circuits of materials, institutions and relationships that bypass film altogether.

For example, we notice that costume draws on the work of tailors. Some of them are dressmen who do some tailoring directly on set, while others are '*filmi*'[1] tailors or independent tailors who work on contracts especially for the film industry with some work for private clients on the side. Others though are perfectly ordinary tailors who work for menswear stores, or for themselves, or in a fashion designer's atelier. Others still work for *dresswalas* or costume supply shops that also rent out costumes for films and theatre productions, as well as for school and religious pageants. I have wondered what the result would be of making inquiries among ordinary tailors in a neighbourhood of a few criss-crossing streets, to see how many had made at least one article of clothing on request for a TV or film production. Anecdotal evidence suggested that this was surprisingly common, while at the other extreme, seamstresses and stitchers working in the global apparel industry, whose work in factories and sweatshops fuels fashion retail in chain stores and marketplaces in India, were also implicated in the production of Hindi film costume.

Having come to grips with the spatial distribution of these phenomena, it is important to acknowledge that the same constraints on researching dispersed workspaces applies to the work itself. In filmmaking, time is never not in short supply and yet the time that is built into the work of foraging for clothes, fabricating costumes (even when a dedicated '*filmi*' tailoring shop sells itself as a 24/7 concern) is at a certain point irreducible. Filmmakers nowadays do not have to go all the way into South Mumbai (the city proper) for everything they need as more and more facilities and retail stores pop up in the suburbs nearer to studios and the Film City back-lot. On the other hand, as the city grows and congestion increases, even the time to travel within the suburbs stretches to almost absurd lengths. For these reasons, an entire sub-industry of assistants or enterprising independent go-betweens have taken on the job of shuttling people and things from one place to another, in essence managing some of the vexing problems of time that the industry is subject to.

Unlike filmmakers, anthropologists do not have much recourse to these facilitators. They have to deal with limits on the absolute amount of time one has to conduct face-to-face and on-site research; and on the hours in the day that can reasonably be spent on the work itself as opposed to travelling, preparing and processing, as well as all the mundane tasks associated with daily living. Ethnography today is still a largely solitary calling with only the investigator and one or two assistants at work on a given project. But it is in situations like film costume research that the potential of a team begins to suggest itself. Just as go-betweens and agents alleviate the frantic and time-wasting dispersal of effort in filmmaking, so anthropologists working collaboratively could prevent any of them frittering away the large amounts of time it takes simply getting from one place to another. Until conventional modes of working alter to accommodate such scenarios, we can reassure ourselves, that ethnographic research does not start and end with interviews and site-specific observations. Rather anthropology insists, to the frustration of some internal review boards[2] that are not used to such a flimsy notion of work boundaries, that fodder for analysis appears almost from the moment that one begins to set about finding places to go and people to talk to.

Sherry Ortner (2009) makes just this point in her study of independent American filmmakers when she argues that the frustrations she endured in trying to secure interviews or to develop a starting point for participant observation revealed much to her about the politics of access in the Los Angeles media environment, such as how the availability of practitioners is constrained, and what terms are set upon how and when one meets. In my case, designers' offers of interview times were complicated by the unpredictable demands of their jobs, although very few actually said they preferred not to talk to me. I am sure that my status as an older, white academic made it easier for me to secure meetings and perhaps also made it possible for me to negotiate meetings directly with designers themselves. Very rarely was I asked to work with a go-between, a secretary for example, indicative of a more general tendency for direct interactions for certain people. For other practitioners, the main challenge was to find time and a venue to meet. On set, only senior workers could be confident of being able to invite me to the studio and to have time to talk without interruption. In fact, the majority – in-charge personnel included – opted to invite me and my assistant to their homes or to come to my assistant's home, where our discussion could be freer. Even so, time constraints, overseas shooting and 'shopping' made some people effectively unreachable.

Mobile phone technology, email and social media have helped to solve many problems of access, bringing practitioners into play who would otherwise be consistently elusive. American costume practitioners have complained to me that the ability to send photographs of costume immediately to production means that mid- and upper-level management can micro-manage costume decisions in ways that were simply impractical in the past. These kinds of trends are harder to discern in the Mumbai context, where centralized decision-making has yet to displace diffused authority vested in different departments to bring a film into being. But texting (which was already immensely popular among designers, directors, actors and so on by the early 2000s), smartphone photography, plus old-fashioned calling – made immeasurably easier and more convenient by mobile phones leapfrogging over landline technology – have given more scope for interactive consultation. They have also made phone interviews feasible in ways that were unimaginable during my first Indian fieldwork in the late 1980s.

Practitioner Perspectives in Costume Analysis

Interacting with and talking to designers in Hindi film allows the investigator to root the visual evidence of costume in its proper historical and socio-cultural context. Consider for example, one of the most celebrated (even notorious) features of the Hindi film industry, its fantastic and multiple costume changes. These changes peak in song sequences where, as Grimaud (2003: 232) has argued, the pace of changes serves to intensify the emotional relationships that the songs depict. Stars appear in one new outfit after another, with relatively little concern about creating a credible 'wardrobe' of clothing that a character might actually wear if the film's world were a 'real' one.

It is possible and not at all inaccurate to discern in the rapid and exuberant costume changes of mainstream films a desire to create spectacle. But talking to designers reveals other causes at work. Even in the present, with more 'rational' financing plans in place, payment is delayed and often fails to materialize altogether. In the past, this problem was chronic and the intensive production schedule of the 1980s probably pushed the entire system to breaking point. With unreliable and risky financing, films could rarely be planned wholly in advance. Instead, each film proceeded by fits and starts as resources became available. In response, film personnel worked on more than one film at once, often several at a time, in order to be employed and to better their chances of being paid. Stars stingily gave out dates between the several films they were making. As a new shooting schedule approached and resources were freed up to make sets and costumes, it was far easier to create costumes from scratch than to put great effort into managing the finer points of continuity. It is not that nobody cared about continuity, although curiously this was a job that by all accounts was informally distributed to several personnel – the direction team, the dressman or even the actors themselves. Rather, that if a new costume would do that's what got made, meaning that each shooting schedule was in some sense a new beginning.

These revelations do not only flow from asking designers to explain costumes as they are portrayed on screen; they also come from asking about the minutiae of conceiving and executing a design. This is in effect to inquire into the pragmatics of costume design and the endeavour brings into sharper focus the extreme fragmentation of costume design as an industrial activity. I have noted already that making costume entails touching down into organically dispersed places like fabric markets, boutiques, costume supply shops and embroidering workshops. But this is not the fragmentation I mean. What I have in mind is the result of multiple designers tapping fashion and apparel networks for these services separately, without the benefit (or restriction) of a cohesive costume department. The effect of a predictably organized department is to solidify conventional procedures, occupational categories and workflow channels that operate faster and more efficiently. It is not that every production 're-invents the wheel' because there is always someone with some idea of procedure based on long experience. But the possibility of ad hoc practice is far greater and there is also a much deeper reliance upon textile and apparel industries that largely function outside of and in ignorance of film needs.

The costume case is extreme, but fragmentation is familiar in all aspects of Hindi film production or what Madhav Prasad has famously dubbed its 'heterogeneous' mode of production, in which all contributions to film production are worked on in parallel, to converge only when shooting commences (Prasad 1998). From the 1990s onwards, shifts in economic policy towards encouraging the growth of consumer capitalism in India coincided with new models for film financing. These in turn bolstered calls for 'reformed' business practices and rational managerial practices, described in the film industry as 'corporatization' (Ganti 2012). Costume designers pulled away from stressing their fashion credentials or defining their work as a form of celebrity service. Designers had always professed to be designing for the character, a claim that was by no means contradicted by stars' preferences to have their own, personal designer. What changed was a growing preference, at least rhetorically, for prioritizing the needs of the film over either characters or actors. At the same time, assigning responsibility to a single designer for an entire film became more common, as did a philosophy of costume that stressed 'realism'.[3] In keeping with these goals, designers started delegating responsibility to assistants to be their representatives on set, essentially installing a layer of practitioners above the dressmen. Executive decisions by dressmen are fewer as a result, although it is by no means clear that all the obstacles to 'rational' practice have been eliminated, or that this is even desirable (Wilkinson-Weber 2006).

The intractability of all the different elements of a film – costume, set construction, properties, location management – either to centralized administration or to hierarchical relationships by department remains. The resilience and ubiquity of the informal sector in the Indian economy, the need for highly specialized, local knowledge in order to make the best use of both formal and informal production inputs, continues to depend upon each 'department' operating with a considerable degree of autonomy. As yet, the reasons for this are not fully understood. In part it is because the system still doesn't support regular and predictable payment; in part it is because there is enormous inertia to overcome turning a reactive system into a proactive one; in part it is because the business of making films in Mumbai necessarily involves communication and co-operation across enormous linguistic, educational and cultural gulfs. Film practitioners come from a wide variety of social and regional backgrounds, with educational levels ranging from no more than two years of schooling to post-graduate degrees and extremely diverse competencies in understanding and speaking several languages. There are good reasons to believe that the persistent delegation of at least some decision-making is in fact, the most reasonable thing to do.

It becomes obvious then that what will be missing from a designer-oriented account is the kind of distribution of authorship that a dispersed system entails. In any film industry, we may want to know how a set of ideas is brought into wearable form and how the costume is dealt with after the designer delivers the costume to production. Given the equivocal authority of the designer in Mumbai and if we are to know more about why costume appears as it does in films, it is crucial. How then to reach into the other layers of costume production and management that lie beyond the designer?

Distributed Authorship

It is clear from the preceding remarks that the study of costume in film industries around the world cannot move beyond the ethnocentric presumption that the way costume is 'done' in the American or European industry is the standard against which others must be measured. Assuredly the basic models for 'how to make a film' have emerged from these quarters, but the economy and society into which any film industry is rooted, as well as the history of labour relations within different industries themselves will inevitably generate different solutions. I learned the Hindi film system from asking designers not just about what they thought, but also about what they did, eliciting details on the path a costume followed from the drawing board (so to speak) to the actor's body. As to whom to contact at pivotal points on this path, only one or two designers were forthcoming, perhaps because most of them thought these other practitioners of little interest, or perhaps because they were concerned about what they might say to me.

Formal resources for finding personnel were few and very limited. Some names could be gleaned from professional talent sources such as the annual publication *Film India*, in which personnel in several (though not all) film categories are listed with their addresses and contact numbers. This was helpful in getting inquiries started, but the listings, while reasonably thorough for actors and directors, are extremely sparse and idiosyncratic in other categories, with industry stalwarts named next to individuals who haven't worked in film for years, have only worked in one or two productions at most or have been dead for several years. Without doubt, the best way to find more practitioners to talk to came from asking interviewees for suggestions of their own. Not only did this so-called 'snowball' method (Bernard and Bernard 2012) yield an ever-increasing crop of subjects, it also allowed me to understand the various points of contact that existed between different professionals. If dressmen recommended make-up artists, what was their connection? What kind of information could they offer in advance about a new interviewee's experience? In all interviews, I was careful to ask about communication among costume and look workers – when did they talk, what did they talk about, what transactions of materials or payment went on? – as well as moments of co-operation and disagreement.

All kinds of details of an interview situation carry import: the setting, the sharing or offering of food and drink, the availability of pictures and other supporting evidence, the stated or implied integration of the speaker into the industry, the extent to which they can be said to be underscoring hegemonic discourse. It is hard to overstate how important listening is to the job. Open interviews are better than highly structured ones but it is not enough to allow the interview to stray away from some standardized, orienting questions. The valence of certain questions, for instance, may be cast into doubt or at least complicated, as more and more accounts are accumulated. For example, it became clear that the actual title of a film for which a costume was made was highly salient for a designer, but less so for dressmen (particularly if recalling a film made sometime in the past) and hardly at all for a tailor and embroiderer, suggesting key differences in how each practitioner connected their work as a professional matter to the identifying features of the industry at its highest levels and in the public mind (in which film titles loom large). At the same time, designers seemed to be indifferent audiences and consumers of films, professing little knowledge of the films for which they had designed costumes since they had 'no time' to spend on film viewing. On the other hand, a roomful of rural migrant embroiderers emphatically nodded their assent when asked whether they went to see films and if they enjoyed doing so.

Interviews need to be flexible enough to change direction in response to what the interviewee states, or implies is important to them, in acknowledgment of anthropology's goal to destabilize 'accepted wisdom' and pronouncements from authority as to the way things are or should be. On general issues of design, for example, dressmen and tailors had less to say than designers, to the point that one might think they had nothing to say at all. Asked to elaborate on the 'how' of costume production – solving problems of garment construction, flattering the star body, finding costumes when what one had was lost or mislaid – they opened up. The cultural meaning of the interview as a discursive form is relevant here as well. Interviews are so well integrated into the media ecology of Hindi filmmaking and marketing that their structure and expectations are already well-known. This has both benefits and drawbacks for the researcher. On one hand, when talking to practitioners who are not often invited to give interviews, one needs to work harder to establish (and later to interpret) terms for the to-and-fro of conversation. On the other, accomplished interview subjects manage the conventions of the interview so well that the interviewer has to work much harder to maintain any mutuality in the encounter.

Talking to other costume workers and observing, even for a short time, activity on set during filming underscores the fact that costume is more than simply a garment that is constructed with a particular character in mind. This is the costume as the designer sees it but it is not how the dressman interacts with it. For him, the costume is defined by its need for repeated renewal – storing where retrievable (if the dressman's memory serves), cleaning when soiled, repaired when damaged, starched and ironed before wearing. The dressman's effort is single-mindedly focused on preventing the costume from doing what clothes naturally do, that is alter and age. Yet the dressman is also required to do those forms of ageing that the character or film demands, so that the costume looks as though it has been subjected to traumas that have in fact, never happened. These are dimensions of costume that are rarely the subject of analysis and yet they are essential to the 'function' of costume in film narratives. Some designers now co-ordinate ageing and distressing themselves. Outside of India, textile artists and ager/dyers specialize in just these kinds of material 'special effects'.

Unlike a handful of anthropologists who have now produced work based on participant observation in the actual making of films, I was unable to find a credible participant position that would bring me directly into the heart of costume production. Participant observation is always recommended if it is feasible, because of how it draws the investigator into cultural processes that often unwittingly escape a cultural practitioner's ability to describe them. An alternative is to find ways to actively engage practitioners in the project itself, propelling the investigation beyond the bounds of traditional social science approaches into practice-based research. Undoubtedly, more work needs to be done to bring anthropological research into conversation with the practice-based work of theatre and art departments.

The Value of Anthropology

Taking on board the practitioner viewpoint can be disarming as one realizes how poor the fit may be between professional self-image and academic analysis. Every costume designer I have ever met has said they design for the character; who and what that character ultimately is comes from the film's director (widely referred to in the Hindi industry as 'the captain of the ship'). This view of costume design and of the professional relationship between designer and director is taken so seriously that designers may rebuff any effort to elicit purposes and meanings that supersede the brief.

Whatever their intentions may be, however, there is no escaping the fact that once screened and distributed, a film's images allow for interpretations that stray far beyond the filmmakers' intentions (and not all of these interpretations come from scholars: highly culturally literate audiences invest in this kind of interpretative work all the time). Even so, some necessary constraints on the form these interpretations take needs to come from a more sophisticated understanding of the processes of costume production so that results and intentions are not confused. For example, the designer can have no influence upon last-minute costumes either commissioned or purchased by dressmen, the replacement of damaged items with new ones obtained by dressmen, or decisions by stars to wear something other than the proffered costume. We can surely not attribute intent without some qualification if a designer has to make a costume with whatever is available with only a few hours' notice, instead of what might have been available had the costume been ordered days or weeks in advance. Sometimes such improvisational events are accepted with a shrug of the shoulders; at other times they are met with bitter resentment.

But the requirement of anthropological analysis is not to privilege one attitude or the other. The dressman's sense of his professional does not fully coincide with the designer's view of him and neither does the tailor's. It is not the case that one is wrong or the other is sacrosanct. Academic analysis does not merely reproduce the art world of costume production; its job, when done properly, is to illustrate how what the audience sees grows out of material acts and recurrent interrelationships in which both conflict and co-operation occur.

Notes

1. '*Filmi*' is a term that can simply mean 'related to film' or may be a reference to commercial film excess – a '*filmi sari*' is one that exposes more of the body than would ordinarily be appropriate.
2. In America, IRBs or internal review boards in universities are responsible for vetting projects using human subjects to ensure that they meet ethical guidelines for research.
3. I use the term 'realism' here, because this is the term that designers themselves use. It is not overtly related to any theoretical meaning of realism in film history.

References

Abu-Lughod, L. (2008), *Dramas of Nationhood: The Politics of Television in Egypt*. Chicago: University of Chicago Press.

Bains, L. and C. M. Wilkinson (2015), 'The Character in Question: How to Design Film Costumes in India', in Ilana Gershon (ed.), *A World of Work: Imagined Manuals for Real Jobs*, 146–63. Ithaca: Cornell University Press.

Becker, H. S. (1982), *Art Worlds*. Berkeley: University of California Press.

Becker, H. S., R. R. Faulkner, and B. Kirshenblatt-Gimblett, eds. (2006), *Art from Start to Finish: Jazz, Painting, Writing, and Other Improvisations*. 1st ed. Chicago: University of Chicago Press.

Bernard, H. R. (2012), *Social Research Methods: Qualitative and Quantitative Approaches*. Thousand Oaks, CA: Sage.

Bourdieu, P. (1993), *The Field of Cultural Production*. New York: Columbia University Press.

Caldwell, J. (2006), 'Cultural Studies of Media Production: Critical Industrial Practices', in *Questions of Method in Cultural Studies*, 109–53. Malden, MA: Blackwell Publishing.

Eicher, J. B. (2000), 'The Anthropology of Dress', *Dress* 27 (1): 59–70.

Ganti, T. (2012), *Producing Bollywood: Inside the Contemporary Hindi Film Industry*. Durham, NC: Duke University Press.

Grimaud, E. (2003), *Bollywood Film Studio: Ou Comment Les Films Se Font à Bombay*. Paris: CNRS Éditions.

Hansen, K. T. (2004), 'The World in Dress: Anthropological Perspectives on Clothing, Fashion, and Culture', *Annual Review of Anthropology* 33 (January): 369–92.

Hardy, K. C. (2015), 'Constituting a Diffuse Region: Cartographies of Mass-Mediated Bhojpuri Belonging', *BioScope: South Asian Screen Studies* 6 (2): 145–64.

Hesmondhalgh, D., and S. Baker. (2011), *Creative Labour: Media Work in Three Cultural Industries*. London and New York: Routledge.

Marcus, G. E., and M. M. J. Fischer (1999), *Anthropology as Cultural Critique: An Experimental Moment in the Human Sciences*. Chicago: University of Chicago Press.

Martin, S. J. (2012), 'Of Ghosts and Gangsters: Capitalist Cultural Production and the Hong Kong Film Industry', *Visual Anthropology Review* 28 (1): 32–49.

Mayer, V., M. Banks, and J. T. Caldwell (eds) (2009), *Production Studies: Cultural Studies of Media Industries*. New York: Routledge.

Ortner, S. B. (2009), 'Studying Sideways: Ethnographic Access in Hollywood', in V. Mayer, M. Banks, and J. T. Caldwell (eds.), *Production Studies: Cultural Studies of Media Industries*, 175–89. New York: Routledge.

Pandian, A. (2015), *Reel World: An Anthropology of Creation*. Durham, NC: Duke University Press.

Prasad, M. M. (1998), *Ideology of the Hindi Film: A Historical Construction*. Delhi: Oxford University Press.

The Hindu (2014), 'SC Allows Women to Work as Make-up Artists in Bollywood' *The Hindu*, 4 November edition.

Wilkinson-Weber, C. M. (2006), 'The Dressman's Line: Transforming the Work of Costumers in Popular Hindi Film', *Anthropological Quarterly* 79 (4): 581–608.

Wilkinson-Weber, C. M. (2012), 'Making Faces: Competition and Change in the Production of Bollywood Film Star Looks', in A. Dawson and S. Holmes (eds.), *Working in the Global Film and Television Industries*, 183–98. New York: Bloomsbury Academic.

Wilkinson-Weber, C. M. (2014), *Fashioning Bollywood: The Making and Meaning of Hindi Film Costume*. New York: Bloomsbury Academic.

Snapshots

3.3 Hollywood Costume: A Journey to Curation

Deborah Nadoolman Landis

Costume design is a central component of cinematic storytelling. The role of the costume designer is profound, yet simple to define; costume designers help bring the people in the movie to life. This core message is the subject of my research, teaching, publishing and curating. After spending the first twenty years of my professional life as a costume designer, in mid-life I shifted to scholarship as parenting became more challenging when my children became teenagers. Significantly, my doctoral dissertation at London's Royal College of Art (Nadoolman Landis 2003), allowed me the unique opportunity to co-ordinate my thoughts on costume design's key contribution to storytelling and international popular culture.

As a practitioner, it was clear that the public and the entertainment industry misunderstood the costume designer's role. This was evidenced by our inequitable compensation and credit that trailed far behind our creative collaborators (production design and cinematography). And, there were a multitude of forces undermining the field. The fashion press, ambivalent about costume design and in debt to advertisers, regarded costume designers as product placement providers for fashion labels. Without the advantage of public relations firms, label-less costume designers have sometimes been denigrated as 'frock queens' and/or confused with personal stylists. Costuming for modern comedy and drama productions has been dismissed as 'shopping'. Often deliberately invisible, contemporary design provides some of the best costuming on small and large screens. In the recent past, scholarly fashion and film theorists have cultivated the philosophy of spectatorship while neatly superseding the costume practitioners, whose creative practice and process remained uncredited in their books and journal articles. Women should credit women. Lately, this fashion for hiding costume design credits in academic writing seems to have ebbed.

Five years of intensive doctoral research galvanized my costume activism. But at that time, there was no way to know the course of my journey. My commitment grew as a two-term[1] president of the Costume Designers Guild (CDG), Local 892. Dominated by women, costume carries the diminished status of 'women's work' and has been relegated to the margins of film and fashion history. While the story of women executives, producers, directors and writers has begun to be explored, labour history has largely ignored the women working in the Hollywood crafts.[2] In 2003, I represented Local 892 at the labour contract negotiations between the AMPTP[3] and the IATSE (whose membership was – and still is – overwhelmingly male). I arrived armed with a keynote presentation with comparative wage and gender bar graphs. This keynote provided sound evidence that costume designers continue being harmed by entrenched gender bias and were contractually and systemically underpaid. It became depressingly clear that the value of the costume designer was defined by a lack of respect from both the AMPTP and our own IATSE. That moment was cathartic.

Frustration ran high amongst my colleagues. With management bound by collective bargaining and unwilling to challenge the rigid constraints of the union contract, costume designers were informed that our status as 'non-mandatory hire'[4] was 'settled' precedent. After unproductive conversations with studio management and the IATSE, it was clear that costume designers needed to take control of our own narrative and our future. With the support of the Costume Designers' Guild (CDG) Executive Board, my tenure as president took giant organizational leaps in areas that were more hospitable to change. With the Board's agreement, I founded the CDG's magazine *The Costume Designer*[5] and nurtured the Costume Designers' Guild Awards which continue to provide a robust public platform for the field.

In 1974, I visited the Metropolitan Museum of Art's (Met) Costume Institute exhibition, 'Romantic and Glamorous Hollywood Design', curated by Diana Vreeland. The Met's exhibition created a surge of interest and publications around Hollywood costume design.[6] In 2004, I was given the chance to co-curate[7] '50 Designers/50 Costumes: Concept to Character' at the Academy of Motion Picture Arts and Sciences (the Academy). As editor-in-chief of that catalogue (Nadoolman Landis 2004), I provided a first-person interview with each costume designer whose work was on view. The designer's voice has been a keystone in my teaching, publishing and curation. Before the internet there was little access to designers talking about their creative process. A practitioner-centric exhibition was a natural extension of my professional life as designer, union leader and academic. Every museum exhibition provides an immersive environment in which to tell a complicated and provocative story. Done well it can be transformative for an artist, for a field and for the visitor.

After curating an additional (smaller) costume exhibition for the Academy,[8] navigating studio archives and communicating with collectors, in 2007 I submitted a proposal to the Victoria and Albert (V&A) Museum in London. If Mrs Vreeland's 1974 blockbuster exhibition was all about the clothes, my proposal for an exhibition entitled 'Hollywood Costume' would illuminate the costume-design process and celebrate the costume designer. The exhibition outline was built from the Power Point file that I created for the 2003 contract negotiations with the IATSE. Its original purpose was as a persuasive political tool for increased wages. This presentation made an authoritative case for the legitimacy and sovereignty of the field. 'Hollywood Costume' presented the role of costume design as understood by costume designers and in addition by our most valued and intimate collaborators: directors and actors. This message was re-inforced in the galleries by leveraging interviews with cinematic masters such as Martin Scorsese, Quentin Tarantino, Mike Nichols and Tim Burton. Acting veterans Robert DeNiro and Meryl Streep also spoke passionately about their own reliance on costume design to disappear into the people in the screenplay.

With over one hundred costumes from sixty lenders, including private collectors, studios, museums and archives, designers and directors, the exhibition took five years to assemble. When it closed at the V&A after fourteen weeks,[9] it was the most successful show in the museum's long history, with over 265,000 visitors. 'Hollywood Costume' closed in 2015 after touring to Melbourne and Phoenix and having premiered at the Academy's unfinished museum in Los Angeles. The *Hollywood Costume* catalogue won a major prize,[10] which serves as a legacy for this once-in-a-lifetime show.

Public engagement is imperative if a paradigm must shift. Every occasion has the potential to educate outside of the classroom. And like costume design exhibitions, costume designer panels boost public awareness and help to unravel the mysteries of the creative process. Inaugurated in 2010, the UCLA David C. Copley Center hosts 'Sketch to Screen'. This free panel which is open to the public includes nominees for the Oscar for Best Costume Design and the designers of the most provocative films of the year. A diverse audience of students, faculty and guests are provided with the insights of and access to the most distinguished costume designers working today. These panels have now proliferated as an international master class, which I moderate each year. In 2017, Swarovski, the Academy and the Copley Center co-hosted 'Costume Design: à la Francaise' at the Mona Bismarck Foundation in Paris with five prominent French costume designers[11] in French, with simultaneous translation into English. In 2018, 'Disfraces y Diseñadores de Vestuario' (Costumes and Costume Designers) held in Madrid with the Academia de las Artes y las Ciencias Cinematográficas de España (Academy of Cinematographic Arts and Sciences of Spain), Spanish costume designers[12] engaged in a lively discussion in front of a sold-out audience. In October 2019, the Rome Film Festival hosted their first panel of Italian costume designers.[13]

Tying the world of costuming together strengthens our community, raises our prestige, lends support to our colleagues and re-inforces our shared language.

Publishing also provides the historic framework and artistic context for the discipline. Unsurprisingly, my lens is practice-based. *Dressed: A Century of Hollywood Costume Design* (2007) celebrates costume design through a chronological overview. *Hollywood Sketchbook: A Century of Costume Illustration* (2012) is the first book to capture the purpose, the people and the history of film costume illustration. Focal Press' *Screencraft* (2003) and *FilmCraft* (2012) series (now published in multiple languages) present the unique perspectives of working costume designers in their own words. The *Hollywood Costume* (2012) catalogue contains provocative essays by design practitioners, costume collectors, historians, directors and archivists. When asked to provide chapters for volumes as varied as *Women Designers in the USA, 1900–2000* (2000), *Swarovski: Celebrating a History of Collaborations in Fashion, Jewelry, Performance, and Design* (2015), *Italy in Hollywood* (2018) and *Pink! A History of Pink in Fashion, Art and Culture,* (2018) my essays re-state the purpose of costume design as doctrine. The upcoming three-volume *Bloomsbury Encyclopedia of Film & Television Costume Design*[14] with over two hundred international contributors seeks to establish and secure costume design's role in motion picture history.

Teaching is the intrinsic element of a comprehensive strategy to introduce costume design as a pre-requisite for cinematic storytelling. While president of the CDG, it became clear that this should begin with educating student filmmakers. All university film programmes need a fully integrated film design curriculum as part of their core curriculum. Costuming for student films is universally trivialized and an afterthought. A conservatory approach mirrors professional film production where all the crafts work in unison. Ironically, this consolidation is found in traditional university theatre programmes, but is missing in film departments. The benefits are exponential: filmmakers learn that their characters don't arrive on the set fully formed; rather, they are that way by design. Currently, *all* University of

California, Los Angeles (UCLA) graduate filmmakers attend a mandatory class in costuming upon entry to the programme. These directors design[15] the costumes for their short films as they are guided through the steps of the creative process. The UCLA Copley Center publishes an updated annual list of graduate costume design students and costume alumni that is distributed to local student directors. Once filmmakers understand the power of costuming it becomes an indispensable tool for storytelling.

Costume design education requires an army of committed faculty to extend its reach. In 2014, the David C. Copley Center launched the 'Dorothy Richards[16] Costume Educators' Luncheon' to provide easier access to film and television industry professionals. Many faculty members encounter students clamouring for film and television design courses, but without access to the professional costume-design network and with a lack of departmental support at their home institutions, delivering on this promise becomes difficult. Richards' presenters include union representatives, designers and professionals working with state-of-the-art 3D printing and construction, dyeing, digital illustration and software from emerging tech companies. Current and updated syllabi are shared freely with a candid discussion around university and professional practice. The Richards luncheon is a forum for design education and a think tank for new approaches to teaching costume.

It is gratifying to witness the success and the influence of this long-term and multi-pronged approach to pedagogy. Through publishing, local and international panels, conferences, film festivals, university teaching and museum exhibitions, the scholarship and popular interest in and engagement with motion picture and television costume design has grown exponentially. The last five years has seen an explosion of awareness. YouTube now features interviews with costume designers, industry publications handicap costuming awards, the CDG website hosts on-line interviews and it is now common for studios to engage costume designers to promote their productions. As a practitioner and as a scholar, my goal has been to define and clarify the purpose of costume design. The creation of personality (identity) is our primary role; the creation of clothing is secondary. Wage equity, artistic recognition and the union contract remain a huge challenge and an ongoing battle. Every interview provides a costume designer with a powerful opportunity to re-frame the language and the conversation around the field. This comprehensive strategy and vision is imperative. Raising the value of our contribution raises the value of our collaboration. Ultimately, costume designers must change the paradigm together.

Notes

1 2001–07.

2 In addition to costume design the crafts include: production design, make-up/hairstyling, sound (mixing and editing), editing, cinematography, visual effects and music (score and song).

3 AMPTP (Alliance of Motion Picture and Television Producers); IATSE (International Alliance of Theatrical Stage Employees).

4 Under the rules of the contract no union production is obliged to hire or give credit to a costume designer.

5 The Costume Designer's Guild Magazine was launched in 2005.

6 Elizabeth Leese, *Costume Design in the Movies: An Illustrated Guide to the Work of 157 Great Designers* (1976); David Chierichetti, *Hollywood Costume Design* (1976); Dale McConathy, *Hollywood Costume: Glamour, Glitter, Romance* (1976).
7 Co-curators: Costume designers Judianna Makovsky, Jeffrey Kurland.
8 'Dressed in Color: Technicolor Costumes', 2009.
9 20 October 2012 to 27 January 2013.
10 Kraszna-Krausz Award, 2013.
11 Panellists: Madeline Fontaine, Pierre-Yves Gayraud, Fabienne Katany, Pierre-Jean Larroque and Anaïs Romand.
12 Panellists: Clara Bilbao, Tatiana Hernández, Pedro Moreno and Cristina Rodríguez.
13 The event was supported by Swarovski. Panellists: Daniela Ciancio, Eva Coen, Stefano De Nardis, Gabriella Pescucci, Carlo Poggioli.
14 Expected date of publication: 2020.
15 First-year filmmakers break down their six-page screenplays, write biographies of each character and create mood boards and sketches.
16 Dorothy Richards's commitment to education found focus in the Brandeis National Committee in Los Angeles where she eventually served as president. In 2014, her daughter Karen Richards Sachs established this fund to honour her mother's legacy.

References

Chierichetti, D. (1976), *Hollywood Costume Design*. New York: Harmony Books.

Leese, E. (1976), *Costume Design in the Movies: An Illustrated Guide to the Work of 157 Great Designers*. Bembridge: BCW Publishing Limited.

McConathy, D. (1976), *Hollywood Costume: Glamour, Glitter, Romance*. New York: H. N. Abrams.

Nadoolman Landis, D. (ed.) (2003), *Screencraft: Costume Design*. Burlington, MA: Focal Press.

Nadoolman Landis, D. (ed.) (2004), *50 Costumes / 50 Designers: Concept to Character*. Beverly Hills, CA: Academy of Motion Picture Arts and Sciences: Academy Imprints.

Nadoolman Landis, D. (2007), *Dressed: A Century of Hollywood Costume Design*. New York: Collins Design.

Nadoolman Landis, D. (2012a), *Hollywood Sketchbook: A Century of Costume Illustration*. New York,: Harper Design.

Nadoolman Landis, D. (2012b), *FilmCraft: Costume Design*. Boston: Focal Press.

Nadoolman Landis, D. (2012c), *Hollywood Costume*. London: V&A Publishing.

Nadoolman Landis, D. (2015), 'Performance Costume', in *Swarovski: Celebrating a History of Collaborations in Fashion, Jewelry, Performance, and Design*, n.p. New York: Rizzoli Books.

Nadoolman Landis, D. (2018a), 'Hollywood Begins, 1908–1929: Clothes, Costume & Couture', in Ricci, S. (ed.), *Italy in Hollywood*, 410–35. Milan: Skira - Museo Salvatore Ferragamo.

Nadoolman Landis, D. (2018b), 'Panavision Pink: Deceptively Demure', in Steele, V. (ed.), *Pink! A History of Pink in Fashion, Art and Culture*, 101–13. London: Thames & Hudson.

Nadoolman Landis, D. and Pat Kirkham (2000), 'Designing Hollywood: Women Costume and Production Designers', in Kirkham, P. (ed.), *Women Designers in the USA, 1900–2000: Diversity and Difference: Jacqueline M. Atkins … [and Others]*, 246–67. New Haven & London: Yale University Press.

3.4 'The Getting of Wisdom': Learning from Anna Senior

Jennifer Gall

When filming ends, the artificial world created on set vanishes along with the wardrobe department. Remarkably, with the wrap of Baz Luhrmann's 2001 film, *Moulin Rouge* at Sydney's Fox Studios, the set, with its giant, lavishly decorated elephant was bull-dozed in readiness for the set construction crew to build a world for the next movie about to begin production on the lot. Some special costume items were kept by the film's stars and the rest were returned to Bazmark's office for storage, before ultimately finding a home at the National Film and Sound Archive of Australia (NFSA) and Sydney's Powerhouse Museum.

This snapshot examines movie costumes through the eyes of the award-winning Australian designer Anna Senior and interprets evidence from her oral history interviews. Senior's unfailing resourcefulness, working within slim budgets in makeshift premises on location, is characteristic of the way in which the Australian film industry operates to produce extraordinarily original films outside of the affluent Hollywood studio system. She describes the process of dressing actors using the language of colour, fibre-texture and astute judgement about how different fabrics move on the body so that they may communicate the script's narrative. From a curatorial perspective, I will describe how a costume from *My Brilliant Career* (1979) functions as the textile 'skin' that transforms Judy Davis into Sybylla Melvin and as the lifeless object that is preserved within archival vaults when the performance is over and the actor has moved on.

Anna Senior (born 1941) has designed costumes for twelve major feature films – notably, *My Brilliant Career* (nominated for an Academy Award for best costumes); *The Getting of Wisdom* (1977); *Phar Lap* (1983) and *Breaker Morant* (1980). She also designed costumes for television movies and mini-series, as well as theatrical and opera productions in Australia and in the USA receiving two Australian Film Institute (AFI) Awards. Currently, she designs for the Canberra Repertory Theatre and for private commissions. Senior asserts that a costume designer differs fundamentally from a fashion designer. On a film production, a designer must be self-sufficient when creating costumes with the ability to problem solve questions about how to depict a character through clothing and initiate ideas rather than simply follow a static pattern to create a fashionable item. The garment is created to support the character's identity and is not an independent artwork. Senior's opinion resonates with Pam Cook's reflection that 'the quest for exactitude and historical authenticity … illuminates the significance attached to costume by the film makers, both as a vehicle for spectacle and as a means for supporting narrative realism and cinematic illusionism' (Cook 1996: 51).

Costume design for film, as defined by Senior requires a unique combination of skills: independent spirit; the ability to 'harmonize' with the diverse personalities of director, producer, cast, crew and technical assistants; a highly developed ability to improvise on the job and adapt design quickly to the dictates of character and set and above all else, organizational capability.

Senior describes how she learned the critical ability to cultivate an overarching vision of how a film would come together. Costumes for key characters must appear to age over time as the narrative unfolds, but as films are not shot in chronological order the designer must keep a meticulous record of each appearance of the costume by creating continuity documentation for reference. These images and notes record exactly what accessories appeared in a particular shoot, what happens to the garment and how these details will influence the film sequence before and after. Where there are multiple characters to clothe, such as the gaggle of school girls with their numerous corsets, petticoats, night-gowns, black stockings and shoes in *The Getting of Wisdom,* the task of keeping each character's outfit intact becomes an added challenge.

A film character is a constantly moving figure and often several versions of a costume must be made so that the actor will look heroic, ravishing, distressed or immortal in a variety of poses, such as riding a horse, languishing on a sofa, climbing a tree, entangled in an amorous embrace or engaged in physical combat. Getting inside the character is imperative before embarking on costume construction – what Senior calls 'dressing people from the inside out'.[1] Inhabiting the character in terms of the emotional journey they will make is the starting point and then, through historical research creating underwear to support not only the outer garment but also provide a physical reminder for the actor of the era in which their character lives.

Age of Consent (1969), Senior's first film taught her that thinking 'inside the character' would provide solutions to questions about how to clothe the actor. Helen Mirren's costume required a simple and figure-flattering design, the kind of effect that the drape of cotton jersey would create. In 1969, however, the fabric was expensive and hard to source in Australia. Senior eventually found a striped version in David Jones's department store for the then extravagant price of fifteen dollars per metre. She then bleached the fabric to subdue the stripes and re-dyed it a soft pink to create seven costumes, representing the passing of time on the sun-drenched far-north Queensland beach. 'Never leave home for a movie without the dye pot'[2] became Senior's enduring axiom. Wondering how to define the waist and yet keep the garment looking natural, Senior imagined what the young girl would have fashioned for herself and hit upon a twisted rope belt with a few shells attached.

Colour is used by Senior to convey emotional nuances, such as in the film *The Getting of Wisdom* (1977). Laura Rambotham's strident red dress and matching double-dahlia hat were deliberately finished with clashing green braid to convey Laura's internal discord as she carves her rebellious pathway through boarding-school life. Serendipitously, the centenary of Liberty of London in 1975 precipitated re-production of a number of original Liberty fabrics and the red floral fabric chosen by Senior was one of these – resulting in an authentic and visually startling costume: a perfect fit for Laura's unconventional character (Figure 3.4.1). A valuable resource for sourcing patterns from

Figure 3.4.1 *Susannah Fowle as Laura Tweedle Rambotham arriving at school in the strident red Liberty print dress and 'double-dahlia' hat in* The Getting of Wisdom *(1977). Number 2246-0044-002. National Film and Sound Archive of Australia.*

this era was *Madame Weigel's* paper patterns, originally available to nineteenth-century Australian women through a catalogue that offered purchase by mail order.

The length of a shoot determines how the whole design process will unfold. For a film like *Robbery Under Arms* (1985) with a three-month schedule, it was possible for Senior to go to a tailor very early in production and order 200 pairs of generic period trousers, jackets, waistcoats and shirts. Following casting, the fine art of selecting and crafting distinctive pieces with particular dyeing and finishing was undertaken with the leading actors in mind. Thinking expansively is key to a successful project, in terms of having sufficient costume resources to cater for all eventualities when filming begins. Senior has remarked: 'You have to start big and then pull in and focus'.[3]

My Brilliant Career (1979), under the artistic direction of Luciana Arrighi was a demanding project given the tight six-week shooting schedule, constant moving between locations and budget constraints. Costumes were worked out as shooting progressed. Senior recalls that the team literally finished the last frock on the last day of the shoot. Wherever they moved to film, it was a matter of setting up a work room, a dye room and a wardrobe department in a hired hall. The early twentieth-century costumes were created using period garments and elements of 1900s clothing and accessories. The striking red parasol used by Sybylla in the boating scene was an antique possession of Senior's (Figure 3.4.2). Sun damage had resulted in the fabric perishing along the spokes and the frayed fabric was replaced by Senior with strips of antique black lace, thus creating a prop that is more visually effective than the original item. The parasol signals Sybylla's transition from tomboy to lady – a process which is only partially effective, as she cannot repress her instincts sufficiently to prevent her from upsetting the boat and catapulting herself and her handsome companion

Figure 3.4.2 *Judy Davis as Sybylla Melvin in the white dress with red antique parasol worn for the boating scene,* My Brilliant Career *(1979). National Film and Sound Archive of Australia.*

(Sam Neill) into the water. As there was only one version of the cream outfit (on productions with larger budgets there are multiple versions of key costumes prepared), it had to be whipped off after each take and carefully dried in readiness for the next attempt. Miraculously, the treasured red parasol never fell out of the boat.

The outfit Anna Senior created for Judy Davis to wear as the heroine, Sybylla, in the boating scene is now housed in the National Film and Sound Archive of Australia (Title No. 360619) and it was displayed throughout 2017–18 as one of the centrepieces of the travelling exhibition I worked on, 'Starstruck: Australian Movie Portraits'. In this context, audiences observed the costume as a disembodied garment, quite still. Standing in close physical proximity to the outfit, visitors remarked on its small size, the tiny waist and the evidence of the slight build of the actress who wore it. For many, this was the first time they looked beneath the onscreen illusion of characters who fill the frame and appear larger than life.

Visitors to the exhibition also interrogated the construction of the outfit in a way not possible when viewing the film. What might appear to be a one-piece gown in the film is in fact, a cream coloured long-sleeved blouse with lace around the shoulders, neck and wrists with a matching cream full-length skirt. Close observation reveals a rip (repaired) on the hem that occurred during filming. When viewed with a forensic eye in the gallery environment, the costume, which will never be worn again, becomes an artefact and not as originally intended Sybylla's 'skin' brought to life by Davis's moving body; but the very absence of the living actor elevates the outfit, which shows the lingering marks of her presence into an almost sanctified relic.

Figure 3.4.3 *The cream dress as displayed in* Starstruck: Australian Movie Portraits *(2017–18). National Film and Sound Archive of Australia*

As a curator, I observed that when people moved through the exhibition they compared the costume with the version depicted in photographic still images and observed the way in which the garment was re-interpreted in photographs for publicity purposes in posters and lobby cards. Ultimately, at the end of the exhibition and on return to Canberra, the costume was removed from the mannequin by the conservator and returned to its costume box at the NFSA. Here, it was laid flat and the weight of the fabric supported with archival packing materials to prevent stress-related damage, thus preserving the costume for future generations. Sybylla's ensemble whether off the screen, on display, or in storage inhabits completely different dimensions to the world it was created to be worn in, but the transition from garment to treasured artefact is enthralling nonetheless.

Clothing a star such as Judy Davis is only one part of the costume designer's task. Talking about strategies for being prepared to clothe a vast cast of extras at the beginning of a shooting schedule, Senior cites *Phar Lap* (1983) as a film with many crowd scenes. In this case, she cut out many dresses to a size twelve with a big seam allowance – 'the magic number!' – as 'it's easy to go up or down to fit characters'.[4] Her pattern for the 1930s dresses involved the ingenious re-purposing of a vast personal collection of large silk scarves into the front and back panels and the handkerchief-hemline skirt.

Films such as *The Odd Angry Shot* (1979) and *Breaker Morant* (1980) involving many uniforms and blood-soaked stuntwork posed a different kind of challenge. The uniforms were painstakingly researched to accurately re-create small details of design and embellishment, and sets of ageing garments were made for the central characters. But in addition, the effect of bullet and shell wounds needed to be synthesized as well as inventing internal mechanisms to dispense liberal quantities of blood on impact of the bullets. In the 1979 release *Money Movers,* stunt-trousers were required to simulate the effect of rifle shots to a character's backside. A condom filled with a kilo of mincemeat fitted over a metal plate wired for sound formed the basis of this gruesome visual effect.

For film scholar Stella Bruzzi, 'the most interesting debates surrounding the involvement of fashion in film still centre on the question of exhibitionism and art; whether clothes should perform a spectacular as opposed to a subservient visual role in film; and whether those same costumes should remain functional intermediaries to narrative and character or stand out as art objects in themselves' (1997: 8). In each of her interviews over thirty years, Senior re-iterates that successful costuming is not about spectacle but instead, perfection is achieved when the garment looks completely contemporary with its era, the colours matched or dyed to blend into the background textures of the set rather than stand out, so that costume and character are inextricably one. 'That's what I am aiming for – when the costumes become part of the characters.'[5]

Notes

1. Interview with Anna Senior by Joyce Agee, 1985, NFSA. Title No. 395571.
2. Interview with Anna Senior by Jennifer Gall, 2018, NFSA. Title No. 1524975.
3. Interview with Anna Senior by Joyce Agee, 1985, NFSA. Title No. 395571.
4. Q&A at the NFSA, pre-screening talk with Anna Senior and Jennifer Gall before *The Getting of Wisdom*, January 2018 and interview with Anna Senior by Joyce Agee, 1985, NFSA. Title No. 395571.
5. Q&A at the NFSA, pre-screening talk before *The Getting of Wisdom*, January 2018.

Bibliography

Bruzzi, S. (1997), *Undressing Cinema: Clothing and Identity in the Movies*. London and New York: Routledge.

Cook, P. (1996), *Fashioning the Nation: Costume and Identity in British Cinema*. London: BFI.

3.5 Design for Television: Costume and Contemporary Clothing

Chrisi Karvonides-Dushenko

An interview was conducted between costume designer Chrisi Karvonides-Dushenko and Sofia Pantouvaki on 7 June 2018. The following excerpt focuses on the designer's work for the HBO television series *Here and Now*, an American drama series created by Alan Ball (executive producer), consisting of ten episodes and starring Holly Hunter and Tim Robbins. The series premiered on HBO on 11 February 2018 and aired for one season. The plot focused on issues confronting a contemporary multi-racial family in the area of Portland, USA and its many topics included race and mental illness.

CKD: Chrisi Karvonides-Dushenko
SP: *Sofia Pantouvaki*

SP: You have worked extensively on costume for television. We would like to discuss one of your recent projects, the series Here and Now *(2018) starring Holly Hunter and Tim Robbins and your design process therein. How did you create the characters? Can you share some insights on your work with contemporary costume, as well as your collaboration with the actors?*

CKD: In this series, Holly Hunter and Tim Robbins are a married couple living in Oregon who have four children. Three are adopted from different countries [Liberia, Vietnam and Colombia] and one is their biological child. It is one of those projects where it's present day Oregon-/Los Angeles-inspired clothing that you use. In such a case, you really have to work with the characters and why they make certain choices. There are pages in the script where we want to allude to or hint at where that character is going in the course of that scene or that script day and then there are times where we want to hold the cards back and not expose what their intentions or motivations are for the day, because it is a mystery.

However, this is also one of those situations where you have to work very closely with the actors to help them settle on costume choices when the clothes are 'not who they are' in their own lives. This is a constant problem when you do contemporary clothing. They have certain colour palettes they gravitate to, or a certain silhouette but that is who they are in life; you as a practitioner, you are constantly reminding them, 'is this the choice that your character would make in this scene?'

So, one of the very important things is to set up a space, an environment, a fitting room that helps them remove themselves from who they are as a person or what their day was about and to get them into focusing on the script. It is 'crazy' with television because every ten days we film a new script. This

Figure 3.5.1 *Costume illustration by costume designer Chrisi Karvonides-Dushenko for Holly Hunter as 'Audrey Bayer' for the series* Here and Now *(HBO, 2018), Courtesy of Chrisi Karvonides-Dushenko.*

show was even more complicated, because we had one director directing two episodes at a time, so that meant when the actors walked into the fitting, I wasn't just fitting one episode, I was fitting two episodes at the same time.

We would establish everybody's clothes in Oregon during the exterior shooting: we had four days of shooting there, every ten days. The first four days we would establish all the characters' key looks, shoot the exteriors in Oregon, travel back into LA and then film all the interiors in Los Angeles. So then six days of interiors, two episodes at once. There were fifteen to sixteen main characters, but then you had hundreds of background characters and probably another two- or three-dozen day players who just appeared in one episode at a time. Normally, what I would do is focus first on my top six characters. I would do the fitting either the day before the script read-through, where they would read two scripts at lunch, or I would do it the day after the read-through, or the day off. Those three days were kind of the sweet spot when the actors could be really focused. Then you had a space.

SP: Did you use that time because then the actors had their brain focused on the specific scenes and on the specific moments of that character? Would you grasp the opportunity that they had to focus mentally and then get their attention and also physically prepare them?

CKD: You start to figure out … certain performers are really good in the morning and certain ones are better at the end of the day, or with some of them you just have to deal with things during their lunch break. We were filming on a Paramount Studios lot, so the trailers are right there, so the actors are essentially captive for that twelve-hour shooting day and you can work it out with your assistant directors to make sure that you get them when you need them.

The first episode, the pilot is very dicey, because you try to figure out everyone's personalities, their preferences, how long they can tolerate being at a fitting. Some of the actors, like Holly Hunter – our fittings were five to six hours long, two episodes at a time. She is a unique performer [the likes of which] I have not met before. She is all about the text and the visual and she is hunting for the visceral response to the scene in the clothing and it is not clothing; it's like a veneer, whether she wants to *not* show what her character's motivations are or she *does* show them.

Figure 3.5.2 *Costume illustration by costume designer Chrisi Karvonides-Dushenko for Holly Hunter as 'Audrey Bayer' for the series* Here and Now *(HBO, 2018), Episode 110. Courtesy of Chrisi Karvonides-Dushenko.*

Figure 3.5.3 a-b *Costume- fitting photographs with actress Holly Hunter for the character of Audrey Bayer for HBO series* Here and Now *(2018), Episode 102 'scene 54, playing piano with Haley', taken by costume designer Chrisi Karvonides-Dushenko on location at Paramount Studios, Hollywood, CA. Courtesy of Chrisi Karvonides-Dushenko, with permission of Holly Hunter.*

She worked really hard to not be herself, she wanted [to be] softer; the silhouette was softer, ruffled, chiffon, sheer, the colours were totally different; she wanted florals but not to the point where it was chaos, but she played a mother who had four children and she was in education and they were fairly successful. So [the actress Hunter] would work through each and every scene, but you had to be very careful not to get her distracted and to stay focused and pull her back in.

I would start by doing tear sheets, I would get maybe one day where I could shop at all the department stores myself and do the sweep, pulling key items that my assistants go and pick up. On that show, I had three shoppers, other people who would shop for me … one shopper, my assistant costume designer would do the second big sweep, the overall arch of looking for coats, pants, or I would find blouses, pants, coats, scarves. I had another shopper who would deal with the underwear, the pantyhose, the right bra for everybody, which is always challenging. And then I had another one; that person would also take care of shoes. Because of this demanding shooting schedule, you needed to get complete outfits, because sometimes the costumes were stuck on a trailer for the three days travelling back to Los Angeles, so I needed doubles or it was raining up there, so I couldn't risk. I had to get a new pair of shoes for most of these outfits, because by the time I was done shooting with that outfit, the shoes were already destroyed from the rain up there … and so we had the doubles.

The other thing is that you want it to not be Los Angeles, so when I was in Oregon I kept shopping in the stores up there: What do women in Portland, Oregon buy – because I didn't want to buy things that don't exist up there, even though we were shooting in LA […]

I don't like doing all high-end [fashion], I like to keep it real by bringing things back in from Target or from H&M and I remind some of them, 'hey, if Michelle Obama buys her clothing at Target, we can all do

Figure 3.5.4 a-b *Costume- fitting photographs with actress Holly Hunter for the character of Audrey Bayer for HBO series* Here and Now *(2018), Episode 102 'family meeting and Indian dinner', taken by costume designer Chrisi Karvonides-Dushenko on location at Paramount Studios, Hollywood, CA. Courtesy of Chrisi Karvonides-Dushenko, with permission of Holly Hunter.*

that, too'. You know, it is more grounded in reality and we are not just some screen actor that has nothing to do with the viewers' reality.

SP: How do you start your design process? When do you start visualizing characters and how they may dress?
CKD: When I read the script, I think of it like a painting. There are key moments and I'll put a ticket at the top, a little sticker on the top [of the page]. If I have the whole family together, then it's the most important that I have got to figure out, that everybody has their own place on the colour wheel or the whole family ends up neutral and maybe Holly is in a primary [colour] … and everybody wants to wear black, but not everybody can wear black (laughs). So, you've got to figure out: who can I push over into grey, who could I push into the navy? You see, it is not a show that is all about black; it's a domestic [story] in a home! Then, there is all the colour in the background that you have to keep constantly remembering. Or, when you're outside in Oregon, there's so much green that I have got to pull back, I lose green most of the time, because of the green out there. For example, there was a picnic: I know the picnic is going to be in the grass, it is a long scene, they are most likely going to find a place where there is an umbrella of shade from the trees. So I now have all that green coming down; how can I make them … magic – that they kind of reflect that light? One of the actresses is African American and when she wears coral, it makes her skin glow. I wanted that [impression] but I didn't want her to be that bright when she was at her office before she ran to join the family for the picnic. So then we put something dark [on top], a jacket that was darker then she would take that off, tie it at her waist and then I would get the coral, so I got the particular light that sort of completed that composition.

And then Holly: I wanted somehow to have a blouse on her that picked up colours off her whole family, to make it feel like her pulling everybody back together, because the whole family was falling

Figure 3.5.5 *Watercolour rendering by costume designer Chrisi Karvonides-Dushenko of the picnic scene for* Here and Now *(HBO, 2018). The rendering depicts the actors dressed in their costumes and represents the designer's colour and pattern composition. Courtesy of Chrisi Karvonides-Dushenko.*

apart and she was like the cohesion, pulling it back together. So I found a blouse that was blue chiffon, that had coral, that had the lime green, it had all these bits [of colour] in it, sort of a peasant blouse. She loved it. It worked! (laughs) I was like, 'okay, here we go'.

So each time that I read the script, I try to figure out where my big scenes that are going to have the key composition are and how I can lead up to that composition. And then it's a new script day and some people end up sleeping at somebody's house, so they stay in those clothes, some people start the day fresh again … or I have one character, the son, who's very dour and getting really depressed; he is always in black, that's sort of a given. By keeping him in the black, I push everybody else into another palette.

SP: Do you have time to try things and do fittings? How is your collaboration with actors during the fitting?
CKD: When we do the fittings, we work really carefully with the actor to keep them focused on who their character is. There are times where there are certain actors where this does not happen. It's not always magical, there are times where it doesn't happen or they have issues with their body or their physicality, so I think ok, if we're not going to have that dialogue then fine … Some actors really don't want to process their look; for instance, one actor hates doing fittings, so we can just barely get through it. I can't even get him to change his pants, so we Photoshop the bottom half for the continuity photos and at least we get the shirts because the producers want to see what we are doing.

The whole time in the fitting, I feel like a ring master because there's myself, there's the tailor, my assistant costume designer is coming and going in the room and sometimes the speciality costumers, if they have to age things or paint something. It is a little bit crazy and you want to keep it really calm and not get them flustered. Then there is like a chaos … (laughs) … Wherever I go, I even have portable fittings, I try to have some kind of lights that help to light the space. [During fittings] I also prefer to take the photos with a good camera as opposed to my phone; there is something psychological, the performer starts to feel like they're back on camera on set. I always start taking the photos of them while talking about the key scene or the dialogue; I try to get them to channel their character as I take the pictures. It is very important for us when you do film or TV because what happens is, many times, I don't get that conversation with the director one-on-one, many times I have to email all of this information.

SP: How do you use the photographs that you take during a fitting?
CKD: I set up a PowerPoint presentation and we have a template. We have each episode: as I break down the script, my assistant edits the template and on the bottom of the PowerPoint she sets up for example – 'episode 102' – and she names it, 'Holly Hunter, picnic scene', 'Holly Hunter going to bed', 'Holly Hunter having an argument with her husband', 'Holly going to the gym'. So each slide is a blank slide with that text. Then as soon as I get the pictures from the fitting, we slam the pictures into those slides and then that goes off to the producers. What I try to do many times is to get the slides printed and I run to lunch and meet the producers as they break for lunch with the slides actually printed – it is too slow to do it on my phone, I've got to have it in my hand – and I say: 'So, how do you feel about this?' and 'do you think that this works?' You know they don't get a lunch break.

Figure 3.5.6 a-b *Costume-fitting photographs with actress Holly Hunter for the character of Audrey Bayer for HBO series* Here and Now *(2018), Episode 103, 'waiting for Greg', taken by costume designer Chrisi Karvonides-Dushenko on location at Paramount Studios, Hollywood, CA. Courtesy of Chrisi Karvonides-Dushenko with permission of Holly Hunter.*

SP: Would you like to say how you developed some other characters in this series?
CKD: The character who is the gamer: in life, he is a painter and he wanted to incorporate this into part of his clothing; for instance, he draws and paints on his clothes. My son does the same thing; he does video animation; [so I said,] 'do you want me to start incorporating these paintings in here?' and then his own paintings ended up as part of the scenic elements as well. So we had this chaos on his clothing as if he did it himself – you know how kids draw on their clothes when they sit in school and they are bored.

SP: Did you have time – this actually requires some collaboration, no? To get into that idea in advance and develop it before the actual shooting started, or did you work on this idea in-between all the other things? How do you deal with time?
CKD: This is all happening at the same time: you are loading two fifty-three foot trucks and shooting two, three locations a day and you're packing and then there was not enough time to take the principals' clothes. The trailer would travel to Oregon with what we needed for all the shooting up there, but it took three days for them to drive up there … so [sometimes the principals' clothes] flew with me.

There's the logistics of making this happen and the pace when you do TV, you know there is no time. I have one hour with each of these actors to come up with all of these ideas and then it has to be distributed.

SP: With whom do you collaborate the most, with whom do you share your ideas and design decisions?
CKD: In television, the writer/creator is the main producer; they are called 'show runners' and their clout is comparable to a film director's. So, just as usually your film director has the last word, your show runner on a TV show has the last say. However, with HBO we have a situation where they nurture the writers and

the process of writing and developing a script and help give them the leeway to create their vision. So they are intrinsic to the visual decision-making process. HBO has an incredible pool of directors who are very accomplished and established directors in the industry. When I was with Ryan Murphy on *American Horror Story* he had the first and final say on all visuals. Murphy was the show runner, writer and creator. [In *Here and Now*] the directors barely had the opportunity to have a conversation with the design teams. So all the collaboration was with our show runner, which was challenging. Yet I still go to the directors to give them an overview: 'This is what you can expect'. It is very different obviously from when you do opera, which is all about the collaboration with the director and the other members of the design team.

SP: To what extent do you actually collaborate with the TV team, do you have any time for creative meetings, is there any collaboration in advance, or does everything happen during the production?

CKD: The sweet time is the pre-production, especially when you do a pilot, because doing the TV pilot you are creating the character. The most rewarding [phase for a designer] is doing the pilot ... In the pilot there is a lot of collaborating; during that time, I often get to be part of the location scouting; so that means that all of us went to Oregon. We were together for breakfast, lunch and dinner in the vans. During that time, there are opportunities to discuss character and what is the motivation; why they want to do that story in Oregon; what is the charm. That is usually a week doing a location scout like that and there I also get to spend a lot of time with the production designer and get to be good friends with the assistant director because they help you with the logistics daily. It is very important that you have a very good relationship with the production designer and the cinematographer. Because you may prepare this whole scene, a huge scene and then nothing is shown, they don't film it ... it happens.

SP: Has this happened a lot to you – to do work that is not shown in the final cut – and if it happens, is it mainly because of improvements, let's say, on the narrative during editing?

CKD: It is true, it's all about the narrative. We actually had it happen on two very large scenes that we did. We did three hundred people in cosplay-comic attire for a convention. And then we had to double it, so that they were all in regular crazy clothing and then 150 of them had duplicates of the same outfit, totally covered in grey ash and in the end ... it got in the way of the story and you only see ten of them – but we had done 150 people. Identical outfits, huge costume outfits, all the t-shirts, everything – t-shirts, shoes, socks, pants, everything doubled, all the handbags, all the hats, you know the swag bags, everything covered in grey ash. But it was gone, just gone. It was so disappointing.

SP: What has your experience offered you? Has it improved your skills, for example in quick reading, or in having this kind of awareness of the whole? Designing costumes for television requires a brain that functions in multitasking all the time, being aware of finance, but also people's psychology and planning and where people are and what is happening concurrently, and so on. Do you rely more on experience, or do you think this also comes from your natural way of thinking things?

CKD: I am lucky. I am one of those people who is good at it. I have done television for so long, [this type of work involving] ten whole scripts every day. I get it, I read it and I've got it down to a system where I can make it happen ... I think it is a combination of both. I have done television for almost thirty years now. I love doing TV. But the one piece, the one secret piece is when I get the script: then everybody has to stay away. Because

I am also dyslexic – so reading has its challenges; but I love to read – I have to sit with the script. It is like a blank canvas and I need it to be. I will just go to some place quiet, but I need to take time for each scene. It is like, 'what do you see, what do you feel?' I want to get this visceral response. It's like when you start a painting you know and you look at the environment: is it just scenery with the trees and the ocean, or what do you feel from the light? That's what I want from the words. I read the words [in the script] and I try to feel it.

SP: You mentioned earlier about creating a space for the actors to focus. Were you referring to the space for the fitting? Or, were you referring to a kind of dressing room, let's say?
CKD: A space for the fitting. But there are plenty of times where I end up doing the fitting in a hotel room or in the trailer … Sometimes, I have been in a state park doing the fitting in the bathroom there. I mean, you just try to find a way to channel calmness and come up with the character and keep the actors to focus on character and to not have angst about their body, or the fact that they haven't acted in a while, or they didn't do their hair right or something … To just keep them focused on who this character is. It is really interesting, when I was working with opera singers, I would do the fitting the same way and we would take the photos and I would talk about the moment that they are singing in the scene or how they're going to dance. They all had, the first time we did it, this look of surprise. I don't think they had encountered that before (laughs). But, the more that I can show them [of the costume] in the context of the story, the easier it is to have a director see it coming and agree. If some actor is standing there and they look like they are really over it and they look bummed out, I am not going to get the approval; we are not going to get there. Also, we do have the luxury with television to fit a couple of extra things in case it doesn't work. We need to have options, so there is always a plan A, B and C. We do not really do that in opera.

SP: I am also interested in ethical issues and sensitivity, on how you work with actors in terms of collaboration; in terms of making them feel safe, creating some kind of creative environment, for them to find their way.
CKD: I think first, is that I am a mom (laughs). I have been at it for a long time. I am bossy as well, (laughs) but I think producers and directors will gravitate towards designers who meet those needs. I try to get to a place where even though there is chaos, the minute I walk into that space to do the fitting, all I need to focus on is this person standing in front of me. I have to turn everything off and just be one-on-one with this person. I do depend a lot on personal intuition and trying to take in what I can, about who they are or what is going on with them.

SP: Do you have any time to discuss your work with your colleagues? Tell us briefly whether you feel you work in a 'typical' manner with costume design, or if have your own mode of working?
CKD: I love it when we work at the studios, when we are at Warner Brothers or at Paramount because then we see how all our colleagues are working … I have a very different system from my colleagues. It's just as we discussed.

Section 4

Costume and the Body

4.1 The Body as the Matter of Costume: A Phenomenological Practice

Donatella Barbieri

Design and the Phenomenal Body

Proposing the notion of the designer's own 'mind-full' body as critical to a costume-practice-led methodology of performance-making, this chapter draws on movement and materials workshops that I have adopted and devised to expand costume practice, research and pedagogy since 2004. Such practices are considered via perception and the Merleau-Pontian philosophy of the body, thus framing costume here as phenomenological. While I have deployed parts of this research into the founding of the Costume Design for Performance[1] MA at London College of Fashion (LCF) in 2006, other workshops scrutinized here were devised for invited participants who were practitioners, researchers and educators. They form part of a long-term research aim to re-define costume as agent and instigator in making performance. Curriculum development and research into the agency of costume in performance are intertwined and are both initially informed by three research projects.[2] Firstly, the AHRB funded 'Designs for the Performer' exhibition (2002–05) questioned the established exclusion zones and hierarchies of traditional design practice. Secondly, the cross-institutional, international and devised production of *LES/Forest* (2005) proposed alternative processes to those of mainstream practice. Thirdly, my participation in the École internationale de théâtre Jacques Lecoq's *Laboratoire d'Étude du Mouvement* (L.E.M.) in 2005, saw a new emphasis upon the engagement of participants' bodily movement through material interaction. More crucially, these initiated an on-going practice of devising material-movement workshops as a radical departure from traditional designing that is the subject of this chapter.

The study of established costume-design practice through interviews with influential UK-based costume designers[3] made evident a process that added significant meaning to performance making. Via the in-depth analysis of a single production, each designer participating in 'Designs for the Performer' (2002–05) articulated how costume may shape the show. Their detailed agency in the development of numerous costumed bodies of large scale and impactful productions[4] was evidenced in this research project. However, hierarchical professional structures involving several specialisms, contractual responsibilities including producing sets of costume drawings well in advance, tight production schedules and stretched budgets precluded the open-ended indeterminacy that an experiential physical workshop entails. These highly efficient structures presume a semiotic approach (Pavis 2003) in which characters are represented through the fixing of 'signifiers' in costume drawing, rather than embodied through a process of movement, improvisation and material performativity in which space and one's own body are fundamental components. In these contexts, the demarcation line between moving bodies and costume-producing bodies is never breached.

The performers and artists I have associated with over a period of fifteen years to develop workshop-based research, some of whom I engage with here, are practitioners who regularly devise their practice through physical and material workshops, in fields including live art, contemporary dance, Butoh, *commedia dell'arte*, physical theatre, mime and dark clown. The L.E.M. pivotal to my research, (Barbieri 2006 and 2007) was conceived in 1968 by Jacques Lecoq (1921–99) while teaching somatic approaches to architecture at the École Nationale Supérieure d'Architecture de Paris La Villette – and one of his students, Krikor Belekian (Scheffler 2016: 180). I return to Lecoq later in this chapter, specifically to his 'neutral mask' improvisations, central to the École Jacques Lecoq approach.

Similarities with the L.E.M. exist with the costumes for *LES/Forest* (2005 – in collaboration with Jana Zbořilová, Czech theatre designer and Professor of Costume Design at the Academy of Performing Arts in Prague, Theatre Faculty, DAMU, her students, and a group of my BA Costume students from London College of Fashion), devised from temporal explorations of form, movement and materials. The design students' own bodies in movement in the early developmental stages of their designing, which included workshop sharings, shaped the design process. Only once prototypes had materialized, did performers and choreographers join in the process of creation of the forty-five-minute physical, non-verbal performance for the Disk Theatre, Prague. Created through motion, the costumes provided impetus for movement that went beyond character and narrative to produce a meaningfully engaging sensory experience for the viewer. Such design-led performance making, as in the expanded scenography described by Arnold Aronson, found itself 'at the centre of interactive networks' in which it was 'at once a tool, a system, a process and a generative organism for understanding' (2017: xvi).

Having started as a somatic approach for architects, the *Laboratoire d'Etude du Mouvement* (L.E.M.) has become an optional part of performer training on the relationship between movement and spatial dynamics at the École Jacques Lecoq. Adapted into physical design workshops as a means to generate a different approach to costume, it enables an understanding of the body in movement as a means through which to design in relation to form, material and space. Traditionally, the explorations offered by physical theatre workshops and laboratories are part of the continuous professional development of performers' versatility and not specifically developed for costume designers. This chapter exposes the value of adopting approaches such as the L.E.M. in a phenomenology of design, as these can be transformative of practice itself.

In *A History of the Theatre Laboratory* (2018), performance scholar Bryan Brown focuses on the Russian tradition, with significant laboratory (or workshop) practices established in the early twentieth century by Meyerhold ([1979] 2016) and Stanislavski ([1936] 2013). The latter's individual re-examinations of theatre-making, alongside its values and purpose, drove experimental approaches that also typify subsequent practitioners' own experiments 'in a space of labour where knowledge cannot be divided from the act of producing it' (Brown 2018: 6). The centrality of *doing* within the protected creative space of the workshop enables the investigation of alternative imaginings of performance and the 'development of theories and artistic techniques' (Brown 2018: 201) to which the responsive bodies of participants are critical. My research proposes a transformative and expanded practice of costume that considers one's own body in movement as fundamental, concrete, kinetic and affective material amongst materials.

The approach to the body that I adopt for this analysis can be understood through phenomenology. Initially expounded by Edmund Husserl (1859–1938), a contemporary of Meyerhold and Stanislavski, phenomenology questioned Descartes' (1596–1650) separation of mind and body which was at the core of much Western philosophy. The latter's privileging of the objective and detached mind, which surveys the world through representations such as semiotics and language, eschews a true material engagement based on physical and material interaction. In Husserl's phenomenology, human subjective experience is the grounds from which to develop understanding, while the lived body is the medium for perception (1999a: 227). Furthermore, his 'phenomenal' inter-subjectivity, 'the constitution in me of others' (1999b: 84) in which 'worlds' may be constituted between subjects (1999b: 85) is relevant to bodies considered as workshop participants not least because of the 'endless openness' it proposes (1999b:108), nurturing an embodied imagination that is arguably critical to design. The relationship between subjectivity and objectivity in design for performance practice is beyond the remit of this study. Let us note that, unlike an *a-priori* mapping of the production of traditional design practices, *subjectivity is foregrounded* in the physical plunging into the world. Therefore, a phenomenological frame of such workshops is required.

Maurice Merleau-Ponty's (1908–61) approach to phenomenology, while building on Husserl's articulation of 'the interconnection between mobility, action and conscious life' (Welton 1999: xi), was also informed by the effects on cognition of surviving soldiers who fought in the First World War, corresponding to Jacques Lecoq's physical re-habilitation of injured soldiers through movement following the Second World War (Foley Sherman 2016a: 63). Both went on to establish that knowledge is generated primarily through the perceiving body; Merleau-Ponty through phenomenology and Lecoq though performance. For Lecoq, the study of movement is meaningful beyond work with performers, as 'everything moves' which endows it 'with life, giving it authority' (2000: 187). Merleau-Ponty considers that 'the union of the soul and the body [...] is accomplished at each moment in the movement of existence' (1962: 102), specifying that '[i]t is never our *objective body* that we move, but our *phenomenal body*' (Merleau-Ponty 1962: 121, my emphasis). If the objective body is the grounding for a solely semiotic and Cartesian approach, it is the phenomenal perceiving body that must be foregrounded in the study of movement materialized in a devising through costume.

Intentionality, Material Agency and the Perceptive 'Flesh'

Experiencing is the source of action, prior to any rationalization as the phenomenal body's motivation for movement and action is not thought, but rather is a response 'to either a desire to achieve something or in response to something external' (King 2017: 33). For Lecoq, performance is 'embodied action and only subsequently language' (Evans and Kemp 2016: 3) as '[t]he body knows things about which the mind is ignorant' (Lecoq 2009: 8). Bodily perception precedes movement, thought and language, explained by Merleau-Ponty in terms of the pre-reflective intentionality that comes before the 'intentionality of act'. He writes, '[w]e found beneath the intentionality of acts [...] another kind which is the condition of the former's possibility: namely an operative intentionality already at work before any positing or any judgement' (1962: 498). Corey Anton explains that 'before – as well as underlying – any categorical thought [...] there is a playful, absorptive character to our understandings' (2001: 30). For Merleau-Ponty, engagement with this non-judgemental, playful and absorbing intentionality is central to artistic practice, as it is '"an art hidden in the depth of the human soul", one which, like any art, is known only in its results' (1962: 429).[5] Practitioners such as Will Schrimshaw apply an explicitly material phenomenology to reveal an artwork's operational workings through the responsive body, engaged via 'the material reality of immediate affective experience' (2017: 116). Theorizing around immersion, sound and contemporary art, Schrimshaw builds on Michel Henry's *Material Phenomenology* (2008) which draws attention to the potentiality of materials as 'purely sensuous, lived experiences that are subjective impressions', as matter 'gives itself to form in order to be informed, constituted and apprehended by it' (2008: 11). Such responsiveness of material reveals its agency and demands attention as the focus of interaction with the perceiving body.

While not directly exposing the agency of materials, in his unfinished, last publication *The Visible and the Invisible* (1968), Merleau-Ponty explores the phenomenon of perception as a two-way exchange between body and world, proving a foundation for later studies around material performativity[6]. Perception 'emerges in the recesses of a body' (1968: 9) and can be understood as 'flesh of the world', through which reversibility is at work between the perceiving and the perceived as 'things pass into us as well as we into the things' (1968: 123). Our 'flesh', or perception is in a reversible relationship with the tangible world, which is felt, seen and perceived through it:

> because my eyes which see, my hands which touch, can also be seen and touched, because, therefore, in this sense they see and touch the visible, the tangible, from within, because our flesh *lines* and *even envelops* all the visible and tangible things with which nevertheless it is surrounded, the world and I are within one another. (Merleau-Ponty 1968: 123, my emphasis)

James Mensch brings attention to Merleau-Ponty's use of the French word *tapisser* 'to cover, drape, line or wallpaper' (2012: 81–2) 'our flesh' and our perception. An intertwining of materials and the body through movement and perception can explain how our phenomenal body may be perceptually 'grasped' as it 'surge[s] towards' the perceived (Merleau-Ponty, 1962: 23) and 'it must plunge into the world instead of surveying it' (Merleau-Ponty, 1968: 38). Materials, in this relationship, have the power to expose states of being and emotions. Draping, immersing, surging and grasping; perception engages the physical imagination and dissolves the self into the space of its perception.

The Imaginative Body and Space of the Neutral Mask

> [i]f bodily space and external space form a practical system [...] it is clearly *in action that the spatiality of our body is brought into being* [...]. By considering the body in movement, we can see better how it

inhabits space (and, moreover, time) because *movement is not limited to submitting passively to space and time, it actively assumes them*. (Merleau-Ponty 117: 1962, my emphasis)

Alongside the body, essential elements of the physical theatre workshop (or laboratory), are movement, space and time, defined to separate from the everyday body and directly engage the phenomenal body. A Merleau-Pontian moving body actively *assumes* space and time as 'it is in action that the spatiality of our body is brought into being' (117: 1962). In Lecoq's 'neutral masks' workshop, the leather mask engenders in the wearer a state of receptiveness, thus enabling the embodiment of space and time through the performer's own physical imagination within the workshop context.

Unlike the L.E.M. – rarely practised and under-theorized optional aspect of the Lecop methods – the neutral mask is critical to École Jacques Lecoq actor training, widely practised and the subject of scholarly studies since the 1970s. Scholar and theatre-maker Laura Purcell-Gates (2017) defines neutral mask as a pedagogy, by connecting it to practitioners before and beyond Lecoq, while Jon Foley Sherman, one of a number of École graduates who have gone on to devise their own workshop practices, recently published phenomenological studies on the topic (2016a, 2016b). Lecoq's collaboration with sculptor Amleto Sartori in the 1950s enabled the devising of the leather, streamlined modernist mask. In *The Moving Body: Teaching Creative Theatre* (Lecoq 2002), the neutral mask is second only to exercises intended to 'delay the use of the spoken word' (2002: 36). If, 'beneath every mask […] there is a neutral mask supporting all the others', (2002: 38) then the material-neutral mask aligns itself with a pre-reflexive and pre-verbal state of being, as 'beneath the intentionality of acts […] another kind which is the condition of the former's possibility: namely an operative intentionality already at work before any positing or any judgement' (Merleau-Ponty, 1962: 498). Engaging what Lutterbie calls 'the mind-full body'[7] (2011: 56), the neutral mask extends 'a pure economy of movement' to the body in 'a sensual and physical relationship with the world and its matter' (Murray 2003).

Observing the Neutral Mask at Work[8]

The performer stands in the empty workshop space holding the neutral mask. Stilled, her gaze is on the eyes of the leather mask that she is holding in her hand. Reversibly, her face and that of the mask mirror each other; in the space between 'things and perceivers' involvement with each other […] the perspective is shared by both' (Foley Sherman 2016b: 63). The mask's skin-like surface may intensify a 'shared perspective' with the holder. The feel of the leather under her fingers may equate to her own bodily flesh in a perceptual exchange in which as 'things pass into us, we into things' (Merleau-Ponty 1968: 123). As the eye holes are rendered central to its minimalist surface, the mouth of the mask is open. If closed, 'it would act as a marker of separation and would suggest something the mask keeps apart from its environment' (Foley Sherman 2016a: 57). Evoking a temporary kinship with the holding body while breaching the separation from the world, body and mask together may then contain, in its entirety, the temporal arc of the exercise. The symbiosis with this permeable mask creates the condition for 'porous bodies taking on their environment' (Foley Sherman 2016a: 44) in an exploration of space that movement generates.

Having donned her mask and now supine, sleeping, she is invited to 'wake as if for the first time'. A series of initial encounters are verbally prompted by the workshop leader, including the embodiment of elements, materials and colours (Murray 2003: 75). She may then journey 'standing in the sea, across a beach, through a forest, up and down a mountain, across a stream and onto a plain' (Foley Sherman 2016a: 42). The invisible is rendered visible though body and space via displacement of the air that exists in-between, as the performer is prompted to move with words such as: 'I am facing the sea, watching it, breathing it. My breath moulds itself to the movement of the waves and gradually the picture shifts as I myself become the sea' (Lecoq 2002: 44). Breath, as air or wind is rendered gestural and material in a corporeal interaction that performs 'sea' bodily. Her breathing, moving body becomes scenography, charged with its own material substance, as 'bodily space and external space' are intertwined through movement.

The neutral mask's work changes from when held to when worn. A catalyst for an expanded, imaginative body while being held, its neutralizing of the face draws attention to the body in movement while worn. Having initially engaged the performer's touch, sight and perception – her 'flesh of the world'– in a reversible relationship, its role transforms in its wearing to supporting the assumption and creation of space through the body in movement. Sartori and Lecoq's discoveries that transformed physical theatre[9] continue to enable, sixty years on, what Foley Sherman calls non-reflexive astonishment (2010) in physical performers' workshops. To apply the principles of material performativity that have guided my own practice however, participants may start with pliable objects or raw matter. They may lend itself to matter 'in order to be informed, constituted and apprehended by it' (Henry 2008: 11) through their responsive bodily movement. As such, time, space and movement may be generated *between* materials and body.

Material Desires

As one of the participants in live artist Tim Spooner's two-day workshop 'A Hole in the Shape of Something'[10], I was part of a group who were able to explore how material performativity may be enacted. If the artist's own body is in a reversible relationship with materials, Spooner, who has designed costumes for Lea Anderson's *Ladies and Gentlemen*[11] and produced solo performances and art installations, asked the twelve participants, largely live artists and performers, to connect with the object or material's intention, while minimizing attention paid to the human in the interaction. As materials and objects had been placed on the stage of the Toynbee Studio Theatre in East London, Spooner's revealing of the liveness of materials, evident in his own practice found expression in individual extended exchanges between participants and objects. He asked how senses and emotions may be engaged through the feedback that participants received from matter and objects. We were not to conceptualize, just to be and do in a process that required trial and error, seeking the most economical way to express the material's intentions through its movement. The question was: what are the desires of the material?

Lecoq's materials in movement workshop perform a different function. Simon Murray notes the range of movement rhythms in the performers' 'becoming' or 'being' through materials in motion, including rubber, steel, glue and earth (Murray 2003: 75). Providing diametrical opposites in trajectories between states, the material behaviours invite an excessive use of body 'becoming' them, as materialization of movement does not, to quote Merleau-Ponty, submit 'passively to space and time', but rather assumes it (1962:117). The resulting improvised action has direct immediacyand as such, the assuming of material behaviour may generate emotional responses. For example, Lecoq notes how, when overstretched and then released, elastic materials are nostalgic for a return to their initial shape, even though they may not quite succeed (2002: 89). Crucial as they may be to Lecoq's physical practice, these imagined materials however, having communicated their desires which are then absorbed into the phenomenal moving body of the performer, disappear. Conversely, Tim Spooner minimized the attention on the body by entering into dialogue with the movement of materials, which themselves assume the Merleau-Pontian entanglement of space and time through movement, almost displacing the human while nonetheless evoking human emotions through their performance.

My practice considers the body as real, live, spatial, visible, tangible, kinetic and affective material amongst materials of the workshop, as such, it brings together both of these perspectives. In a transformative and expanded field of costume research, the aim is to embed specific material performative qualities through costume from the start, which may, in turn engage the body of the performer in movement and be equal partners in the performance. An empathic relationship with carefully selected elements is nurtured from the beginning in workshops, designed to be attentive to the behaviour of materials, while bodies are rendered phenomenal, mind-full or, to borrow Foley Sherman's term, porous. Workshops such as these are structured according to a number of tasks that progressively immerse participants into material embodiment through the act of doing.

Since participating in the L.E.M. in 2005, I have learnt by doing, by devising my own workshops, collaborating with movement practitioners or participating in their workshops. Following on from the blindfolded clay figure task intended to engage a material and phenomenal body, in the section below, I apply a phenomenological perspective to selected moments that provide examples of how a bodily exchange with materials exposes phenomenological practising.

The blindfolded clay modelling task which I borrowed from my participation in a second Complicite' interdisciplinary workshop 'Photography, Image and the Body'[12] (see Barbieri 2007) with photographers, performers and visual artists, introduced an immersive materiality through clay. Sitting around a large table, each participant was asked to don a blindfold. Thus, temporally blinded they made a figure of a body, a version of their body, from a lump of modelling clay that had been placed in their hands. The sensory feedback received from the clay guided the figures being shaped under their fingers as perception was channelled through touch. Upon shedding their blindfolds, the participants were often surprised by the unexpected human shape that greeted them. Expressive and unruly modellings populated the table, embodying a group of diverse participants made from the same clay.

Figure 4.1.1 *Clay figures made by participants in the 'Photography, Image and the Body' workshop while wearing a blindfold in September 2006. Photograph by the author.*

The blind handling of clay shapes the sense of a body other than the everyday one, a porous body, perceiving as much as being perceived through touch. If it established a body/clay relationship, *Moving/Drawing* (2007) (devised by me with movement director Lilo Baur and fine artist Charlotte Hodes and for which design students from across the University of the Arts London registered) addressed drawing as movement and vice-versa. One set of drawings was made around the 'bamboo pole task', intended to develop a sense of extended perception. Pairs of participants held a cane at one of its extremities, each applying pressure via the tip of their index finger so that it would be held up between them while in motion. Movement escalated and de-escalated through the level of pressure exerted by one or the other of the participants from their end, in turn stepping forward to direct it or being guided through turns and twists. Through such unstable tension, they held on to the cane while walking it along the floor or making it fly above head. The resulting improvised dance could be multiplied and entangled with each pair joining others. While each participant was pushing gently into their respective end of the cane through their index finger in order to keep it from dropping to the floor, the cane lost its objective status and began to be part of their extended 'scope and radius of touch' (Merleau-Ponty 1962: 165). And as it appeared to guide the movements of the connected participants' extended bodily perception,[13] their bodies may have felt to them at certain points, as tail extensions of the cane.

The latter was also demonstrated by a short experiment referring to Merleau-Ponty's experiencing of his own body:

> If I stand in front of my desk and lean on it with both my hands, only my hands are stressed, while the entire body trails behind them like the tail of a comet. It is not that I am unaware of the whereabouts of my shoulders or back, but these are simply swallowed up in the position of my hands, and my whole posture can be read so to speak, in the pressure they exert on the table. (Merleau-Ponty, 1962: 115)

Applying Merleau-Ponty's later articulation of reversibility, as he presses into it, the desk might be pressing back into his hands as his dynamic body becomes 'as an attitude directed towards existing or possible task' (1962: 114). Drawing activities following such an exercise can result in expressive and dynamic line work with regard to plasticity, exaggeration and energy.

Drawing and Movement into Design took place in 2008 at Eastbourne House Arts Centre, London. It was aimed at practitioners from a range of different disciplines and was advertised as a workshop run by myself and Marie-Gabrielle Rotie to explore the relations between drawing, movement and space. Butoh movement expert Rotie plunged the participants into two-metre squares of drafting papers, or 'skins' in a slow sub-merging and re-emerging of bodies through paper, while spaces, cocoons and monsters merged into one another and separated, as the paper, which had been used for drawing tasks by the participants, gradually disintegrated during what had appeared to be an evenly matched slow dance between bodies and paper. I have since used smaller squares of paper in a 'waking for the first time' exercise in which the paper then leads movement, as much as it is led by movement.These paper exercises help to materialize a Merleau-Pontian perceptive 'flesh', extended through sheet materials. Participants' heads are draped with a sheet of either fine white tissue paper which is animated by their breath, the beginning of a 'waking up' through a mirroring breath/material motion. The room then becomes filled by buoyant cloud-like paper being followed by bodies, until the fluttering is suddenly rendered still by the paper floating to the ground, ending the dance with the vitalized paper. In a 'doing' that does not immediately reveal its meanings, phenomenal bodies and material intertwine. Elemental materials such as sheets of paper, clay and bamboo sticks are used to awaken playful empathic exchanges with materials, to enact an equality between the performativity of bodies and matter in the confines of the workshop.

Figure 4.1.2 *Paper 'skins' in the 'Drawing and Movement into Design' workshop held at Trinity Laban Conservatoire of Music and Dance in August 2008. Photograph by Marie-Gabrielle Rotie.*

Rendering the Body Porous

To permit one's own body to become malleable matter requires a safeguarding through a preparatory warm-up that also anticipates a responsive physical imagination. Lilo Baur, during the warm-up for the 'Moving/Drawing' workshop in 2007 at LCF, applied a Feldenkrais[14] method focused on the anatomical body in which small, precise movements engaged the whole body and expanded bodily awareness. For example, a pair of workshop participants walked slowly together, one carried in their hands the weight of the other's head, letting go after a few minutes. After my partner released their hold of my head, I continued to feel lifted and light, while pointedly aware of my body as material and malleable. Here, much like Lecoq's intention to embed 'rich deposits' of embodied, physical knowledge in his students (2009: 46), a more than decade-old bodily sensing of lightness is recalled by its memory. In the chapter 'Awareness through Movement of The Elusive Obvious', Moshe Feldenkrais relates an ancient Chinese proverb 'I hear and forget. I see and remember. I do and understand' (1981: 89).

A heightened corporeal awareness was achieved in the 'Drawing and Movement into Design' (2008) workshop through Butoh movement led by Marie-Gabrielle Rotie. Chinese philosophy scholar

Pao-Yi Liao for whom the study of perception and Butoh explain one another, compares a 'merging with the universe' shared by many ancient philosophies from Asia, with a phenomenological '*transformation* both of the external object or space into a subjective field and of the *phenomenal body* into a thing-like object with the texture of materiality' (1999: 95, Liao's emphasis). The condition for Butoh's 'state of emptiness' through which such bodily 'encountering and transforming' may occur (1999: 61) is arrived at through an emptying of 'the aggressive ego of self' (Liao 2006: 113). A Butoh exercise described by Liao, also deployed in a variant form by Rotie in 'Drawing and Movement into Design' (2008), is 'Insect Biting'. From a standing position with bent knees, the participant slowly moves forward while imagining insects crawling from underneath the floor through her body. They are gradually eating away at her 'joints, the ears, the eyes, and hair' leaving only the skeleton. As they 'come out of the body, and fill the entire space, so as to make no difference between the inside and outside of the body', the insect 'functions in the same way as the lines or eyes, representing the relationship between the body and the environment' (1999: 218). Here, 'eyes' refers to an exercise previously discussed by Liao, 'Walking with Eyes', which invites participants to imaginatively place 'eyes' on different parts of the body, which can then push it into directions defined in relation to the space (1999: 216). By the same token, 'lines' also refers to the Butoh exercise simply entitled 'Walking', with the body imagining itself gradually separated into 500 sliding pieces being pulled in different directions by lines which 'spread within the whole space' and allow 'body and space to merge and become one' (1999: 215). For an expanded practice of costume that engages with embodiment, such merging of the body and space is instructive, as '[t]he Butoh costume is like throwing the cosmos onto one's shoulders. For Butoh, while the costume covers the body, it is the body that is the costume of the soul' (Hoffman and Holborn [1987] quoted in Barbieri, 2017: 28).

In 2007, the first year of the Costume MA at the London College of Fashion, Marie-Gabrielle Rotie's initial collaboration with student designer Kumiko Takeda,[15] who had participated in Butoh workshops in her native Japan, later extended to the movement direction of several of the performances produced with the students. While most of the coursework does not align itself to Butoh specifically, aspects of its practice continue to engage designers and collaborating performers. In the one-to-one physical workshops I currently organize with Peta Lily,[16] identification with costume as environment, or 'cosmos onto one's shoulders' in improvisations around its materiality remains one of the approaches to which we return, as Lily's movement direction, renowned for Dark Clown and Archetypal characters performers' workshops, draws on a wide range of schools of movement including Butoh's. The MA demonstrates bodily movement's connection with costume in the range of applications by its graduates, which, beyond costume design, include design-led experimental performance making, costume-led site-specific and site-responsive performance-making and costume as artistic practice.

My own costume-led collaboration with performer Mary Kate Connolly was also influenced by Butoh. In our 'Old Into New' performance (2011)[17] Connolly appeared to have been internally consumed by insects biting into the deep folds of her skirt pleats, that, once cut open by her from an initial bound and sculptural form, defined a dance in which different parts of her body led the transformation from elegantly contained to monstrously unruly states of being. An understanding of the body as material informed the 'Wearing Space' physical workshops for Prague Quadrennial of Performance Design and Space 2015 (Barbieri 2016). The warm-up devised with Connolly, the suddenly stilled, silent, shut-eyed, standing bodies of participants were calmly and verbally encouraged to consider their breathing as a letting-go of their everyday selves. In her warm-up, an awareness of the body from the inside, beginning to move just one bone at a time, in a sequence through which each joint could gradually be re-discovered, led to the eventual raising of one's own foot to take a first ever step with the body rendered, in Merleau-Pontian terms, phenomenal. Interdisciplinary groups of participants, including designers, performers, visual artists, professors and students became engaged in a pre-reflexive encountering of the world created within the workshop. We ran three full workshops and I was a participant in the first two, becoming a leader in the last, channelling Connolly's verbal qualities and scripted prompts, which she had allowed me to record previously. Once the first few very slow steps forward had been taken, participants were invited to gently open their eyes, which to this participant meant experiencing the familiar space anew. While this immersive warm-up shared aspects of the neutral mask's (waking for the first time), of Butoh's (the emptying of the everyday self) and of Feldenkrais (attention to anatomy and small but precise movements that effected the whole body), my physical memory was of a renewed consciousness around materials and objects we had placed neatly around the workshop space. In the process of rendering my body porous, receptive and mind-full in the creative process so as to be plunged into the potentialities of matter, I was aware of my body being matter that 'gives itself to form in order to be informed, constituted, and apprehended by it' (Henry 2008:11), thus rendered conversant with other matter such as the objects in the workshop space.

Extended, Material Perception

The L.E.M. (2005) introduced a way of moving through objects made during the two-week workshop by individual participants in an iterative process that oscillated between movement and fabrication (Barbieri 2006; and 2007). Materials used for the latter were elemental (e.g. corrugated cardboard, balsa wood, string, bamboo, paper) resulting in impermanent though timeless constructions and body-extending forms intended to direct its movement. These materializations of expanded movement enabled participants to experience their body as material, spacious and dynamic. Objects were mostly destroyed at the end of the L.E.M. as the drive was to embed deep deposits in the physical memory. Nor did the majority of movement objects survive Rotie's Butoh movement in 'Drawing and Movement into Design' (2008). For the latter, paper '"skins" and pre-made "body – extensions" [. . .] which further the boundaries of the body and articulate the space and physicality of the performer' (Henry 2008: 11) were made by me with the help of assistants in the weeks leading up to the workshop. Large paper skins, conical limb extensions, unfolding forms and large fan-like paper attachments were destroyed during the work with participants in a workshop beginning with Butoh's emptying of the ego exercises. As a participant, I moved through a pervasive sense of melting into the patch of floor designated by a paper skin, while invited to perceive by Rotie's recited poetry, lines of imaginary insects reaching inside my limbs. Equally, inter-subjective connection with the other participants, with whom I shared a similarly materialized and embodied experience remains potently vivid ten years on, as does the sound of scrunching and tearing paper filling the room alongside that of charcoal scratching on it. Performer and phenomenologist Suzan Kozel, in her chapter 'Process Phenomenology' in *Performance and Phenomenology* (Kozel, 2015), writes that:

> All reflection is past reflection, even if that event happened 10 seconds ago, and events from 10 years ago are not necessarily phenomenologically or experientially stale. This opens the suggestion that phenomenology relies on a sort of corporeal, experiential archiving. (2015: 57)

Kozel's corporeal archiving is aligned to Lecoq's deep deposits of bodily memory and Feldenkrais' understanding through doing and therefore remembering. Likewise, materiality holds on to gestural intentionality embedded in a physical/material memory through the reversible relationship with the perceiver encountered in the workshop. In the creation of objects prior to a workshop, even when these were ultimately destroyed, the relationship with the raw materials remains full of potentiality, holding memories of previously made objects or intent to create new ones. Such performative interaction persists in physical memories, fuelling further interdisciplinary material encounters.

Conclusion

While effective within the conventional production process, an approach to costume design that initially explains itself through a set of character drawings as a detached, external overview of a set of bodies may deny the creative force that is implicit to matter in movement, be it human or non-human. This chapter has proposed ways in which pre-reflexive phenomenal bodies, including the designer/performance-makers' own bodies, may be plunged into a process of discovery in an expanded practice of costume that is spatial, dynamic, malleable and discursive. Such porous practice can permit boundary transgression in instigating ways of working through costume while re-claiming the space of the rehearsal room as a design space, through an open-ended interaction with materials and wearable performative objects that we call 'costume'. A perceiving, responsive and transmitting body that reflects upon the on-going and constant change of human experience both inside and outside rehearsal rooms and making workshops is critical to the work that costume can 'do' and to defining costume's own agency before, during and beyond the performance.

Notes

1. Agnes Treplin has led the MA Costume at LCF since 2010.
2. See also 'Costume Re-Considered' (Barbieri 2012) and 'War, Revolution and Design' (Trimingham and Barbieri 2016).
3. The designers were Nicky Gillibrand, Pamela Howard, Birgitte Reiffenstuel, Elizabeth Jenyons, Emma Ryott, John Bright, Sandy Powell, Lucy Orta, Lez Brotherson and Marie-Jeanne Lecca.
4. Selected interviews were re-visited with the designers as part of the research process for *Costume in Performance: Materiality, Culture and the Body* (Barbieri 2017: 193–211).

5 Merleau-Ponty is citing Immanuel Kant's *Critique of Pure Reason* (1999) in which he concludes that only with difficulty may we understand how impact is built into artworks.
6 See for example Joslin McKinney (2015).
7 He is referring to philosopher of dance Maxine Sheets-Johnstone's definition, which she preferred to the expression 'embodied mind'. See 'Embodied Minds or Mindful Bodies? A Question of Fundamental, Inherently Inter-related Aspects of Animation' (2011).
8 Observations drawn from witnessing of the mask at work in 2005 as part of the L.E.M., cross-referenced against Lecoq's (2002), Murray's (2003) as well as Foley Sherman's writing on the subject (2010, 2016a and 2016b).
9 On the re-discovery of leather in relation to L.E.M. and to the Victorian clown see 'Performativity and the Historical Body' (Barbieri 2013). On the grotesque see Chapter 3 in 'Costume in Performance' (Barbieri 2017).
10 'Arts Admin's Weekender Lab: A Whole in the Shape of Something, by Tim Spooner'. See https://www.artsadmin.co.uk/events/4102 (accessed: 3 February 2019).
11 Anderson has discussed how costume enabled her to establish rules in her own performances, (Connolly 2017) as she collaborates with highly influential costume designers, such as multiple Oscar winner Sandy Powell and live artists including Simon Vincenzi and Tim Spooner.
12 On this workshop see Barbieri (2007: 7–9). It was organized by Natasha Freedman, Complicite's then education and marketing director, photographer Sarah Ainslie and movement director Lilo Baur.
13 On the notion of cognition and scenographic practice, see Melissa Trimingham (2017).
14 Moshe Feldenkrais was a scientist and an engineer who established therapeutic movement methods that promoted awareness of the whole body (Feldenkrais 1981).
15 Takeda's performance (2007) drew from Oscar Wilde's *Salomé*. While the costume was designed along Butoh lines, the performer was a capoeira specialist working with Butoh movement and ideas.
16 See http://www.petalily.com/workshops.html (accessed: 3 February 2019).
17 Devised for Prague Quadrennial 11, 'Extreme Costume Talks', Prague and the UK exhibition opening performance also at PQ11. Movement by Mary Kate Connolly, performance concept and costume design by Donatella Barbieri, realized with Claire Christie and assisted by Emily Ni Brohim. Funded by Prague Quadrennial and London College of Fashion: University of the Arts London, supported by Simona Rybáková and the Society of British Theatre Designers. See http://ualresearchonline.arts.ac.uk/4967/ (accessed: 3 February 2019).

References

Anton, C. (2001), *Selfhood and Authenticity*. New York: SUNY Press.

Aronson, A. (2017), 'Forward', in McKinney, J. and S. Palmer (eds), 2017. *Scenography Expanded: An Introduction to Contemporary Performance Design*, xiii–xvi. London and New York: Bloomsbury Academic.

Barbieri, D. (2006), 'An Exploration of the Application of the Laboratoire'. *Costume Symposium 2006: Academic Research Papers*. Bournemouth: The Arts Institute at Bournemouth.

Barbieri, D. (2007), 'Proposing an Interdisciplinary, Movement-Based Approach to Teaching and Learning as Applied to Design for Performance-related Areas'. In *Prague Quadrennial 2007,*

Prague, 14-24 June, 2007. London: London College of Fashion. Available from: http://ualresearchonline.arts.ac.uk/1755/ (accessed: 2 April 2019).
Barbieri, D. (2012), 'Costume Re-Considered'. *Endymatologika 4*, 'Endyesthai (To Dress): Historical, Sociological and Methodological Approaches, Conference Proceedings'. Athens: Peloponnesian Folklore Foundation.
Barbieri, D. (2013), 'Performativity and the Historical Body: Detecting Performance Through the Archived Costume', *Studies in Theatre and Performance* 33 (3): 281–301.
Barbieri, D. (2016), 'Costume Before and Beyond the Production: The Spacelab Costume Workshops at Prague Quadrennial, 18-28, June 2015', *Studies in Costume & Performance* 1 (2): 199–207.
Barbieri, D. (2017), *Costume in Performance: Materiality, Culture and the Body*. London and New York: Bloomsbury Academic.
Brown, B. (2018), *A History of the Theatre Laboratory*. London and New York: Routledge.
Camilleri, F. (2013), 'Between Laboratory and Institution: Practice as Research in No-Man's Land'. *TDR/The Drama Review* 57 (1): 152–66.
Connolly, M. K. (2017), 'Hand in Glove: Reflections on a Performed Costume Exhibition and the Stories behind the Garments', *Studies in Costume & Performance* 2 (1): 9–25.
Evans, M. and R. Kemp eds (2016), *The Routledge Companion to Jacques Lecoq*. London and New York: Routledge.
Feldenkrais, M. (1981), *The Elusive Obvious*. Capitola, CA: Meta Publications.
Foley Sherman, J. (2010), 'The Practice of Astonishment: Devising, Phenomenology and Jacques Lecoq', *Theatre Topics* 20 (2): 89–99.
Foley Sherman, J. (2016a), *A Strange Proximity: Stage Presence, Failure, and the Ethics of Attention*. London and New York: Routledge.
Foley Sherman, J. (2016b), *Space and Mimesis*, in M. Evans and R. Kemp, (eds), *The Routledge Companion to Jacques Lecoq*, 83–90. London and New York: Routledge.
Fraleigh, S. H. (1999), *Dancing into Darkness: Butoh, Zen, and Japan*. Pittsburgh: University of Pittsburgh Press.
Henry, M. (2008), *Material Phenomenology*, trans. S. Davidson. New York: Fordham University Press.
Husserl, E. (1999a), *The Essential Husserl: Basic Writings in Transcendental Phenomenology*. Bloomington, IN: Indiana University Press.
Husserl, E. (1999b), *Cartesian Meditations*, trans. D. Cairns. Dordrecht/ Boston/London: Kluwer Academic Publishers.
Kant, I. (1999), *Critique of Pure Reason*, trans. & eds. P. Guyer and A. W. Wood. Cambridge: Cambridge University Press.
Kemp, R. (2012), *Embodied Acting: What Neuroscience Tells Us About Performance*. London and New York: Routledge.
King, I. (2017), *The Aesthetics of Dress*. New York: Springer.
Kozel, S. (2015), 'Process Phenomenology', in M. Bleeker, J. Foley Sherman and E. Nedelkopoulou (eds), *Performance and Phenomenology: Traditions and Transformations*, 54–74. London and New York: Routledge.
Lecoq, J. (2009), *The Moving Body (Le Corps poétique): Teaching Creative Theatre*, trans. D. Bradby. London and New York: Bloomsbury Academic.
Liao, P. Y. (2006), 'An Inquiry into the Creative Process of Butoh: With Reference to the Implications of Eastern and Western Significances', doctoral dissertation, Trinity Laban Conservatoire of Music and Dance, City University, London.

Lutterbie, J. (2011), *Towards a General Theory of Acting:Cognitive Science and Performance*. New York: Palgrave Macmillan.

McKinney, J. E. (2015), 'Vibrant Materials: The Agency of Things in the Context of Scenography', in M. Bleeker, J. Foley Sherman and E. Nedelkopoulou (eds), *Performance and Phenomenology: Traditions and Transformations*, 121–39. London and New York: Routledge.

Mensch, J. R. (2012), *Ethics and Selfhood: Alterity and the Phenomenology of Obligation*. New York: SUNY Press.

Merleau-Ponty, M. (1962), *Phenomenology of Perception*, trans. Colin Smith. London: Routledge.

Merleau-Ponty, M. (1968), *The Visible and the Invisible*, Followed by *Working Notes* (1964), trans. Alphonso Lingis. Northwestern University Studies in Phenomenology and Existential Philosophy, Evanston, IL: Northwestern University.

Meyerhold, V. ([1979], 2016), *Meyerhold on Theatre*, E. Braun (ed. and trans.). London: Methuen Drama.

Murray, S. (2003), *Jacques Lecoq*. London: Routledge.

Pavis, P. (2003), *Analyzing Performance: Theater, Dance and Film*. Ann Arbor: University of Michigan Pres.

Purcell-Gates, L. (2017), 'Puppet Bodies: Reflections and Revisions of Marionette Movement Theories in Philippe Gaulier's Neutral Mask Pedagogy', *Theatre, Dance and Performance Training* (1): 46–60.

Scheffler, I. (2016), 'A Brief History of the L.E.M', in M. Evans and R. Kemp (eds), *The Routledge Companion to Jacques Lecoq*, 179–92. London and New York: Routledge.

Sheets-Johnstone, M. (2011), 'Embodied Minds or Mindful Bodies?: A Question of Fundamental, Inherently Inter-related Aspects of Animation', *Subjectivity* 4 (4): 451–66.

Shrimshaw, W. (2017), *Immanence and Immersion: On the Acoustic Condition in Contemporary Art*. New York and London: Bloomsbury Academic.

Stanislavski, C. ([1936] 2013), *An Actor Prepares*. Edinburgh: A&C Black.

Trimingham, M. (2017), 'Ecologies of Autism: Vibrant Spaces in Imagining Autism', in J. McKinney and S. Palmer (eds), *Scenography Expanded*, 183–96. London and New York: Methuen Drama.

Trimingham, M. and D. Barbieri (2016), 'War, Revolution and Design: Exploring Pedagogy, Practice-based Research and Costume for Performance through the Russian Avant-garde Theatre', *Studies in Theatre and Performance* 36 (3): 269–80.

Welton, D. (1999), 'Introduction: The Development of Husserl's Phenomenology' in *The Essential Husserl: Basic Writings in Transcendental Phenomenology*. Bloomington, IN: Indiana University Press.

4.2 The Body as Site: Interdisciplinary Approaches to Dress in/as Performance

Jessica Bugg

Introduction

Very little has been written on the lived experience of dress in contemporary dance, where its relationship to the body is particularly active, not only because of its aesthetic symbolism, but also its physical, kinesthetic, experiential and bodily engagement in movement. It is the opportunity afforded at this interface and the embodied potential of dress in and as communication that I address here. As Andrea Eckersley explains, the effects of art works or in this case, garments are 'transmitted' both 'in and through the art, in the viewer's body' (Eckersley 2017:180). But more than this, dress as bodily practice in the context of performance is affective, resonant and transformative. It is felt, embodied and re-embodied by those that wear, view, design and make it in both its production and reception.

The expanded role of costume in performance has developed significantly over the past decade, supported by a growth of research into the agency of costume, most notably in the UK, Finland and Australia. Nevertheless, dress in dance remains relatively underexplored in publications on performance, with a few notable exceptions: Carter and Fensham (2011); Barbieri (2012 and 2017); Anderson and Pantouvaki (2014); Helve and Pantouvaki (2016); Trimingham (2011); Bugg (2014; and 2016) and Mackrell (1997). Outlets for discussing costume research have also developed through conferences such as 'Critical Costume' and the inception of the Intellect journal *Studies in Costume and Performance*, founded in 2016 by Donatella Barbieri, Sofia Pantouvaki and Kate Dorney. These platforms and the new research coming out of PhD studies in related areas points to the significant potential of further practice-oriented research to continue expanding the emerging field.

This chapter reflects on the development of interdisciplinary, embodied and performative methods in my own practice-based research that have enabled inter-connected approaches to design and communication. I have been particularly interested in activating the lived experience of dress as a tool in the development of body-sited concepts and movement and exploring the performative dynamic between designers, wearers and viewers. Here, I summarize these methods that have involved thinking, practising and researching in the active site of the body to understand the lived experience of dress both *in* and *as* performance.

Interdisciplinary Methods to Understand the Bodily Experience of Dress

Yuniya Kawamura discusses the methodological dominance in fashion and dress research by cultural studies scholars and social scientists and the relative lack of anthropological methods used today, particularly in connection to practice-oriented research (Kawamura 2011). This, Kawamura suggests, is unhelpful and can negate the cross-disciplinary methodological investigation that is essential to the study of dress and its corporeal significance, particularly in performance. She (2011:13) affirms that 'we can regard fashion/dress studies as an interdisciplinary area of knowledge' that has only come into being, precisely because of 'theories and research findings that cross traditional boundaries' and the subsequent merging of 'multiple, different methodological strategies.' In practice-oriented research there is arguably even more need to engage multi-methods to effectively navigate the study of dress production and consumption. Dress functions across disciplines and in all cases in its direct relationship to the body. In the multi-sensory experience of performance, dress is mediated in and through human activity. To understand such relational aspects, particularly in performance it is necessary to ask both ontological and epistemological questions, to uncover tacit knowledge and lived experience and to locate this within theoretical, psychological and sociological frameworks. Such a complex and dynamic research area therefore demands a challenging mix of research methods and an openness to different fields and disciplines.

The methods I use within my current research grew out of my PhD (Bugg 2006), which sought to unpack the experiences of wearers and viewers of conceptually informed dress in communication. The scope of the research traversed fashion, art and performance and began in an increasingly transdisciplinary climate in the late 1990s and early 2000s. Dress and fashion research methods at this point were situated largely in social sciences or cultural and historical studies frameworks and it was necessary for me to navigate this methodological lineage alongside the central role of practice in my research. Much of the study involved the development of methods and ultimately a methodology through which I could garner knowledge through practice and between disciplines. I reflect here on the development of these embodied methods through the production of dress-centred performance and dance films.

Practice-related research approaches to fashion and design were nascent at that time and there was still a tendency to perceive the pure sciences and social sciences as superior, offering perhaps more objective methods and measurable research outcomes. From the 1990s and into the early twenty-first century things were changing and as Baz Kershaw et al. (2010: 63) recall, this thinking was beginning to filter into various disciplines, particularly within fine art, design and performance (ibid). It was an exciting, but uncertain time for developing understanding of approaches for practice as research (PaR) and this new thinking enabled the development of methods that afforded enquiry and knowledge about the lived experience from the practitioner's perspective (Kershaw et al. 2010: 63). These 'fresh methods of melding art and scholarship' and the emerging definitions of practice-based or practice-led research focused on a 'post-binary commitment to activity (rather than structure), process (rather than fixity), action (rather than representation), collectiveness (rather than individualism) and reflexivity (rather than self-consciousness)' (Kershaw et al. 2010: 64–5). Such approaches challenged the dominant methodologies in science, social science and cultural studies, which were generally less concerned with process. It was in this shifting terrain that I began to interrogate and situate my developing methods, to enable the exploration of the body and dress in a range of contexts through multi-modal approaches.

My experimental practice challenged a purely semiotic reading of dress, moving towards an understanding of its experience and the complex relationship between designer, wearer and viewer of concept-led clothing design. The research started in a practice-based mode where knowledge was created partly through the practice itself. It increasingly became practice-led with creative artefacts, becoming tools through which I could engage with the lived experience of wearers and viewers in a range of contexts and understand the nature of my own and others' practice. The research questions responded to a developing hypothesis that alternative and cross-disciplinary approaches were emerging in 'experimental fashion' design that were concept- and context-led, as opposed to being solely driven by aesthetics, consumption and trends. Research questions broadly addressed the relationship between the body and dress in a range of performative contexts seeking to understand the role of designers, wearers and viewers in the constructions of meaning.

The interdisciplinary and bodily nature of my study obliged me to draw on methods from performance, fashion, dress studies and art, as well as social science and psychology in relation to scholarly writing on the body to critically position and explore my work in that context. In this process, my own embodied knowledge of practice and experience of dress was 'brought to bear on other forms of knowledge' (Kershaw et al. 2010: 121) that in turn led to new understandings of practice, experience and methods. The multi-method designed throughout my PhD research (Figure 4.2.1) employed an ongoing dialogue and ultimately a seamless integration of theory and practice, where theory fed into practice and practice generated both data and theory. This research informed the theoretical framework, the focus of interviews with leading contemporary practitioners working in related contexts with clothing as communication, and likewise the semi-structured interviews with wearers and audiences.

Methods of analysis developed and tested in the early stages of the research were formalized in three practice case studies and two live practice applications. The case study approach enabled me to be objective and to organize the large quantity of work generated, as well as draw out a focused analysis of the 'how' and 'why' questions (Yin 2003: 1) that were emerging. This enabled me to observe and reflect on practice, to analyse live situations both during and after the fact, to study interaction between people and their surroundings and to observe and analyse the experiences, feelings and behaviours of participants in context. Each case followed a fixed structure that defined the boundaries in relation to both the research questions, interviews and findings from the previous case. Typically, individual case studies focus on a very specific and singular activity (Denscombe 2003: 30). Here however, they explored a range of complex and interrelated factors reflecting the nature of the research.

Garments were designed to communicate concepts or behaviours and sought to test ideas and uncover knowledge of their affect and perception in a range of disciplinary contexts and scenarios on differently trained wearers' bodies. In this way, I reflected on the role of my own practice within the

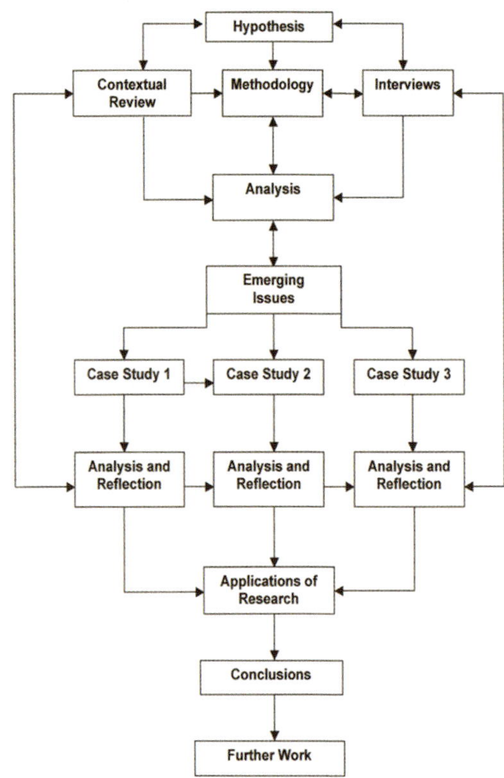

Figure 4.2.1 *Jessica Bugg, research design and multi-method methodology, 2006.*

broader research. Through reflection both in and on my practice, as heralded by Donald Schön (who from the 1960s worked across reflective practice and organizational learning) (1991) I could observe, reflect and analyse my practice and the affect and perceptions of other participants. This enabled me to combine 'creative doing with reflexive being' (Kershaw 2010: 64) and this was controlled through the careful development of different types of data retrieval formats that served as a structure throughout the research. Each scenario within each case study was recorded by video or photography and reflective notes were taken. Wearers were asked to improvise in response to wearing the garments, in particular performative contexts, and at no stage were any of the participants informed of the design concepts and intentions of the research.

All respondents were asked the same standard questions and the responses were recorded for each individual garment in each context. This included design data, context data and details of wearers' and viewers' backgrounds/training. It also documented the wearers' behavioural, perceptual and emotional responses to the design concept and experience of wearing in the context/location. This enabled comparative and content analysis between each garment in each of the contexts and subsequently all the findings were synthesized into the case study conclusions. These were then drawn into a matrix designed to record a summary of responses from wearers and viewers in each scenario. This led to a model of the interactive and performative relationship between participants and the impact of dress in a range of contexts and on differently trained bodies.

Developing Methods, Dress and Performance in the Site of the Body

In my recent work, I have focused on the relationship between dress and the moving body to develop understandings of dress in performance, particularly in contemporary dance. Dress in dance has tended to be restricted by its primary focus on ease of movement, as opposed to engaging with the wider phenomenological experience of dress in performance. The research responds to the fact that dress often plays a supporting role to the choreography, as opposed to being active within its development. I have established embodied methods that extend design and performance through an embodied understanding of the dressed body in performance. Deep practical engagement with the dressed body as a creative site led to integrated approaches to design, movement and communication. Knowledge has been derived from the lived and experiential aspects of dress, informing its expanded potential and developed agency in performance through design. Such approaches also seek to enable designers, wearers and viewers to achieve greater agency in the development of performance and aim to extend communication through dress both in and as performance.

I tend not to classify my work as 'costume', perhaps because I originally trained in fashion design and maybe because it can imply theatricality, covering or changing an individual's identity or the process of locating a wearer in place and time. The term 'clothing', whilst not as loaded, imbues a utilitarian functionality as something that is separate or applied to the body. This is at odds with my practice, which concerns the interactive embodied and sensory aspects of dress in movement and through experience, where the body and dress can become inseparable, or where dress can 'alter the body itself' (Eicher et al. 2008: 6). The word 'dress' in this sense, as Kawamura suggests (2011: 10), provides not only 'dress items and practice', but also 'the relationship of this form to the body'. This offers a more active, bodily understanding of the materials and communication produced in my practice and research. Here I use the words clothing and dress, as appropriate to the context of the discussion. My interest in dress in dance extends beyond ergonomic or aesthetic approaches, focusing on a more 'mindful body that acts and resists' (Johnson and Foster 2007: 115) in its complex relationship to dress through lived corporeal and temporal experience and embodied design and performance approaches.

The methodologies developed are specifically designed to further investigate and extend knowledge of the communication between bodies that design, wear and view dress in performative contexts. I examine the means through which design approaches across disciplines can be re-thought in the context of the body and how practical and theoretical approaches to embodied clothing design and communication can be extended through cross-disciplinary dialogue and analysis. My work aims to demonstrate how the agency of dress could be more active in the making and reception of contemporary dance in live performance, dance, film and curatorial

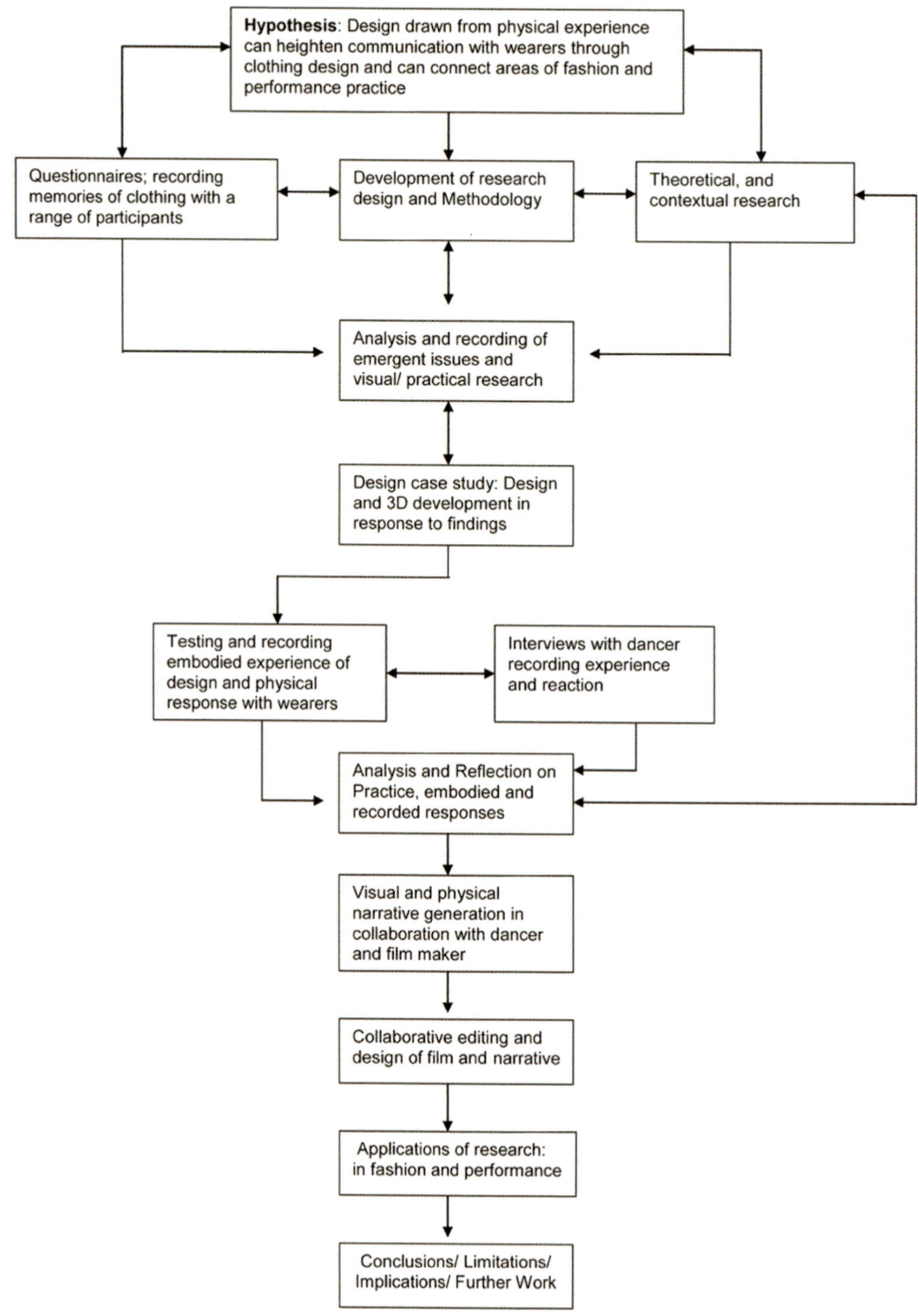

Figure 4.2.2 *Jessica Bugg, methodology for the* Emotion Collection *(2012).*

contexts. Functioning in a phenomenological framework the research seeks to understand the lived experience of dress in performance, employing a practice-led and grounded theory approach that does not start with a 'pre-conceived theory in mind', (Strauss and Corbin 1998: 12) but rather with a broader field of investigation.

Data collection is generated throughout the design process and is documented in the form of video footage and images that record practice and semi-structured interviews with all participants, as well as material and theoretical research, observational analysis and case-study design. An iterative dialogue is afforded between the lived experience of designers, performers and viewers through practice that is in conversation with ongoing theoretical research in areas such as cognitive science, psychology, embodiment, memory, kinetic, haptic and sensory perception and phenomenology. In my processes, image, form and the material properties of dress are inextricably bound up with lived bodily experience. The research demonstrates how this can be activated as an integral part of developing performance, enabling deeper ideation and reflection in practice for all participants involved. This deeper engagement with the bodily experience of dress leverages cognitive, physical, psychological, sensorial and embodied understandings of the subject and can extend the performance itself.

Embodied Design Methods in and through Practice Research

Here I reflect upon three of my more recent practice-led research projects as case studies to articulate and demonstrate my current methods in context. Each project has evolved a nuanced methodology that enables an analysis of the particular research questions and each is informed by the findings of the previous project.

The *Emotion Collection* project (2012) proposed that design drawn from the physical experience and memory of clothing could heighten communication with wearers and viewers through design and connect areas of fashion and performance practice. Here, I aimed to extend an analysis of the relationship between garment design for performance and experimental fashion. I worked to expose a hybrid area of practice emerging between the two disciplines in respect to both design methods and communicational strategies, to understand and extend the potential for using emotional and physical triggers in garment design to communicate with wearers and viewers in contemporary performance contexts. All of this had the more general effect of questioning the role of narrative in dress and performance.

The designs generated and tested here were informed by a series of interviews that sought to uncover lived experience and memories of dress, leading to the design of a dress-centred performance. This work was inspired by a chance encounter with a discarded shoe, within which a personal and embodied narrative was inscribed. For me, this written narrative had a resonance in its relationship to the impressions left of the body that had worn the shoe and in turn instigated an exploration of embodied narratives in dress. A diverse range of participants were interviewed about their memories and emotions connected to dress and this sample was drawn from a call on social media. The semi-structured approach to interviews enabled emerging knowledge to be unpacked through the course of an interview. The questions were drawn from emergent themes in my previous research and were informed by theoretical research into emotion, memory and dress. Stories of wearing dress and associated memories were analysed through discussion and in some cases photographs, or material examples of particular garments. Interview participants talked about the sensory aspects of wearing, re-calling textures, smells, colours and the way garments felt on the body, describing the associations, feelings and memories evoked (Bugg 2014: 44). This information was then analysed through content analysis that enabled the identification of shared or connected experiences and memories in relation to wearing. Two performative garments were developed from these narratives and design inspiration was derived and deconstructed from the information gleaned.

The garments were tested and explored with a dancer who devised a response to wearing them while moving (Figure 4.2.3). The dancer's experience and interpretation was captured on film and through an interview following each experimental workshop. Analysis of this 'experiential' data, in turn, informed the creative direction and development of the performance and the shooting and editing of two short films, produced in collaboration with the dancer and a filmmaker. The films focused on the sensory and emotional bodily narratives leveraged between body and dress, seeking to form a dialogue between the clothing, 'performing' body and the viewer by visually and physically suggesting narrative and tapping into the sensory, visual, experiential and collective memory of dress. This work placed costume at the centre of the production process, rather than as

Figure 4.2.3 *Jessica Bugg, the* Emotion Collection: *Black Point Dress (2012) © Marc Craig photographer.*

an applied element and enabled the designer to utilize the embodied experience of dress in both the generation of performance and the art direction of the films. The narrative of both the design and the subsequent films were non-linear, non-specific and deconstructed from the lived experience of interview participants and the dancer, aiming to engage viewers in a dialogue with dress and the body through the potential of shared experiences.

This project started to reveal how design drawn from physical experience could heighten communication through what I was coming to understand as embodied design methodologies. The methodology developed through this research (Figure 4.2.2) enabled me to demonstrate how dress could become 'central to the conceptualization, development and communication process', as opposed to being applied to a communication or performance. This led me to understand that dress could be much more than an applied visual element in dance as a 'generator of performance through design' (Bugg 2014: 46).

Within this work, the body is understood in an holistic sense where the mind is embodied and the body is a lived, experienced and socially connected entity; it is also a creative site and a method for working with materials and modes of communication. Dress is understood as both a tool for the body in performance and as an extension and inseparable part of the body through the lived experience of wearers and viewers in and through movement. My work has demonstrated that the materiality and form of dress resonates visually, physically, cognitively, sensorially and emotionally in the site of the body and between bodies in performance (Bugg 2016:169–93). In conclusion, my approach to design and performance generation, here, is one of thinking and making 'through the body' and dress, as opposed to 'for the body' and the body itself is understood as a creative, active and interactive site.

Drawing with the Body and Cloth

In a subsequent project, *Drawing with the Body and Cloth* (Bugg 2013), I worked with a dancer to develop design and movement in response to the painting *A Detail from The Tempest* by Peder Balke, painted in approximately 1862. We worked in experimental laboratory situations in the National Gallery London, developing a specific methodology in and for the site of the body, that of the designer and performer (Figure 4.2.4). Drawing was used as a theoretical frame and tool to connect the designer and dancer's creative processes and enable the development of garment design and movement as a fully integrated and iterative practice. This three-dimensional temporal drawing process working with and experiencing the resonance of body and cloth moved on from the suggested narratives or intentions incorporated into the garments that had been explored in the *Emotion Collection*. I aimed to extend methods for developing clothing centred performance; to develop an integrated approach to clothing design in contemporary dance and to explore the connectivity between embodied design and drawing methodologies and practice.

I was inspired by Maxine Sheets-Johnstone's perspective (2009: 30) that 'thinking in movement' is 'the incarnation of creativity as process' where no 'artistic product exists in advance or in arrears'. In other words, form and movement were developed simultaneously in the project in real time through the exploration of the designer and dancer's lived and bodily experience (Figure 4.2.5).

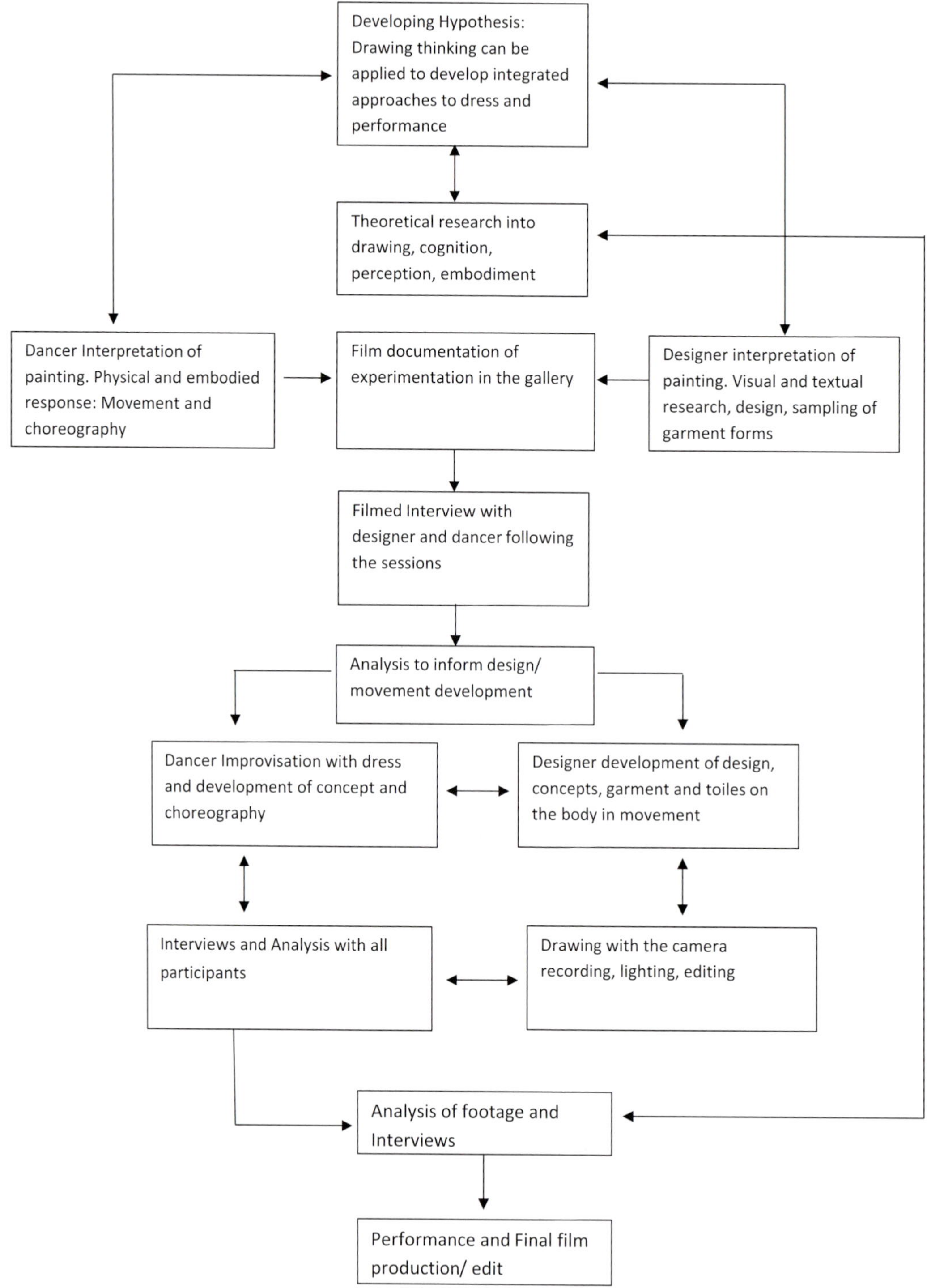

Figure 4.2.4 *Jessica Bugg, methodology for* Drawing with the Body and Cloth *(2013).*

Figure 4.2.5 *Jessica Bugg,* Drawing with the Body and Cloth: Grey Waves *(2013) © Roy Shakespeare photographer.*

This methodology enabled both to share in a dialogue in the form of words, movements, materials and forms within the creative process, integrating the sensory, experiential perception, cognitive and physical responses of both participants. This approach aimed to eradicate the distinction between material form, the body and movement within the creative process. Here, the act of sketching was both a thinking and practical process that in the words of Tim Ingold (2013: 108) enabled us 'to correspond with the world' in and through the lived experience of designing and making dress-centred performance 'not to describe it, or to represent it, but to answer it'. We were able to mix and connect our 'own sentient awareness with the flows and currents of animate life', (Ingold 2013: 108) enabling materials and processes to become interconnected and ultimately indistinguishable from the body. The lived experience of the wearer's engagement activated the materiality and form of the garments and their relationship to the body, triggering cognitive processes and physical responses that in turn extended the body. The project revealed how dress could be developed as integral to the dance and become 'an active agent in connecting visual, physical, cognitive and sensory experience' in the process of making a holistic work (Bugg 2016: 169–93).

Perceiving Dress: Optical Laces

The third research project that I reflect on here is *Perceiving Dress: Optical Laces* (2014) that explored the relationship between clothing, movement, experience and perception to again inform the design of a performative garment, movement, performance and short-film production. The dress was specifically designed to encourage and uncover the relationship between the tactile, aesthetic and physical experience for the wearer. The proposition of the research built on ideas that had emerged in *Drawing with the Body and Cloth* (2013) relating to the potential for the dancer's sensory exploration to resonate in the viewers' experience of the dress in performance. This research drew on writings about performance and technology, interactive art, empathy, embodiment, performance and cognition: Fischer-Lichte (2008); Broadhurst and Machon (2011); Noland (2009); Shapiro (2011); Foster (2011); Shaughnessy (2012). Here, I aimed to develop an analysis of how dancers navigate between visual and experiential aspects in the development of dance; to extend devised approaches to design, performance and sensory communication through dance and the body and to extend an analysis of viewers' embodied and sensory engagements with dress in the mediated context of dance film.

The design of the dress responded to the findings of the previous project *Drawing with the Body and Cloth*, where dancers were shown to be engaged in movement, not only with the feeling of garments on their bodies, but also with the way they looked. Whilst it had emerged that this was not necessarily a conscious consideration for the dancers, there were questions about how the aesthetics of dress and its relationship to experience was bound up with their perception and response. The dress was designed in such a way as to be both an extension of the sensate body and a tool for the dancer, offering visual and wider sensory and experiential opportunities through its construction (Figure 4.2.7). It was made from shoe laces and was created to achieve an optical visual effect in movement. The weight and sound of the garment were enhanced through its design to offer further exploration of sensations in movement, which enabled the researcher to question and explore how the body mediates between visual and wider sensory experiences in performance.

The methodology for this work (Figure 4.2.6) differed from the previous project in that its methods were simplified to engage the dancer in the research process. She was presented with the garment for the first time in the performance studio, where she improvised without direction and her physical responses were filmed. A semi-structured interview followed the performer's physical response and this enabled her to reflect on how the dress had affected her movement and how she had worked and felt whilst performing. The interview questions probed where that movement had come from and what she was feeling and thinking as she moved in the dress, 'her awareness of the visual aspect of the dress and what her sensory experience was in movement' (Bugg 2014: 74). The dancer also engaged with the film footage and reviewed her movement from the improvisation session. She was then taken back into the studio to develop a response to the garment in motion and the film footage shot to produce the footage for the short film. The interviews were then analysed in relation to the two sets of film footage that were produced in the experimental development workshops. The researcher in the role of creative director worked with the filmmaker and editor to edit the film, which was directly informed by the dancer's verbal and physical responses to the garment in performance and her reflections during the interview. The film's edit and its treatment sought to further heighten

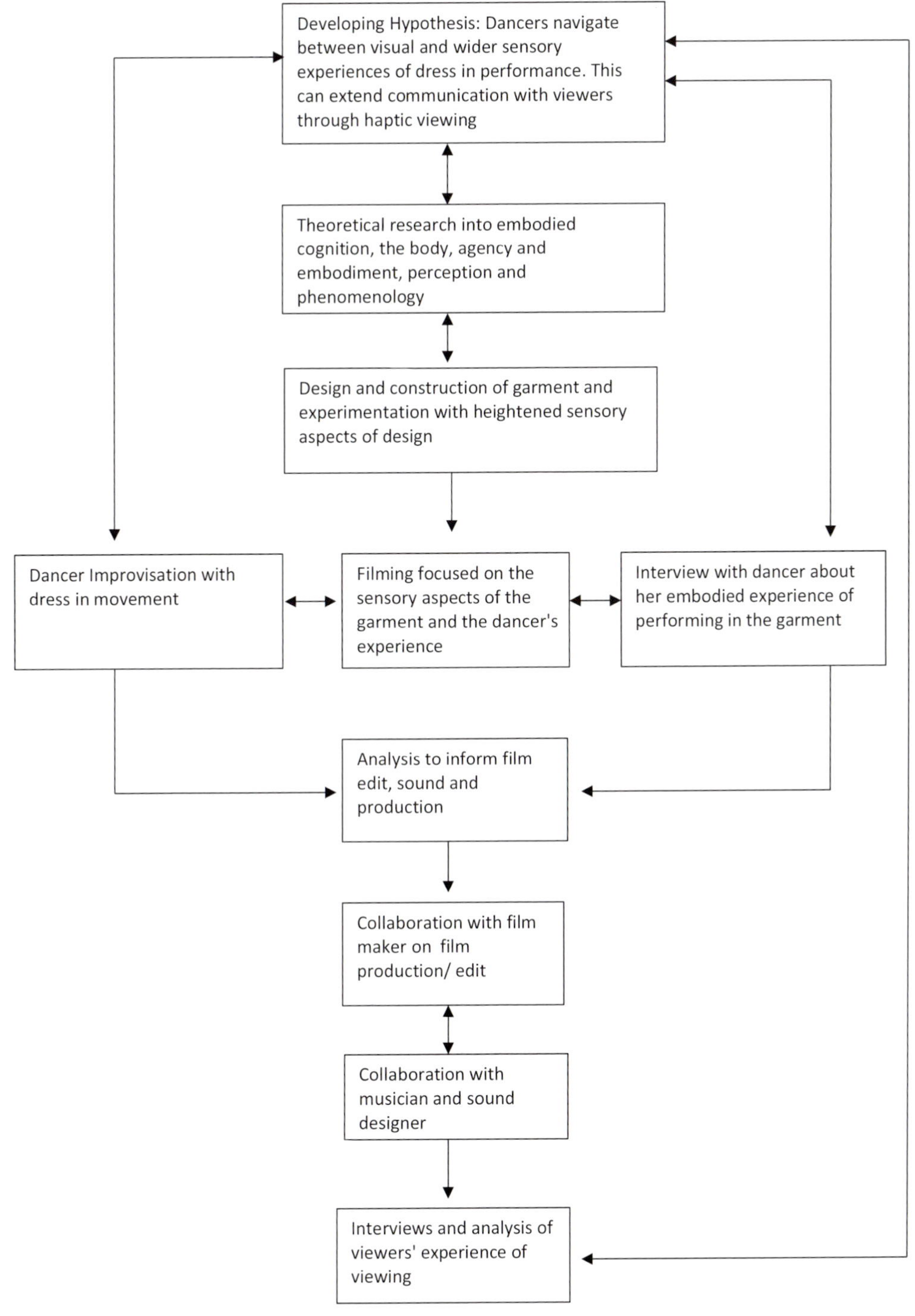

Figure 4.2.6 *Jessica Bugg, methodology for* Perceiving Dress: Optical Laces *(2014).*

Figure 4.2.7 *Jessica Bugg,* Optical Laces *in movement (2014) © Rene Lindell photographer.*

sensory responses and optical qualities for the viewer. Collaboration with musicians also enabled the sound of the shoelaces while moving to be laid back into the soundtrack and a bespoke musical score was created to further enhance the immersive experience. This film itself enabled subsequent research into the way that viewers engage with dress-based performance in film. A selection of viewers were recruited to complete an online questionnaire in response to watching the film. A viewers' workshop was also held at Aalto University with a group of postgraduate students to analyse their responses to the films. Viewers' experiences were then analysed to inform further research. The viewers' feedback suggested that aspects of their response had developed from the lived experience of the dancer and could become re-activated in what Cook would term 'the mimetic relationship between viewer and sensuous object' (Broadhurst and Machon, 2011: 107). The research demonstrated that there is greater potential to develop performative and experiential engagement with dress through the mediated context of film as opposed to creating a secondary or diluted experience.

Conclusion

The body-sited and mixed-methods research approaches discussed here have enabled transdisciplinary research and analysis of the body and dress in performance contexts. Research methods and critical and theoretical frameworks have been brought together in different ways to enable an interrogation of the complex performative dynamic that is activated between the bodies that make, wear, experience and interpret dress in performance. This has generated new research questions and processes in an iterative dialogue in the course of this ongoing enquiry. Practice has remained central to my research; creative processes have generated data in the context of the body in performance, the analysis of which has led to new approaches and understandings. Theory has also informed and been generated through practice and hypotheses that have been tested and developed throughout the research process.

The research has responded to the proposition that there are significant opportunities afforded in body-sited design and communication strategies. This has been questioned using phenomenological and practice-led investigations of how designers, wearers and viewers can be more meaningfully connected through an experiential bodily understanding of the creative process of making dress and performance as integrated practice. The methodologies developed through this research have contributed to knowledge of the active, experiential and transformative relationship between dress and the body in the process of making dance. The research has also exposed the potential of phenomenological frameworks and embodied methods in the development of dress, dance and communication that can inform practitioners and researchers across dress- and performance-related disciplines.

References

Anderson, A. and S. Pantouvaki, eds. (2014), *Presence and Absence: The Performing Body*. Oxford, UK: Inter-Disciplinary Press.

Barbieri, D. (2012), 'Encounters in the Archive: Reflections on Costume', *V&A Online Journal* 4. http://www.vam.ac.uk/content/journals/research-journal/issue-no.-4-summer-2012/encounters-in-the-archive-reflections-on-costume/ (accessed: 18 February 2019).

Barbieri, D. (2017), *Costume in Performance: Materiality, Culture and the Body*. London: Bloomsbury Academic.

Broadhurst, S. and J. Machon, eds. (2011), *Identity, Performance and Technology: Practices of Empowerment and Technicity*. London: Palgrave Macmillan.

Bugg, J. (2006), 'Interface: Concept and Context as Strategies for Innovative Fashion Design and Communication: An Analysis from the Perspective of the Conceptual Fashion Design Practitioner', PhD thesis. London: London College of Fashion, University of the Arts London.

Bugg, J. (2014), 'Dancing Dress: Experiencing and Perceiving Dress in Movement', *Scene* 2 (1–2): 67–80.

Bugg, J. (2016), 'Drawing with the Body and Cloth', in A. Reiley and S. Zoubir-Shaw (eds), *Embodied Performance: Design Process and Narrative*, 169–93. Oxford: Inter-Disciplinary Press.

Carter, A. and R. Fensham, eds. (2011), *Dancing Naturally; Nature, Neo-Classicism and Modernity in Early Twentieth-Century Dance*. London: Palgrave Macmillan.

Denscombe, M. (2003), *The Good Research Guide: For Small-scale Social Research* Projects, 2nd ed. Philadelphia: Open University Press.

Eckersley, A. (2017), *Practising with Deleuze: Design, Dance, Art, Writing, Philosophy*. Edinburgh: Edinburgh University Press.

Eicher, J. B. (2008), *Global Perspectives on Dress, Culture and Society*. London: Fairchild Books.
Eicher, J. B., S. L. Evenson and H. Lutz (2008), *The Visible Self: Global Perspectives on Dress, Culture and Society*. London: Fairchild Books.
Fischer-Lichte, E. (2008), *The Transformative Power of Performance: A New Aesthetic*. London: Routledge.
Foster, S. L. (2011), *Choreographing Empathy*. Abingdon: Routledge.
Helve, T. and S. Pantouvaki (2016), 'Sharing 'Untamed Ideas: Process-based Costume Design in Finnish Contemporary Dance through the Work of Marja Uusitalo', *Scene* 4 (2): 149–72.
Ingold, T. (2013), *Making: Anthropology, Archaeology, Art and Architecture*. Abingdon: Routledge.
Johnson, D. C. and H. B. Foster, eds. (2007), *Dress Sense: Emotional and Sensory Experience of the Body and* Clothes. Oxford: Berg.
Kawamura, Y. (2011), *Doing Research in Fashion and Dress*. London: Bloomsbury Academic.
Kershaw, B., L. Miller and J. Whalley (2010), 'Practice as Research: Transdisciplinary Innovation in Action', in B. Kershaw and H. Nicholson (eds), *Research Methods in Theatre and Performance*, 63. Edinburgh: Edinburgh University Press.
Mackrell, J. (1997), *Reading Dance*. London: Michael Joseph.
McKinney, J. and H. Iball (2010), *Researching Scenography*, in B. Kershaw and H. Nicholson (eds), *Research Methods in Theatre and Performance*. Edinburgh: Edinburgh University Press.
Noland, C. (2009), *Agency & Embodiment: Performing Gestures/ Producing Cultures*. Cambridge, MA: Harvard University Press.
Schön, D. (1991), *The Reflective Practitioner: How Practitioners Think in Action*. London: Routledge.
Shapiro, L. (2011), *Embodied Cognition*. Abingdon: Routledge.
Shaughnessy, N. (2012), *Applying Performance: Live Art, Socially Engaged Theatre and Affective Practice*. Basingstoke: Palgrave Macmillan.
Sheets-Johnston, M. (2009), *The Corporeal Turn: An Interdisciplinary Reader*. Exeter: Imprint Academic.
Strauss, A. and J. Corbin (1998), *Basics of Qualitative Research: Techniques and Procedures for Developing Grounded Theory*. London: Sage.
Trimingham, M. (2011), *The Theatre of the Bauhaus*. Abingdon: Routledge.
Yin, R. K. (2003), 'Case Study Research: Design and Methods,' in *Applied Social Research Methods Series*, 3rd edn, Vol. 5. London: Sage.

4.3 'Aware-Wearing': A Somatic Costume Design Methodology for Performance

Sally E. Dean

Introduction

Close your eyes. Can you sense your clothing touching you? And that you are touching your clothing?

This chapter will address and define the importance of 'Aware-Wearing', a somatic act developed by the author in collaboration with the costume designers and visual artists Sandra Arroniz Lacunza and Carolina Rieckhof. It is proposed here as a significant research methodology for costume design and costume-based performance practices. The central aspects of 'aware-wearing' include dressing and undressing, walking, the sense of touch, the role of the performer-spectator and the materiality of both bodies and costumes. Based on examples derived from my ongoing somatic and interdisciplinary artistic research entitled the *Somatic Movement, Costume & Performance Project*, I focus on how one particular 'Somatic Costume™', the 'Furry Heart Protector' (2015–18) evolved through three inter-related creative stages: design, workshop and performance. These stages are non-linear and cyclical. They work with the somatic-based methods described here to 'inhabit' the costume, with the aim of focusing on how the *experience* of costume effects and 'affects' bodies (*affective* being a philosophical term not simply equivalent to emotions). The aim is to further speculate on how we write about, design and perform costume as a 'wearer' opposed to as a 'viewer', inviting scholars, practitioners and spectators to become active participants in a live multi-sensorial costume experience.

There is little research into costume designers' and scholars' experiences and perceptions of costume while wearing it. 'While dress cannot be understood without reference to the body and while the body has always and everywhere to be dressed, there has been a surprising lack of concrete analysis of the relationship between them' (Entwistle 2000: 324). The act of consciously wearing is a practice of embodiment – and a return to the emphatic relationship between costume and the body. Embodiment is noted here as 'the act of incorporating and bringing visible expression to, the materiality of lived experience' (Dean and Nathanielsz 2017: 180). Body and costume move each other in metaphorical and literal manners. The multi-sensorial, intersubjective act of wearing allows subjects to increase their experience and understanding of their bodies, costume and environment as well as the inter-relationships between the three zones. Wearing becomes the bridge to knowing and knowledge, a powerful untapped research methodology in the field of costume design and costume-based performance. What if costume designers, performers, directors/choreographers, spectators and scholars wore costumes during all phases of the design, performance and writing processes and asked themselves, how does what I wear affect my body and perceptions? How does the costume affect how I sense, notice, move, act, feel, think, create and write?

The *Somatic Movement, Costume and Performance Project*

The *Somatic Movement, Costume and Performance Project* led by Sally E. Dean was founded in 2011. Somatic Costumes are created through collaborative acts between envinroment, materials, wearers and spectators. They are designed to integrate the key principles from somatic movement practices that advocate conscious awareness. By noticing movement habits, wearers are open to the potential of re-patterning their psychophysical selves and creating new ways of moving, being, performing and designing. Internal or 'kinesthetic' experiences of the body become the design and choreographic starting point, as opposed to the costume's external form or movement.

The term 'somatic' refers to Thomas Hanna's use of the older classical term in the 1970s – an experiential, holistic approach to the body that supports body-mind integration and process-based learning (Hanna 1988). Somatic movement practices were prominent in the fields of education, dance and therapy. The 'somatic body' or soma is defined as a sentient, perceiving being(s). It begins with the senses. The senses are the gateway to meaning, knowledge and knowing and act as the interface between the interiority of the body and the external world. They are also a way of accessing the materiality of the body, and a key principle in somatic practice. Internal experience is not just imagined, but 'real' and physical. The difficult concept of body materiality is defined here as the 'stuff that the body is made of' (referencing archaeologist Tim Ingold's phrase 'the stuff that things are made of', [Ingold 2011: 20]) as well as the ideas used by the outdoor-movement artist and scholar Paula Kramer in *Dancing Materiality* (Kramer 2016). I also build upon and add elements of the movement practitioner and writer Sandra Reeve's 'ecological body' into my re-definition: a somatic body is a changing body in relationship to a changing environment and context that is in a 'state of flux' and participation (Reeve 2011: 17–22). The somatic body is therefore a body in, of and created by relationships.

Somatic Costumes are embedded with sensation and imagery in order to evoke a specific psychophysical awareness, or 'kinesthetic body consciousness' in wearers through the sense of touch. Storm writes that 'kinesthetic body consciousness is awareness of the body's movement, position, and level of muscular tension. It is achieved through perception of muscle and joint movements and through the senses, primarily the tactile; the auditory is also frequently involved, and all of the senses can play a part' (Storm 1987: 306).

As an example here, we designed the *Balloon Hat* to bring awareness to the volume and buoyancy of the skull. In this project, wearers are placed in the role of performer. The project's aim is to adjust the tendency for costume to be considered within a subordinate and 'scopophilic' role in which 'looking' and the role of the spectator is privileged. For example, scholarly writing about costume may lean towards the third person – writing about someone else's experiences of costume, or writing from an imagined experience of costume as opposed to the materiality of both the body and costume and their meeting while wearing it. By practising 'aware-wearing' writers place themselves in the role of being 'inside' the experience instead of 'outside' the experience they observe.

For costume designers there are specific results from 'aware wearing' that activate and re-activate the design process. By 'aware-wearing' the costume they are designing, they may notice the kinesthetic attributes of the costume which will inform the movement, quality, body position, emotional 'affect' and character of the wearer. For instance, a designer wears a costume he/she has been designing for a performer and may notice some of the following: the shape of the costume, the texture, the sound, the movement of the material, the weight, the quality of touch and its effects and 'affects' on the body. As an example, if the shape of the costume affects the shoulders to curve inwards and hunch forwards, this will not only create a physical position for the body, but also an emotional affect and character.

I have applied key somatic practices from my background and training to this project: Skinner Releasing Technique (American: Joan Skinner), environmental movement (British: Helen Poynor), Amerta movement (Javanese: Suprapto Suryodarmo) and Scaravelli yoga (British: Giovanni Felicioni). Each somatic practice instigates psychophysical awareness in the body through different focuses: Skinner Releasing Technique utilizes poetic imagery; environment movement accesses the outdoor environment of south-coast England; Amerta movement combines imagery, environment and ritualistic sites from Java; and Scaravelli yoga integrates external body forms with internal sensation and imagery.

The Importance of Wearing: Touch

The *Somatic Movement, Costume and Performance Project* approaches the somatic body as inherently multi-sensorial, where all senses are inter-connected and related. Philosopher Michel Serres refers to this dynamic sensorial overlap as the 'mingled body' (Serres 2008). Anthropologists of the senses remind us that the senses are not necessarily biological, but are also social-cultural-historical constructs. Sensorial classifications, rankings and definitions lie beyond the classical, Aristotelian sensorial model of the five senses (touch, taste, sight, hearing, smell).

This project commenced with the least-researched sense, the sense of touch, or the 'haptic' (including the tactile, the kinesthetic or kinesthetic body consciousness and proprioceptive senses), whilst simultaneously incorporating many other sensations. The haptic provides our sense of touch and implies a participant's active engagement in the experience (Grunwald 2008: vii). It receives sensory information from two receptors: our mechanoreceptors (responding to mechanical pressure or distortion) and thermo-receptors (responding to changes in temperature). These receptors are found on both the skin (cutaneous inputs) and in our muscles, tendons and joints (kinesthetic inputs) (Lederman & Klatsky 2009: 1439). The kinesthetic sense is our perception of the conjoined body and its movements. The material, texture, weight, form and movement of the 'somatic costume' itself typically creates a direct and tactile kinesthetic experience for the wearer. For example, if the costume is heavy, the person will experience a corresponding 'heaviness' in their body.

We begin with the touch of the costume in order to re-balance the sensorial hierarchy derived from Western culture and society, in which vision dominates. How do we design, starting, not from the visual imperative and what would such a costume resemble, when touch and 'affects' on bodily perceptions are prioritized? This remains an under-researched area for costume design.

How Do We Wear? Daily-Life Wearing vs. Aware- Wearing

There are two types of wearing, 'daily-life wearing' and 'aware-wearing'. 'Daily-life wearing' is the way we use our bodies and our garments in daily life. Daily-life movement can often be habitual. I brush my teeth, but I might not be aware of how I brush my teeth or even what I am experiencing in the process. How do my teeth feel while being brushed? Can I sense the rhythm of it, the movement, the sensation it creates in my gums? Instead, brushing my teeth is something I need to get done. I might even daydream in the process, thinking of the last paragraph I wrote in this chapter for example.

The way we brush our teeth becomes, then, a metaphor for daily-life wearing. Applied to costume, if I am wearing high-heels, I may no longer be aware of how it is affecting my psychophysical experience.

Once we begin to notice the costume´s impact on bodies, we transition into 'Aware-Wearing'. aware-wearing is a somatic approach to wearing that invites wearers to bring attention to their perceptions and experiences of themselves, the costume, others and the environment. First, it includes the process of sensing, listening and noticing – to the costume, the body and the meeting in between. This can be both in movement and in stillness. Verbal instructions may be given to support somatic experiences such as 'notice that your skin is touching your costume and your costume is touching your skin'. This leads to awareness and consciousness.[1] With awareness and consciousness there is choice – wearers change how and what they are wearing to create a desired experience or effect.

Aware-Wearing is more akin to how the body is accessed and utilized in performance practices as opposed to those of daily life. Aware-Wearing is similar to Barba and Savarese's term 'extra daily-life technique', how bodies are used in performance versus 'daily-life technique' or daily-life wearing (Barba and Savarese 1999: 9). In extra daily-life technique, the wearer has the potential to access their body beyond the habitual patterns created through social-cultural conditioning. The context of performance also heightens awareness for the wearer in relationship to spectators. If you know someone is watching – it heightens your awareness of what you are doing. In Aware-Wearing, the spectator is always present.

In this somatic approach, a spectator can exist within anything: the costume, the wearers, the environment, spirit and within oneself. The spectator's location can be internal and/or external and may operate in a state of flux:

I touch/see the costume
The costume touches/sees me
We touch/see each other -
As I touch/see the sky through my heart
The sky touches/sees me through one ray of sunlight

One method that we utilize in the *Somatic Movement, Costume and Performance Project* that instigates Aware-Wearing is somatic walking – activating an internal and/or external spectator. This internal spectator is cultivated through walks with eyes closed that are often slow and constant and supported through touch and the act of dressing and undressing. We also support integrating the internal and external spectator through silent walks in public environments, where the spectator is in a state of flux. The trees can become the spectator, oneself or the passerby. Walking also activates Aware-Wearing through movement – a change in body position or location which can change our perspective.

Aware-Wearing advocates the relationality of costume. I use the term 'costume' because it implies an inherent relationship to both the performer and spectator. Costume can act as a verb or noun, allowing it to operate in two important roles as an action or subject. Theatre scholar Aoife Monks Aoife Monks uses the term 'costuming' to imply its important role as an activator of experience and perception between the costume and performer, a role that requires relationship – there is no costume without the actor (Monks 2010). Building on Monks's definition of costume, I define it further: Just as there is no costume without the performer, there is no performer without the spectator, the witness to the performative event. This costume definition then pre-supposes a dynamic and important relationship among all three – performer, spectator and event/space/environment.

The 'somatic costumes' that result from this approach find resonance in the work of the late Brazilian artist Lygia Clark and her 'Relational Objects' (Brett 1994). Her *Nostalgia of the Body* series (1964) aimed to re-orient art from the object, to bodies and senses. Clark's multi-sensorial objects to touch and wear were intended as experiences with wearers and therefore their value existed in that interaction, as opposed to in the object itself. Here, I emphasize that costumes and bodies have their own agency and materiality – they are both autonomous and inter-connected as 'intermaterial confederations' (Kramer 2016: 6). This approach builds on Nicolas Bourriaud's theory of 'relational aesthetics' (Bourriaud 2002) along with 'expanded scenography', which includes 'relationality' as one of its three core principles (McKinney & Palmer 2017: 9). Relationality in expanded scenography extends not only to humans, but also to the environment and, I propose here, animate and inanimate objects and spirit.

Touch in Wearing: Costume and Body

How and where is the costume and body touching? By practising Aware-Wearing, wearers may focus on different aspects of touch between the costume and body that inform the kinesthetic experience of the wearer. These touch patterns include the following and evoke particular physical and psychological responses in wearers, depending on how they are used/combined:

- *Temperature of touch*: warm, cold, etc.
- *Weight of touch*: heavy/deep, firm, light, or no touch (the space between the costume and body). An example of light touch is wearing a balloon inside a t-shirt while standing. If the body position changes to lying down on the balloon, the weight of touch changes to firm.

- *Location of touch*: where is it located on the body? Is the location a point, a surface or surrounding a body area from all sides? For example, wearing tight leggings would act as compression touch (heavy weight) with a location of surrounding the legs from all sides.
- *Direction of touch*: is the touch moving towards the body (push) or away from the body (pull), or in many directions at once? For example, in the 'Balloon Hat for Two People', the head of one wearer may be pulled by the costume (the material moves away from its contact on the body) when the other wearer pulls away from their partner.
- *Texture of touch*: the quality of the material such as smooth, itchy, slippery, or the quality of the moving body such as sticky, coarse or soft.
- *Time of touch*: is the touch intermittent or constant?
- *Movement of touch*: how is the material moving on/with/without the body and the body moving on/with/without the material?

During wearing, the impact of the touch upon the wearer over time can be experienced as less significant than when first wearing the costume. To re-activate the touch's presence, Aware-Wearing can be applied, by bringing awareness to an aspect of touch listed above, as well as changing the costume's touch by changing the body position (e.g. from standing, to sitting, to lying) or moving (e.g. walking). The how and where of touch can also affect the timing of movement. Aware-Wearing is also activated through dressing and undressing.

Figure 4.3.1 *'Balloon Hat for Two People' designed by Carolina Rieckhof in collaboration with Sandra Arroniz Lacunza. Performers: Soile Makela and Tanja Eloranta.* METAworkshop - Somatic Movement and Costume Workshop *led by Sally E. Dean, Teatteri Metamorfosi at Helsinki, Finland, 2015. Photograph by Helena Leminen.*

Dressing is an extension of wearing. Like wearing, it can be an 'aware' or 'daily-life' approach. The act of dressing acts as the transitional, liminal place – where the costume is put on/taken off as well as the place before/after touching the costume. It also instigates how we dress/undress and the many ways we can enter/exit a costume.

In somatic movement and costume workshops as well as performances, shedding the costume and moving again without the costume, can be as significant as wearing it. For example, during a workshop, one wearer first described the 'Elastic Costume' as constricting, but upon removing the costume she found new freedom: 'moving in new ways which were entirely unexpected' (participant feedback, Dean 2011: 179). This also happened with the 'Pointy Hat Costume': 'new movements appeared when you removed the hat' (participant feedback, Dean 2011: 179). Wearers are left with an 'invisible costume' – sensing the costume's presence even in its absence. Aware dressing and undressing, including being dressed by another, can not only heighten awareness, but also evoke a sense of ritual.

What are you wearing today? Close your eyes. Is there a sense of weight, compression or lightness coming from your costume?

Evolution of the 'Furry Heart Protector Costume': Design, Workshop and Performance

To illustrate the collaborative somatic approach applied within our Aware-Wearing research methodology, I now focus on one 'Somatic Costume'. The 'Furry Heart Protector Costume' went through three inter-linked stages of creation: design, workshop/s and performance. It aimed to raise questions such as where can and does design begin? What is the significance of experiments with the moving body, nature and the material by a 'somatic instigator'? Somatic instigators bring awareness to bodies including matters of quality, orientation/direction, space, movement, relationship, volume, weight, dynamic and musicality. For example, 'the weight of the tailbone towards the ground' would bring both a weight and orientation/direction awareness.

The design stage of the 'Furry Heart Protector' began amidst nature, by the sea in 2015, during Helen Poynor's collaborative and somatic 'Walk of Life Training workshop', Beer, UK (http://walkoflife.co.uk/helen.htm). I was experiencing a profound loss that initiated an intuitive-movement investigation into understanding/experiencing boundaries of the heart, literally and metaphorically, which led to the designing of a 'Somatic Costume'. While lying on the stony beach, resting on my back, listening to the sounds of the tide coming in, I began sliding and gathering stones on top of my body. Their texture, weight and temperature – heavy, slightly damp and cold, solid and smooth ancient mineral beings – created a deep inner comfort. My hands gathered more and more stones, piling them over my body, as if burying myself I am enveloped by stones. I gathered the most stones on top of my heart. Then came the revelation, 'I need a heartprotector'. The contact of the weight and substance of the stones, near the 'heart' area, created a feeling of protection – but also physically provided a direct-felt sense of:

Figure 4.3.2 *'Furry Heart Protector' designed in collaboration by Sally E. Dean and Sandra Arroniz Lacunza. Audience from* Something's in the Living Room, *created and performed by Sally E. Dean. Chester University, UK, April 2016. Photograph from video still by Dan Williams.*

- the front of the upper torso and the front of the heart
- the back of the upper torso and the back of the heart
- the space and layers in-between

Besides the volume of the upper torso encompassing the heart area, the sense of weight and orientation to the ground became apparent. This instigated dis- and re-orientation, because typically I experience my heart orientated more towards the sky. Metaphorically, I was discovering the 'feet of my heart' (ground), not just the 'wings of my heart' (sky).

To translate this experience involving stones into a costume design and to bring the process from outdoors into the dance studio, two dancers were invited to 'dress me' by taping one stone about the size of my heart to the front and the back of my chest – the metaphoric, not anatomical site of the heart. Then, two dancers were invited to be dressed in this prototype costume during the workshop. The location, weight and size of the touch of the stone became critical elements on the dancer's psychophysical experience. For example, a stone over 2 pounds was described as 'too heavy', reducing the dancer's ability to move, the weight orientating the dancer to the ground and into stasis. A stone under 1 pound was called 'too light' and its presence was more difficult to feel. The costume needed stones weighing 1–2 pounds to create the desired kinesthetic effect.

From the dance studio, the process moved to a make-shift costume design studio where costume designer/visual artist Sandra Arroniz Lacunza and I collaboratively created the 'Furry Heart Protector Costume', a wearable square pocket resting on the front and back of the heart, where stones can be inserted through velcro openings at the top. The front pocket is covered with soft grey fur material.

Our design process started through a somatic approach – inviting the costume designer to experience the material of the stone and to share her bodily perceptions. Here, I add the words of collaborator Sandra: 'While I am lying on the floor, the stone's pressure on my chest when placed near my heart, relates to a strong and pleasant touch, while your body feels more and more relaxed' (Notes from Lacunza: 1 April 2018).

The key design elements were the pocket, adjustable elastic straps, velcro and fur. The pocket became another way of easily housing the stones without tape and held in place by elastic straps on top of the shoulders and near the ribs. The pockets also added an element of dressing – the stones could be removed while the pocket remained, allowing wearers to sense the difference of the stone's absence and presence as part of the overall experience. This dressing element and the addition or removal of a stone in the costume added a further ritual quality to the experience, that was in turn explored in the performance stage.

The elastic straps were made of a material that allowed for movement, dispersing the weight carried in the straps through the material and the wearer's body itself, rather than one specific point (for instance at the top of the shoulders). The use of the elastic straps came from the idea of creating a 'bra-like structure' for the pocket attachment. The elastic straps both attached the pocket to the body and in turn translated two important haptic elements of 'the stone experience':

Figure 4.3.3 *Taking the stone out, 'Furry Heart Protector', designed in collaboration by Sally E. Dean and Sandra Arroniz Lacunza. Participant from 'Clothing as Portals of Perception' participatory talk given by Sally at the Open Platform event, Wellcome Collection, Reading Room, London, March 2017. Photograph by Camilla Greenwell.*

the location of the stone on the body and the magnitude of its impact. The elastic straps were adjustable, allowing the wearer to move them, (making the straps longer or shorter) in order to have the stones rest on each wearer's front and back of their heart, adapting to body size. The touch and weight of the stones became more significant than the touch and sensations of the elastic straps: 'With the elastic straps, you feel their presence less, making you aware more of the front and back of your chest' (Notes from Lacunza: 1 April 2018). Non-elastic straps were also experimented with, but this changed the effect on the shoulders, inhibiting and downplaying the sensations from the stone. 'Velcro also has practical and sensorial importance' (Notes from Lacunza: 1 April 2018). Velcro kept the pocket closed and prevented the stone from falling out. We also chose velcro instead of buttons or snaps because of the ripping sound when opening the pocket, causing vibrations in the fabric and 'felt by the skin' (Notes from Lacunza: 1 April 2018). The sound also emphasized and awakened in the wearer the significance of the transition, that is the taking out of the stones: 'It's almost like a soft "opening" of the skin, to get access to the heart' (Notes from Lacunza: 1 April 2018). It also evoked a ritual sense as if you were 'ripping' the stone, or your heart out of you.

Fake fur, with its soft quality, was added to the front of the pocket to encourage wearers to touch and stroke the front area of their hearts. 'It also softens the touch of the pocket, but not the stone feeling' (Notes from Lacunza: 1 April 2018). We chose the fur together, via the sense of touch. Sandra noticed that 'the same material in different colors has a different touch feeling' (Notes from Lacunza: 1 April 2018). Colour dyeing of the fabric may also change its texture. The touch experience can be affected by the visual aesthetic. Originally, we aimed for fur to evoke an animal's furry breast and later we chose a soft grey fur for its kinesthetic sensation.

The 'Somatic Costume of the Furry Heart Protector' was co-created and designed from a stone; through the different environments of beach, dance and costume studio; through the materials and the people who touched them. Although the somatic costume has both sensorial and semiotic value, the design began from a moving sensorial experience, allowing the symbols and meanings to arise as part of the process but always returning to how the costume affects our perceptions of our bodies. The kinesthetic realm led the process, as opposed to visual/aesthetic ones.

Next, we brought these costumes into workshop settings, inviting wearers to share their experiences of the 'Furry Heart Protector Costume'. Here is a revealing example:

I want to stroke it
Feels cosy and comfortable
Stroking the pocket feels like stroking the heart
The pocket when raising the arms moves up – keeps it in the heart area
Pouch like – kangaroo
Interesting it is so somatic
Feeling of substance in the body when the stone is in the pocket
More strength, expanding body
More substance to the muscles
Sense of carrying volume

Stones feeling light
It encourages movement
– choreographer Jacky Lansley[2]

Experiences from the design process were applied to the workshop setting, such as lying on the floor and sensing the weight of the stone on different areas of the body, before dressing up in the 'Furry Heart Protector' costume.

The dressing and undressing elements were also applied from the design process, but the ritual aspect of it was heightened through walking slowly, with the eyes closed, on beige material, towards a partner, lengthening the time between not wearing a stone to wearing one, amplifying both the difference and significance of these states.

In the performance stage, the Furry Heart Protector costumes are given to spectators to wear in recent performances of *Something's In The Living Room*, inviting them into both the kinesthetic and poetic experience. Aware-Wearing is implemented through spectators dressing and undressing each other in the costumes, as well as their walking journey from the place of dressing into the theatre space. The sensorial aspect of the costume is integrated with a personal semiotic action: spectators write on potatoes with black markers: 'something that you love that you have lost on the back potato and something you love that you found, on the front potato'. (Potatoes replaced stones, because there were no smooth, heavy beach stones in Pamplona, Spain, where the performance took place. Potatoes took on added meaning in Spain, as 'potato' also means 'heart-attack'. We continued to use the potatoes for their ability to create weight, but they also fit into the theme of 'food' for the performance piece). This action originated from the workshop stage, where wearers were invited to choose stones and write intentions on pieces of paper stuck under their stones in an installation and offering of stone and fur.

Figure 4.3.4 *Lying, wearing stones on areas of the body,* Somatic Movement and Costume *workshop, Independent Dance, Monday night improvisation class, Siobhan Davies Dance Studios, London, UK, 2015.*

Figure 4.3.5 *Writing on the potatoes. 'Furry Heart Protector,' designed in collaboration by Sally E. Dean and Sandra Arroniz Lacunza. Audience from* Something's in the Living Room, *created and performed by Sally E. Dean. Chester University, UK, April 2016. Photograph from video still by Dan Williams.*

Figure 4.3.6 *Rock installation,* Somatic Movement and Costume *workshop, Independent Dance, Monday night improvisation class, Siobhan Davies Dance Studios, London, UK, 2015.*

Figure 4.3.7 *Potato installation,* Something's in the Living Room, *created and performed by Sally E. Dean. Chester University, UK, April 2016. Photograph by Spence Cater.*

The performance concludes with performers and spectators shedding their costumes and building a shrine of potatoes as a material, sculptural eulogy.

Conclusion

The act of wearing costumes implies that wearing is research itself. Aware-Wearing advocates for the relationship between bodies and costumes through a somatic, multi-sensorial, performance approach. Once writers, makers, designers and performers become 'aware-wearers', the wearer's experience, as well as the costume itself, gains new material and sensorial value beyond the visual or semiotic. The former stimulates a vocabulary of touch patterns between costumes and bodies that might be further researched and developed, fuelling under-researched links between the kinesthetic, psychophysical and visual effects of costume. The aim is to re-balance the current Western ocular centrism, that prioritizes visual, spectacular and external experiences by advocating experiences that are tacit, tactile and internal. The Aware-Wearing practice also argues for collaborative design and performance-making processes and platforms. Wearing provides an area of shared experiences, lessening the hierarchies between performer, director, designer, writer and spectator. Finally, the acts of wearing and sensing return the centrality of the relationship between costumes and bodies to the forefront of costume design and costume-performance research.

Notes

1 For example, 'I sense the compression of my leggings against my skin and I notice that this brings more three dimensionality to the experience of my legs. I can sense the front, back and the sides. It makes me feel more grounded and connected to the floor.'

2 Carolina Rieckhof. Notes complied in personal conversation with choreographer Jacky Lansley while wearing the costume and talking through her experiences during *Portals of Perception* project. Lacunza and Dean were present. Dance Research Studios, London, February 2017.

References

Barba, E. and Savarese, N. (1999), *A Dictionary of Theatre Anthropology: The Secret Art of the Performer*. London: Routledge.

Barbieri, D. (2007), 'Proposing an Interdisciplinary, Movement-Based Approach to Teaching and Learning as Applied to Design for Performance-related Areas'. London: London College of Fashion. Available from: http://ualresearchonline.arts.ac.uk/1755/ (accessed: 2 April 2019).

Bourriaud, N. (2002), *Relational Aesthetics*. Paris: Presses du Réel.

Brett, G. (1994), 'Lygia Clark: In Search of the Body', *Art in America*, July, 55-65.

Bugg, J. (2014), 'Dancing Dress: Experiencing and Perceiving Dress in Movement', *Scene* 2 (1+2): 67–80.

Classen, C. (1993), *Worlds of Sense: Exploring the Senses in History and Across Cultures*. London: Routledge.

Classen, C. and Howes, D. (2014), *Ways of Sensing*. New York: Routledge.

Dean, S. E. (2011), 'Somatic Movement and Costume: A Practical, Investigative Project', *Journal of Dance & Somatic Practices* 3(1–2): 167–82.

Dean, S. E. (2014a), 'Somatic Costumes™: Traversing Multi-sensorial Landscapes', *Scene* 2(1–2): 81–7.

Dean, S. E. (2014b), 'Amerta Movement & Somatic Costume: Sourcing the Ecological Image', in K. Bloom, M. Galanter and S. Reeve (eds), *Embodied Lives: Reflections on the Influence of Suprapto Suryodarmo and Amerta Movement*, 113–126. Axminster: Triarchy Press.

Dean, S. E. (2015), 'Amerta Movement & Somatic Costume: Gateways into Environment', in S. Whatley, N. Garrett-Brown and K. Alexander (eds), *Attending to Movement: Somatic Perspectives on Living in this World*, 155–80. Axminster: Triarchy Press.

Dean, S. E. (2016), 'Where is the Body in the Costume Design Process?' *Studies in Costume & Performance* 1(1): 87–101.

Dean, S. E. and Nathanielsz, J. (2017), 'An action of Orientation: Skinner Releasing Technique in Reflective Practice', *Journal of Dance & Somatic Practices* 9 (2): 179–94.

Eddy, M. (2009), 'A Brief History of Somatic Practices and Dance: Historical Developments in the Field of Somatic Education and its Relationship to Dance', *Journal of Dance & Somatic Practices* 1 (1): 5–27.

Eicher, J. B. and Roach-Higgins, M. E. (1992), 'Dress and Identity', *Clothing and Textiles Research Journal* 10 (1): 1–8.

Entwistle, J. (2000), 'Fashion and the Fleshy Body: As Embodied Practice', *Fashion Theory* 4 (3): 323–48.

Grunwald, M. (ed.) (2008), *Human Haptic Perception*. Berlin: Birkhäuser Verlag.
Hanna, T. (1988), *Somatics*. Wokingham, UK: Addison-Wesley Publishing Company.
Howes, D. (ed.) (2005), *Empire of the Senses: The Sensual Culture Reader*. Oxford: Berg.
Ingold, T. (2011), *Being Alive: Essays on Movement, Knowledge and Description*. London: Routledge.
Ingold, T. (2012), 'Thinking Through Making'. Video of a lecture given at 'Tales from the North, Conference' at the Institute for Northern Culture in Lapland, 12 April 2012. Available from https://syntheticzero.net/2014/03/12/tim-ingold-on-thinking-through-making/ (accessed: 9 April 2019).
Ingold, T. (2013), *Making: Archaeology, Anthropology, Art and Architecture*. London: Routledge.
Kramer, P. (2016), 'Dancing Materiality'. PhD thesis, available from http://paulakramer.de/wp-content/uploads/2016/06/final_version_PhD_Kramer-copy_small_for_email.pdf (accessed: 3 April 2019).
Lederman, S. J. and Klatzky, R. L. (2009), 'Haptic perception: A tutorial', *Attention, Perception and Psychophysics* 71: 1439–59.
McHose, C. (2006), 'Phenomenological Space: – An Interview with Hubert Godard', *Contact Quarterly* 31 (2): 32–8, Summer/Fall.
McKinney, J. and S. Palmer (eds) (2017), *Scenography Expanded*. London: Bloomsbury Methuen Drama.
Monks, A. (2010), *The Actor in Costume*. Basingstoke: Palgrave Macmillan.
Noe, A. (2006), *Action in Perception*. Cambridge, MA: MIT Press.
Reeve, S. (2011), *Nine Ways of Seeing A Body*. Axminster: Triarchy Press.
Schechner, R. (2003), *Performance Theory*. London: Routledge.
Serres, M. (2008), *The Five Senses: A Philosophy of Mingled Bodies*. London: Continuum International Publishing Group.
Storm, P. (1987), *Functions of Dress*. New Jersey: Prentice-Hall, Inc.

Snapshots

4.4 Costuming the Foot: A Designer/ Performer's Personal Artistic Methods

Alexandra Murray-Leslie

In this 'Snapshot', I present computer-enhanced footwear and apparatus as a way of 'costuming' the foot (Figure 4.4.1). The high heel is a ubiquitous signifier in everyday life, suggesting positions as different from patriarchal oppression to post-feminist liberation. My co-linked design and performance practice takes this over-determined clothing artefact into new realms of performance practice, in which I am often the performer and wearer. The work belongs to the overarching field of NIME (New Interfaces for Musical Expression) integrating a theatrical fashion approach as a way to costume the foot for audiovisual performance. This makes the work 'bidirectional', (Kac 2005) as it has emerged though transdisciplinary means and exists in several transdisciplinary mediums, all of which seek to circulate new modes of communication using my foot devices as lead protagonists with an 'affective value'.

Over the past thirty years, I have developed my own individual style of artistic practice which I describe as 'a personal artistic method'. This approach plays to my unique strengths as a multi-tasking designer, fabricator and performer and my research in imagining ways that the human foot can be coupled with a new type of audiovisual technological costume to perform unusual theatrical events with the feet. I sought to find ways in which we can use that part of the body, our feet, in different ways, rather than just as utilitarian 'stepping machines' (Ingold 2004: 319. Prototyping inventions and iterations become responses to problems and opportunities which are taken on board and unlocked.

The experimental project presented here is part of a larger body of work developed since 2006 which creates high-heeled shoe-based 'instruments' in order to facilitate distinctive audiovisual theatricality, expression and experimentation. My iterations of foot apparatus build on my previous experiences in the international group I co-founded, 'Chicks on Speed', including the 'E-Shoe' and 'High-Heeled Shoe Guitar'. It is the process of research into fabrication, the resulting physical prototype and its visual 'performance', perhaps on stage in a video artwork, lens-based work, in a sports science laboratory or fabrication laboratory during the making process, that is of concern here. An approach dedicated to the integrated understanding of the 'whole' (Jordà 2005) is the key to achieving better artistic results in the physical aesthetic design of wearable digital audiovisual instruments and their effects on dramaturgy and uses in live performance. It is not just the audiovisual foot-based instrument that is important; it is the entire performance and the different types of documentation that result from this process that are equally valuable. Francesca Granata

Figure 4.4.1 *Alexandra Murray-Leslie,* Computer-Enhanced Footwear Prototype 3, *Ars Electronica Festival, 7 September, 2017. Photograph by Wolf-Dieter Grabner.*

has argued that the recording and documentation of such performative acts, which I suggest also include here the performances of 'making' the feet artefacts themselves in fabrication laboratories for lens-based works and music videos, can 'constitute a primary source of a similar order to the garments themselves' (Granata 2017: 12). In this case, a costuming of the foot.

In particular, I investigate the designing of shoe- and foot-based audiovisual instruments and their impact on the practice of the performer's work within a larger performance (*Gesamtkunstwerk*) and how this can further inform further iterations of the foot-devices. This lies at the heart of my practice as a maker and performer, which encourages a flexible research ecology, one that supports tacit understandings, inferred practices and theoretical assumptions that can be made explicit, queried and contested. The aim of the general project is not just about getting better performances or inventing new technology; it is about the creation of new knowledge into technologically assisted theatrical expression concerning computer-enhanced foot costumes. This research can not always be applied to the terms 'method' and 'methodology', which at times attempts to capture new knowledge by codifying and categorizing it. My practice and research seeks rather to establish imaginative *modus operandi*, pushing the boundaries of artistic practice and critical analysis, which requires some consideration of the ontological and epistemological positions that underpin the applied research methods. I carried out practice-based research and action-guided technological experiments including fabrication processes (Figure 4.4.2), pop music/art performances, lens-based works and music videos. According to Linda Candy, 'Practice-based research is an original investigation undertaken in order to gain new knowledge partly by means of practice and the outcomes of that practice' (Candy 2006). New knowledge is produced through artistic practice, as well as the resulting artefacts and processes of creation. The term 'artefact' describes an artistic outcome or object made by the artistic practitioner during a period of research, the outcomes of which may take the form of installations, exhibitions, objects or performances (Bluff 2017). As framed by Candy and Ernest Edmonds, an artefact 'might be an object, such as a table, painting or building. It might exist over time, such as a piece of music or a film. On the other hand, it might be less persistent in time, such as an exhibition or performance' (Candy & Edmonds 2010: 123). In the context of my practice, the artistic artefacts include:

Figure 4.4.2 *Left: Computer-Enhanced Footwear Prototype 3* (CEF P3), *worn by dancer Elizabeth Bressler in the music video 'We are Data', re-mixed by Chicks on Speed and Cora Noava, directed by Alexandra Murray-Leslie, 2016. Right:* Computer-Enhanced Footwear Prototype *(CEF P3); showing outcomes of embedded mylar in every 100 slices of the 3D print. Pier 9 Technology Centre, Autodesk, San Francisco, 2016. Photographs by Alexandra Murray-Leslie.*

- a computer-enhanced foot-based appendage as costume (Figures 4.4.1 and 4.4.2)
- live performances on stage, in the fabrication lab
- sounding choreography motion experiments in the sports science laboratory
- pop music videos[1]
- lens-based works (Figure 4.4.3)

The development of the *Computer-Enhanced Footwear Prototype 3* took place in the Sports Science Laboratory at Pennsylvania State University, the fabrication laboratory, Pier 9 Technology Centre, Autodesk, San Francisco and on stage in public performances in 2016 and 2017. The prototype facilitated audiovisual performance as well as incorporating an accompanying visual spectacle initiated by using the feet in new and different ways afforded by 'performing' the computer-enhanced high-heeled shoes.

There are frequent challenges to address for the existence of an artistic act or object and for it to and change over time. My artistic method builds on the understandings I gained in the performance group Chicks on Speed and involves engaging in a critical transdisciplinary approach to enrich my own investigations. These include the artistic decision-making process of prototyping and performing computer-enhanced footwear. This involves working with an identifiable high-heeled shoe, generally ready-made and practising a culture of 'de-making' (Murray-Leslie 2018), informed by the concepts 'defamiliarization' or 'ostranenie' as expressed by Viktor Shklovsky in the essay 'Art as Technique' (1917) and later Brecht's *Verfremdungseffekt* (alienation or estrangement effect) which was a method he used in order to distance the audience from the artificiality of theatre, breaking through the so called 'suspension of disbelief'.

This work has a strong relationship to a bodycentric object or commodity that we already know and are familiar with. I alter the relationship through changing the physical object by enhancing it with technology. In creating a visual-musical instrument from a shoe, I seamlessly merge fashionable dress with the costume associated with pop music. This becomes a one-off, wearable foot costume, inspired by and simultaneously inspiring contemporary fashion and employing newer methods of integrating DIY circuitry and 3D printing techniques. My method promotes further use on stage to create an audiovisual spectacle, to surprise and engage audiences further, creating a sort of momentary 'climax' within the performance set list. In making bespoke foot costumes, I also take 'ready-made' high-heeled shoes and use them to provoke a new non-market significance, subverting its original fashion-commodity connotation and proposing an alternative to consumer preferences for fast fashion and 'reinvestination' (Meinhold 2013). I invert the conventional association of the high-heeled shoe with male-centred fetishism, both commodity and sexual.

Thus, I have turned the high-heeled shoe into a 'technical apparatus' (Flusser 1999) to extend the foot's capabilities and the potential of such shoes, changing the meaning of high-heeled shoes from status or sexual symbols and instead creating audiovisual instruments for theatrical performance. Miniaturized sensors and circuits enable this. This pairing of technology and a high-heeled shoe becomes strange or bizarre for an audience and creates an expression of surprise or wonder. This, I believe, is integral to maintaining the audience's attention over the duration of a performance and is considered in my artistic method here. The approach also merges fashion and sound, creating a different type of costuming the foot facilitated through digital technologies. Such devices have a way of extending the body and foot's artistic performativity, facilitating a 'wearable performance' element in the specific scene of a larger show (Birringer and Danjoux 2009), something an audience isn't ordinarily used to seeing. Here, the dual role of a visually charged and auditory costume breaks the pattern and expectation of fashionable costume elements, well beyond the expression of a style choice or visual language.

This is not so much about virtuosity, as the way the shoe artefacts have been physically made, performed or documented via the lens or various forms of photo media. The important part is the essence of the idea to use the feet and high-heeled shoes, or foot apparatus, in different ways, and the meaningful iteration of the artefact driving forward, which also embraces DIY aesthetics and failure. For example, the shoes, their performance and the lens-based works convey meanings that exist far beyond the virtuosic document and emit the energy of what was happening on stage in that moment. Similar attitudes are expressed in the artefacts and the way they are performed. This allows radical artistic exploration, going 'off-road' and giving space to the unusual, unpredictable and bizarre processes and outcomes which are sometimes out of one's control when working in a bigger art collective such as Chicks on Speed.

To conclude, I engage with a critical transdisciplinary approach to enrich my own investigations; throughout the artistic decision-making process, prototyping and performing computer-enhanced footwear. I started out wanting to design a high-heeled shoe musical instrument and ended up creating an artistic artefact with interconnected qualities. It became a musical

Figure 4.4.3 *Alexandra Murray-Leslie performing the Objetconnex 500 3D printer whilst fabricating the* Computer-Enhanced Footwear Prototype 3. *A cyborg craft collaboration with Steve Mann, Pier 9 Technology Centre, Autodesk, San Francisco, 2016. Photograph by Steve Mann and Alexandra Murray-Leslie.*

instrument, expressive visual lighting effect, fashionable costume for the feet, new design for a high-heeled shoe, styling element for photo and stage, new and novel 3D printed material and new choreographed playing techniques. The foot-wearables I developed changed the way we move, each pair having their own set of playing styles. Various taxonomies of gestures were created appropriating motions from sports science (used for designing mappings and creating documentary artworks) and pole dancing (used for performance). This method of 'performing making' is both idea-rich and theatrical. It included the visual sampling of language, for example Jeremy Scott's half high-heeled shoe/foot with heel, titled 'Body Modifications' (1996) or Laurie Anderson's lyrics from her song 'Monkey's Paw' (1989, quoted in Balsamo 1996: 18) about buying a pair of 'high-heeled feet'. In testing the idea critically, I talked to global experts and peers from transdisciplinary fields of enquiry such as sports science to gain new insights and apply them to the concept. Each prototyping phase was connected to a workshop collaboration with a technologist, scientist, choreographer, dancer or musician. Technology partnerships, artistic residencies and university research labs all contributed to the rich ecology that became *Computer-Enhanced Footwear Prototype 3*.

Note

1 See the music video 'We are Data Remix' directed by Alexandra Murray-Leslie, music by Chicks on Speed, available at: https://vimeo.com/207064196/04df14ac93 (accessed: 26 March 2019).

References

Balsamo, A. (1996), *Technologies of the Gendered Body: Reading Cyborg Women*. Durham: Duke University Press.

Birringer, J. and M. Danjoux (2009), 'Wearable performance', *Digital Creativity* 20 (1–2): 95–113. Available online: https://bura.brunel.ac.uk/handle/2438/5681 (accessed: 26 March 2019).

Bluff, A. (2017), 'Interactive Art, Immersive Technology and Live Performance', PhD thesis. University of Technology, Sydney.

Candy, L. (2006), *Practice Based Research: A Guide*, Creativity and Cognition Studios. University of Technology, Sydney. Available online: https://www.creativityandcognition.com/resources/PBR%20Guide-1.1-2006.pdf (accessed: 26 March 2019).

Candy, L. and E. Edmonds (2010), 'The Role of the Artefact and Frameworks for Practice-based Research' in M. Biggs and H. Karlsson (eds), *The Routledge Companion to Research in the Arts*. London: Routledge.

Flusser, V. (1999), *The Shape of Things: A Philosophy of Design*. London: Reaktion.

Granata, F. (2017), *Experimental Fashion: Performance Art, Carnival and the Grotesque Body*. London: I. B.Tauris.

Ingold, T. (2004), 'Culture on the Ground: The World Perceived through the Feet', *Journal of Material Culture* 9 (3): 315–40.

Jordà, S. (2005), 'Digital Lutherie: Crafting Musical Computers for New Musics' Performance and Improvisation', PhD thesis, Universitat Pompeu Fabra, Barcelona. Available online: file:///Users/AML/Downloads/Jorda-Sergi-PhD-2005.pdf (accessed: 26 March 2019).
Kac, E. (2005), *Telepresence and Bio Art: Networking Humans, Rabbits and Robots*. Ann Arbor: University of Michigan Press.
Meinhold, R. (2013), *Fashion Myths: A Cultural Critique*, trans. J. Irons. Bielefeld: Transcript Verlag.
Murray-Leslie, A. (2018), 'Demaking the High-Heeled Shoe', in E. Edmonds and L. Candy (eds), *Explorations in Art and Technology*, 163–71. Springer Series on Cultural Computing. London: Springer Verlag. Available online: https://link.springer.com/chapter/10.1007/978-1-4471-7367-0_16 (accessed: 26 March 2019).
Shklovsky, V. ([1917] 1965), 'Art as Technique' in Lee T. Lemon and Marion J. Reiss (eds), *Russian Formalist Criticism: Four Essays*, 3–24. Lincoln: University of Nebraska Press. content/uploads/2015/03/wilde_PhD_exegesis.pdf (accessed: 26 March 2019).

4.5 Costume and the Modernist Body: Fashioning August Strindberg

Viveka Kjellmer

Body and clothing interact, shape each other and come together to create a new whole. Rachel Hann and Sidsel Bech underline costume's important role when they write: 'Costume is critical. It is critical to making performance, critical to spectatorship, critically overlooked within scholarship, notable when in crisis, and a means of critically interrogating the body. It is therefore critical that we discuss costume' (Hann and Bech 2014: 3). The actor on stage depends on the costume for the performance. It visually frames the character portrayed and physically contributes to creating it through its impact on the actor's body and patterns of movement.

Marvin Carlson points out that theatre is largely based on memory-awakening echoes of past experiences in the audience. He calls this phenomenon 'ghosting' (Carlson 2001) and shows how on some level, each theatre set carries the traces of previous sets of the play, as well as past roles portrayed by the actors. But ghosting is not limited to theatrical references, it is cultural in general (Carlson 2001: 96–130). In this study, I use the concept of 'ghosting' to explore how costumes use fashion references. They might position an actor in a visual discourse already known to the audience, emphasizing social meanings for example.

The perception of fashion and fashion images changed in the early 1900s. Both fashion and its images increasingly came to be considered art or forms of artistic expression (Troy 2003; Mackrell 1997) and French fashion magazines spread across the world. *La Gazette du Bon Ton*, for example, was sold in London, New York, Berlin and several other cities (Mackrell 1997: 163). The German fashion magazine *Die Modewelt,* started in Berlin in 1865 and was published until 1909 in fourteen countries (Mackrell 1997: 137–8). The flow of images and fashion magazines across borders shows that there was great interest in fashion and that fashion images were accessible to the general public across of Europe.

Costume Sketches as Visual Culture

Between 1915 and 1918, Swedish scenographer and director Knut Ström created the costumes for a production of August Strindberg's *A Dream Play* in Germany.[1] I will focus on Ström's costume sketches for the main character, the Daughter of Indra,[2] using art-historical analysis to examine how his sketches relate to the visual culture and fashion imagery existing in contemporary illustrations and magazines. This approach highlights how Ström's work visually expressed his modernist and artistic ambitions.

Knut Ström's sketches include both detailed costume sketches and paintings of the entire scenography, where Ström tried out overall patterns of colour and shape for his set designs.[3] In other sketches, the Daughter of Indra is dressed in a bright bluish-green, straight, long-sleeved dress. The cold green colour of the dress stands out against the dark background. In some of the sketches, she wears a purple dress of similar design. The purple hue stands out as much as the blue-green, both differing clearly from the dark palette of the interior and other costumes in the sketches. The colours become a sign of how much the Daughter of Indra fails to blend in with the humans. It is notable how the blue-green and the purple dress are both very similar in shape and colour to dress designs appearing in contemporary fashion illustrations.

Examining aspects of materiality opens up new ways to understanding these sketch materials. Gillian Rose and Divya Tolia-Kelly (2012: 4) point to the importance of examining the relationship between the material and visual aspects of culture and its consequences for both image and interpretation. This line of thought is fundamental to my analysis of the sketches and is a way to capture in writing how Ström used the material aspects of colour and form to design costumes. The material traces that the working process left in the sketches also reveal their making and I read them as non-textual sources of Ström's work. When the sketches are analysed from a material perspective,

Figure 4.5.1 *Knut Ström (1915). Scenography sketch for* A Dream Play, *The Daughter of Indra and the Officer with the Mother. Courtesy of the Swedish Museum of Performing Arts, Stockholm.*

the *process* and Ström's experimentation with colour becomes visible. His use of the shapes and colour schemes of contemporary fashion illustrations emerge and Ström's sensitivity to the wider visual culture of fashion is revealed.

The Modernist Body

Caroline Evans argues in favour of a definition of the modernist body that includes the re-negotiation of the ideal female body that occurred in the early 1900s. Instead of the curvy corseted body, a leaner, more boyish physical ideal was introduced. Evans demonstrates how fashion shows played a major role in this development by introducing the element of movement into fashion discourse. Fashion was now seen as clothing on a body in motion, rather than lifeless garments (Evans 2013). Such thinking has been the basis of distinctions made about women and modernist fashion, from Paul Poiret to Madeleine Vionnet, for several decades and can be found in the writings of Elizabeth Wilson, Anne Hollander and Evans and Thornton. I propose that it is this new view of women's bodies, that leaves an imprint on Knut Ström's visual thinking concerning the body and costume in his sketch material.

Figure 4.5.2 *Knut Ström (1915). Scenography sketch for* A Dream Play. *The Daughter of Indra and the Glazier in front of the Growing Castle. Courtesy of the Swedish Museum of Performing Arts, Stockholm.*

In Figure 4.5.2, we see the Daughter of Indra depicted with her back turned to the viewer and her arms raised high. Her body points upwards, towards the sky in contrast to the person standing at her side, who is bent towards the earth. The lines of the dress and the outstretched arms, marked by the green colour of the sleeves, mirror the upward-striving flowers around her. The sweeping, slightly elliptical shape of the dress represents a clear departure from the curvaceous female body, delineating instead an elongated, slender shape.

A contributing factor to the new silhouette was that the tightly-laced corset, with a narrow waist, diminished. But a new body ideal demanded other types of underwear. The laced corset was replaced by body stockings, compressing the body and making it appear slimmer. Evans shows that the corset-less body began to spread as an ideal as early as 1910 and had its final breakthrough in 1914 (Evans 2013: 201–14). The new ideal meant a different body shape. Postures and ways of moving also changed. The sketch of the Daughter of Indra discussed above, in green with raised arms shows exactly this: a freer position in which she can straighten her body and reach towards the sky.

Short Hair as a Sign of the New Woman

Aoife Monks (2010) argues that the costume is paradoxical, both an inseparable part of the actor's body on stage and also an outfit that can be removed and viewed separately, but still linked to the character. She calls costume 'a body that can be taken off' (Monks 2010: 11). Monks describes how clothing can trigger a bodily reaction in the viewer. Taking the corset as an example, she shows how a garment can communicate on multiple levels: symbolically by communicating confinement, but also physically in our own body when we imagine how it feels to wear a tightly laced corset (Monks 2010: 24). This highlights that theatre costumes are more than just dress and how they create a visual, but also a physical link between what we see and what we may experience in our bodies. The viewer who sees the Daughter of Indra in an elliptical dress without a visible waistline understands how the body has been released from the laced corset and can move in a completely new way.

The new silhouette came with a new hairstyle. Short hair on women was shockingly new. Earlier generations of women wore hairstyles made up of long hair that was never cut (Zdatny 1997). Ström chooses to depict the Daughter with cropped hair. Short hair on women was not common in 1915 when Ström made these sketches. It foretold a new type of woman and thus signalled social change. Women's cropped hairstyles did not spread among the general public until the 1920s. Before then, it was the avant-garde, like film stars who wore short hair. Indra's Daughter's cropped hair is an example of 'ghosting', where the hairstyle carries a meaning borrowed from the world outside of the theatre and signifies both the avant-garde and social change. From a fashion perspective, the cropped hairstyle symbolized the new sporty and youthful fashion, as with the slender silhouette. Ström chose this visual trope in the costume sketches to indicate that the Daughter of Indra represented something other than the established and accepted. Thanks to the wide distribution of the fashion press and fashion images, it is reasonable to assume that a theatre audience would recognize this silhouette and understand what it meant.

In conclusion, Ström's costume sketches draw on fashion as a driving force for modernist change. The sketches reveal how he captured lines, poses and colouring that were also visible in contemporary fashion illustrations. A recognizable visual language, seen in fashion magazines and illustrations of the time 'ghosts' his costume sketches. Fashion and theatre have much in common and both areas underwent significant renewal in the early twentieth century. Knut Ström was visually creative and sensitive to these trends and he contributed to the renewal of the theatre. The new ideal female body and the attention it attracted fitted well with the visual innovation that characterized the modernist reformist theatre where Ström felt at home. His design choices both reflected and contributed to the rise of the New Woman.

Notes

1. See my longer study 'Fashioning A Dream Play: On Knut Ström's Costume Sketches, 1915–18 from a Fashion Perspective' (Kjellmer 2016) in the volume *Dream-Playing across Borders: Accessing the Non-texts of Strindberg's* A Dream Play *in Düsseldorf, 1915–18 and Beyond.*
2. *A Dream Play* concerns the daughter of the god Indra, who descends to Earth to learn about human life. She tries to assimilate, but fails and ultimately returns to her father to tell him about the misery of humankind.
3. The sketch materials consist of pencil drawings and small paintings in water colour and gouache, depicting costumes and set designs. These sketches are in theatre archives in Sweden and Germany; others are owned by the Ström family.

References

Carlson, M. (2001), *The Haunted Stage: The Theatre as Memory Machine*. Ann Arbor: University of Michigan Press.

Evans, C. (2013), *The Mechanical Smile: Modernism and the First Fashion Shows in France and America, 1900–1929*. New Haven and London: Yale University Press.

Hann, R. and S. Bech, (2014), 'Critical Costume', *Scene* 2 (1–2): 3–8.

Kjellmer, V. (2016), 'Fashioning *A Dream Play*: On Knut Ström's Costume Sketches, 1915–18 from a Fashion Perspective', in A. von Rosen (ed.), *Dream-Playing across Borders: Accessing the Non-texts of Strindberg's* A Dream Play *in Düsseldorf, 1915–18 and Beyond*, 92–121. Gothenburg: Makadam.

Mackrell, A. (1997), *An Illustrated History of Fashion*. New York: Costume & Fashion Press.

Mirzoeff, N. (2009), *An Introduction to Visual Culture*, 2nd ed. London: Routledge.

Monks, A. (2010), *The Actor in Costume*. Basingstoke: Palgrave Macmillan.

Rose, G. and D. P. Tolia-Kelly (2012), 'Visuality/Materiality: Introducing a Manifesto for Practice', in G. Rose and D. P. Tolia-Kelly (eds), *Visuality/Materiality: Images, Objects and Practices*, 1–11. Farnham: Ashgate Publishing Ltd.

Troy, N. (2003), *Couture Culture*. Cambridge, MA and London: MIT Press.

Zdatny, S. (1997), 'The Boyish Look and the Liberated Woman: The Politics and Aesthetics of Women's Hairstyles', *Fashion Theory* 1 (4): 367–98.

Section 5

Costume and its Collaborative Work

is well articulated, but the creative practice of technical staff and the period of costume realization is less theorized (Wilkinson-Weber 2004: 582; White 2015: 1; Hunt and Melrose 2005).[2] The primary responsibility of costume technicians, be they makers, cutters or drapers, managers, buyers or craftspeople is consistently articulated as design interpretation or translation (Arnold 1973: 215; Bicât 2006: 54; Cunningham 2009: 12). While this interpretative position is usually designated rather than defined, it can be extrapolated as implying that the design, whether a render, sourced image or described idea, is read as a text by technicians, who then translate this vision into an object conveying the same meanings.

While the terms 'translation' or 'interpretation' are used interchangeably in much of the discussion about the costume technician's responsibilities, Linda Pisano differentiates between them, stating that, 'the role of cutters and drapers is to interpret the designs. Not merely translate them, which can imply duplication' (2017: 163). While I extend this interpretative position to all costume technicians, not just cutters and drapers, I concur with Pisano's allusion to the creativity inherent in costume realization. Pisano's semantic distinction can also be understood as a reference to the longstanding tension between word-for-word or sense-for-sense translation. Walter Benjamin, re-iterating an argument put forward by St Jerome in 342 AD, maintains that the translator's task is to convey the original work's meaning or intention and he encouraged fidelity to sense over fidelity to words (Benjamin 1996: 258–60). When applied to costume, during realization, technicians will read and make creative judgements regarding different aspects of a design and how these should be interpreted. Thus, costume interpretation is a creative as well as technical process. This perspective is emphasized by Shura Pollatsek, who suggests that 'costume technicians do not merely execute the design, they add their own artistry as they interpret it' (2016: 2), a point scenographer Pamela Howard re-iterates, stating that 'the costume drawing is a mark of respect for the artistry of the costume maker … and should leave enough room in its interpretation for the individuality of the maker to contribute to the finished item' (2009: 166). According to Maggi Phillips and Renee Newman, 'the "creative judgement" process is critical to the interpretation of design', with each costumer likely to generate a unique interpretation that relies on what they can derive from the render and conversations with the designer, alongside their own research, knowledge and aesthetic understanding (2017: 10).[3] Hunt and Melrose alternately conceptualize the judgements that technicians make as operating in three arenas. They term these the 'technical-real' (what is physically possible?), 'fictional-affective' (what best serves the story or performance needs?) and 'human-real' (how to navigate this choice in relation to other agents in the production) (2005: 73). The latter requires emotional intelligence, so it is a requirement to apply existing knowledge, gained via experience, to new scenarios that support the costume technician's abilities to resolve unfamiliar problems and interpret new designs. In their interpretation, technicians rely not only on a comprehensive understanding of the designer's vision to make creative judgements, but also their experience and costume-construction skill to make technical ones.

Practitioners assessing and responding to situations, changing their practice to make sense of new situations or provide new solutions is a process conceptualized by Donald Schön as reflection-in-action (1983: 54–61). In the context of design, architectural theorists Adrian Snodgrass and Richard Coyne similarly suggest that design interpretation begins with pre-conceptions and expectations and that these projections are not merely the 'arbitrary production of the subjective imagination but derived from experience bought to bear on clues scattered throughout the [design] situation'. They go on to argue that this experience arises from skill, tacit understanding and 'a network of practices, institutions, conventions, aims, tools, expectations and a multitude of other factors' (Snodgrass and Coyne 2006: 39). The comprehensive articulation of resources used in interpretation is further supported by Eckhart and Stacey's research in to fashion knitwear realization, in which technicians not only use the designer's render, mood boards and inspiration images to make creative judgements, but also their experience gained from working previously with garments, their knowledge of their knitting machines and yarn properties, all elements that find equivalents in costuming practices. In this way, a technician's existing knowledge and previous experience facilitates their initial interpretation of the design.

This interpretation is continually evolving. On-going discussion between technicians and designers, new information and material choices change their understanding of the design parameters, an example of Schön's concept of 'backtalk' in which design is a 'reflective conversation with the materials of the situation' (1983: 172). As aspects of the costume are resolved, understanding of the whole design is also improved. This dynamic dialogue emulates a hermeneutic circle, as articulated by Martin Heidegger and expanded upon by Hans-Georg Gadamer in which an understanding of parts builds an understanding of the whole, which is also revised as new aspects are considered (2004: 236). Expanding on Gadamer's theorizing, Snodgrass and Coney suggest that design understanding develops by a:

> back-and-forth interplay between the parts and the whole. Interpretations of the parts modify the projection, which in turn plays back to modify the interpretations of the parts. This process is fluid, repetitive and continuous … leading eventually to a clarification of the projection. (Snodgrass and Coney 2006: 46)

While not explicitly referring to Gadamer's hermeneutic circle, Schön emphasizes that to develop an understanding of design needs, 'attention must oscillate between the "whole" and the "unit", the global and the local' (1983: 93). Evident in the costume workshop, the cyclical interplay between parts and the whole to drive design understanding articulated by these theorists, is a valuable way to understand the nuances of costume realization.

The parts and the whole of a costume can be considered in several ways. There are the individual characters' costumes, each of which are complete in themselves but relate to others to make up the whole sartorial world. Thus, the choice of material or style in one costume might be replicated or precluded in another. There are the garments that make up each costume, which combine to create meaning and inform choices, such as a style or colour of shoe determining the accompanying hosiery choice. Deconstructed further, the manufacturing techniques, structure or material choices of one aspect of a costume element will impact upon other components of the design, such as the choice to use a heavily beaded silk chiffon that determines the amount of flare a dress can withstand before the thin fabric risks being torn by its own weight. The interplay between these many parts and the whole informs the technician's interpretation and facilitates an evolving understanding of the designer's vision as choices are made during the realization. This cyclical process is facilitated further by the costume's iterative cycle of production, as items are sourced or made. It is a creative process that responds to implied meanings as much as to literal details, and in order to successfully interpret them the technician must collaborate closely with others in their team as well as designers.

Costume Collaboration, Subjectivity and Dialogic Design Development

I argue here that for each production a unique shared 'aesthetic language' is created and the process of building this language both creates and clarifies the costume's design. The need to create a common scenographic 'visual language' in order to collaborate successfully, has been discussed by others (Howard 2009: 159; Pantouvaki 2010: 71; Curtis 2014: 74). Here, the term 'aesthetic language' is employed as it emphasizes the haptic nature of costume, aligning it with the 'aesthetic logic' of a staged world as discussed by Barbieri (2017: xxiii). This collaboration and the creation of aesthetic language occurs not only between designers and technicians, but also amongst technicians: either in a hierarchical mode, such as the guidance provided by a cutter to a maker, or in a peer exchange such as when several technicians brainstorm solutions to style an intractable wig, or collectively interpret an aspect of a dress design. In so doing, they clarify and communicate their individual perspective on the design's aesthetic language within their team.

Design interpretation is consistently emphasized as individual and subjective in costume texts (Ingham and Covey 1992: 166; Nadoolman Landis 2003: 124; Newman and Phillips 2017). Applied to this chapter's concept of a shared aesthetic language, this suggests that during the design realization process, there are many versions of the costume design which can exist concurrently in the workshop. These versions physically reside in the illustrated render and the compartmentalized written articulations in the costume plot or budget, as well as in the minds of the designer and technicians. Beyond the workshop, there are many more versions of the design in the minds of performers, directors, audiences and others. The congruence between the audience's expected version and the realized design has already been argued as essential to the success of the production (Walter 2017: 154). This chapter suggests that the congruence between the versions held in the mind of the technician and designer determines the relative success of the realization and the ease of the production process. But how does this congruent understanding combine with a subjective interpretation?

The solution is to consider costume collaboration as dialogic, a term coined by structuralist Mikhail Bakhtin. Richard Sennett summarizes this as a process of exchange, during which mutual understanding or awareness of individual views is established (2013: 19). This dialogue is considered by Hans-Georg Gadamer to be integral to interpretation, emphasizing that while interpretation is individual, interpretations become meaningful when they are convincing, coherent and have an inter-subjective value (Grondin and Plant 2003: 124). This dialogic process builds a convergent understanding of the production's aesthetic language between the participants. It is important to note for the conceptualization of the process that a *convergent* rather than *converged* understanding is established. The subjective nature of design interpretation makes an identically convergent understanding of the design unlikely. These interpretative positions are, however, brought together over the iterative realization process to a point at which differences in perspective are no longer easily discernible. This dialogic design-language-building process is facilitated to the cyclical process of costume realization, as costumes are iteratively built or sourced. This correlates with studies of other design practices, such as Tomes, Oats and Armstrong's study of graphic design communication and translation. They found that the 'iterative nature of the negotiation and adjustment of design means that the sub-processes involved do not take place in a set sequence. Rather they tend to recur throughout the progression from initial idea to agreement on the final design' (1998: 136). In the process of sourcing, selecting, returning, or pattern-making, toiling and making, the understanding of the design vision improves but also evolves. Aesthetic and technical choices are made by the technician in response to this dialogue, which again extends the collaborative conversation.

Another complication in this convergent understanding of a production's design is the evolution that naturally occurs as a 2D drawing is transformed into a 3D object. The contingent nature of costume realization is evident in the design evolution that occurs during the costume's material transformation and the discoveries and challenges posed by rehearsal. The material qualities, technical realities and changing needs of the production influence the design in both small and significant ways, causing it to evolve as rehearsals progress. Thus, there is an evolving location of convergence over the design realization period. For example, during rehearsal a blocking movement turns out to be more energetic than expected, requiring a robust costume that stretches. Alternatively, a fabric is found that is deemed 'perfect' for the character but no longer suits the previously planned style of garment, or a costume may overshoot the budget envisaged and thus money has to be saved on another. These changes fit into the aesthetic, dramaturgical, psycho-social, functional, technical and logistical parameters of costume design as identified by Suzanne Osmond elsewhere in this volume. As the production process creates a moving target for the design outcome, it requires on-going communication to ensure that all agents are 'across' (support) the changes. For instance, the decision to change a fabric in the fitting room will be communicated and discussed with others in and beyond the workroom such as makers, buyers, directors, lighting designers and choreographers.

Communicating a Shared Aesthetic Language

A shared aesthetic language is established and expanded during the realization process by the four communication modes used in costuming. Heather Milam writes that in the costume workshop 'communication happens in three ways. Through conversation and explanations, through the rendering, sketch and research and through gesturing' (2017: 176) and Pisano suggests these visual, verbal and social-communication skills are necessary for collaboration (2017: 150). In addition to this trio, I suggest that materials, especially the costume itself, are an important mode of communication. As found and built objects, rather than drawn or inscribed ones, costume's haptic qualities differentiate them from visuals. Each of these four modes encompass a variety of communication practices. Figure 5.1.1 outlines some of the more readily identifiable practices, although by no means

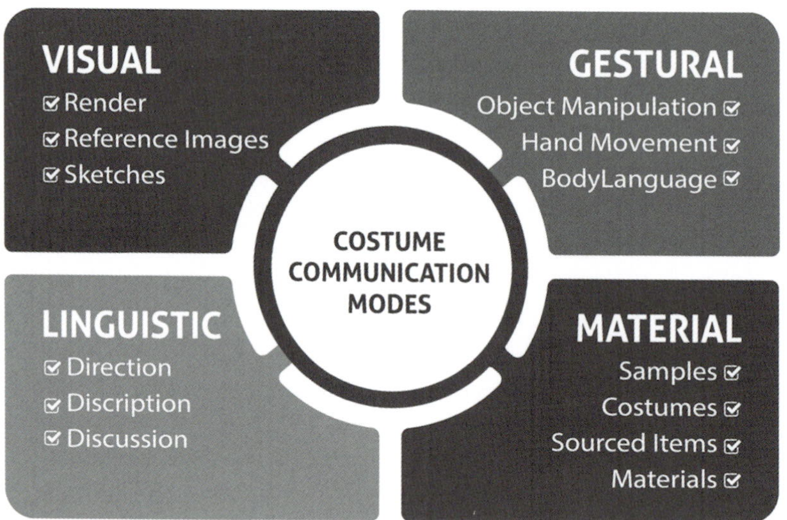

Figure 5.1.1 *Costume communication modes. Diagram by Madeline Taylor*

claims to be an exhaustive list. Discussing the strengths of each of these four communication modes will clarify how they support the development of a shared aesthetic language.

Visual communication practices are commonly privileged in costume literature, with the design render consistently identified as the most significant articulation of the design vision (Cunningham 2009: 143; Curtis 2014: 207). This is evident by the reverence with which design renders are held, both during the production process and very often after the event. The designer usually uses the render to start the aesthetic conversation about the design, although, as Pantouvaki has identified, the render may not always be representative of this vision (2010: 70). This may be due to rendering skill, or the difficulty of conveying three-dimensional materiality via two-dimensional media. Whether representative or not, alongside the render, additional visual research such as photos or illustrations regarding garments, materials or styling are often used. Eckert and Stacey discuss this practice in the fashion industry, stating that 'pictorial displays of a range of instances' allow technicians to learn the design parameters by generalizing from these positive instances (2000: 533), a strategy equally applicable to costume practice. Another form of visual communication is the sketches that designers or technicians make of a costume design. This might be of a detail not depicted, or a perspective not shown, such as a back or side view, or in a different form, such as a technical drawing in pencil rather than an expressive idea in watercolour. This re-drawing clarifies the design further and is another way of processing the information.

The gestural and linguistic communication practices of the costume workshop may be more ephemeral, but are equally valuable in conveying information. Communication via gesture includes hand movements, manipulating materials and body language. Hand movements might be as simple as pointing, but can also be used to convey more complex information such as outlining a silhouette in space, or over a human figure to communicate information about shape, scale and fit. More tangibly, this gesture might involve material manipulation, such as moving a strap or pinning up a hem. In this way, the gesture provides an example of the preferred position or shape for a costume. While not a practice unique to costume communication, body language such as facial expression has been established as the most accurate indicator of feelings or attitudes towards a subject (Mehrabian 2011: 193). Designer Stephen Curtis discusses how the flick of an eye, or a change of tone tacitly communicates an attitude or response (personal communication), while Tina Bicât suggests that a performer's body during fitting will communicate costume issues unconsciously (Maclaurin and Monks 2014: 129). Sensitivity to, and understanding of, body language is therefore vitally important to the collaboration. Linguistic communication can be in written or spoken form. Examples of descriptive practices in costume include the para-text on a design render, such as the name of performer or scene it is used in, or the verbal articulation of the characteristics that might make up a sought-after pair of jeans, such as 'low rise dark indigo flares'. Alternatively, this description could convey dramaturgical information regarding the character's situation or attributes. Communication of ideas via discussion or explanation supports an articulation of the design, which allows space for responsiveness to others and a dialogical process as highlighted previously.

The final communicative practices identified are those facilitated by the materials of the costuming process, including samples, sourced items and existing costumes. These items not only form the costume, but are useful communication tools. In sampling for fabrics, for example, the materials chosen and offered will convey a wealth of information about the design vision, or the sampler's interpretation of it, as well as the tactile qualities desired for the costume. These aspects can only be suggested by the render. Similarly, information about the construction, fit or form of the costume can be efficiently conveyed by selecting an existing garment to replicate a manufacturing technique or design aspect. These various communication practices of costume help to establish the shared aesthetic language of the design.

Establishing this shared aesthetic language begins at the first design presentation, where the designer initiates the conversation with their design vision, renders and research. During the design presentation, the visually communicative render and other materials are displayed, but alongside this is a linguistic description of the works and the aesthetics they create. Over the production period, the designer and technicians create a shared aesthetic understanding that builds on and clarifies these initial images and ideas. Like learning any language, creating this shared aesthetic requires the participants to establish the vocabulary and syntax of the designer's vision in which design elements such as texture, colour and line provide the vocabulary and the syntax for how these elements are combined or put together. While the designer leads the conversation, both they and the technicians are equally active in this process, employing the four different communication modes in different combinations. This is consistent with the findings of various studies into design communication (Tomes, Oates, and Armstrong 1998; Ulusoy 1999). Schön addresses the issue in his studies of architectural design, suggesting that his own linguistic metaphor, in which drawing together and talking to each other make up 'the language of design' (1983: 80). In his discussion thereof, he emphasizes how linguistic and visual communication combine to establish a shared understanding of a design. Referring back to the four communication modes identified in Figure 5.1.1, it is important to note that the exchange Schön analyses to evidence this 'language of design' communication, also relies on pointing and draws on source material. Thus, while Schön leaves out discussions of gesture and materials in his formulation, they are evident in his data (1983: 81). These visual, gestural, linguistic and material communication modes, each of which encompass many practices, are used to create a shared aesthetic language, discussed below within a series of collaborative mechanisms.

Negative Scoping

Architectural theorist Chris Alexander proposes that it is often easier to identify and justify the design misfit than it is to articulate why a design is aesthetically pleasing or 'correct', stating that 'the concept of good fit, though positive in meaning, seems very largely to feed on negative instances; it is the aspects … which are obsolete, incongruous, or out of tune that catch our attention' (1973: 22). Applying this idea to collaborative costume practice, I argue that as suggestions or ideas are exchanged, negative scoping allows the participants to build a shared basis of understanding as inappropriate approaches, objects or their properties are identified and rejected. Negative scoping, as an aesthetic language-building mechanism, relies on a dialogic interplay of spoken discussion and material objects to clarify the scope of the design aesthetic.

It is useful here to use director Nancy Meckler's conception of 'offers', a term she uses to describe the suggestions and ideas of others in the collaborative process (Neill 2017). Negative scoping in the costume workshop comprises the costume technician making 'offers' that fit within their initial understanding of the preferred options, which are then rejected or accepted by the designer with justifications as to why. Over the course of the exchange, the technician responds to these justifications, modifying offers to fit the design requirement parameters that are established with each interaction, a process illustrated by Figure 5.1.2. In this process, with each offer, technicians gather information and then reflect on that information in combination with their expertise and experience, using this to drive the next offer. A largely tacit practice, this cycle aligns with Schön's 'reflection-in-action', in which he suggests that practitioners draw on their previous practice, which provides 'a repertoire of expectations, images and techniques' and teaches them 'what to look for and how to respond' (1983: 60). This corresponds with Tomes, Oates and Armstrong's graphic design practice research in which it was found that in the design process 'the respective personal understandings of the negotiators are what is used to find commonalities, in an ongoing process of *offering* for critique and modification' (1998: 136; emphasis added). This common understanding is both created by and in turn creates the shared aesthetic language of the production, a dynamic model of interpretation, revision and response.

This mechanism is used throughout the costume realization process. A common example of its employment is the sourcing or selecting of materials or ready-made garments, whether new or from stock. In this process, the materials are vital signifiers, containing a store of information that can be parsed into individual components to clarify the ideal aesthetic. For example, a length of fabric may be critiqued for its drape, fibre content, care requirements, reflective ability, weave, colour, texture, print, opacity and embellishment, just to name a few properties. In rejecting certain qualities of the fabric over others, tacit acceptance is often presumed for the unnamed qualities and the

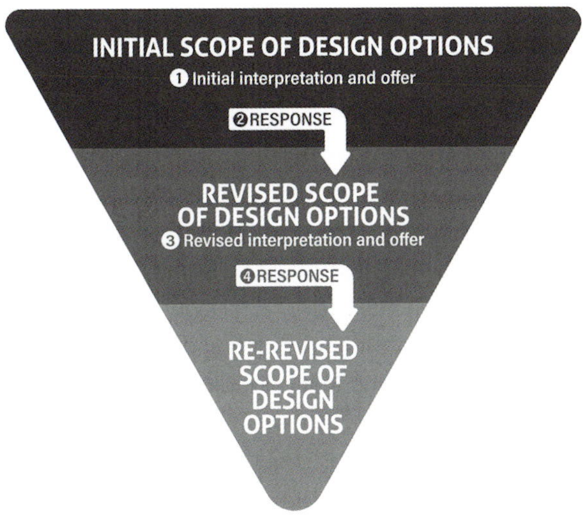

Figure 5.1.2 *Negative scoping mechanism. Diagram by Madeline Taylor.*

costumer will respond accordingly in future offers. The responsive nature of these interchanges and the exchange overall as diagrammed, additionally corresponds to Gadamer's previously discussed hermeneutic circle. This correlation evidences another way in which the creative interpretation of costume technicians is embedded in costume process.

The process of sourcing a specific costume item provides a concrete illustration of negative scoping in practice. Asked to find a man's black leather belt for a business-suited character, costume buyers will use their knowledge of the production and the other garments depicted in the design render to choose a belt that would be suitable for business attire and offer this to a designer. In their response and rejection of this initial offer, designers might say that the buckle is 'a bit too shiny' or 'too large' and the leather 'looks too plasticky'. This would then be interpreted by the technician as a request for something that a wealthier, but more understated man would wear. The buyer would then select new belts, possibly incorporating finer grained leather, more delicate stitching and a simpler or less reflective buckle. This selection uses their technical knowledge regarding comparative weights and grains of leather or leather-stitching techniques which is then translated into cultural and social understandings of significations of wealth. Within this, are also creative judgements regarding how a buckle might simultaneously connote wealth and an understated personality, which characteristics are dominant and how a belt's various constituting components, such as its materials, design and manufacturing techniques might combine or be altered to convey this message. In selecting the most appropriate option from this latest round of belts, the designer communicates information about the character's design which can then be taken by the technicians, interpreted and applied in future offers for this character. This could relate to practical aspects, such as trousers with belt loops fitting the selected belt, but also creative considerations, i.e. the pattern or material of a tie that would be consistent with this characterization. The choices regarding one character also build the aesthetic understanding of others and so each choice clarifies the aesthetic language of the production. For example, a business competitor character might be described as 'wealthy and flashy'. The understatement of the first belt will then be used as a base-level marker for a comparative understanding of 'flashy'. This exchange and the many like it, that build a shared understanding of the production's aesthetic, usually operate at a tacit level. If discussed at all, the offering and responses are couched in figures of speech, such as 'Is this in the world?'

The unconscious employment of negative scoping means that there is little awareness of the impact this mechanism might have on inter-personal relationships. While negative scoping is vitally useful in clarifying a design and its constitutive elements and thus, the aesthetic of the production, it is important that its participants understand that it is easier to identify negative rather than positive design aspects or, as explained by Alexander, 'wherever an instance of misfit occurs … we are able to point specifically at what fails and to describe it' (1973: 23). To regularly have ideas and contributions rejected could be detrimental to a technician's self-efficacy or their relationship with the designer. Once it is known that negative aspects are easier to identify and describe than the positive ones, however, it becomes easier to recognize that an offer's rejection is part of the costuming process, rather than a reflection on the candidate's creative judgement. Knowledge of this mechanism also emphasizes the importance of providing reasoning for a negative response, as this supplies valuable information that can be used to inform future offers. As the shared aesthetic language of the production is established, technicians are empowered with additional information that can be employed to inform each offer and contribute more substantively, as in the next mechanism outlined.

Provisional Sampling

Provisional sampling is another identifiable collaborative mechanism. This takes a more tangible form than negative scoping and exemplifies the costume technician's interpretative responsibilities. The most significant instance of this mechanism is the toile: a costume prototype made up in cheap material so that the design can be fitted, tested and perfected. Provisional sampling is enacted not only in whole garments, however, but also its elements. This could equate to pinning trim onto a costume for the designer's approval before it is permanently attached, or art-finishing several swatches of material before applying paint to the completed costume. Another instance may be a buyer purchasing several similar shirts to provide more options in a crucial fitting. Provisional samples may be requested by the designer or implemented by the technician, but the material and aesthetic choices are made primarily by technicians, reflecting their interpretation of the designer's vision.

The toile or other sample is a physical manifestation of the technician's design interpretation. The presentation of this sample to the designer can be considered another form of 'offer'. Provisional sampling often employs all four modes of aesthetic communication simultaneously, but the material costume or its stand-in is at the centre of the process. Dow et al.'s research supports this positioning, stating that prototypes help people summarize their ideas, demonstrate their progress and expertise, bring to the surface implicit design vocabulary and ground group communication and decision making (2011: 2807). The creative choices made over the course of the toile's production are often justified by verbal discussion and gestures that manipulate and display different aspects of the sample. Shown from different perspectives, such as how it is fastened or worn, the toile displays the progression of the technicians' thought process and how their interpretation responds to the design vision or functionality. As an offer, the provisional sample usually prompts discussion between designers and technicians which further illuminates and clarifies the design aesthetic. In this discussion, the sample is rarely rejected outright, but aspects are critiqued and plans are made for its modification. As such, this provisional sample contributes significantly to the development of a costume design. Recent studies at the Stanford Design School have highlighted the value of provisional sampling or prototyping. It was found that iteratively prototyped designs outperform non-prototyped designs, with more iterations producing better results, but that production schedules and budgets 'often discourage iteration in favour of realisation' (Dow and Klemmer 2011: 124). This tension plays out in costume with provisional sampling often requiring significant time and resources. Due to these costs, provisional sampling usually commences once the design has been clarified and often occurs after significant discussion and visual communication, during which the technicians establish that they have understood the design parameters. Provisional sampling is one of the ways in which trust is built between technicians and designers. The creative choices made by the technician are evident in the provisional sample. Designers use these samples and how closely they match their expectations of what the sample should look like to assess the technician's interpretation and understanding of the parameters of the design vision.

Within the provisional sampling mechanism and costume practice more broadly there are divisions with respect to creative responsibility, but these boundaries are generally tacitly, rather than explicitly defined and regulated. I recently observed a costume supervisor asking a costume maker to trim several hats, suggesting that she create three versions, with the trimmings to be pinned on and shown to the designer. These provisional samples were to 'first make sure we are on the same page', an allusion to the shared aesthetic language being created for the production. This regulation of creative decision-making illuminates the boundaries demarcating roles, responsibilities and artistic judgement in the costume workshop. The costume technician is given creative freedom to trim the hats as she believes aesthetically suitable, but this suitability is provisional, needing approval before being firmly constructed. In another instance, an enthusiastic costume technician suggested a change in a toile fitting that the designer responded to non-committally. In the debrief following the fitting, she apologized for this interjection and made it clear that she thought she had over-stepped her role, an example of how these boundaries are internalized and self-policed by those who work within them. Rather than disagreeing, the designer accepted the apology, indicating that they had agreed with this assessment. For Gay McAuley, in her ethnography of the production process, protocols around decision-making, what could be decided by the technical team, what could be decided by designers and what needed to be referred to the director were unclear (2012: 111). McAuley's inability to discern the boundaries of decision-making responsibility is arguably due to her outsider status. Sennett discusses the role of the workshop as a space of learning, in which tacit knowledge is absorbed through on-the-job training and observation (2009: 77). Learning the scope of a role's responsibilities and what is beyond its remit is a tacit process that is usually acquired on the job. Part of becoming a professional costumer is learning to recognize the boundaries of such creative responsibility. It remains a rich topic of further research to identify additional mechanisms of costume collaboration and interpretation.

Conclusions

This chapter has argued for a new perspective on the processes and practices of costume realization, positioning the collaborative dialogue between technician and designer as not only creating the three-dimensional costume, but also a convergent understanding of the design's aesthetic language. This dialogue relies on four modes of communication: visual, gestural, material and linguistic. Using the concept of 'aesthetic language', the interpretative responsibilities of costume technicians and the design process as a highly social interaction are emphasized. The mechanisms of negative scoping and provisional sampling assist in reaching an understanding of how this shared aesthetic language is generated, as they are usually tacitly practised. Their employment requires not only understanding the material costume and how it is created, but also the emotional intelligence to navigate the collaborative process. Through the study of communication and collaboration within costume realization, the tacit knowledge and expectations embedded in costume practice are highlighted. From this newly enhanced understanding we gain the opportunity to improve our work.

Notes

1. In this document, Monks calls for a more holistic and collegial approach to costume research that values and studies the process of costume, not just its outcomes.
2. While the chapter focuses on costume technicians and designers, this should not be read as implying that only they contribute to the costume's design. Performers, directors, choreographers, production managers, stage managers and others all contribute to costume's development as it is realized, while others such as suppliers and audiences implicitly inform design choices (Pollatsek 2016: 39; Walter 2017: 154).
3. The importance of cognitive interpretation to the success of the physical design realization has been found in similar research in fashion (Eckert 1999: 36–7).

References

Alexander, C. (1973), *Notes on the Synthesis of Form*, 7th ed. London: Oxford University Press.

Arnold, J. (1973), *A Handbook of Costume*. London: Macmillan.

Barbieri, D. (2017), *Costume in Performance: Materiality, Culture, and the Body*. London; New York: Bloomsbury Academic.

Benjamin, W. (1996), *Walter Benjamin: Selected Writings*, M. P. Bullock and M. W. Jennings (eds), Vol. 1. Cambridge, MA: Belknap Press of Harvard University Press.

Bicât, T. (2006), *The Handbook of Stage Costume*. Ramsbury: Crowood.

Cunningham, R. (2009), *The Magic Garment: Principles of Costume Design*, 2nd ed. Long Grove, IL: Waveland Press.

Curtis, S. (2014), *Staging Ideas: Set and Costume Design for Theatre*. Sydney: Currency Press.

Dow, S. and S. Klemmer (2011), 'The Efficacy of Prototyping Under Time Constraints' in C. Meinel, L. Leifer and H. Plattner (eds), *Design Thinking*, 111–28. Berlin: Springer Berlin Heidelberg. https://doi.org/10.1007/978-3-642-13757-0 (accessed: 18 March 2019).

Dow, S., J. Fortuna, D. Schwartz, B. Altringer, D. Schwartz and S. Klemmer (2011), 'Prototyping Dynamics: Sharing Multiple Designs Improves Exploration, Group Rapport, and Results', in *Proceedings of the SIGCHI Conference on Human Factors in Computing Systems*, 2807–16. CHI '11. New York, NY, USA: ACM. https://doi.org/10.1145/1978942.1979359 (accessed: 15 March 2019).

Eckert, C. (1999), 'Managing Effective Communication in Knitwear Design', *The Design Journal* 2 (3): 29–42. https://doi.org/10.2752/146069299790225306 (accessed: 15 March 2019).

Eckert, C. and M. Stacey (2000), 'Sources of Inspiration: A Language of Design', *Design Studies* 21 (5): 523–38. https://doi.org/10.1016/S0142-694X(00)00022-3 (accessed: 16 March 2019).

Essin, C. (2012), *Stage Designers in Early Twentieth-Century America: Artists, Activists, Cultural Critics*. Basingstoke: Palgrave Macmillan.

Gadamer, H.-G. (2004), *Truth and Method*. Translated by J. Weinsheimer and D. G. Marshall, 2nd ed., Continuum Impacts. London; New York: Continuum.

Grondin, J. and K. Plant (2003), *The Philosophy of Gadamer*. London: Routledge.

Howard, P. (2009), *What Is Scenography?* 2nd ed. London: Routledge.

Hunt, N. and S. Melrose (2005), 'Techne, Technology, Technician', *Performance Research* 10 (4): 70–82. https://doi.org/10.1080/13528165.2005.10871452 (accessed: 20 March 2019).

Ingham, R. and L. Covey (1992), *The Costume Designer's Handbook: A Complete Guide for Amateur and Professional Costume Designers*, 2nd ed. Portsmouth, NH: Heinemann.

Maclaurin, A. and A. Monks (2014), *Costume: Readings in Theatre Practice*. Basingstoke: Palgrave Macmillan.

Malloy, K. (2014), *The Art of Theatre Design: Elements of Visual Composition, Methods, and Practice*. London; New York: Focal Press.

McAuley, G. (2012), *Not Magic but Work: An Ethnographic Account of a Rehearsal Process*. Manchester; New York: Manchester University Press.

Mehrabian, A. (2011), 'Communicating without Words', in C. David Mortensen (ed.), *Communication Theory*, 2nd ed. London: Transaction Publishers.

Milam, H. (2017), 'In the Costume Shop', in Melissa Merz (ed.), *The Art and Practice of Costume Design*, 175–96. New York: Routledge, Taylor & Francis Group.

Monks, A. (2014), 'In Defense of Craft: A Manifesto', *Scene* 2 (1–2): 175–8. https://doi.org/10.1386/scene.2.1-2.175_7 (accessed: 20 March 2019).

Nadoolman Landis, D. (2003), *Costume Design*, (Screencraft). Burlington, MA: Focal Press.

Neill, H. (2017), *Theatre Voice: Nancy Meckler*, Theatre Voice, London. http://www.theatrevoice.com/audio/nancy-meckler/ (accessed: 15 March 2019).

Newman, R. and M. Phillips (2017), '"You Are No Longer Creative When You Give up": Technical Theatre's Creative Sleight of Hand.' *Behind the Scenes: Journal of Theatre Production Practice* 1 (1). http://journals.sfu.ca/bts/index.php/bts/article/view/8.(accessed: 20 March 2019).

Osmond, S. (2017), 'Book Review: *Unbuttoned: The Art and Artists of Theatrical Costume Design*', *Studies in Costume & Performance* 2 (1): 95–102. https://doi.org/10.1386/scp.2.1.95_5.(accessed: 15 March 2019).

Pantouvaki, S. (2010), 'Visualising Theatre: Scenography from Concept to Design to Realisation', in Monika Raesch (ed.), *Mapping Minds*, 67–75. Oxford: Inter-Disciplinary Press.

Pisano, L. (2017), 'Costume Collaboration' in Melissa Merz (ed.), *The Art and Practice of Costume Design*, 149–74. New York: Routledge, Taylor & Francis Group.

Pollatsek, E. S. (2016), *Unbuttoned: The Art and Artists of Theatrical Costume Design*. New York: Focal Press.

Schön, D. (1983), *The Reflective Practitioner: How Professionals Think in Action*. New York: Basic Books.

Sennett, R. (2009), *The Craftsman*. London: Penguin Books.

Sennett, R. (2013), *Together*. London: Penguin Books.

Snodgrass, A. and R. Coyne (2006), *Interpretation in Architecture: Design as a Way of Thinking*. London: Routledge.

Tomes, A., C. Oates and P. Armstrong (1998), 'Talking Design: Negotiating the Verbal–visual Translation', *Design Studies* 19 (2): 127–42. https://doi.org/10.1016/S0142-694X(97)00027-6 (accessed: 15 March 2019).

Ulusoy, Z. (1999), 'To Design versus to Understand Design: The Role of Graphic Representations and Verbal Expressions', *Design Studies* 20 (2): 123–30.

Walter, H. (2017), 'A Footnote in History: Irving's 1876 *Othello*', *Studies in Costume & Performance*2 (2): 137–56. https://doi.org/10.1386/scp.2.2.137_1 (accessed: 17 March 2019).

White, T. R. (2015), *Blue-Collar Broadway: The Craft and Industry of American Theater*. Philadelphia: University of Pennsylvania Press.

Wilkinson-Weber, C. (2004), 'Behind the Seams: Designers and Tailors in Popular Hindi Cinema', *Visual Anthropology Review* 20 (2): 3–21. https://doi.org/10.1525/var.2004.20.2.3 (accessed: 15 March 2019).

5.2 Fitting Threads: Embodied Conversations in the Costume Design Process

Suzanne Osmond

Much attention has been paid over the past few decades to the crucial role that collaboration plays in professional design practice, particularly in the disciplines of architecture and industrial design (Lawson & Dorst 2009; Brown 2013; Markopoulos et al. 2016). The role of effective and nuanced communication in creative collaboration is a well-established principle, although less attention has been paid to the role of non-verbal forms of communication within design expertise. This chapter contributes to filling a gap in analytical scholarship regarding the collaborative interaction that occurs within performance-making in the disciplinary practice of costume between costume designer, draper/maker and performer in the design process. The introduction of a framework through and by which non-verbal forms of communication can be analysed gives another perspective on costume design expertise in research, practice and education.

My analysis proceeds through observation, thick description (a term derived from anthropology and ethnography) and conclusions in which the non-verbal aspects of communication are foregrounded. In order to do this, I introduce the term 'embodied conversation' to refer to the specific phenomenon of collaborative interactions that occur on and around the body of the performer in the costume design process.[1] The iterative processes of research, ideation, sketching, rendering and technical drawing form key stages in the creative collaborations that costume designers carry out with directors, makers, performers, artists and other creative professionals. It is in the costume fitting process, however, that a significant part of the collaborative design process occurs and in which the role of non-verbal forms of communication is amplified. By specifically focusing on these 'embodied conversations' in the dynamic relational setting of the fitting room, the aim is to develop discipline-specific analytical tools with which to further understand the embodied and tacit inter-relational forms of knowledge that costume designers employ.

I use an action research methodology consisting of observational research, surveys and interviews with costume professionals. The research aims to understand how specific practices are to be understood 'in the field' and then to have these insights available for systematic theorizing (Denzin and Lincoln 2008: 290). I propose below a schematic framework for identifying and analysing non-verbal forms of design communication based on communication theory and recent findings in the cognitive sciences that relate to the embodied creative process.

Collaboration and Communication in the Costume Design Process

Costume designers typically operate in a physically immersive, materially oriented space that includes a high interpersonal dimension. In common with their colleagues in other design professions, the skills and experience they bring to the role include 'the integration of reason with observation, reflection, imagination, action and production' (Nelson and Stolterman 2003: 18). In addition to these fundamental design skills involving cycles of research, ideation and realization, costume designers bring specific knowledge of historical and contemporary clothing forms, specialized technical and managerial skills, as well as context-specific expertise in both visual and verbal communication. These contexts may range from live performance to film, from intimate independent theatre productions to main stage spectaculars and include a plethora of conceptual and dramaturgical approaches, as well as diverse contemporary and historical references. Most distinctive for the costume designer, compared with other design disciplines, are the design processes that occur on and around the body of the performer. The performer's body provides the practical, narrative and ideological site upon which the collaborative and creative processes of costume design coalesce. As well as the function of the body of the performer within the collaborative process, the body of the designer and also that of the maker/s display that which Barrett (2010: 145) calls 'situated knowledge'. This knowledge is produced at the intersection of experience, practice and theory and is manifested in verbal as well as non-verbal forms. These forms of communication can be considered as 'embodied conversations' that occur between bodies and other material and spatial actors in the design process. The ultimate 'conversation' occurs in the subsequent stage of a production between the costumed performer and the audience as a manifestation of the design process.

Yet the costumed body, whether on stage or regarded within the continuum of the wider creative process, is not a fixed entity. As Monks (2010: 20) notes, when audiences look at a performer in costume they see multiple bodies 'emerging continuously throughout the course of the performance'. For performance philosopher Esa Kirkkopelto, the performing body on stage is both a real object and a dramaturgical component (2016: 50). The costume designer's work can be seen as progressively resolving these two entities: attending to both the 'real' body of the performer and to the fictional, dramaturgical body of the character or role (Monks 2010; Pantouvaki 2010). Monks (2010: 19–25) has discussed the complexity of the 'real' actor's body as a series of bodies or processes: the working body, the aesthetic body, the self-expressive body, the character's body, the sensate body and the historical body. In the context of a costume fitting, the costume designer applies their skill proportionally to each of these aspects of the performer's body, whilst also engaging in multiple channels of collaboration. The iterative processes of 'fitting' any costume involves the resolution of diverse aesthetic, technical, representational, functional, logistical and narrative aspects of the costumed body in performance. This complexity plays out with its greatest intensity in the temporally and spatially defined spaces of the fitting room. The fitting room has been described variously as a classroom, a creative laboratory, a therapy session and a 'rather awkward experience' (Freer 2015). Broadway costume designer William Ivey Long calls it a 'sacred space', a space which holds intimate secrets kept with the solemnity of a Hippocratic oath (Ahrens & Viagas 2006: 206). It is usually a small enclosed space, where dressed and half-dressed bodies, unfinished garments, unresolved tensions and the rhizomic processes of artistic collaboration coalesce – generally in front of a full-length mirror – which further amplifies the intensity and complexity of the event.

In most cases, the costume design process begins on the two-dimensional plane. The conversations and collaborations that lead up to a finished costume-design rendering typically involves the contributions of the director and other members of the creative team. Once a costume begins to be materially realized, the contributions of makers, supervisors, specialist craftspeople and the performers themselves become integral to the process; all individual collaborators bring along their own embodied processes, tendencies and technologies. This complex process might occur iteratively over the course of several costume fittings, usually occurring in a time period synchronous with the rehearsal period. Each fitting typically lasts between twenty and thirty minutes, whilst more complex designs might require an hour or more to fit and resolve multiple layers of garment or multiple costumes. Typically present in the fitting room with the performer and designer are one or more costume professionals; this usually includes the principal maker (usually a tailor, draper or cutter) and may also include an assistant, the costume supervisor and various specialty makers such as shoemakers, milliners and finishing artists.

The costume-fitting process involves a number of physical, practical and conceptual issues. These include the exercising of power and hierarchical structures, information dissemination, collaborative decision-making, creative problem solving and the implementation of often highly specialized craftsmanship. Designer Michael Wilkinson explains how the fitting room figures within his creative process:

> I love the dialogue that happens in the fitting room and to see the actor become transformed by the clothes, to see what they're drawn to intuitively, and to see what they might be surprised by when we try clothes on in the fitting room. It's sort of a real Exploratorium, the fitting room. (Wilkinson in Blackwell 2014: n.p.)

Wilkinson highlights the fact that the collaborative interactions and opportunities that arise in and around the fitting process generate a significant proportion of the design decisions of costume designers. Unlike most other elements of performance design, the crucial early stage decision-making that costume designers engage in on the body of the performer cannot be tried out in a model box. Such decisions cannot be easily rendered in 3D digital form, tried out in the rehearsal room, mapped on a technical drawing or simulated in the performance space. Costume renderings, although they provide a strategic focus for costume designers and those involved in their realization, exist solely in the world of representation until they are realized on the actor's body in three dimensions. As Academy Award winning designer Tim Chappel states, 'there can be a costume without a rendering, but there can't be a costume without a fitting' (Chappel interview 2017). He goes on to imply that the 'embodied conversations' that occur in the fitting room are substantially more important than the costume rendering in determining the various success factors that the process must facilitate.

As any costume professional will attest, creation on and around the messy, fragile and unstable performing body can be challenging, more so when it also involves the integration of other messy, unstable bodies and multiple objects. The somatic physicality of the performer renders the costume design process a deeply complex negotiation, involving the psychological aspects of the performer, as well as the imaginative responses projected by them and the director/choreographer into the character or the role they are portraying. It is in this nexus between the sensory, emotional and the material components of performance that the use of nuanced non-verbal communication skills becomes a crucial aspect of professional practice. These 'embodied conversations', I argue, are a specific competency of professional costume designers and are worthy of attention from scholars, practitioners and pedagogues.

Examples of research into the embodied aspects of design communication and decision-making are scarce. Theories, concepts and models of the design process in established areas of design-thinking scholarship, such as architecture and industrial design, tend to prioritize the procedural, strategic and methodological parts of design practice with the aim of improving innovation, sustainability and profit. The embodied nature of user experience is certainly a focus in the current research into design thinking, however this has precluded consideration of the ways in which design knowledge is held in and expressed through the body of the designer.

As the following section demonstrates, considering design expertise within the context of arts-based research methodologies yields a more generative set of models and frameworks for considering how costume designers practise their expertise.

Costume Design Expertise

Research into what designers actually 'do' has been the focus of inquiry in the more established design disciplines such as architecture and product design since the 1990s when the intuitive and creative processes of designers began to attract attention as a focus of inquiry in other areas of scholarship and education. Inquiry into the nature of design thinking and design expertise aimed to make explicit the creative processes designers engage in with the aim of improving practice and outcomes (Lawson 1997; Lawson and Dorst 2009; Cross 2011; Dorst 2011). This body of knowledge contributes to a discussion of the ways in which costume designers 'do' design in its articulation of the generative nature of design thinking and the processes by which designers use their skills to move from divergent to convergent design decision-making processes.

A striking omission from most of the literature and research on design decision-making is consideration of the body: specifically the role of the designer's body in the design process, the creative intelligence associated with the 'secondary' senses of touch, smell and taste and, of relevance to this chapter, the role of non-verbal communication in collaborative design interactions. Drawing on key developments in cognitive science regarding embodied cognition, Lindgaard and Wesselius (2017) have recently extended current thought about design thinking by bringing theoretical attention to the role that the senses play in design expertise. They claim that 'ambivalence towards the role that feeling plays in thinking may be one source of the ambiguity of design thinking'. (2017: 90).

Detailed research and scholarship into the types of knowledge transfer costume designers engage in during creative collaborations has begun to be explored by Pantouvaki (2010) in relation to the designers' collaboration with performers, as well as the creative role of the maker's hand in collaborative design decision-making. In this volume, Madeline Taylor (2019) analyses specific nuanced characteristics of the creative relationship between the costume maker and designer. In terms of embodied costume design practices, practice-led researcher Sally Dean has also proposed in this volume a collaborative method of costume design that occurs during the act of performance itself. Choreographer and designer Tina Bicât offers a practitioner's perspective on the collaborative costume design process in devised theatre and provides a useful set of guidelines and background information to the designer about collaborating with performers in the fitting room. When considering the performer's body and the kinaesthetic aspects of costume, the movement it affords the performer and the movement of the costume in response to the performer's body, Bicât (2012) offers a more empathetic and relational set of guidelines for designers in working with performers' bodies than most similar instructional texts.

Recent theories and models of practice-based research in the arts offer ways to consider the forms of knowledge that costume designers employ by recognizing the role of embodied practices in creating artworks, artefacts, performances and other cultural texts. Nelson (2013: 37) proposes that professional practice in the arts exists within the nexus of three modes of highly context- dependent formations of knowledge: know-how, know-what and know-that. The know-that and know-what are defined as expositional forms of knowledge that can be gained from formal education and experience and can generally be readily transferred and explained. In Nelson's model, as in Gilbert Ryle's 1940s model on which it extends, the know-how is also referred to as procedural knowledge or the knowledge exercised in the performance of a task. Ryle ([1949] 2009) had argued for a distinction between 'knowing how' and 'knowing that': 'Knowing how' describes the ability to carry out tasks which Ryle argued was different from knowledge of facts and processes. This enaction incorporates consideration of experiential, tacit, haptic and embodied forms of knowing and is often harder to explain and transfer. These forms of knowing are linked to embodied processes involving all the senses, as well as to discrete actions and reactions.

Three Dresses, One Performer: An Example of Observational Research in the Fitting Room

As part of the larger action research project that informs this chapter, I engaged in a number of observational research sessions in order to gather data about costume design expertise in the context of the fitting room. I chose to focus my observations on large-scale opera companies as this gave both scope and access to high-level professional design practitioners. The data gained in these observational sessions was analysed in combination with surveys, interviews and my own reflective practice and tacit knowledge of the costume fitting process. One of the advantages of my professional background was, firstly, the ability to negotiate access to costume fittings and, secondly, to engage in the process of data gathering with a nuanced awareness of the situation. By developing a series of 'thick descriptions' of the fittings I observed, I was able to 'make the familiar strange' and interpret it 'from a position of empathetic understanding' (Blanche et al. 2006: 321).

The following is an account of one such costume fitting, subjected to interpretative analysis using the two frameworks articulated in this chapter. The first maps the design domains attended to (the dramaturgical, the aesthetic, the functional, the logistical, the technical and the psycho-social) and the second provides an analytical framework for considering the non-verbal embodied forms of communication: vocalics, kinesics, proxemics, haptics, chronemics and oculesics.

Tim Chappel is running late to his fitting with the new lead performer in Opera Australia's operetta *Two Weddings, One Bride* – a tardiness he later reveals to me as strategic. The fitting room at Opera Australia is one of three, set away from the busy costume workroom, each divided by a deeply hemmed calico curtain. The rooms are slightly larger than most fitting rooms, giving the space necessary for the larger size of costumes common in the context of a national opera company. The room also contains a context-driven selection of materials. A rack containing the costume items to be fitted: a mix of calico toiles, half-finished garments and tulle undergarments. A table contains boxes of pins and safety pins, a bag of stockings and socks, rolls of cotton tape in various widths and scattered pens and paper. A box of artificial flowers on the carpeted floor sits besides a collection of shoes drawn from the company's vast stock.

I'm the first to arrive. I wait in the small room on one of the three chairs placed at the side of the room. The costume supervisor arrives with the young female opera singer who is taking over the lead role in *Two Weddings, One Bride* in two months' time. They are followed by Samuel St Aubyn, a cutter who has worked at Opera Australia for the last five years. He wears an apron, self-fashioned it references a tradesman's apron. Sam's tools of trade include a cluster of safety pins, scissors, tape, clippers and a tape measure round his neck. The performer looks relaxed and expresses pleasure to be having the fitting as her first performance in the role is not far away and there is a lot of 'stage business' involving the costume which relies on her being very familiar and confident with the way the garments go on and off her body whilst in performance.

Sam begins to pin the performer into her first costume; his manner balances friendliness with professionalism. It's the same professional attitude a hairdresser or beautician might adopt as they function professionally in the bodily regions usually associated with social relatedness and intimacy. The costume supervisor Cassandra Pascoli chats amicably to the performer as Sam makes some adjustments to the first dress. She discusses the jewellery and accessories Tim has chosen and the image the company may have chosen to publicize the cast change.

Julie Lea Goodwin is the second performer in this role, so the costumes are familiar to the team. All the problems involving how the costume changes and stage business are 'choreographed' have been solved in the previous iteration. The focus here is very much on making sure they fit this body and that the performer is comfortable, given that the coming on-and-off of costumes on stage is vital to several comedic moments.

Tim arrives and the atmosphere in the fitting room changes. Sam almost visibly stiffens and becomes wholly professional. His manner is consultative, respectful and at times gently chiding of Tim for his 'hands on' approach to handling the costume. Tim, having come from a costume-making background is confident in his handling of the garment and interactions with the performer. Each time he 'goes in' to manipulate the garment on the performer and suggest a solution, Sam responds by communicating the implications of that move. For example at one stage, Chappel stands side-by-side with the performer, peers into the mirror and clasps his hands around her waist to gesture the waist coming in a little to accentuate the silhouette, the silhouette being more visible in the distance presented in the mirror than close up. Sam responds with a reminder that two dresses are being worn over the top of each other and that this will influence how small the waist can be.

Both designer and maker spend some time focused on the sweetheart keyhole neckline and in reducing the amount of gape given the layers involved (Figure 5.2.1). Again, Sam stands back to let Chappel skillfully manipulate the neckline. He then moves in and pins the agreed amount out on two panels to bring the garment in closer to the performer's body. Noise from the other two rooms necessitates participants leaning in at times and focus close attention on their exchanges. Cassie comes in and out gathering accessories and attending to the plethora of details involved in organizing all the costumes for this production.

The third garment to be fitted is a wedding dress (Figure 5.2.2). This is in the second-fitting stage and is in the final fabric. The train of this dress has to be torn off by wedding guests as part of a choreographic routine, so Sam has constructed a series of magnets around the waistband which secure the parts of the train firmly enough for Julie Lea to spend most of the second act in this dress, whilst still allowing them to be removed, all without damaging the lace or tulle.

During this fitting, Tim does one thing that strikes me as exemplifying the ways in which costume designers work creatively in the liminal spaces between their own bodies and those of the costumed performers. Once the details of how the wedding bodice fitted were resolved and attention moved to the skirt and the functions it had to perform, Tim sang a few notes of the 'champagne aria' and enacted the tearing-off of the skirt pieces as he drifted

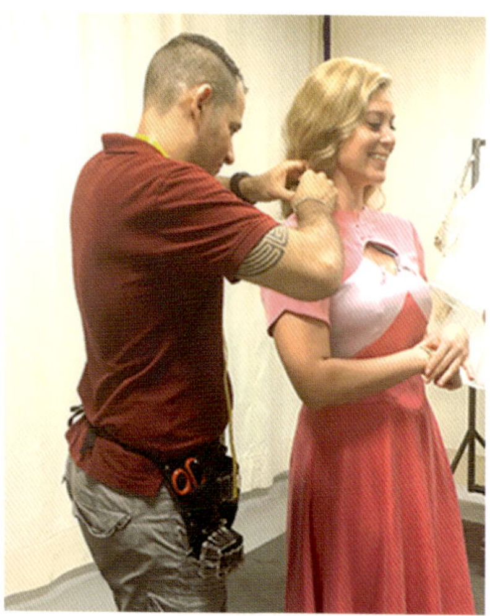

Figure 5.2.1 *Costume fitting for the role of 'Girofla/Giroflé' in Opera Australia's production of* Two Weddings, One Bride *(2017). Costume-cutter Samuel St Aubyn (left), performer Julie Lea Goodwin (right). Costume Designer: Tim Chappel. Photograph by Suzanne Osmond. Courtesy of the author.*

Figure 5.2.2 *Costume design from* Two Weddings, One Bride. *Costume Designer: Tim Chappel, Opera Australia 2017. Courtesy of Tim Chappel.*

around the static performer. In doing so, he is using his body to simulate the actions the garments will be exposed to in performance, but he is doing something else as well. By inserting himself bodily into the functionality of the design, he is moving from abstraction (the idea of the costume in the sketch) to specific embodied action (the actions of the performance).

S. Osmond, Opera Australia Costume Department, March 2017.

Analysing the Costume Fitting

In this thick description of a few minutes of a costume fitting at Opera Australia, the types of communication and knowledge being shared and negotiated to move the design process forward occur within several intersecting domains. I propose that these domains are: the dramaturgical, the aesthetic, the functional, the logistical, the technical and the psycho-social. This schema proposes that each act of verbal and non-verbal communication within the collaborative design process is concerned with one or more of these domains. Table 5.2.1 outlines these domains and relates them to particular aspects of the design realization.

Table 5.2.1 Knowledge Domains in the Costume-fitting Process

Domain	Key Questions
Dramaturgical	How does the design relate to the internal world of the production? How does the design relate to the external world of the production? How does the costume assist with the creation of narrative?
Aesthetic	How does the costume appear? How does it appear on the performer?
Functional	What does the costume afford the performer? What does the costume afford the character/role/narrative? What does the costume afford the audience/spectator?
Logistical	How should tasks be sequenced? How can issues of cost, time and scope be resolved?
Technical	What are the specific methods of construction, materials, tools and techniques required?
Psycho-social	How can the team and its individual members manage the performer's expectations, as well as collective (the team's) goals and expectations? How can the team members build trust, manage conflict, ease tension and encourage collaborative problem solving?

In generating the initial framing data for this research, I sent out a number of surveys to prominent costume designers. One question concerned the degree to which they rated the importance of addressing the *logistical* aspects of the process during a costume fitting. Most designers responded that considerations around task sequencing, cost and time were of minimal importance to them during a costume fitting. Here, I encountered a reflexive moment in which I questioned the degree to which my personal subjectivity (as a professional costume supervisor) might bias the significance of the project management functions of a costume fitting. When triangulating the data gained from observational research sessions, however, I found empirical evidence of a greater focus on task sequencing and management functions expressed by the majority of the observed costume designers. Although gender and age may have played a role in the ways in which both designers used the costume fitting as an arena in which to posit possible logistical and organizational solutions, it nevertheless raises further opportunities for research into the organizational and project management aspects of design collaboration.

The use of the term 'dramaturgical' to encompass the representational and narrative functions of performance costume recognizes the role that costume plays in creating dramatic compositions, whether on stage or in alternative performance contexts. The responsibility of performance costume to communicate the circumstances, attitudes, atmosphere, narrative and characterizations within performance is widely recognized. Costume integrates with the body of the performer to represent the internal (psychological) and external (sociological) worlds of the production, giving audiences access to the dramaturgical meanings of the performance. From a broader sociological perspective, the term has been influentially used as a metaphor by Goffman (1999) to refer to 'impression management', a person's efforts to create specific impressions in the minds of others. It has been used more recently by Barbieri (2017: 175) to refer to Oscar Wilde's nuanced construction of the sartorial aspects of his characters: the 'dramaturgy of costume' refers to the representational techniques that costume designers use to create 'embodied, cultural, social, artistic and historical narratives' (Barbieri & Pantouvaki 2016: 7).

The *aesthetic* elements of costume include the application of design principles and context-driven aesthetic concerns. In a costume fitting, this might include consideration of the effects of lighting, skin tone, scale and contrast and the effect that the juxtaposition of various other objects (other performers, scenic elements, accessories and props) has on the design. Curtis concluded his problematization of the role of the designer in his text *The Designer: Decorator or Dramaturg* by claiming a middle ground in which the designer is equally responsible for the synthesis of 'image, aesthetic and meaning' (2016: 7).

Crucial moments of collaborative decision making about *functional* aspects of costume occur both progressively and iteratively at various stages of the design process: in the initial conversations with the director, in formative discussions with the performers, in the discussions with makers, in rushed exchanges in corridors, in the costume-fitting process and finally in the technical and dress rehearsals. In each case, costume designers are called upon to negotiate, resolve and revise parts of the design that are integral to the embodied nature of performance.

The degree of technical skill a costume designer holds will inevitably influence the confidence with which they approach technical problem-solving and manipulation in a costume fitting. This is an area where the differences between procedural and expositional knowledge about cloth, cut and fit become evident. Distinct from the procedural embodied knowledge held in the body and perceived in action, expositional knowledge is the result of skills and processes acquired as a result of formal education and/or apprenticeship. Costume designers who have received formal training in pattern cutting, draping and costume construction may have at their disposal a greater vocabulary of techniques and technical knowledge. There was a great degree of difference in this respect in the designers I interviewed for this study. This level of expositional knowledge does not, however, have a direct correlation to the skill of the costume designer.

The degree to which designers are able to negotiate, initiate and facilitate the collaborative process provides perhaps the greatest point of difference between practitioners. When asked in the interview that followed my observation session about the way he collaborates with performers, Chappel shared: 'you wouldn't succeed unless you were a person who's nurturing, you have to be a natural nurturer. That is why we do it. It's just an extension of our personality type' (Chappel interview 2017). These psycho-social aspects of design expertise are evident in a designer's communication style and the ease with which they use the fitting event to build trust, manage conflict and ease latent or overt tensions. As an example of this type of expertise in action, I refer to the situation above, in which a potentially awkward and problematic situation was diverted through Chappel's expertise in collaborating with performers, a characteristic he refers to as 'nurturing'. The way in which Chappel interacted with the performer's body was more akin to the way in which a doctor might press on a part of the body to determine a reaction, yet the interaction had nothing of a clinical character.

Conversely, and highlighting the risks that this socially intimate context poses, Dan Potra, (Australian costume designer with an international professional practice) expressed a fear of designing costumes earlier in his career due to the risk of mis-communication with performers:

> I used to hate designing costumes until about 15 years ago – because I just didn't know how to handle the performers. I just didn't understand what they wanted – and the kind of unspoken words used to really unnerve me until I realised that actually the best way to approach a fitting is like a hairdresser. … And the whole thing is about listening … making the performer aware that his or her concerns are taken into consideration. (Potra Interview 2017)

Designer Sofia Pantouvaki shared the importance of building an empathetic relationship, in which she encourages the performer to feel that the way the fitting goes 'is something that relates directly to them. … This gives them a sense of calmness … it is not only 'my worry' [the performer's], it is also a common stress, shared with the designer, so that feeling of sharing, I think, builds a positive moment of joint effort towards a goal. (Pantouvaki interview 2017)

Non-verbal Forms of Design Communication

The previous section has provided a schema for recognizing and analysing the various concerns that are attended to during the costume design process and in particular during the costume-fitting process. From an embodied perspective, a research model of the collaborative communication in the costume-design process would focus on the use of verbal and non-verbal language within these domains in the form of speech, gesture and touch. Although these forms of knowledge and means of verbal and non-verbal communication are present in all phases of the costume-design process and indeed within all design processes, the costume-fitting event provides a tight temporal and spatial site of focus.

The following section aims to create a framework for analysing the various modes of non-verbal communication that occur during the costume-design process, the ways in which collaborators communicate their intentions and engage in rich 'embodied conversations'. Communication theory offers a number of useful categories of non-verbal communication. In Andersen's (2008) survey of these, he identifies eight non-verbal codes. The embodied interactions above, are considered within several of these categories of non-verbal communication: vocalics, kinesics, proxemics, haptics, chronemics and oculesics.

These forms of communication exist almost wholly as tacit knowledge in that they are only made visible in practice. Polanyi's theory of tacit knowledge recognized that knowledge that is known, but cannot be easily articulated or transferred is 'beyond language' and can only be expressed in practice (Polanyi 2013: 5). The development of specialty technical language is the result of what Polanyi would call procedural knowledge, in that it is taught in colleges and universities andpicked up from professional practice. Non-verbal forms of language are not, however, traditionally taught in tertiary settings. It is unlikely that any student has been explicitly instructed on how to gesturally communicate 'I need this to be fuller at the back'. These forms of embodied communication are a central characteristic of the creative collaborative process and are worthy of analysis, given their prevalence in practice and the crucial role they play in communicating concept into reality.

Kinesics

In observing designers during fittings, it was striking how much of an integral role that body language and gesture plays in design communication. Designers' hands tend to play a central role in fittings in particular. In the situation described in the fitting at Opera Australia, hands fluttered, mimicked forms, indicated silhouettes and gestured spatial relationships.

Gestural communication is also an important aspect of the way in which performers react to the costume in a fitting. Designer Sofia Pantouvaki, among others, observed that even though she begins her collaboration with the performer before rehearsal 'the fitting is a moment for understanding how the character will move, how he or she will stand' (Pantouvaki interview 2017). Chappel's physical interactions and mimicking of the dancer's interactions with the singer in pulling off her skirt engages directly with the functional aspects of the costume and provides an embodied understanding of how costume supports movement.

Vocalics

In communication theory, para-language refers to the vocalized, but non-verbal aspects of communication. Vocalics is the study of para-language, which includes the vocal qualities that accompany verbal messages, such as pitch, volume, rate, vocal quality and verbal fillers (Andersen 2008). In transcribing the costume fittings I observed as part of this study, a great deal of the transcription is made up of utterances such as appreciative 'aaahs', tentative 'hmmms', 'uh huhs' in agreement, clicking sounds, loud inhalations and exhalations, laughter and sighs. Put together, they provide a rich vocabulary of non-verbal forms of communication, which at the time of their utterance, portrayed meanings that were sharply definitive and unequivocally understood.

Proxemics

The study of proxemics focuses on the ways in which relational configurations of space and distance influence how people communicate and behave. Smaller spaces with a higher density of people often lead to breaches of socially agreed thresholds of personal space. The configuration of space and how close participants stand to each other in the fitting room forms a text which establishes hierarchies and influences behaviour. Filmer and Rossmanith's study of the ways in which theatrical spaces inform actors' experience and influence the dynamics of theatrical presentation itself determined that the dressing room plays a vital role in the formation of performer subjectivity. To them it directly influences the ways in which hierarchies and relationships are formed and maintained within the continuum of a performance run (Filmer and Rossmanith 2011). Although the fitting room was not considered directly in their study, many of their insights are directly relevant to understanding the space of the fitting as an influential non-verbal text. Indeed, the dressing room is often the site of costume fittings being situated close to the action of technical rehearsals and performance. Fittings often occur in custom-designed, 'jerry-rigged' fitting rooms or in specially designed costume trailers, but they also occur in crowded backstage wings, kitchens, bedrooms, hotel rooms, hallways, bathrooms, classrooms, tents and public spaces. The ambiguity of the dressing room has been a feature of Western European art and literature for centuries, emphasizing the slippage between costume and fashion, performance and life. It marked a liminal or transitional zone in societies as varied as Stuart England or nineteenth-century Paris. The sub-division of space into a smaller private space and the inclusion of a prominent mirror is a common feature of such spaces. One of the dual aims of this spatial construction is to afford two types of proximal relationship: one in which the maker and designer are able to engage with the costumed body up-close and another, in which the mirror is utilized to replicate the audience's proximity to the costumed body.

Haptics

Historian Elizabeth Harvey notes that the sense of touch 'evokes at once agency and receptivity, authority and reciprocity, pleasure and pain, sensual indulgence and epistemological certainty' (Harvey 2003: 2). Touch operates at many levels, including functional-professional, social-polite, friendship-warmth and love-intimacy (Andersen 2008).

Other than sight, touch is perhaps the most critical sense being activated in a costume fitting. Fittings are the point at which the tactile properties of the costume become apparent for the performer and the haptic properties of the costumed performer becomes apparent to the designer and maker. Susan Davis, costume shop manager at the Seattle Opera, notes that she pays particular attention in fittings to the ways in which a performer 'picks at or keeps touching' parts of the costume, 'as this can be a good indication that something feels odd' (Davis in Merz 2017: 190).

Chronemics

Chronemics provides insights into how the use of time creates and sustains 'order, control, efficiency and production' within non-verbal communication (Bruneau 1981: 104). When applied to the temporal framework of the costume-fitting process it is possible to develop further perspectives on hierarchies, emotional interactions and the characteristics of professional knowledge. The economics of most production contexts dictates a rehearsal period as quick as possible to rehearse a performance to a satisfactory level, usually somewhere between four and six weeks, depending on the scope of the production. During this rehearsal period, the time allocated for costume fittings is pressed between busy daily rehearsal schedules and other commitments such as publicity calls, other departmental calls, coaching and meetings. The tight temporal frame in which a fitting occurs influences the intensity of verbal and non-verbal interactions between those involved. Costume fittings are commonly scheduled back to back in thirty- to fourty-five-minute intervals. This pattern makes the most of the design and production teams' time and minimizes the impact on the rehearsal room.

The chronemic code active in a typical fitting room tends to place the performer's time as most valuable, followed by the designer and then the costume department staff, including the cutter. This code is visible in the way in which performers are rarely left waiting for a fitting to occur and in which fittings are usually held in clusters for the convenience of the designer, who may not be on-site continuously. One of the characteristics of people's relationship to time is manifested in lateness, earliness and the degree of temporal flexibility assumed or allowed to them. Generally, these factors relate to politeness, value and power (Burgoon, Guerrero and Floyd 2016: 199). Higher-status individuals generally have greater flexibility in terms of their use of time. As an Academy Award-winning designer, Tim Chappel could be seen to occupy that position in the situation described above. Chappel's previously mentioned lateness, however, reveals another dimension of expert knowledge that manipulates time in a nuanced manner to promote professionalism and increase morale:

> I generally try and leave a good ten minutes for the cutter and actor to be alone before I come in. Because I have been a cutter, I know there's nothing worse than you're just getting the dress on the person and everybody has got an opinion. It's like 'give me a God damn second to sort out what I need to sort out first and then you can have an opinion', so I just leave them to it. (Chappel interview 2017)

Other aspects of the chronemic code that might present opportunities for further analysis of the costume-design and production process, are the relationships between time and value in the costume workroom and the differences between perceptions of time in film and live-performance production.

Oculesics

In the semi-private space of the fitting room, performers look into the mirror and at the point of their gaze a character is manifested. Looking (or not looking) is one aspect of non-verbal communication between performer, designer and costume maker that can have great potency in the context of the fitting room. Despite the degree to which they have been involved in the development of their costume, a performer's initial reaction to their costumed image in the mirror can range from delight to horror. This moment provides an opportunity for the designer and costume department to address the performer's needs and expectations, especially when these may be a source of dissonance. Designer Julie Lynch explains the significance of this dynamic in relation to a performer, who, throughout the entire fitting and construction phase refused to look at himself in the mirror in a costume that comically exaggerated his body. Rather than arising from an insecurity about his appearance, the performer was engaged in a sort of embodied characterization experiment in which he only desired to engage with the kinesthetic and functional aspects of the costume until it was completed. She explains:

> For his Trinculo costume, he tested it as it was being built, internally exploring how it felt and how it worked. However, he left his judgement of the external aesthetic until it was complete, trusting the designer with the image, and then responding to it as a spectator might. (Lynch 2017a:149)

An awareness of the types of looking that performers engage in once confronted with an image of their costumed body, is something that astute costume designers intuitively gauge and respond to, as a cue to building trust and creative collaboration.

A specialized type of design looking is central to the costume-fitting process and to the costume design process in general. The complexity of this looking provides a fascinating focus for the study of costume design language, collaboration and the creative process. The looking that designers do in the fitting room tends to have a more binocular characteristic. The designer's gaze shifts from being focused directly on the costumed body, to focusing at the same time on its image reflected in the mirror. The designerly gaze imaginatively collapses the space between materiality and representation and between cloth and character. Through squinting, staring, stepping back and shifting focus designers imaginatively replicate the gaze of the audience, whilst also balancing the image in the mirror with their own internal (and external) visualization of the costume design.

The insights gained in this study are focused on the phenomenon of the costume fitting, but have resonances for the entire costume-design and realization process. As Lynch explains, the process of collaboration begins long before the costume fitting and spills out into other spaces in the processes of performance-making such as the rehearsal room.

> I see the fitting also going on as a continuum of the rehearsal room. I then go and sit in the room and I imagine them in the costume (...) So the fitting is a sort of continuance of the process. (Lynch interview 2017b)

In using the methodologies of action research and in creating a discipline-specific set of tools for the analysis of non-verbal forms of communication, this inquiry has explored the complexity and diversity of verbal and non-verbal communication employed in the costume design and realization process in the space of the fitting room. The approach foregrounds the embodied nature of design practice and design knowing. It also offers an alternative model to consider design expertise as being embedded in multi-sensory contexts beyond that expressed in verbal and written language and in visual communication. In offering a means for further investigation of the ebb and flow of power, information, decision-making, creativity and craftsmanship that occurs in the costume-realization process, the fitting room achieves new significance as a site of dynamic interaction in the costume-design process.

Note

I would like to thank Professor Sofia Pantouvaki and her colleagues at Aalto University for providing the opportunity for the postdoctoral residency that enabled this research within the 'Costume Methodologies' research project with funding by the Academy of Finland. I was greatly helped there by Susanna Suurla, Tua Helve, my colleague Dr. Phoenix Thomas, the Costume in Focus (CiF) research group members and Aalto University staff. I would also like to thank the Swedish Royal Opera staff who allowed me access to their workplace. Thanks also to Opera Australia staff, Rebecca Ritchie, Samuel St Aubyn, Cassandra Pascoli and Lyn Heal. The following designers gave their time to be interviewed and their words provided a valuable resource: Tim Chappel, Dr Julie Lynch, Stephen Curtis, Dan Potra and Professor Sofia Pantouvaki. I would also like to thank the editors of this edition, Distinguished Professor Peter McNeil and once again Professor Sofia Pantouvaki, for her rigour, brilliance and tireless advocacy for the field of costume studies.

1 The term has been used elsewhere within academia to refer to a number of concepts around human–computer interactions (McKinney et al. 2009).

References

Ahrens, L. and R. Viagas (2006), *The Alchemy of Theatre*. New York: Playbill Books.

Andersen, P. (2008), *Nonverbal Communication*. Long Grove: Waveland Press.

Barbieri, D. (2017), *Costume in Performance: Materiality, Culture and the Body*. New York Bloomsbury.

Barbieri, D. and S. Pantouvaki (2016), 'Towards a Philosophy of Costume', *Studies in Costume and Performance* 1 (1): 3–7. DOI: 10.1386/scp.1.1.3_2.

Barrett, E. (2010), 'Foucault's "What is an Author": Towards a Critical Discourse of Practice As Research', in E. Barrett and B. Bolt (eds), *Practice as Research: Approaches to Creative Arts Enquiry*. London: I. B.Tauris.

Bicât, T. (2012), *Costume and Design for Devised and Physical Theatre*. Ramsbury: Crowood.

Blackwell, K. (2014), 'Michael Wilkinson on Making Costumes for Iconic Characters', *Austin Way*, 14 November. Available online: https://webcache.googleusercontent.com/search?q=cache:LcEO-CwkZTgJ:https://austinway.com/michael-wilkinson-on-reinventing-iconic-characters-through-his-costumes+&cd=6&hl=en&ct=clnk&gl=au (accessed: 25 March 2019).

Blanche, M. T., K. Durrheim and D. Painter (eds) (2006), *Research in Practice: Applied Methods for the Social Sciences*. Cape Town: Juta and Company Ltd.

Brown, D. M. (2013), *Designing Together: The Collaboration and Conflict Management Handbook for Creative Professionals*. USA: Pearson Education.

Bruneau, T. (1981), 'Chronemics and the Non-Verbal Interface' in M. Ritchie Key (ed.), *The Relationship of Verbal and Nonverbal Communication*, 101–18. The Hague: Mouton Publishers.

Bruneau, T. (2009), 'Chronemics', in S. W. Littlejohn and K. A. Foss (eds), *Encyclopedia of Communication Theory*, Vol. 1, 97–101. Thousand Oaks: SAGE Publications Ltd.

Burgoon, J. K., L. K. Guerrero and K. Floyd (2016), *Nonverbal Communication*. New York: Routledge.

Chappel, T. (2017), Interview with Suzanne Osmond, 23 March, Surry Hills, Sydney, Australia.

Cross, N. (2011), *Design Thinking: Understanding How Designers Think and Work*. Oxford: Berg.

Curtis, S. (2016), *The Designer: Decorator or Dramaturg?* Strawberry Hills: Currency Press.

Dean, S. (2016), 'Where is the Body in the Costume Design Process?' *Studies in Costume and Performance* 1 (1): 97–111. DOI: 10.1386/scp.1.1.97_1.

Denzin, N. and Y. Lincoln (2008), *The Landscape of Qualitative Research*. Los Angeles: Sage Publications.

Dorst, K. (2011), 'The Core of 'Design Thinking' and its Application', *Design Studies* 32 (6): 521–32.

Dorst, K. and N. Cross (2001), 'Creativity in the Design Process: Co-evolution of Problem-solution', *Design Studies* 22 (5): 425–37.

Filmer, A. and K. Rossmanith (2011), 'Space and Actor Formation', *Theatre Research International* 36 (3): 228–39.

Freer, A. (2015), *How to Get Dressed: A Costume Designer's Secrets*. New York: Ten Speed Press.

Harvey, E. (2003), *Sensible Flesh: On Touch in Early Modern Culture*. Philadelphia: University of Pennsylvania Press.

Goffman, I. (1999), *The Presentation of Self in Everyday Life*. New York: Doubleday.

Kirkkopelto, E. (2016), 'Joints and Strings: Body and Object in Performance', *Performance Philosophy* 2 (1): 49–64.

Lawson, B. (1997), *How Designers Think*. Oxford: Architectural Press.

Lawson, B. and K. Dorst (2009) *Design Expertise*. Oxon: Routledge.

Lindgaard, K. and H. Wesselius (2017), 'Once More, with Feeling: Design Thinking and Embodied Cognition', *She ji: The Journal of Design, Economics, and Innovation* 3 (2): 83–92.

Lynch, J. (2017a), *Costume's Mirror up to Nature*, PhD thesis, University of Sydney, Faculty of Arts and Social Sciences. http://hdl.handle.net/2123/18800 (accessed: 24 March 2019).

Lynch, J. (2017b), Interview with Suzanne Osmond, 22 March, Kensington, Sydney, Australia.

Markopoulos, P., J.-B. Martens, J. Malins, K. Coninx and Liapis, eds (2016), *Collaboration in Creative Design: Methods and Tools*, Switzerland: Springer.

McKinney, J., M. Wallis, S. H. Popat, J. Bryden and D. Hogg (2009), 'Embodied Conversations: Performance and the Design of a Robotic Dancing Partner', in 'Undisciplined! Design Research Society Conference 2008', Sheffield Hallam University, Sheffield, UK, 16–19 July 2008. Availiable online: http://shura.shu.ac.uk/481/1/fulltext.pdf (accessed: 24 March 2019).

Merz, M. (2017), *The Art and Practice of Costume Design*. New York: Routledge.

Monks, A. (2010), *The Actor in Costume*. Hampshire: Palgrave Macmillan.

Nelson, H. and E. Stolterman (2003), *The Design Way: Foundations and Fundamentals of Design Competence*. Englewood Cliffs, NJ: Educational Technology Publications.

Nelson, R. (2013), *Practice as Research in the Arts: Principles, Protocols, Pedagogies, Resistances*. Hampshire: Palgrave Macmillan.

Pantouvaki, S. (2010), 'Theatrical Costume: Dressing the Role: Dressing the Performer', in I. Papantoniou (ed.), *Endyesthai (To Dress): Towards a Costume Culture Museum*, Athens, Peloponnesian Folklore Festival, 109–17. Available online: https://www.academia.edu/1958418/Theatrical_Costume_Dressing_the_Role_-_Dressing_the_Performer (accessed: 19 March 2019).

Pantouvaki, S. (2017), Interview with Suzanne Osmond, 13 April, Aalto University Library, Helsinki, Finland.

Polanyi, M. (2013), *The Tacit Dimension*. Chicago: The University of Chicago Press.

Potra, D. (2017), Interview with Suzanne Osmond, 8 March, Kensington, Sydney, Australia.

Ryle, G. ([1949] 2009), *The Concept of Mind*. London: Routledge.

Weise, W. (2006), 'Seeing and the Difference It Makes: Ocularity, Gender, and Space in Swift's and Montagu's "Dressing Room" Satires', *Women's Studies* 35 (8): 707–38.

Snapshots

5.3 Haptic Descriptions: Costume Design by Gillian Gallow and April Viczko

Natalie Rewa

This snapshot focuses on examples of costuming in Canada by designers Gillian Gallow and April Viczko that demonstrate a shift in attitudes to the role of costumes concerning the engagement of the spectator and the dynamism of costume itself. Their designs emphasize a range of visual and textural vocabularies so that the spectator imbues them with specific elements and consequently attributes to the costumes the status of interpretative environments in themselves. The designs engage the spectators in a form of active, albeit 'silent' description of these details that is simultaneous with the performance and such acts of observation reverberate in the wider context of the reception of the production. Drawn in closer by the visual 'touch' of the costumes observed from afar, the spectators take note of the autonomous narration engendered by the costumes within the production. In doing so, they also attend to the on-going negotiation with the costumes and by the performers as crucial to meaning making. The interventions discussed here are of two types: Gillian Gallow designs costumes by addressing the imperatives for the production: 'what has to be performed'.[1] Gillian Gallow's design for *An Octoroon* (2017) by Branden Jacobs-Jenkins at the Shaw Festival, Niagara-on-the-Lake, Ontario, Canada, emphasized the racialization of figures.[2] And when she designed for a revival of the opera *Louis Riel* (2017) by Harry Somers and Mavor Moore (first produced by the Canadian Opera Company in 1967 as a Centennial project), the costumes attested to the production's dynamic effort towards re-situating the historical narrative that looks back to the nineteenth century by the more recent cultural knowledge witnessed by the Truth and Reconciliation Commission (2008–15).[3] The design strategy deployed by April Viczko, my second example of a type of intervention, draws attention to a near-scientific interspecies analysis for potential ecological stylization of performance. Viczko's costume residency at the Banff Centre for Arts and Creativity (2018) curated a far-reaching interaction amongst the production departments to achieve a sympoeisis in the age of the Anthropocene.[4] Viczko's costumes for *Slime* by Byrony Lavery demonstrated an initiative 'to induce a transformation', (Haraway 2016: 130) rather than despair at the historical past or current ecologically destructive observations of human devastation. Designs by both Gallow and Viczko affect protocols of performance-making, bringing the performativity of costumes directly into a choreography of emboldened attitudes to embodiment. Designing, fitting and wearing the costumes challenge long-accepted cultural narratives through costume-driven strategies.

Gillian Gallow: 'Costuming Addresses what has to be Performed'[5]

Gallow's costume designs demonstrate a strategy to keep conflicts in play without resorting to an explanatory individualism; such 'labour' [cultural work] is assumed by the costumes in recent productions including *Louis Riel* (Canadian Opera Company, 2017), *An Octoroon* (Shaw Festival, 2017) and *Idomeneus* and *Orlando* (both Soulpepper Theatre, 2018). As Gallow explains of the costume design for *An Octoroon*:

> As much as costuming is about understanding character, I believe it is also about recognizing the audience's view of the world and characters through costume. *An Octoroon* by Branden Jacobs-Jenkins confronts the audience with the power of costume. When the black playwright cannot find any white actors willing to play the slave masters, he puts on white face and plays the roles himself. Furthermore, a white actor puts on red face to play the indigenous character and the indigenous actor puts on black face to play the slaves. In the world of the play, they become these characters, but the audience sees a deeper story weighted in the wrongs of the past and the continued racism of today. I chose to heighten the impact of the costume by playing heavily into the stereotypes the play confronts. The indigenous character, although dressed historically accurately was literally washed fully in red. The kind-hearted slave master was blonde-haired and dressed in white. And the elderly amenable black slave was inspired by minstrel show costumes.[6]

In the case of *Louis Riel*, Gallow's design similarly tunes the interpretative environment (Stewart 2011: 446). This production by the Canadian Opera Company marked a significant watershed in costume design. It was programmed as a revival fifty years after its première as part of a season that also commemorated Canada's 150 years of existence during the 2016–17 season. Gallow's costumes amplified the production's interrogation of the telling of the Métis' relationship with the late nineteenth-century colonial government.[7] There is little inclusion of a contemporary historical understanding of the Métis' political position within the opera and therefore the costume design intervened effectively to adjust this within the visual narrative. The costumes silently 'challenge' the expression of power relations by the continuous presence of a created choral figure of the Land Assembly throughout the opera and in the scenes between Riel and the colonial officials. The presence of the Land Assembly marks an expanded approach to production design, whereby the inclusion of First Nations and Métis communities become integrated into the performance. Gallow's costumed presence of the Land Assembly became a predominantly relational instantiation of the operative groups, effective not only historiographically, but also and perhaps more significantly, as an active contemporary re-inscription of territorial colonial conflict as more than one between individuals and one that is not yet resolved. The contemporaneity of the design for the costumes of the Land Assembly is in contradistinction to the historicized costumes of Riel and the colonial officials. Such costumes allow for a consciousness of 'propositions not available before' (Haraway 2016: 128) and highlight the complexity of processes of resolution that are neither, nor are likely to be completed by the end of the performance. Gallow's costumes underlined a fresh cultural perspective by costuming the 'physical chorus' (non-singing and unscripted) of Métis and Indigenous people in a bold red cloth; these costumes by their resemblance to contemporary clothing insist on a *living presence* of the Métis and First Nations, conceptualizing *survivance* (Vizenor 1999: vii). While the 'Land Assembly' does not intervene in the action of the opera, their presence and the differentiation by their costuming maintains the complexity of political negotiations as a reminder of what was *not* written into the libretto. This Land Assembly made for a formidable silent presence on the stage throughout the production in an effective, non-emphatic choreography by Santee Smith in counter-distinction to the vocal representation of parliament or the settlers. The costumes narrated *survivance* – the confluence of survival and resistance expressed by vibrant First Nations and Métis populations – and served to re-inforce active forms of actualizing self-expression simultaneous with the largely unchanged libretto. Thus costumed, the Land Assembly provided spectators with living renunciations of dominance, tragedy and victimry and made explicit what was absent in the original dramaturgy of 1967.[8] Consequently, with the inclusion of several Indigenous performers within the para-operatic action, the production acknowledged and emphasized performers and performance by First Nations and Métis artists who have developed new performance, and others who have been integral to the recuperation of traditions that have become part of the cultural landscape of these territories, also called Canada, over the last fifty years.

Figure 5.3.1 *Original costume sketch by Gillian Gallow of 'Wahnotee' in* An Octoroon *(Shaw Festival, 2017). Courtesy of Gillian Gallow.*

Figure 5.3.2 *Patrick McManus as 'Wahnotee' and Ryan Cunningham as 'Paul' in the production of* An Octoroon *by Branden Jacobs-Jenkins at the Shaw Festival (2017). Photograph by David Cooper.*

Moreover, Gallow's costuming re-draws the iconic images of Métis leader Louis Riel in his encounters with European settlers, as well as that of the political architects of the country. Costumes for the figures of the colonial government similarly took up bold colours and textures against the backdrops of projections of architectural plans for government buildings, rather than their materialization as onstage structures. Conceptualizing costumes as 'a choice that makes an impact on others',[9] Gallow's costumes play out the power dynamic employing the contemporary reading of fashion choices/narratives in her choice of bold plaids, for example, for the politicians, rather than referring to the palettes of well-known/worn portraits. Together with choreography by Santee Smith,[10] the costumes contributed to re-drawing the lines of interaction in public spaces beyond simply ghosting in the silenced figures by animating all the spaces of the production. Such re-orientation of perspectives locates the opera in competing forms of depictions that by their simultaneity open up not only space, but time, to inhabit their implications.

For the characterless *Idomeneus* (2018) by Roland Schimmlpfenning, Gallow chose images from protest marches from which she created an analogue to an *identitilessness*. Focusing on how to find a balance after society is ripped apart, these costumes perform an erasure of all pre-conceived notions of identity – of either class or individuality – and an insistance on the person of the actor who is always present. Gallow notes that she forged a fresh relationship to the text by the costumes that were not determined by the past cultural markers, but rather by contemporary clothing dyed a variation of grey and painted over with streaks of white and grey. The effect was as if looking at the performance through a scrim, as the performers emerged in their various groupings dictated by the speeches. The set consisted of a sand-filled rectangle and individuality was immediate, as footsteps in the sand were concomitant with the ephemerality of ghosting in speech.

Gallow's costumes bring to the forefront the complex narratives that maintain the *differend*[11] and actively allow the costume to remain enigmatic and therefore a matter of active significance.

April Viczko at the Banff Centre: *Sympoeisis*

The experience of costume designer April Viczko in May–June 2018 signals an integrated, technologically interactive scenographic dramaturgy responding to our current critical age. Viczko's on-going costume research into wearable art became central to a three-week production residency at the Banff Centre for Arts and Creativity in Banff, Alberta, Canada. The Centre commissioned a co-production of *Slime* by Byrony Lavery in collaboration with The Only Animal (a theatre company based in Vancouver):

> The process of creating *Slime* was extraordinary. The various departments of production at the Banff Centre were as invested in process as in product. This was a liberating experience as a designer. It meant that a milliner and a programmer would work together to decode the costume sketch to create pathways for wires and processors on a lightweight base to accommodate actor comfort, action and electronics. The dressing of the final look with feathers and wefts of blonde hair to match the actor were efforts by millinery and the wigs department. The wardrobe became a place of 3D printing, dyeing, painting, sewing, pattern drafting, and Arduino programming. What continues to amaze me months later is how simple it was to execute a complex design; how investment in process lead to a compelling stage product.[12]

The action concerns the third 'Slime' conference where delegations of animals address the threats to life by the impact of climate change. Viczko's animation of components within the costumes brought the otherness of organisms into performance, a symbiopoesis[13] that continued in the production by the rejection of an infatuation with the 'sound of our own human voices' by a biophony of animal vocabularies (sourced from animal sound archives). With Arduinos, fibre optic wires for LEDs and a 3D printer integrated amongst the sewing machines of the wardrobe, these technologies became central to the conceptualizing of costuming as fresh sites of performance. Viczko's design facilitated a new materiality for the human performers, so that a headdress would not only glow, but could light up in multiple colours, a mesh tattoo on the forearm of a costume could be activated by an LED switch and a 3D printer could manufacture other components of the costumes.[14] The effect of the residency unsettled the silos of production design, as such costuming brought together the wardrobe, video, lighting and carpentry shops. As Viczko opined, her design was manufactured by 'colonizing each department',[15] so that rehearsals often featured seven technicians editing and/or rehearsing the work of the costume: the wardrobe department was expanded as these new materials were brought into play in the architectonics of channels to accommodate the wires, situating pockets for the Arduinos and insulation against the heat of the batteries, similarly the wig and millinery departments were challenged by LED and video animations.

Figure 5.3.3 *Costume Drawing for 'Ola',* Slime *(2018) by April Viczko. Courtesy of April Viczko.*

Such collaboration on enabling the design emphasizes the complexity of these assemblages and how they make productive strides in drawing attention to discontinuities between technologies and performance. The technological animation of these costumes also addresses the scale of production and the possibilities for re-orienting departments for production. Invoking a hapticity of the luminescence of non-human matter, for example, Viczko's programme for this residency took the opportunity to re-calibrate the spacing and the timing of the performance of a costume

Figure 5.3.4 *Lisa Baran in* Slime, *Banff Centre of Arts and Creativity (2018). Photograph by Donald Lee.*

and its collaboration with the performer, that is, the costume in itself proprioceptively re-sites a performance. Viczko's approach to costume at Banff maps a series of fresh entanglements of matter and meaning that delve into the performance of the Anthropocene with distinct modes of performance.

Notes

1. Gillian Gallow, interview, 24 August 2018. Gallow's reference was to the pragmatic choices made in designing the costumes for *Orlando* (straps for wigs and visible zippers for quick changes), which also reveal how narrative strategies are transferred to the materiality of the costumes.
2. 'The process of manufacturing and utilizing the notion of race in any capacity' (Dalal 2002: 27).
3. From the nineteenth and throughout the twentieth century, children of First Nations families on Canadian territories were regularly removed to residential schools as a form of federal cultural policy. The Truth and Reconciliation Commission (2008–15) sought to document the history and lasting impact of the Indian Residential Schools. The testimony of survivors, in

addition to the documents comprise the *Truth and Reconciliation Report* (2015). Its ninety-four *Calls to Action* (see: http://www.trc.ca/websites/trcinstitution/File/2015/Findings/Calls_to_Action_English2.pdf) constitute a substantial programme to begin the process of redressing the policy's harm to all areas of social and cultural life in order to begin a process of conciliation between First Nations on these territories and subsequent immigrants. The production of the opera in 2017 was imbued with a substantial review of the cultural consciousness following the Truth and Reconciliation Commission and was especially evident in Gallow's costuming of the Land Assembly (a created composite figure for the production).

4 *Sympoeisis* refers to an endorsement of increased efforts to 'work with' other species collaboratively. Seen as a specific imperative in the current geological period – the Chthulucene or Anthropocene – when the human impact on the planet has been the greatest and new forms of 'working with' are imperative.

5 Gillian Gallow, interview, 24 August 2018. See note 1.

6 Gillian Gallow, email correspondence, 21 September 2018.

7 Throughout the production, Peter Hinton directed an emphasized Indigenous and Métis presence: by an opening monologue by Indigenous activist Cole Alvis, by including a song by contemporary singer Jani Lauzon, and by the performance by Buffalo Dancer Justin Manyfingers to replace the written bar-room scene. In this way the 2017 production began to historicize the presentation of Métis (Aboriginal and European) figures and to re-define the actions of Métis leader Louis Riel, who actively led the resistance from 1869 through to 1885, as well as the colonial government's lack of regard for the Métis' right to land in treaties in Manitoba and Saskatchewan.

8 Director Peter Hinton was influenced by the Resistance 150 movement that created art works in response to the Canada 150 movement with the motto 'Remember, Resist, Redraw.'

9 Gillian Gallow, interview, 24 August 2018.

10 Santee Smith is a Kahnyen'kehàka (Mohawk) artist of the Turtle Clan. She is the founding artistic director of Kaha:wi Dance Theatre and Chancellor of McMaster University, Canada.

11 The attention to an artistic practice which maintains distinct and oppositional positions without an imperative for consensus in a public space. By making 'visible what the dominant discourse tends to obscure and obliterate', it characterizes such spaces as actively agonistic (Chantal Mouffe 2007: 4).

12 April Viczko, interview by Skype, 31 July 2018.

13 A co-habitation of human and other life forms, which creates a figure in performance that is distinctly a new performing life form, rather than a representation of animal-likeness.

14 'The headdress for Ola was created by a milliner, programmers, electricians, prop-makers and wig technicians. It was created to respond to the actor's movements by sensors triggering various lights within the antennae. We ended with three pathways of lights: 1) a glow of white mini- LEDs controlled with a switch by the actor, 2) connected to an accelerometer and RGB LEDs and 3) RGB LEDs set at a programmed cycle. The movements of the actor had to be very pronounced with the kind of sensors we had available. However, the proof of concept was thrilling'. Email correspondence with April Viczko, 28 August 2018.

15 April Viczko, Skype interview, 31 July 2018.

References

Dalal, F. (2002), *Race, Colour and the Process of Racialization: New Perspectives from Group Analysis, Psychoanalysis and Sociology*. New York, NY: Brunner-Routledge.

Haraway, D. (2016), *Staying with the Trouble*. Durham, NC: Duke University Press.

Mouffe, Chantal. (2007), 'Artistic Activisms and Agonistic Spaces', *Art and Research* 1 (ii): 1–5.

Nolan, Yvette (2015), *Medicine Shows: Indigenous Peformance Culture*. Toronto: Playwrights Canada Press.

Stewart, K. (2011), 'Atmospheric Attunements', *Environment and Planning D: Society and Space* 29: 445–53.

Vizenor, G. (1999), *Manifest Manners: Narratives on Postindian Survivance*. Lincoln, NE: University of Nebraska Press.

Glossary

Differend A term used by Jacques Derrida (*Le Différend,* 1983) to denote a wrong or injustice that arises because the discourse in which the wrong might be expressed does not exist. Chantal Mouffe argues for artistic practices that create spaces which allow for conflicts to become present and expressed by other means: she terms spaces where resolutions are not mandated as agonistic. Costuming can become active in enabling a re-characterization of space as one in which alternate expressions of wrongs or injustices are articulated otherwise.

Identilessness Derived from a dramaturgical observation that social and cultural roles can be unhinged, setting whole populations adrift in terms of their relationship to each other and to structures of power.

Proprioception Awareness of the body which becomes crucial to affect movement and specific use of the actorly body when costumes are designed; the actor learns to negotiate the costume in the space of the performance.

Survivance The term introduced into First Nations literary studies by Gerald Vizenor (1999), emphasizing the narrative strategies that weave together stories of active survival and resistance to forces of oppression. For a discussion of examples in First Nations dramaturgy in Canada see 'Survivance' (chapter 2) in Yvette Nolan (2015).

5.4 The Costume Designer´s 'Golden List' of Competence

Christina Lindgren

How can we secure broad, deep, relevant and advanced competence for the costume designer of the future? This question has been a key question for me during the past six years.

I started teaching as Professor in Costume Design at Oslo National Academy of the Arts (KHIO) in 2013, the same institution at which I myself had studied ten years earlier. In Norway, costume design studies are part of a joint programme with fashion in the design department of KHIO. Upon starting my new role in 2013, the costume design part of the study had been on hold for some time: there were very few students interested in costume and no mandatory courses. My work instructions were: 'your responsibility includes everything concerning costume design on both the bachelor and master level'. I set to work.

At that time, fashion and costume studies at KHIO were artefact-based with emphasis on aesthetics, i.e. value judgments connecting material, form and techniques. My fashion design colleagues often said: 'Clothes are clothes'. By this, they meant that a garment is primarily a designed object and *how* the garments are used is not the main question. The argument was, that the competency requirements for the two types of designers (fashion designers and costume designers) were the same. I expressed my disagreement here, as I see costume as a complex, dynamic entity consisting of four components: body, garment, action and context (Figure 5.4.1). This was the start of the process of defining *what* kind of competence elements a costume-design education should provide. In order to do this, I needed a tool: a list, accessible to everyone, that would make visible the competencies required by a costume designer. I called it the 'Golden List' of Competence in Costume.

This list was assembled by first considering my own practice and that of my colleagues and secondly, by examining curricula for costume design education at the bachelor's and master's level elsewhere. The list was then reviewed by the Costume Design Working Group of the Norwegian Association of Performance Designers, consisting of costume designers Else Lund and Gjøril Bjercke Sæther. After establishing the list in a Norwegian context, an international context for best practice was required next. I workshopped my list at the Costume Design Sub-commission of the Performance Design Commission at OISTAT (International Organization of Scenographers, Theatre Architects and Technicians) while at World Stage Design 2017 (WSD 2017) in Taipei.[1]

During this event, the list was discussed amongst an international group consisting of approximately sixty students, professionals or educators. The participants came from different continents, countries

Figure 5.4.1 *Costume generating dance. Photograph from the biannual 'Clothes for Dance Laboratory' in the frame of artistic research of Professor in Choreography, Anne Grete Eriksen and Professor in Costume Design, Christina Lindgren. An interdisciplinary research of dancers, choreographers and costume designers. Dancers: Charlotte Utzig and Anita Suzanne Gregory, Costume Design: Kristine Gjems and Choreography: Heidi Jessen.*

and contexts. Two questions were raised: 'What competence is missing from this list and what could be removed?' We also considered the question: 'Costume design stands with one foot in the field of design and art and the other in the performing arts. In what department should costume design education be located and why?' After group discussions, the results were shared in a plenary session that was audio-recorded; the list was further revised based upon the comments collected in this discussion. I therefore feel that the list is robust and well considered.

The main points concerning the costume designer's list of competence were the following:

Firstly, that the costume designer needs to get a 'bird´s-eye perspective' on a new performing arts production in order to be a responsible partner. When they work on different productions with different collaborative partners, costume designers must conceptualize the design that will best contribute to the production. To do this, they need terminology, tools and methods in order to achieve an overview of the other contributors' ideas early on, as well as of the possibilities that the context creates. When costume designers have a 'bird´s-eye perspective' of the situation they are capable of contributing more to the performance's development. They can use this information to make informed decisions and thereby carry responsibility for their contribution and for the artistic entity as a whole. This is as much a necessity for the costume designer as it is for all the partners in the creative team.

Regarding the question of costume studies' affiliation, the participants of WSD 2017 noted that costume design education is most often situated within theatre studies. The students who participated in that discussion observed that the best-suited department is the one where costume students can easily collaborate in creative teams. They argued that costume designers work collectively in their professional practice and therefore need to develop their collaborative skills during their education, while fashion designers tend to work in a more individualistic way when building a new concept or 'collection'. Based on the common understanding of an obvious affiliation for costume design within the performing arts studies, all of the participants emphasized the need for future costume designers to secure access to competence in visual arts more widely, as well as access to specific workshops for costume making. One of the educators argued that in the United States of America, studies located in theatre departments can generate a gender bias towards costume designers within the performance-making team, including in relation to what a costume designer earns. When located in a fine arts department, costume design students tend to be seen as instigators of new ideas and products, she argued. The participants agreed that the matter of affiliation also depended on resource allocations.

The issue of 'artistic signature' was added to the list of competence. The WSD 2017 discussion group emphasized the importance of the costume designers' ability to 'drive their own work' in order to be able to actively participate as artistic collaborators. They argued that if the collaborators know a designer´s style, the designer will be able to attract like-minded collaborators. They suggested changing the term 'a personal artistic signature' to 'an artistic signature'.

Originally, the list included the competence of 'autonomy'. The group of professionals suggested adding 'flexibility' to this point, since the work of the costume designer is part of a collaborative process, a tendency and way of working which gains increasing prominence in most professions around the world, but is not always reflected in secondary and tertiary education. Costume designers require space in the creative process to 'hear' their own voice and come up with their own ideas, but at the same time they also need to learn how and when to abandon ideas. One group of students suggested that a costume designer also needs to be prepared for failure, in other words, pro-risk not risk-averse, since they generally work collaboratively; the results of such work do not come easily or directly, but through a playful and creative process that can be frustrating and thrilling alike.

One group of professionals suggested adding 'knowledge of how the body and costume works in motion' to the list of skills, instead of simply the generic term 'fitting'. They argued that costume designers need skills and knowledge of how the body and costume work together *in motion* (hermeneutics) in order to visualize how a costume interacts with a body; this kind of knowledge is connected to understanding how costume design can generate stories, sensations and images and how costume communicates a narrative without a text.

Participants also observed that the costume designer´s area of practice is currently expanding and therefore the need for costume-design competence also relates to these new developing contexts. Many participants felt that a wide understanding of performance art, installation and environmental design methodologies was important. Therefore, the discipline's requirements would extend to understanding the history and theory of film and media, digital and web-based modes of cultural production including 'internet-based performance where costume design is already being practiced'. For these reasons the educators questioned the classic term 'dramaturgy' and suggested revising it to 'insight into traditional and new forms of dramaturgy'.

Other suggestions were elaborated upon and discussed at this international meeting. Through the experience of sharing, discussing and revising the list, it became evident that the snapshot of expected competence is surprisingly similar around the globe. Since it is of major importance that the list is in line with the competencies required in contexts where costume design is practised, it will require further revision and updates at future events including World Stage Design or the Prague Quadrennial.

The list that has been created is a shared, dynamic and updated tool. Since I first began to compile it, I have articulated and refined its potential purpose and use. It can be a tool to work systematically with study plans within educational contexts, to identify and complement tutors' competence and to conduct surveys amongst alumni concerning the relevance of their education. In institutions where costume design is integrated into fashion or scenography education, the list can also be useful to map the specialized and overlapping competencies. It can assist students in identifying their personal areas of competence, as well as their individual fields of interest. It serves as a tool to define the breadth of competence required to educate costume designers in new areas and contexts; this is particularly important when the organization bears a 'national responsibility'[2] for the field of costume design.

As I write, there is no conclusive answer as to the question of how to secure broad, deep, relevant and advanced competence for the costume designer of the future. And yet, I wish to offer this workshopped tool for composing a rich curriculum with the potential to enable students to develop as strong members of a creative team across a wide field, in which costume design is and will be practised.

The Costume Designer´s 'Golden List' of Competence

1. Creativity

- A singular artistic expression
- An artistic signature
- Autonomy and flexibility
- Courage, curiosity and imagination
- Willingness to be vulnerable to failure and to accept risk

2. Skills

- Various techniques of costume design (including the techniques of drawing and painting)
- Convincing presentation skills to back up ideas in design and drawings
- Technical costume drawings
- Vocabulary of design terms
- Knowledge of costume making
- Basic pattern design and modelling

- Knowledge of materials
- Understanding the body form in fittings
- Knowledge of how the body and costume work in motion
- Co-operation with performers on character development, or other forms of the costumed body
- Knowledge/skills of making material and garments through weaving, knitting and other material creation techniques
- Knowledge/skills to transform material and garments through dyeing, embroidery, patina and other material-elaboration techniques
- Skills in applying new technologies to the costume design and making processes

3. History and Theory

- General humanistic education, including cultural, social, economic and political histories
- History and theory of art, design and fashion
- History and theory of scenography and costume design
- History and theory of theatre, dance, opera, film and other forms of performance
- Dress history, costume history, textile history, historical costume
- Text or discourse analysis, character analysis
- Insight into traditional and new forms of dramaturgy
- Knowledge of and skills for critical thinking in the field of costume design
- Knowledge of and skills for critical thinking in the field of performance, art and design
- Concepts of gender and race identities and their representation in a performative setting
- Sensitivity to cultural appropriation and the asymmetry of colonizer/colonized
- Consciousness and awareness of the social, political and historical context of the performance

4. Design Methodology

- General knowledge of materials, form, tools and techniques
- Knowledge and experience of perception
- Conceptual and realized costume design processes
- Methods for visual storytelling/visual dramaturgy
- Methodology of the design of period costumes
- Use of storyboards and knowledge of continuity in film and television
- Knowledge concerning how costume design works in the entities of theatre, dance, opera, film/television
- Knowledge concerning the specific possibilities and limitations of costume design in the entities of theatre, dance, opera, film and television
- An ability to acquire a 'bird's-eye perspective' on costume design across the performance as an entity

- Ability to predict, consider and communicate the effect of a costume design on a performance's unity
- Responsibility for the costume as a contribution to such unity
- Ability to generate a performance starting from the costume design
- Knowledge and skills to implement costume in a performance
- Familiarity with a range of methodologies for costume design for theatre, dance, opera, film, television, new media, performance art and other performative and installation environments
- Familiarity with a range of methodologies for a field that extends to film, media, and internet-based performance where costume design is being practised
- Methods for using new technology/knowledge of new technology
- Research methodologies such as artistic and design research, as well as the older disciplinary practices of the university.

5. Knowledge of the Other Visual/Spatial Areas of Performance Design/Design for Film

5a) Basic knowledge of scenography

- General knowledge of scenography materials, form, tools and techniques of scenography
- Familiarity with methods for analysing space and context
- Technical drawing, model building
- Deep understanding of the relationship between costume and space

5b) Basic knowledge of lighting design

- Light qualities: visibility, distribution, colour, intensity, movement
- Lighting design methods
- Lighting design techniques: lamps, dimmers, filters and special effects
- Understanding of the relationship between costume and light

5c) Basic knowledge of make-up and mask design

- Character development, techniques and style, expressions
- Understanding the relationship between costume and mask
- Understanding the relationship between costume and make-up/hair
- Understanding of the spatial relationships between mask/body/environment

6. Knowledge in the Field of Competence of the Collaborative Partners

- Basic knowledge of directing, choreography, directing for opera, directing for film
- Basic knowledge of acting, dancing, singing, acting for film, puppetry, object manipulation

7. Advanced Niche Knowledge

- Advanced knowledge of costume for theatre, dance, opera, film and other forms of performance

- Understanding of costume in a global perspective; how costume's contribution is perceived and appreciated in different countries and cultures, past and present

8. Co-operation

- Experience various forms of collaboration; with various artists on performances in theatre/dance/opera/film
- Skills for co-operation with an artistic team on the development and realization of ideas and concepts
- Skills for co-operation with the workshops
- Skills for communication with performers in fittings and dress rehearsals
- Personal skills, such as respect and perseverance
- Communication skills
- Ensemble ethics
- Knowledge and experience of theatre history and culture
- Knowledge of the costume designer's rights regarding copyright, crediting, salary and working conditions
- Knowledge of social responsibility relating to the use of images by other artists
- Knowledge of principles of equity and diversity

9. Project Organization

- Budget and time allocation
- Planning the design process, including production, costume tests, dress rehearsals, cost adjustment, re-cycling of materials and sustainability
- Leadership in supervising the costume production
- Logistical planning
- Ability to source materials
- Use and maintenance of costumes
- Securing the sustainable production, maintenance, repair, upcycling and re-cycling of the costumes in a wardrobe

Notes

1 The costume programme during this event was facilitated by the leadership team of the OISTAT Costume Design Sub-commission, Simona Rybáková, Rosane Muniz and Sofia Pantouvaki.

2 This applies to countries where an educational institution is responsible for costume design education. For example, in Norway, the Oslo National Academy of the Arts is the only institution offering costume-design education and holds a so-called 'national responsibility' for developing new professionals for this field.

Section 6

Costume and Social Impact

6.1 Exploring Rossini's Berta: Young Audiences and the Agency of Opera Costume

Sofia Pantouvaki

Performance is a form of art that children can fully grasp. Through the synthesis of artistic forms, narrative and expressive style, performance excites children's imagination, incites their thinking and activates their emotional world. Children tend to be motivated to actively participate in live performance through theatrical action which stimulates their spirit and mind, their sensations and judgement by reflecting models and ideals and gives examples of wider educational affection on their characters. Performance takes on a special role for young audiences,[1] becoming 'an index of ideology' (Grammatas 1999: 160),[2] suggesting rules of life and models of ethical behaviour and discussing directly or indirectly issues related to human personality. Frequently, the emphasis is put on the positive aspects of life in ways that tend to become didactic at times, whereas elsewhere, performance may have clear pedagogical aims in terms of help-seeking and empathy. According to Theodore Grammatas, theatre can become 'a weapon for the emancipation and education of young audiences – with all the positive or negative meanings these notions may convey' (1999: 108). Shifra Schonmann notes that the theatre 'offers a language of universal symbols that should be understood by the young viewers. This then is a pedagogical criterion' (Schonmann 2006: 137).

Of special importance within the context of theatre for young audiences is its social and cultural function. Helen Nicholson remarks that theatre is a cultural institution, which helps 'to shape forms of participation' in which theatre-makers continue 'to encourage children and young people both as artists and as citizens' (Nicholson 2011: 85). Therefore, theatre is not only an intellectual, educational and emotional experience, but also a socially engaging event and a cultural experience that entails artistic and aesthetic elements; the 'aesthetic experience is fundamental in [a child's] development', as Schonmann observes (2006: 44). These complimentary perspectives of theatre for young audiences form the core of the project analysed here.

This chapter focuses on a costume-based activity within the opera project 'Interactive Opera at Primary Schools' led and co-ordinated by the Greek National Opera (2012–15). The project used a new professional staging of Gioachino Rossini's *The Barber of Seville* as a stimulus for schoolchildren aged nine to twelve to interact creatively with an opera performance. Enthused by the narrative, the music and the characters of the *Barber of Seville* and Rossini's life, the children were involved in the design and making of a costume element which complemented the costume of one of the characters on the stage, Berta. Here, I discuss the children's creative and collaborative process, providing an analysis of the costume items produced, including the visual and material means employed and the themes which emerged. I use the concept of 'creative interaction' to explore the multi-layered agency of opera costume and especially its function as a form of expression, a social agent and a pedagogical tool. My research showed that by introducing a 'costume-thinking' process that involved analysis, interpretation, design and implementation, the children were invited to actively participate in the creation of an operatic character which boosted their artistic expression, activated cultural exchange and enhanced their social integration.

'Interactive Opera at Primary Schools': An Artistic and Educational Project

In 2011, Greek National Opera (GNO) undertook a research project co-funded by the European Union with a joint artistic and educational scope entitled 'Interactive Opera at Primary Schools.'[3] The project was conceived as a fully professional version of Gioachino Rossini's *The Barber of Seville*, staged as an incentive for schoolchildren to 'interact with' i.e. to participate actively in and contribute to an opera performance that took place at their school. The children of the participating primary schools prepared before the arrival of the GNO team during their school art classes and joined in the final preparation and presentation of the performance during the opera team's two-day visit to their school. The project became part of the integrated curriculum in Greek primary schools[4] in the frame of three art-related subjects taught at the primary level under the umbrella of 'Aesthetics Education': music education, drama education and visual arts education.

For the needs of the project, the GNO employed professional artists and educators and commissioned a creative team to create a new, abridged adaptation of Rossini's *The Barber of Seville* for young people. The team comprised a stage director,[5] two scenographers (one of whom was myself, also costume designer for the project), a lighting designer and a choreographer.[6] The artistic team also included three music conductors, a small-scale orchestra ensemble (the GNO Educational Programmes Orchestra), six dancers and a multiple cast of opera singers for eight main roles.[7] Five expert educators[8] worked with the schoolchildren in workshops relating to specific areas of the project: music and voice, rhythm and movement, drama, visual arts, lighting and scenography. The educators' role was essential not only from a pedagogical viewpoint, but also for the evaluation of the project as they collected systematic feedback in situ. The production team included set constructors, painters, prop makers, costume makers, wig makers and a technical team that ran the performances while on tour, consisting of stage technicians, a lighting crew, dressers, hair/wig and make-up artists, a stage manager and a tour manager. A unique and important aspect of this project was that every team member, including the opera singers, the musicians in the orchestra and the technicians were involved in the educational activities of and with the children, led by the GNO educators.

'Interactive Opera at Primary Schools' toured 150 public schools over five school years from May 2012 until October 2015. It had a broad impact and benefited over 44,000 pupils and 735 primary school teachers.[9] The project had multiple aims, summarized by the GNO co-ordinator of educational programmes, Dr Nikos Xanthoulis (2012) as:

- to introduce children throughout Greece to the art form of opera, an art that comprises many arts; to engage the aesthetic criteria of young audiences through a new professional production of high artistic merit
- to familiarize youth with the making of a musical production by actively engaging them in it; to introduce the various professions related to opera (both on stage and backstage)
- to offer a production especially made with the contribution of the schoolchildren, for the children of their home town, in their own school environment, addressing their fellow pupils as opera spectators
- to provide, through concrete activities, schools all over the country with a guide to drama and music education that can also be developed in the future beyond the specific project.

According to the external evaluation report results collected after the first phase of the project, the children continued to talk about this experience both at school and at home for a long time after the opera had visited their school (TEC S.A. 2013: 64).[10] The teachers commented that the project provided them with a tool for an 'open school' and 'surpassed their expectations' (TEC S.A. 2013: 64). They praised the 'impressive' collaboration of professionals from diverse fields including the technicians, who are usually invisible with the children (TEC S.A. 2013: 64) and applauded the experience as an orchestration of all the arts (TEC S.A. 2013: 62) and the entire spectrum of colours and sounds, which 'was fascinating' (TEC S.A. 2013: 64). Overall, the feedback collected emphasizes the value of the interaction between the pupils and opera professionals, as well as the significance of the scenographic and costume objects that the pupils constructed and the fact that these were used in the performance (TEC S.A. 2013: 91).

Children and Performance Design in the Context of *The Barber of Seville*

The collaborative features of performance-making, aesthetic and sensorial engagement, as well as the collective experience of attending performances are perspectives taken into consideration in planning the activities of the 'Interactive Opera at Primary Schools' project as a whole. The importance of the visual and spatial aspects of performance and the vital role of human representation, evident through acting/singing and costume put an emphasis on the role of design-related activities in this project, which required the participation of the schoolchildren through team work and the production of collective artworks.

Visual language is of huge importance in performance for children. Images create visual relationships to the world of fantasy and connect imagination to reality. Grammatas remarks that 'child spectators are capable of simultaneously partaking of imagination and reality', creating a visual world 'according to their needs' (1992: 47). As Schonmann notes:

> in the process of watching a play, the child is not creating an imaginary world that takes the place of the real world, but is witnessing a reality that is created in front of his eyes, in the here and now on the stage. The child as a spectator needs to be mature enough to understand the *as if* situation as a part of the theatrical language. (Schonmann 2006: 40)

Therefore, with the contribution of design elements, the young audience participates in the action, engages in dialogue with the performance and experiences a sense of life created on the stage (Pantouvaki 2008). Maureen Cox, author of *The Pictorial World of the Child* argues that children brought up within a social setting 'cannot help but be influenced by the culture that envelops them, and this includes the visual images they see' (Cox 2005: 2). The communication of ideas by means of design and music is often achieved without the requirement of a particular cultural background. A stage image acquires a self-reliance that becomes the language of the messages contained in a performance (Grammatas 1999) and ideas are then communicated through scenographic and embodied metaphors (Pantouvaki 2008; and 2018) as well as viscerally (Barbieri 2017).

The visual world for this staging of *The Barber of Seville* was based on the *commedia dell'arte* tradition which was used as a motive and expressive code. The scenographic concept provided an easily transferable wooden stage which offered a physical space for the performances,[11] as well as a dramatic space for the action. Although not based on *commedia dell' arte* stock character elements, the costume design was inspired by *commedia* touring troupes that traditionally used old and recycled garments.

The costumes were artistically elaborated (dyed and aged) to look used and the design included some colourful visual elements and deliberate modernizations such as the use of contemporary striped socks, an element that added a feeling of playfulness to the design.[12]

The cut and forms of the costumes were drawn from a broad range of centuries, starting from the late Renaissance or sixteenth century, with elements identified in the costume of Dr Bartolo signifying the 'old spirit', and mixed with costumes based on fashions from later centuries such as the Baroque period of the seventeenth century, in the decadent elegance of Don Basilio, the music teacher's costume; also, to the Rococo style of the eighteenth century in the disguise of Count Almaviva as a singing tutor. Figaro's (the barber's) costume was based on male dress from the early nineteenth century (the post-French Revolution period) identifying – in comparison to the other male characters – the spirit of a new age.

The costume of Berta, a servant to Dr Bartolo, was inspired by a simplified version of a Renaissance dress, thus relating to the spirit of Dr Bartolo's home. The dress had detachable sleeves attached to the bodice by laces, two skirts and an underskirt (Figure 6.1.1). Its colour palette was monochromatic, in dark green, functioning as a background colour. This costume included an apron, which indicated

Figure 6.1.1 *Costume drawing for the character of 'Berta' for the opera* The Barber of Seville, *Greek National Opera (2012). Courtesy of the author.*

Berta's status as a house worker and which was offered to the children as an unfinished costume element for them to design. Costume takes on vital importance here for the children's engagement with the performer (in this case, the singer) during live performance. It becomes an active mediator by creating connections between the narrative and performing body through design, interpersonal understanding and human representation.

Costume as a Participatory and Pedagogical Tool

By combining professional performance and education, the 'Interactive Opera at Primary Schools' project offered the professional performance designers a challenging, enriched and expanded role. This extended beyond designing a new production as a collaborating artist and member of the creative team, addressing an educational aspect, for which the designer becomes a contributing researcher and educator.

My background experience in designing performances for children, combined with my research in theatre and education specifically on the impact of scenography upon young audiences (Pantouvaki 2008) was crucial in responding to this new, integrated role which required proposing and planning, not only the sets and costumes, but also the educational activities relating to the performance's design. Nicholson (2011: 87) remarks that 'the experience of seeing the work of professional theatre-makers contributes to [the children's] artistic development'. Children are typically involved in performance as active performers (acting, reading verse, singing, etc.) and this immersion in the theatrical event is usually their first insight into the making of live performance.[13] The project analysed here enabled the children to participate in the meaning-making process of performance, not only by developing creative activities but mainly by integrating the children's design input into the opera performance. This resulted in an opera designed *for* and *with* the children concentrating on 'its own artistic form and its aesthetic merits' (Schonmann 2006: 10).

From the multiple perspectives of the designer, researcher and educator, we addressed the following questions: How could the children participate in and actually contribute to the design of the opera? Could the children create and even construct part of the scenographic elements? Could the children experience the creation of an opera performance, instead of only watching the final outcome? This process resulted in the creation of three specific actions which became a new tool for creatively engaging school children (Pantouvaki 2012b) and integrating the principles of design for performance into education for young people.[14] These participatory actions addressed the main areas of design for performance – the sets, the props, the lighting and the costumes – as a framework for teamwork, social interaction and learning. Through these the schoolchildren interacted with the performance by becoming *co-creators*, specifically *co-designers* of the final outcome that was presented on stage.[15] The pupils' contribution affected and shaped the visual aspects of the opera performance and especially the representation of one of its characters, Berta. This made each individual show and each representation of Berta different from the next.

Active participation and creative engagement was therefore, the proposed form of interaction. The costume-based activity was generated through collaborative work encouraging the children to collaborate with their classmates. When the opera team arrived at their school, the creators of the apron would present it to the opera educators and to the opera singer performing the role, explaining their approach to the character of Berta. On the following day, the singer wore the apron on stage, together with the rest of her costume. It is important to note that this activity brought the children into direct collaboration with the technicians (Figure 6.1.2) as well as with the professional opera singers.[16] The children's involvement in the role of co-designer was intended to value both the work on stage, as well as the work backstage. The teachers commented that the pupils' eagerness

Figure 6.1.2 *The children present and deliver their apron to the dressers of the Greek National Opera. First Primary School of Itea, 14–15 November, 2012. Photographer: Aris Kamarotos. Courtesy of the photographer.*

to fulfil this task shows that alternative role models can be developed for the children's future (TEC S.A. 2013: 64).

Finally, through the realization and completion of the specific objects, the aprons that they designed and made, the schoolchildren achieved a tangible material outcome. This means that their creative contribution was appreciated and became part of the performance in a concrete way. The teachers observed that the children were enthusiastic about the fact that their own creations were directly integrated into the performance that was performed the next day as a part of it (TEC S.A. 2013: 63). This shows the significance of offering the children creative responsibility as active agents and the possibility of undertaking a task that they would take full control of.

Designing an Operatic Character from the Children's Creative Perspective

Berta is Dr Bartolo's housekeeper, a soprano role in Rossini's *The Barber of Seville*. She is a small ('secondary') character in the opera, singing only in five scenes; to engage the children in the design of such a character was a deliberate choice, aiming to show that not only the main characters are important in a story. Berta's words, according to the libretto, centre on commenting on the various events in the house with a focus on Dr Bartolo's actions (aria: 'What a suspicious old man!') and her main aria ('The old man seeks a wife') comically criticizes 'love, which makes everyone go mad' (Sterbini [1816] 2019). However, the teachers[17] mainly worked with the children on analysing the character through the music and plot as a whole, taking into consideration Berta's professional identity and her role in the story as a housekeeper. The costume element they worked with, an apron, supported this direction.

This interaction through costume engaged the children in the design and making of Berta's apron which complemented her costume on stage. The apron was prepared as a 'blank' canvas for expression, offered to the children by the costume designer as a concrete material object that they could (co-)design, becoming co-creators of the character. The choice of the apron as the element for this costume-based creative interaction was a successful one, given that all the participating children – from all the geographic areas of Greece that the project had visited, with children from diverse ethnic and cultural backgrounds – were familiar with this type of garment. The apron is a readily recognized garment to children from a wide variety of places and from everyday situations, which range from the intimate environment of their homes (their family members wearing aprons to cook) to images of popular culture (e.g. television celebrity chefs) and events from their local cultural environment (particularly those involving local folk dresses, which include an apron in most regions of Greece). According to the teachers, the apron was one of the means that 'deconstructed the myth that opera is an unfamiliar type of performance for children' and showed that instead, an operatic character can be 'really familiar' (TEC S.A. 2013: 65).

Inspired by the narrative of the opera and the music, the children analysed Berta by trying to visualize her and suggesting what she might look like, what she would enjoy and what kind of a costume she might wear. They had no visual references for the costume design except Figaro's image, which became the project's logo and was printed on the materials that they received in advance. The guidelines sent to the teachers suggested allowing the children freedom, but included a tip: that 'Berta might like stripes' although 'this is not compulsory if the children pick a different approach' (Pantouvaki 2012a: 44); this suggestion was taken into consideration by some of the teachers when discussing the project with their pupils. As Schonmann (2006: 67) notes, 'the child's awareness that the play is a fiction must be ensured. The aesthetic response rests on the imaginative involvement of the child'. Our approach intended to leave the children's imagination as free as possible.

Costuming transforms the imagined character of the story into an embodiment on stage with a concrete physical appearance. The schoolchildren were introduced into a costume thinking process, i.e. a process of thinking about the representation of human character through costume, via the following stages: presentation (of the character); reaction; discussion (exchange of ideas); interpretation (possible pathways for the design); participation (active engagement); communication (expression of meanings) and reception. This led to the shaping of a design for the costume. The process of creation is in general, 'an existential experience that enables openness and growth, only if it is not intentionally designed to contain learning aims' notes Schonmann (2006: 42). Here, the children worked freely at the boundaries between fantasy and reality, applying meanings and ideas from real life and real people to the character of Berta: for them she is a believable character. To be able to conceive the act of interpretation and subsequently the act of design, the children had to unpack the concept of 'aesthetic distance' (Schonmann 2006) and explore how it is constructed through design. Decoding the conventions of the stage and proposing ways for human representation – on a small scale, through this one costume element – for a professional singer was an advanced creative process for the young participants aged nine to twelve.[18] Through playing and experimentation with materials and compositional elements from the visual arts, they were able 'to make distinctions between the real and the imaginary world' and be involved in 'high-level thinking operations' (Schonmann 2006: 107) developed through their exploration of costume. The diverse stage representations of Berta stemmed from the children's 'own ways of seeing and knowing the world' (Schonmann 2006: 20) and afforded them one layer of mediation, through their role of co-designer in the creation of an operatic character, which influenced the presentation of the performance.

Through the process of interpreting Berta's character, the children were offered a chance to discuss all the characters in the opera. The on-going dialogue between the children and the character continued to develop until the children met the singer who would perform, i.e. make the character come alive on stage. The encounter between the young designers and the opera singers impersonating Berta was significant as a stage of communication. One of the elements the children were impressed by was 'how a regular person becomes/is transformed into an artist' (TEC S.A. 2013: 61). Through their active involvement in the process of costume designing, the children also learned to distinguish the role from the real performer.

Costume as Expression and Communication: Results of the Children's Design Process

Helen Nicholson claims that 'all imaginative and challenging theatre extends children's cultural education' (2011: 87). Analysing Berta as a fictional human character provided the children with an opportunity to discuss human habits, tastes, wishes, behaviours and relationships. In the theatre for young people we should not 'destroy the depth of the ideas that emerge', remarks Schonmann (2006: 100).[19] One of the strong aspects of this project was that it embraced a diversity of ideas that emerged directly from the participating children. The success of this project lies therefore, in the fact that the children's ideas were allowed space for expression and remained untouched and raw and were integrated as such. Teachers reported that this activity offered their pupils a sense of self-confidence, including those who were not particularly confident in their studies.[20] The key to comprehending the difference of this children-influenced process, as opposed to an adult-led interpretation process, is in understanding that 'children interpret the world differently from adults because they see it on their own terms' (Waksler 1986 quoted in Schonmann 2006: 43); this interpretation is based on their own concerns and uses means that are familiar to them.

The children worked with materials and techniques that were already known to them, such as painting and handicrafts. The apron was sent to the schools in advance, already cut and sewn in the required dimensions and the schoolchildren were invited to paint and decorate it freely using colours or mixed media, or any other technique and materials of their choice.[21]

How were the children inspired to design Berta's apron? The analysis of the produced costume items reveals a diversity of themes that range from visual and decorative patterns that the children applied to Berta's 'sartorial style', to themes that they associated with her personality, such as her love for music, her passion for cooking and her sensibility towards environmental matters. In several cases, the elements that were integrated into the apron were based on the children's interpretation of the

Figure 6.1.3 *Berta (Anna Alexopoulou) with a striped apron. Second Primary School of Karpenissi, 12–13 November 2012. Photographer: Aris Kamarotos. Courtesy of the photographer.*

story of the opera more broadly; such ideas connected Berta to the other characters of the opera (especially Dr. Bartolo, Rosina and Figaro) and generated parallel, complementary narratives born from the children's interpretation of the plot and developing beyond it. Here, I analyse these themes and approaches.

Although only briefly introduced to the teachers, the idea that 'Berta might like stripes' (Pantouvaki 2012a: 44) was embraced by a large number of children as relevant to her 'cheerful character'. Berta was seen by many of the children's groups as a joyful, open-hearted and optimistic person and her affection for stripes – a kinetic, vivid pattern – seemed like a natural 'choice' (Figure 6.1.3). Stripes have been analysed as a ubiquitous pattern, historically associated with people who 'disturb the established order' (such as heretics, prostitutes, madmen, convicts, court jesters and servants and, later, clowns) but over the centuries, especially after the French Revolution, they eventually became a symbol of freedom and free spirit (Pastoureau [1991] 2001: 2). The children were certainly not aware of this analysis of the pattern, but its symbolism, particularly in indicating boldness and playfulness was evident in the documentation of their interpretation processes. Numerous aprons were designed in striped patterns in horizontal, vertical or diagonal arrangements, with narrow or wider stripes, usually in bright colours because this is 'what Berta likes'.[22] In many cases, the stripes were put together with other elements, such as flowers, because 'Berta likes stripes but also flowers'[23] which 'make her apron look pretty'[24] (see Figure 6.1.9). Stripes were also frequently combined with other geometrical patterns such as triangles and circles,[25] parallel curves or dots,[26] as well as rhombuses,[27] a pattern that was familiar to the children from representations of Harlequin, the stock character of the Italian *commedia dell'arte* dressed in stylized patches, presented to them by their teachers.

Figure 6.1.4 *Berta (Anna Alexopoulou) wearing an apron with stripes, flowers and hearts. Third Primary School of Komotini, 28–29 January 2013. Photographer: Aris Kamarotos. Courtesy of the photographer.*

Another strong element in the proposed representations of Berta was colour. The use of bold colours was interpreted as an additional choice of the character ('Berta likes strong colours',[28] see also Figure 6.1.4) as well as a symbol of her personality: the apron is 'cheerful like Berta herself'[29] and 'colourful like the character of Berta'.[30] The children's interpretation of colour relates to liveliness, optimism and a positive temperament. This is also evident in the rare cases where colour was used to 'cheer her up, as in the specific scene she seems sad'.[31] Colour was integrated with an imaginative array of techniques and materials besides painting, i.e. fabrics, ribbons, laces, embroidery and small-scale objects applied onto the surface of the aprons. In several cases, as will be shown later, the apron became a symbol of the character's occupation and her social status. For example, the apron was sometimes embroidered[32] or covered with pieces of velvet and decorated with bows, because 'she lives and works in a noble house', while also holding a kitchen towel (an addition proposed by the children) aged with 'stains', as this was 'where Berta cleans her hands while cooking'.[33] Such realistic elements were also present elsewhere, e.g. when the apron 'should also look old', therefore bearing pieces of fabric looking like patches[34] or in a few exceptional cases, painted in dark colours, because 'in that time period there were no bold colours',[35] an interpretation rooted in the viewing of eighteenth- and nineteenth-century paintings that the visual arts teacher had shown to the pupils.

Flowers were also attributed to Berta's character, as 'she is cheerful and positive, a happy person who likes flowers';[36] 'Berta likes colours and flowers!' and 'for sure there are many flowers in Dr. Bartolo's house and Berta loves taking care of them'[37] (Figure 6.1.5) so 'we wanted to create a "cheery", flowery apron'.[38] The flowers indicate that the apron she wears is 'joyful like Berta', because 'Berta may have a heavy workload and many tasks and responsibilities at Dr. Bartolo's house, but

Figure 6.1.5 *(a) The children presenting their work on the first day of the GNO visit, an apron full of flowers in bright colours; (b) Berta (Alexandra Mattheoudaki) wearing the apron on stage the day of the performance. Third Primary School of Voula, Attica, 22–23 October 2012. Photographer: Aris Kamarotos. Courtesy of the photographer.*

inside her she is optimistic and romantic'[39] (Figure 6.1.6). Romanticism was also the personality trait identified in Berta when roses were used.[40] These brief narratives, collected during the presentation of the aprons by the various children's groups, explain the children's understanding of the floral elements as a symbol of positive spirit, optimism, romanticism and cheerfulness. The implementation of the ideas in some cases were very refined and demonstrated a high level of skill.[41]

In many cases, Berta's apron was directly related to her profession as housekeeper and cook at Dr Bartolo's house. This was indicated by kitchen utensils painted on or attached to the aprons in three-dimensional forms reproducing the objects. These included paper spoons, forks and ladles with which 'she can cook', cut out and glued or sewn on the apron[42] and cutlery[43] drawn with chalk[44] or painted on the apron in a linear, stripe-like composition indicating that 'Berta likes to cook'.[45] Berta's connection to the kitchen is also evident in the numerous representations of food depicted on the apron, including fruit,[46] vegetables (e.g. an aubergine and a tomato[47] as well as real vegetables placed in a pocket added to the apron[48]), cakes[49] and other sweets (desserts) and ice cream,[50] as well as real beans, lentils and rice glued onto it.[51] These elements were inspired not only by the character of Berta, but also the composer Gioachino Rossini himself, who was a 'virtuoso' in gastronomy (Braus 2006). 'It is possible that Rossini loved to eat more than he loved to compose and there are humorous stories about his adventures with food', notes Sweatman (2009: 11), who calls him 'Rossini, the Foodie' (2009: 17). Rossini's culinary talent was made known to the children through a story that the stage director of this project wrote as a part of his director's note. This inspired adding to Berta's apron 'Rossini's recipes'; in a particular case, the teacher searched for recipes of Italian food – including those by Rossini – on the internet, together with the pupils as part of their preparation[52] (Figure 6.1.7).

Figure 6.1.6 *Berta (Eleni Davou) is interpreted here as 'optimistic and romantic' and her apron is designed with a pattern of small flowers. Twenty-second Primary School of Peristeri, Athens, 16–17 October 2012. Photographer: Aris Kamarotos. Courtesy of the photographer.*

Thus the global revival of food culture as popular televisual entertainment and social activity was successfully amalgamated with the opera script and ethos through design.

This interesting combination of food and music was another theme in the design of Berta's apron by the children. The aprons often combine colourful drawings of musical instruments and notes[53] or a large cooking pot from which musical notes and a stave steam out because 'Berta likes to sing while cooking'.[54] Designs of curly staves with musical notes function as an indication that she likes music,[55] while in another case, there is a big G-clef because 'Berta likes to sing or listen to music while cooking' and 'of course, we are also in an opera performance'.[56]

It is also interesting to observe elements of realism that the schoolchildren applied to their designs for Berta's apron. The most significant of these relate to her work at Dr Bartolo's house, especially her role and actions in the kitchen. The type of activities she might be doing are taken into consideration in the following examples: The apron has fingerprints and stains from working in the kitchen[57] and

Figure 6.1.7 *(a) Recipes of Italian food are embedded in this apron, photographed backstage and showing a polyphony of ideas; (b) Berta (Vassiliki Katsoupaki) wearing the apron on stage the day of the performance. Third Primary School of Keratsini, 17–18 May 2012. Photographers: (a) Christina Avgeridi, (b) Andreas Simopoulos. Courtesy of Sofia Pantouvaki (a) and of Greek National Opera (b).*

bears traces of dirt because 'Berta cleans her hands with the apron while cooking'.[58] There are also stains because she 'uses olive oil in her cooking'[59] and because 'Berta cooks fried potatoes and gets dirty from the frying oil'.[60] Another apron bears signs of her hands covered with flour, since 'Berta has been making bread'.[61] In one case, the apron's stripes are not clearly visible because 'the apron is very dirty from use in Berta's tasks'.[62] These lively descriptions of the concept behind the design proposals come straight from the children's everyday reality and their observation of the life around them, at home and beyond.

Other elements of realism relate to the addition of patches which indicate the apron's wear following extensive use[63] and are sometimes reminiscent of Harlequin's patches,[64] as well as patches that Berta herself has added to the apron 'because Dr. Bartolo does not give money to Berta to buy a new one'.[65] Frequently, a pocket was added to the apron.[66] This element has been a simple, yet surprisingly inventive addition by the children that was not part of the original costume design. Here, the children's imagination developed many more imaginative ideas: 'the pocket is for Berta to keep the recipes that Rossini gives her, which he writes on sheet music';[67] 'she needs a huge pocket so she can place her kitchen utensils and anything else she needs';[68] the big pocket 'serves to Berta to place her ladle while cooking'.[69] These pockets have diverse shapes; they are rectangular, semi-circular, but also triangular[70] and even in the shape of an apple.[71] They are made of different fabrics, as well as of pieces of plastic bags because Berta 'likes to recycle'.[72] Several children's groups identified in Berta's character an environmental sensibility and therefore a love for recycling, including with materials from her kitchen, as in the case of flowers made of plastic bottles and caps decorating her apron (Figure 6.1.8).[73] Moreover, the apron serves to carry measuring tapes, needles

Figure 6.1.8 *Berta's apron is decorated here with flowers made of recycled plastic bottles and caps. (a) The children explain their concept to the GNO educator (Venetia Nasi); (b) Berta (Anna Alexopoulou) wearing the apron on stage the day of the performance. First Primary School of Andravida, 19–20 December 2012. Photographer: Aris Kamarotos. Courtesy of the photographer.*

and threads because 'if Berta does every helping task at home, she must also be fond of sewing'[74] (here it is interesting to note that sewing is not considered a 'servant's task' by the children, but rather, a personal hobby).

Of special interest are ideas stimulated by artistic elements that were introduced to the children by their visual arts teachers, such as intensified shapes and patterns from the visual world of *commedia dell'arte*,[75] bold colours citing twentieth-century art movements such as Fauvism (see also Figure 6.1.2)[76] or the technique of graffiti.[77] In a few cases, the aprons were based on the form and patterns of the aprons of local traditional dress from the region or town.[78] Also, a few groups integrated drawings with local references, including depictions of architectural sites emblematic of their hometown as a connection between their life and the world of the opera.[79]

Other significant ideas are those that expand beyond visual representation and reality and touch the sphere of metaphorical interpretation and symbolism. For example, one children's group narrates: 'on the top part of the apron we included a few small clouds [collage] that show Berta's thoughts for all the tasks she has to undertake'.[80] Another apron is drawn in a way that indicates 'two layers of fabric', of which the 'top layer' has an austere pattern in black and white and gives the illusion that it is torn and enables the viewer to see the 'background layer' which is in strong colours and indicates Berta's cheerful self, thus functioning as a window into her personality.[81] Another interesting apron is a metaphorical representation of the fight between good and evil, signified by the use of black and white.[82] Finally, an allegorical design depicts a pocket added to the apron, opening to 'a meadow where from a bee starts its travel to freedom'.[83]

Dialogue, questioning and interpretation offered the children a possibility to 'react to' and 'interact with' an operatic character through imagination and critical thinking and express their thoughts and ideas. This process, in the vast majority of cases, was experienced with enjoyment, 'a long disregarded concept in education' (Schonmann 2006: 176) that enables learning through experience and emotions. The character of Berta inspired diverse options for human representation through the use of colour, the consideration of composition and form, the selection of materials and the integration of ideas and meanings into a physically produced object, offering the children a possibility to think *through* costume. Moreover, the interrelation of narrative, music, food and visual arts enabled the experience of costume as a synaesthetic entity. That is, the children were able to experience one sense modality by stimulating another (Braus 2006), such as 'hearing' colours, 'tasting' sounds and 'touching' feelings. This empowered them to an advanced level of creative expression activated by the process of designing costume.

Opera Costume as a Social Agent

Helen Nicholson remarks that 'performance provides children with an aesthetic space that is socially liberating' (2011: 81). One of the values of the children's costume-based creative interaction with Berta's costume was its frame and proposed work method, which involved the pupils in teamwork. This was developed further by the teachers, who engaged the children in discussions through critical reflection and in evaluating different proposed ideas with a freedom to decide. The teachers emphasized generating multiple-draft proposals and prioritized the pupils' own wishes and critical evaluation, directing them towards making the final choice by themselves, thus giving them responsibility for the final outcome. The apron was eventually the result of either a selection process through which one main idea was implemented or, in several cases, a synthesis of many ideas into one final object. This is clearer if we observe some of the work methods used.

In most schools, the teachers asked the children to first work individually, expressing their personal ideas and then gathered the pupils in a group to discuss the different ideas and to make a joint, collective decision towards the final idea that would be realized. For example, in one school, each child drew their own idea for the apron on paper in small scale and after a collective discussion they chose one idea to apply to full-scale; they then transferred the design to the 1:1 scale using a grid and finally, painted it with acrylic paint.[84] However, the children frequently enhanced plurality and polyphony by choosing to include more than one idea in a single apron (see also Figure 6.1.7); in these cases Berta's apron was a collage of ideas resulting from individual drawings by various children.[85] Such an apron was divided into two parts: half of it is colourful with flowers (top part), while the other half is black and white (lower part) because it was a combination of two different ideas offered by the group of children.[86] Two other aprons included a collection of themes inspired by the opera's story (food, musical notes, etc.) made by various children in small-scale drawings on individual pieces of fabric that were then sewn together onto the surface of the apron;[87] similar combinations of ideas originally drawn in small-scale and later synthesized into full scale were applied elsewhere.[88] In another case, the teacher gave a task to the entire class to design an apron; then, a small group of female pupils evaluated which elements to use in the final design: they decided to select the 'most interesting elements from each proposal', so they picked the colour from one, the stripes from another, the flower and the lace from the other drafts.[89] At this school, the children were so enthusiastic about the result that when the day arrived for them to present and deliver the apron to the opera team, they all stood up together to show that the work was collective and that they couldn't distinguish among themselves any individual creator of the apron.

Such collaborative work was also a part of other methods used, including real-time co-design of the apron. There, the children worked spontaneously and contemporaneously, i.e. painting the outline of the apron concurrently while seated around it in a circle or drawing on the apron in turns by rotating it. This method was particularly important when used in schools with multi-ethnic pupils with varied cultural backgrounds.[90] In collaborating with others through discussions on human nature (habits, wishes, preferences, behaviours and relationships), the children begin to understand the wishes of others and develop skills in respecting and accepting other persons' views (Figure 6.1.9). Therefore, the 'creative interaction' with Berta's costume enriched and encouraged their sense of social empathy.

The open nature of these activities invited all the children to take part, allowing them 'a chance to publicly identify with the school events and by so doing receive necessary and fitting recognition from other pupils and teachers' (Schonmann 2006: 180). The costume-based activity with Berta's apron was embraced by pupils of all genders and the results represented the interpretation of the character by both girls and boys, who usually worked together in mixed teams. In a few cases, female pupils would take responsibility for designing the apron, applying patterns onto it, or colours or decorative elements (e.g. flowers) that are stereotypically related to romantic female characters[91] or based on research in art and dress history.[92] Collaborative work also includes the blending of ideas, e.g. in the creation of an apron with colourful stripes painted by the male pupils of the classroom,

Figure 6.1.9 *The design of Berta's apron as a result of collaboration, discussion and collective decision-making. Third Primary School of Lavrio, 31 October–1 November 2012. Photographer: Aris Kamarotos. Courtesy of the photographer.*

combined with three-dimensional paper butterflies and flowers created by their female schoolmates and placed on the stripes to 'add an additional layer of joy'.[93] Berta's occupation as a cook, as well as the reference to Rossini's close connection to gastronomy were key in engaging all genders in the analysis of the character (Figure 6.1.10). The years during which this project was implemented in the schools followed the rise of male celebrity chefs in Greece, especially after the fame of the male winner of the first season of MasterChef Greece, who became widely popular through the medium of television all around the country. Hence, men as chefs became widely recognized and this led the young boys to find their own role in the work with the apron. The pupils' view, however, recorded in the questionnaires for the purposes of the external evaluation of the project, is that 'boys and girls participated to the same extent' in this activity (TEC S.A. 2013: 30).

Nicholson (2011: 84) claims that theatre education maintains 'its traditional commitment to providing learning experiences that are artistically challenging, socially engaged and egalitarian'. Thinking through costume about the representation of human character in this activity involved the children in dramaturgical interpretation, visual representation and material practice (Essin 2012) through an active, co-authorial role by engaging their imagination, intellectual skills, experiences and emotions. In the theory of multiple intelligences, Gardner ([1983] 2011) claims that interpersonal intelligence (the communication and understanding of other people's emotions) and intrapersonal intelligence (the internal skills, emotions and the understanding of the self) are cultivated through the development of experiential learning activities. This happened here through working with a group of peers with costume as a tool for active participation, interpersonal understanding, expression and learning. Here, the act of participation was a celebratory act, important on both a personal as well as social level.

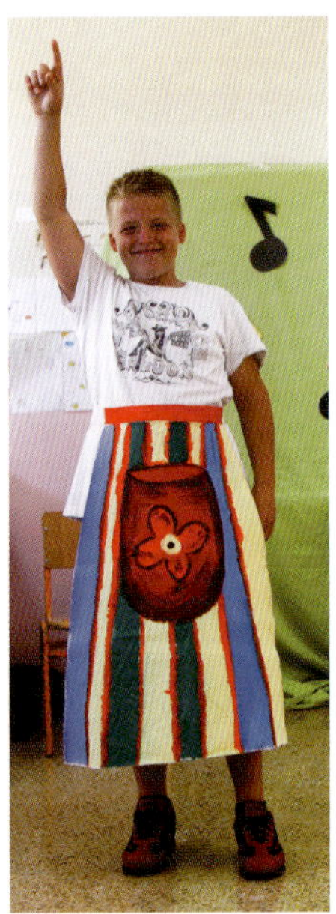

Figure 6.1.10 *This costume-based activity was embraced by pupils of all genders. (a) A young male pupil as a 'chef'; (b) Berta (Alexandra Mattheoudaki) wearing the apron on stage the day of the performance. Twenty-second Primary School of Piraeus, 7–8 June 2012. Photographer: Andreas Simopoulos. Courtesy of Greek National Opera.*

Conclusion

The evaluation report compiled a few months after the implementation of the project's first phase indicates that the teachers felt the project's strongest aspect was its interactive character and especially the opportunity offered to the pupils to create the sets and costumes of the performance (TEC S.A. 2013: 35). The teachers remarked that, through their active participation and embodied experience, pupils were able to recognize the importance of team spirit, collectiveness and professionalism (TEC S.A. 2013: 40).

The children's creative work in co-designing Berta's apron shows a breadth in the understanding of human personalities and a wide range of imagination and interpretation. By considering performance as 'not only a synthesis of the arts, but also the art of synthesis' (Papandreou 1989: 42), the schoolchildren were introduced to collaborative work, to thinking through design and to the synthetic character of making a musical performance. By means of analysis, interpretation, design and implementation, the children developed their own process of 'costume thinking' on an operatic character. This creative process boosted their artistic expression, provoked dialogue, cultural and intellectual exchange and resulted in teamwork beyond divisions of gender towards a common human and artistic goal, achieved through critical perception, problem-solving and decision-making. By engaging the children in an activity that they could fully take control of they were able to complete the task that they had begun. In this way, they truly contributed to the making of the performance, becoming co-designers of the performance and co-creators of the character. This gave them the feeling of responsibility, satisfaction, pride and a sense of accomplishment, all of which are highly important components of a childhood experience.

This example of the 'Interactive Opera in Primary Schools' project proves that when children are given an opportunity to be engaged in the process of staging an opera, they are not only taught about the visual and performing arts, thus acquiring artistic and cultural education (here, specific to the field of costume design), but also undergo a developmental and emancipatory process. Maxine Greene (2001: 7) sees aesthetic education 'as integral to the development of persons – to their cognitive, perceptual, emotional, and imaginative development. We see it as part of the human effort (so often forgotten today) to seek a greater coherence in the world'. Hence the 'creative interaction' with the operatic character in this project generated an aesthetic experience for the child participants and produced a new unique art form based on costume: a co-designed costume that is beyond the reach of the original lead designer. This is shaped within a conceptual framework and becomes a pedagogical tool in a natural, unforced way, offering an opportunity for 'non-educational education' (Schonmann 2006). As the teachers and headmasters commented in their interviews during the project evaluation, 'the students learned so many [new things] without realising that they were taught' (TEC S.A. 2013: 65); in their assessment they referred to the programme as a 'remarkable pedagogical tool' (TEC S.A. 2013: 35). The costume-based activity reached its general goals.

The imaginative artworks produced by the schoolchildren carry their intellectual ideas in concrete visual and material representations that are embedded in the aprons. These costume elements were embraced and taken forward by the opera singers who performed the role of Berta on stage. The singers were inspired to develop new reactions and gestures in response to the children's ideas, providing a next level of 'interaction': that which happens on stage during the live action of the opera.

As this project shows, by creating a platform for co-creation, children were offered a chance to understand human characters and propose ideas for human representation, thus becoming co-authors of new ideas. This took place through an understanding of the agency of costume within the context of opera. On a pedagogical level, the process enhanced a critical pedagogy approach for the development of creative expression through experiential learning. From a sociological perspective, children's creative engagement in performance through costume design has the capacity to re-inforce the bonds among a group of children and contributes to the development of substantial life characteristics within a social frame, such as the acceptance of others' personalities, development of trust, training in active listening, dialogue and active participation, practicing empathy and observation and improving interpersonal and intercultural communication. Such a project offered a chance to develop both education for and about opera (the theatrical medium as a music-based stage art form), as well as education through opera, in which the operatic character becomes a means to reach artistic, pedagogical and social objectives. It is hoped that this paradigm will be adopted and developed further in other contexts, settings and ways as a vehicle to engage, enlighten and educate children through costume all over the world.

Notes

1. The rich and varied terminology used by theatre researchers (Kalogeropoulou & Kangelari 1995; Grammatas 1998; Grammatas 1999; Schonmann 2006; Nicholson 2011), refers to 'children's theatre', 'theatre for children and youth', 'theatre for young audiences' or 'theatre for young people' (Schonmann 2006) involving performances prepared by adult professional or amateur actors and addressed to children (and adult accompanying persons), performances played by children addressed to youngsters and family audiences, dramatized games performed by children and addressed to children, as well as other forms of performance (puppet theatre, shadow theatre, etc.) addressed to them.
2. All translations of non-English references in this text are by the author, unless stated differently.
3. The project was conducted within the framework of the Greek Ministry of Culture's 'Education and Lifelong Learning' scheme and was co-funded by the European Union (European Social Fund) and the Greek state (National Strategic Reference Framework (NSRF) 2007–13).
4. The project 'Interactive Opera at Primary Schools' was implemented in collaboration with schools that operated between 2010–15 as all-day primary schools with a 'single reformed curriculum' (in Greek: *Eniaio anamorfomeno ekpaideutiko programma*). This curriculum was based on actions supporting lifelong learning; it promoted social integration and active participation and aimed at the development of innovation, creativity and an entrepreneurial spirit. This reformed curriculum enriched theatre education, music, visual arts, information technology,

English language and physical education and included experiential actions in thematic areas such as sustainability and recycling, health education especially nutrition, consumer education, environmental education and hygiene, etc.

5 Kostis Papaioannou, a professional theatre and opera director whose background includes opera productions for young audiences with the participation of pupils in schools.

6 Set design by Sofia Pantouvaki and Giorgos Kolios, costume design by Sofia Pantouvaki, lighting design by Christina Kamma and choreography by Themistoklis Pavlis.

7 The opera originally included a double cast of soloists for each of the eight main roles, which eventually grew to become a sextuple-cast due to the length and complexity of the project's implementation which spanned over five artistic seasons (equally, five school years). The singers in the role of Berta were: Anna Alexopoulou, Eleni Davou, Vassiliki Katsoupaki, Alexandra Mattheoudaki and Maria Vlachopoulou.

8 The GNO educators were (in alphabetical order) Christina Avgeridi, Zoe Lymperopoulou, Venetia Nasi, Konstantina Strani and Tatiana Theologou. Their expertise focuses on theatre, music and education, as well as scenography and education (V. Nasi), the latter of which was crucial for the analytical discussions with the children who worked on the costume-based assignment.

9 'Interactive Opera at Primary Schools' was implemented in three phases: phase one at seventy schools (school years: 2011–12 and 2012–13), phase two at fifty-two primary schools (school year: 2013–14) and phase three at twenty-five primary schools (school year: 2014–15). In some exceptional cases, more than one school from the same town participated, resulting in a total of over 150 participating schools. For an overview of the project, see the video by the GNO Education section (2014).

10 The project's success is evident from the participants' responses (pupils, teachers, headmasters, parents, as well as the artistic and technical staff of the opera) to the questionnaires collected for the external evaluation of the project. One of the musicians said, 'the performance was a magical experience for both the children and ourselves; we performed in front of 700 children and there was not a whisper' (TEC S.A. 2013b: 60). The headmaster of one school reported that, for about a month after their participation in the project, they would play opera through the loudspeakers of the school during the breaks (TEC S.A. 2013: 65).

11 This was invaluable, especially at the schools that did not have a school theatre; then, performances took place at the schools' sports gym or outdoors and the scenography itself became the stage.

12 According to statements made by their parents, the mixed period costumes impressed the pupils and were part of their discussions at home (TEC S.A. 2013: 46).

13 The majority of literature and research on the topic of children's theatre or theatre for children/youth or young audiences also focuses on how children experience performance as performers or spectators, not as performance makers or designers.

14 For a more detailed presentation of the project as a whole and the three design-related actions, please see Pantouvaki (2012b; and 2014). The focus of this chapter is on the action relating to costume.

15 Here, the term 'interactive' does not refer to any technological means, but to the children's active involvement (interaction).

16 The enthusiasm expressed by the pupils when they met the opera signers made the singers feel like 'celebrity film actors' according to their statements (TEC S.A. 2013: 58), as the children wanted to talk to them and get their autographs, etc.

17 In most cases, the children worked on Berta's costume with the visual arts teacher, although in some cases they analysed the character of Berta together with the drama teacher and in a few fortunate cases with both of those teachers together (this is not generally possible for practical reasons related to the teachers' overlapping teaching schedules).

18 The children who participated in the specific activity, the design and making of the apron, were from the last two grades of primary school – the fifth and sixth grade – which corresponds to the ages of eleven to twelve. In a few cases, children from the fourth grade (ten-year-olds) also joined.

19 Schonmann is concerned by the 'complicated situation in which the world of the young will always be constructed through the eyes of adults and their perceptions' (2006: 20), because, as she notes, 'children's fiction is not an issue of what the *child wants*, but of what the *adult desires*'. (Schonmann 2006: 20).

20 Remark by one of the teachers from the First Primary School of Michaniona, 15 February 2013, from the feedback collected in situ by the GNO educations for the purposes of this study.

21 Materials include water soluble paints, ribbons, pieces of fabric, lace, paper, chalk (painting with chalk), three-dimensional materials (usually recycled plastic objects), thread, safety pins and small fake flowers.

22 Tenth Primary School of Chania, 1–2 April 2013.

23 Second Primary School of Aegaleo, 5–6 June 2012; Ninth Primary School of Ilion, 2–3 October 2012; First Primary School of Glyka Nera, 18–19 November 2012; Second Primary School of Patras, 13–14 December 2012; Third Primary School of Peraia, 10–11 January 2013.

24 Third Primary School of Lavrio, 31 October–1 November 2012.

25 See e.g. the Fifth Primary School of Karditsa, 5–6 November 2012.

26 See e.g. the Fifteenth Primary School of Piraeus, 24–25 May 2012.

27 First Primary School of Zacharo, 17–18 December 2012.

28 Eleventh Primary School of Piraeus, 1 June 2012; Thirteenth Primary School of Serres, 4–5 February 2013.

29 First Primary School of Itea, 14–15 November 2012; Eleventh Primary School of Kalamata, 29–30 April 2015.

30 Third Primary School of Vrilissia, 30 May 2012; First Primary School of Alimos, 27–28 February 2014.

31 Sixth Primary School of Evosmos, Thessaloniki, 6–7 March 2014.

32 See for example, the Second Primary School of Orestiada, 24–25 January 2013.

33 First Primary School of Raidestos, 8–9 January 2013.

34 Third Primary School of Mytilene, 27–28 May 2013.

35 Fourth Primary School of Tyrnavos, 13–14 March 2014.

36 Second Primary School of Voutes, Herakleion, 11–12 April 2013.

37 Third Primary School of Voula, Attica, 22–23 October 2012.

38 Second Primary School or Messini, 26–27 November 2012.

39 Twenty-second Primary School of Peristeri, Athens, 16–17 October 2012.

40 See for example, Primary School of Kato Kastritsi, 19–20 November 2012.

41 For example, the fifth grade eleven-year-old female pupils of the Fourth Primary School of Ierapetra in Crete (8–9 April 2013) drew the pattern of a flower and used it as a basis to cut out flowers from fabric scraps found at their homes, then placed the three-dimensional flowers on the apron and embroidered their stems. At the Thirteenth Primary School of Larissa, (4–5 March 2013) another group of female pupils created felt flowers that were sewn onto the apron.
42 Fiftieth Primary School of Athens, 22–23 May 2012.
43 Second Primary school of Ilioupoli, 9–10 October, 2012.
44 Third Primary School of Vrilissia, 29–30 May 2012.
45 Collaborative participation of two schools: Primary School of Kerameia and First Primary school of Lixouri, Cephalonia, 10–11 December 2012 (the apron specifically made by the pupils of the latter school).
46 Fourth and Twelfth Primary School of Xanthi, 31 January–1 February 2013 (joint participation of two schools); Tenth Primary School of Neapoli, Thessaloniki, 4–5 March 2014.
47 Fourth Primary School of Nafplion, 6–7 December 2012.
48 Seventh Primary School of Arta, 31 March–1 April 2014.
49 At the Third Primary School of Elefsina (26 March 2013), female pupils embroidered a cake in the centre, surrounded by 'delicious desserts'; they also drew fruit and sweets on small pieces of fabric and sewed them with embroidery stitches at home; there is also 'a blue strawberry because there was no red thread at home!'
50 Primary School of Lakki, Leros island, 3–4 June 2013; Ninety-ninth Primary School of Athens, 17–18 March 2014.
51 Sixth Primary School of Preveza, 25–26 April 2013.
52 Third Primary School of Keratsini, 17–18 May 2012.
53 See for example, the Second Primary School of Nea Smyrni, Athens, 15–16 May 2012.
54 First Primary School of Veroia, 18–19 February 2013.
55 First Primary School of Igoumenitsa, 15–16 April 2013.
56 First Primary School of Ptolemaida, 20–21 May 2013.
57 Fourth and Twelfth Primary School of Xanthi, 31 January–1 February 2013 (joint participation of two schools); Sixth Primary School of Corfu, 18–19 April 2013; Thirteenth Primary School of Xanthi, 16–17 March, 2015.
58 Fourth Primary School of Tyrnavos, 13–14 March 2014.
59 Primary School of Rodolivous, 7–8 February 2013.
60 First Primary School of Kalamata, 10–11 February 2014.
61 Twenty-second Primary School of Larissa, 11–12 March 2013.
62 Second Primary School of Trikala, 8–9 November 2012.
63 First Primary School of Igoumenitsa, 15–16 April 2013.
64 Twenty-sixth Primary School of Larissa, 2–3 March 2015.
65 First Primary School of Pefki, 6–7 February 2014.
66 Twenty-second Primary School of Piraeus, 7–8 June 2012; Twelfth Primary School of Kavala, 5–6 March 2015.
67 Tenth Primary School of Kallithea, 24–25 February 2014.
68 First Primary School of Loutraki, 29–30 November 2012.
69 Second Primary School of Aegaleo, 6 June 2012.
70 Sixth Primary School of Corfu, 18–19 April 2013.

71 Fifth Primary School of Kastoria, 13–14 May 2013.
72 Seventh Primary School of Rethymon, 4–5 April 2013.
73 First Primary School of Andravida, 19–20 December 2012.
74 First Primary School of Papagos, Athens, 29–30 October 2012.
75 Sixth Primary School of Pyrgos, 23–24 November 2012.
76 First Primary School of Itea, 14–15 November 2012.
77 First Primary School of Nafpaktos, 7–8 April 2014.
78 Fourth Primary School of Lefkada, 3–4 April 2014.
79 First Primary School of Grevena, 22–23 May, 2014.
80 One hundred and twenty-ninth Primary School of Athens, 29–31 January 2014.
81 First Primary School of Skiathos, 14–15 March 2013.
82 Second Primary School of Giannitsa, 26–27 May 2014.
83 Primary School of Agios Minas, Thymiana, Chios Island, 29–30 May 2013.
84 Fourth Primary School of Nafplion, 6–7 December 2012.
85 Fifteenth Primary School of Piraeus, 25 May, 2012; Second Primary School of Ilioupoli, 9–10 October 2012; Thirteenth Primary School of Drama, 21–22 January 2013.
86 Second Primary School of Nea Michaniona, 11–12 February 2013.
87 First Primary School of Polycastro, Kilkis, 17–18 January 2013; Fifteenth Primary School of Heraklion, 6–7 May 2015.
88 Fourth Primary School of Peristeri, 27–28 January 2014; First Primary School of Alexandroupolis, 9–10 March 2015.
89 Twenty-seventh Primary School of Ioannina, 22–23 April 2013.
90 Second Primary School of Zefyri, 24–25 October 2012.
91 Second Primary School or Messini, 26–27 November 2012; Thirteenth Primary School of Larissa, 4–5 March 2013.
92 Second Primary School of Nea Peramos, 28–29 March 2013. The teacher at this school said that she directed the pupils towards researching art history and dress history; she asked them to study the elements they found 'about this other time' [Rossini's time], to interpret them and develop something new for the costume. Her female pupils drew the design and embroidered the apron with her help and she said to the educators' team that this activity positively inspired her to do something beyond her daily curriculum and combine crafts with design thinking.
93 Primary School of Velvendos, Kozani, 16–17 May 2013.

References

Barbieri, D. (2017), *Costume in Performance: Materiality, Culture and the Body*. London/New York: Bloomsbury Academic.

Braus, I. (2006), *Classical Cooks: A Gastrohistory of Western Music*. Bloomington, IN: Xlibris, Corp.

Cox, M. (2005), *The Pictorial World of the Child*. Cambridge: Cambridge University Press.

Essin, C. (2012), *Stage Designers in Early Twentieth-Century America: Artists, Activists, Cultural Critics*. New York: Palgrave Macmillan.

Gardner, H. ([1983] 2011), *Frames of Mind: The Theory of Multiple Intelligences*. New York: Basic Books.

GNO Education (2014), *Εθνική Λυρική Σκηνή: 'Η Όπερα Διαδραστικά στα Δημοτικά Σχολεία'* [*Greek National Opera: Interactive Opera at Primary Schools*]. Available at: https://www.youtube.com/watch?v=ohC4Dk09vY0 (accessed: 12 April 2019).

Grammatas, T. (1992), *Ιστορία και Θεωρία της Θεατρικής Έρευνας* (*History and Theory of Theatre Research*). Theatre Research, 1. Athens: Tolidis Bros.

Grammatas, T. (1998), *Θέατρο και Εκπαίδευση* [*Theatre and Education*]. Athens: Telethrion.

Grammatas, T. (1999), *Fantasyland: Θέατρο για παιδικό και νεανικό κοινό* [*Fantasyland: Theatre for Children and Young Audiences*]. Athens: Typothito.

Greene, M. (2001), *Variations on A Blue Guitar: The Lincoln Center Institute Lectures on Aesthetic Education*. New York: Teachers College Press, Columbia University.

Kalogeropoulou, X. and D. Kangelari (1995), *Θέατρο για Παιδιά - Ένας πρακτικός οδηγός* [*Theatre for Children: A Practical Guide*]. Athens: Hellenic Centre of Theatre for Children and Youth (ASSITEJ Greece).

Nicholson, H. (2011), *Theatre, Education and Performance: The Map and the Story*. Basingstoke: Palgrave Macmillan.

Pantouvaki, S. (2008), 'The Effects of Theatrical Storytelling and Scenography on Children: The Case of Children's Theatre in the Ghetto of Terezin (1941–1945)', PhD thesis, University of the Arts London.

Pantouvaki, S. (2012a), 'Παράρτημα για τους δασκάλους των εικαστικών' ['Appendix for the Art Teachers'], in Nikos Xanthoulis (ed.), *Ο κουρέας της Σεβίλλης – Εγχειρίδιο προς τους εκπαιδευτικούς για την διαδραστική συμμετοχή των μαθητών* [*The Barber of Seville: Guidelines to the School Tutors for the Children's Interactive Participation*], 43–6. Athens: Greek National Opera.

Pantouvaki, S. (2012b), 'The Barber of Seville: Creating an Opera Design Project For and By the Youth', in 'The Art of Research IV', Conference Proceedings, Helsinki, 28-29 November, 2012. Available online: https://www.academia.edu/37364546/The_Barber_of_Seville_Creating_an_Opera_Design_Project_For_and_By_the_Youth (accessed: 20 April 2019).

Pantouvaki, S. (2014), 'Scenography as a Means for Youth Education and Creative Interaction in the "Interactive Opera at Primary Schools" Research Project', in A. M. Steijn, A. Penjak and C. Morgan (eds), *Staged Experiences*, 25–34. Oxford, UK: Inter-Disciplinary Press.

Pantouvaki, S. (2018), '"Like Seeing Normal Life": Children's opera *Brundibár* in Theresienstadt (1943–1944) and the Power of Scenographic Metaphors', *Theatre and Performance Design* 4 (3): 173–203.

Papandreou, N. (1989), *Περί Θεάτρου* [*About Theatre*]. Thessaloniki: University Studio Press.

Pastoureau, M. ([1991] 2001), *The Devil's Cloth: A History of Stripes and Striped Fabric*, trans. J. Gladding. New York: Columbia University Press.

Schonmann, S. (2006), *Theatre as a Medium for Children and Young People: Images and Observations*. The Netherlands: Springer.

Sterbini, C. ([1816] 2019), *Il Barbiere di Siviglia Libretto*, English Translation, Opera-Arias.com aria database Available online: https://www.opera-arias.com/rossini/il-barbiere-di-siviglia/libretto/english/(accessed: 10 April 2019).

Sweatman, S. (2009), 'About the Composer', in *The Barber of Seville: Study Guide*, 2009/10 Season, Winnipeg: Manitoba Opera, 11-17. Available online: https://mbopera.ca/wp-content/uploads/2018/10/The-Barber-of-Seville-Study-Guide-Nov.-6.pdf (accessed: 11 April 2019).

TEC S.A. (2013), 'External Evaluation Report of the Action: "Interactive Opera at Primary Schools"', Strategy Consultants, 17 December, Athens, Greece.

Vettas, N. (2017), 'Education and the Greek Economy', in C. Meghir, C. A. Pissarides, D. Vayanos and N. Vettas (eds), *Beyond Austerity: Reforming the Greek Economy*, 309–58. Cambridge, MA: MIT Press.

Xanthoulis, N. (2012), 'Educational Targets of the Programme "Interactive Opera in Primary Schools"' [in Greek]. Paper Presented at the 1st Symposium 'Interactive Opera in Primary Schools', 1 December 2012. Athens: Greek National Opera.

6.2 Designing Hospital Clown Costumes: Psychological and Social Benefits for Finnish Children's Healthcare

Merja Väisänen

This text was developed in close consultation with Susanna Suurla

Introduction

Over the past three decades, hospital clowning has been globally established as a significant support activity in children's healthcare. Hospital clowns, those 'peculiar red noses' interrupt the everyday routines and hierarchies of the hospital environment by creating an atmosphere of merriment through their interactions. Humour and laughter increase children's psychological and physical well-being by reducing fear, stress, anxiety and other effects of hospitalization. The clowns therefore offer sick children a chance to disengage from their illness.

Hospital clowns are easily recognizable due to their appearance and their arrival at a hospital does not go unnoticed. In this chapter, I examine how the clown's appearance influences the social situations between children, parents and healthcare personnel and how integral the clown's costume is to her/his personality and expression. In particular, by designing new costumes for hospital clowns, I study how the visual elements of the clown's appearance affect the encounters between the clown and the child and create specific moments in the hospital space where play and fantasy transpire. The observations are based on a collaborative costume design project entitled 'Hospital Clown Costumes', jointly conducted by the Costume Design major of the Department of Film, Television and Scenography at Aalto University, Finland and the Finnish Hospital Clowns Association between 2015 and 2017.[1] In this project, the Finnish Hospital Clowns' costumes, previously designed and assembled by the clowns themselves, were re-designed based on practice-based research[2] that combined a design process with the performer's experiences. Furthermore, I observe how the visually striking hospital clown's costume is also a type of uniform which performs in correlation with the hospital's wider social structures.

Figure 6.2.1 *Hospital clowns in their new costumes. (From left to right): Costume design modification by Lecturer Merja Väisänen, new costume design by MA student Tiina Hauta-aho, BA students Vilma Väisänen, Mimosa Kuusimäki, Department of Film, TV and Scenography at Aalto University. Courtesy of the Finnish Hospital Clowns Association. Photograph by Juuso Partti, 2017.*

The aim of the 'Hospital Clown Costumes' project was to advance knowledge about the hospital clowns' costumes' psychological, emotional and social impact on the performer, the audience and the broader hospital community. The analysis provided here relates to Lotta Linge's earlier work on the implications of hospital clowning on the well-being of sick children, (Linge 2008; 2011; 2012) as well as Persephone Sextou's (2016) observations concerning the effects of children's theatre on the mental and physical welfare of children in a hospital environment. The psychological and physical effects of humour and laughter and the positive effects of hospital clowns' presence on the well-being of young patients have also been researched in the fields of medicine and social sciences. These studies might include some description of the clowns' visual appearance as non-verbal communication between the clowns and children; however, they fail to analyse how broader aspects of hospital clowns' costume can be deployed and perceived within the healing processes of sick children.

The results provided within this research project enable the hospital clowns to further their understanding of the different means of non-verbal communication that a performance costume provides for the performer. The hospital clown may utilize the costume as a catalyst for attention and discussion, as well as a visual prompt, which assists the children to attain an imaginary world and allows them to momentarily overlook their illness. In addition, the renewed and re-designed costumes define the clowns' position within the hospital community, in turn strengthening their professional identity.

Hospital Clowning

Hospital clowning is a form of socially engaged art foregrounding playful intervention and is used in pediatric and adolescent hospitals to reduce children's distress and facilitate their adaptation to the hospital environment. Hospital clowns, also known as 'clown doctors' are carefully chosen professional performers, who undergo special training in order to work with children in the healthcare environment. Clown doctors use a variety of techniques that include clowning, improvisation, music, magic and puppetry to bring moments of happiness and diversion to the sick children as well as their families and the hospital staff. They collaborate with medical professionals and may also be specifically trained to assist in the child's treatment, for example escorting children to operating rooms and assisting with their blood tests, physiotherapy and even emergency treatment.

The practice of professional clowns working in hospitals as part of the healthcare team began in 1986 in North America. During the 1990s, the practice spread to several European countries.[3] In Finland, hospital clowning began in 2001 when the Finnish Hospital Clowns Association was founded by Lilli Sukula-Lindblom,[4] Tom Lindblom and Ilkka Viippola. In January 2002, the first hospital clown doctors started to work at the Helsinki University Hospital of Pediatrics and Adolescent Medicine, popularly known as the 'Children's Castle'. Since then the programme has extended to all departments of pediatrics and adolescent medicine in the Finnish university hospitals of Helsinki, Turku, Tampere, Oulu and Kuopio. Altogether, the Finnish Hospital Clowns Association has trained fifty professional clown doctors. Each year these clown doctors reach an audience of more than 77,000 chilren, parents and hospital personnel (The Finnish Hospital Clowns Association 2019). All Finnish hospital clown operations are funded by donations and subsidies.[5] Since 2016 the association has developed its artistic, financial and operational areas of activities. The aim of these improvements was to reach the quality standards of the European Federation of Healthcare Clown Organizations (EFCHO).[6] The re-design of new costumes for the Finnish hospital clowns, discussed in this chapter, was the most visible part of that progress and contributed in an on-going manner to the development of the artistic and professional policy within the Finnish Hospital Clowns Association. The association gained EFCHO membership in 2017.

Hospital Clowning as a Form of Performing Art

Hospital clowning is a distinctive form of theatre and performance. Ackroyd (2000) incorporates theatre performed in hospitals under the term 'applied theatre', an umbrella term for many different forms of performative educational practices and community-based participatory processes. Persephone Sextou describes the theatre offered on an individual basis to children in the hospitals as 'bedside theatre performance' (Sextou 2016: 15). McKinney and Palmer (2017) have defined three concepts in order to identify experiences of scenography in an expanded form: relationality, affectivity and materiality. Hospital clowning can be located within this field of expanded scenography, where one of the central concerns is the spectator's perspective and the mode of the encounter. As the hospital clown costume exists across and through all of these aspects, it can be interpreted and read as a form of scenography that re-arranges ordinary hospital space in order to become a place where empathetic encounters may take place (McKinney & Palmer 2017).

Hospital clowns themselves characterize their performing or acting as an encounter or play. The interviewed clowns emphasized that their manner of performing is a meeting with the child, which may also have the characteristics of performing; hence sometimes, but not always, the situation appears to be a performance. Hospital clowns largely encounter children in the patient rooms; however, they also meet them in other varied spaces within the hospital building, such as the pediatric emergency outpatient clinic or in the 'children's day rooms'. One of the interviewees described how, when patients are placed in a space like an audience, the children become more like conspicuous spectators rather than participants. Such situations may develop a very performative tenor and cause the children in turn to expect a 'performance'.

Everyone recognizes the clown with her/his red nose and costume with colourful patterns. This is the surface or veneer of the clown, but who is actually inside the costume? When clowning, the performer 'performs' a character who is her/his own creation. Often the clown's character ensues from the performers' own vulnerabilities, their weaknesses or failures (van der A 2012) and as a result, the clown is a very personal and individually created character. The clown becomes an archetype that one needs to discover oneself. Even though the clown as a character cannot exist apart from the person who performs her/him, she/he can be identified as a character existing in her/his own right. The performer differentiates the clown persona from their own self by utilizing the clown's name and their way of dressing, moving and talking (van der A 2012).

Figure 6.2.2 *Hospital clowns in their new costumes. Costume design by Lecturer Merja Väisänen. Courtesy of the Finnish Hospital Clowns Association. Photograph by Juuso Partti, 2017.*

According to the interviewed clowns, hospital clowns mainly work in pairs except when assisting in the child's treatments. These specially trained clowns' primary task is to support the child's consent to treatment and encourage the child in that situation. This may mean diverting the child's attention away from the procedure or by playing realistically and describing what will actually occur during the procedure. The clown may spend a whole day with a child first, getting to know the child and discussing the upcoming procedure and later, supporting the patient during the treatment by being present.

Like most paired clowns, hospital clowns also play with status relationships in their acting. Traditionally, there are two main status archetypes within the clown community, based on the behaviour of the clown.[7] These archetypes are the 'whiteface clown' who exhibits a relatively high status and the 'Auguste clown', who has a much lower status than the 'whiteface'. When two clowns perform together, they often play with these contrasting statuses: they can keep, share and change these higher and lower roles during their interplay. When they encounter the child, they always position themselves towards the lower-status point and place the child at the top of the hierarchy. The clowns interviewed emphasized that this 'game of clowning' between them, including how they enter the room as a pair helps to create performance situations in which the child is offered a chance to observe and not necessarily participate in the action.

Designing and Researching Hospital Clown Costumes

For this collaborative project, I supervised and co-designed thirty-six individual hospital clown costumes, together with four students from the Costume Design major at Aalto University.[8] Each designer had to design six to nine particular clown costumes. As every costume consists of five to nine components altogether, 250 different items were designed and created within the project.

The aim of the new designs was to unify and refine the visual appearance of Finnish hospital clowns. We replaced their previous ad-hoc and home-assembled costumes in order to enhance their professional identity and elevate their presence within the healthcare setting. Their new costumes fulfill the requirements of a performance costume and concurrently function as work-wear in the hospital environment. This process gave the performers the ability to develop and renew their clown characters in collaboration with the designers alongside the development of the costumes' functional aspects. Through individual interviews, in person and by means of electronic interview formats, we collected information regarding the performers' approaches and practices as hospital clowns, their own perceptions of their clown characters and their wishes regarding the new costumes we were proposing. The performers' main wishes regarding their costumes centred on the garments' functionality, such as their ease of movement, or the need to carry or apply props on and to their costume.

A starting point for creating the new costumes was the clown doctors' witty and expressive names, such as *Kerttu-Leppä* (Bug-Lady, derived from Ladybug, Figure 6.2.3) and *Tiukka os. Pipo* ('Straight', formerly known as 'Laced',[9] Figure 6.2.4). In the designs, we wished to retain some elements from the old costumes which characterized their individual clown persona and that were also recognizable

Figure 6.2.3 Kerttu-Leppä *(Bug-Lady). Costume design by Vilma Väisänen. Courtesy of the Finnish Hospital Clowns Association, Photograph by Juuso Partti, 2017.*

Figure 6.2.4 Tiukka os. Pipo *(Straight née Laced). Costume design by Mimosa Kuusimäki. Courtesy of the Finnish Hospital Clowns Association. Photograph by Juuso Partti, 2017.*

within their clown doctors' names. In the next phase, each designer composed their ideas, based on their collection of preliminary materials and without restrictions; then they shared their ideas with each other. To harmonize the costumes, the design approach taken was that all ideas would be pooled and accessible to all. Each designer also used printed fabrics donated by Marimekko in their designs, most notably in the clown doctor coats. The brand's recognizable visual identity also helped to contribute to a balanced result for the clown costumes.

Our design ideas were presented to the clowns at the association's 2016 summer conference via costume sketches and mood boards. This was part of the collaborative design pre-planning process, through which designers collected feedback before developing their costume designs further. The individual fittings of the actual costumes which occurred during the autumn of 2016 were tangible moments for each clown to look at and experience their new costume. They also allowed us, the designers to see how the clowns' characters became alive through their costume. These were also the moments when both performer and designer were able to test and develop the visual, constructional and functional aspects of the costume at the same time. These moments also indicated how intensely the costumes affected each clown performer and their personal subjectivity. The performers began to act differently as soon as they put their costumes on. Their gestures, movements and ways of reacting and speaking all started to change.

The effectiveness of these costumes was evident when the finished costumes were presented to the clowns at a launch event in February 2017. None of the clowns were able to disengage from their character once they were dressed in the costume, thus also hindering their ability to communicate in a normal manner. The immediate feedback received from the hospital clowns was extremely positive and enthusiastic. They enjoyed both the colourfulness of the new costumes and the use of print fabrics, especially in the re-designed doctor's coats, which had been modified to suit each clown's character. As designers, we felt that we had managed to co-ordinate the clowns' appearance: the costumes appeared more professional and also gained several functional enhancements.

The insights gained during the design process regarding the powerful influence that the hospital clown's costume has on the performer aroused my interest in researching the subject even further. I set out to examine the habits, meanings and influences behind a clown's costume in a hospital context, in order to grasp how to design this complex costume.

Figure 6.2.5 *Finnish hospital clowns' new costumes. Courtesy of the Finnish Hospital Clowns Association. Photograph by Juuso Partti, 2017.*

Following the design process, which lasted from September 2015 to February 2017, I collected performer experiences following a period of wearing the new costumes from 2017 to 2018. The observations that inform this chapter were collected primarily from a group of clowns whose new costumes I designed myself. This group consists of seven clowns who work in the Department of Pediatrics and Adolescent Medicine at Turku University Hospital.[10] Five of these clowns were newly appointed when the project started in 2015, whereas two had been working as hospital clowns since 2001.

This group of clowns was interviewed with regard to their personal experiences, for example, how the costumes influenced them as well as their surroundings.[11] I used a semi-structured interview form which incorporated five themes: working as a hospital clown, the costume of the hospital clown, transforming into the role of a hospital clown, the performance situation and the feedback from the children, their parents and healthcare personnel.

Research Outcomes: The Hospital Clown Costume as a Vigorous Transformer

The hospital clown costume is an affective performance costume, founded on the deeply rooted conventions of clown costumes.[12] The costume is based on the performer's personal clown character and derives its special characteristics from the pre-requisites required for working in the hospital environment and its social structure. The costume holds an indispensable significance for the clown in transitioning to and being within the fictional character s/he embodies. As such, the hospital clown's performance costume is marked by its intense psychological influence and it is deeply connected to the performer.

The clown's red nose, often called the world's tiniest mask, is a tool allowing the performer to transition in and out of the clown character.[13] The hospital clowns interviewed, described getting dressed in the clown costume as a ritual through which the performer transitions slowly from their everyday life to the clown character. The dressing-up into the clown character almost always occurs in the same order, just as the undressing out of the role appears in a reverse order. All the clowns put the red nose on last, since that conclusively transforms them into the character. This psychological power is demonstrated within an act, as the clowns usually remove their red noses when they address healthcare personnel concerning a patient in their office. Only those who have worked the longest do not remove their noses if the children are able to see into the office. One of the clowns explained that when she wears the clown's nose she also has the 'vibe of the clown' in her body and voice which is why she wants to take off the nose. The clowns also described writing their work reports in their own clothing and not in their clown costume, in order to perceive the day's events from an 'external' perspective.

One of the interviewed clowns expressed how she had questioned the role of the costume and the red nose at the Hospital Clowns Association's entrance examinations, wondering why they could not encounter the patients as one person to another. Prior to her work as a hospital clown, she had worked as a dance instructor in different nursing institutions and wore a 'hoodie' (track or field suit top) as her work attire, a garment similar to the clothes she wore in her everyday life. After working as a hospital clown, however, and wearing the red nose and costume, she realized that these elements also provided a psychological shelter to and for the performer.

The clown costume's marked nature protects the performer's psyche from this profession's emotional strain, as it allows the performer to distance his/her personal self from the persona of the clown. The clown character and costume provide a welcome barrier to challenging situations in the hospital setting and casual clothing, according to my subjects, cannot achieve this aim. Because the clown costume is integrally connected to the performer's clown character – in turn tapping into their own personality, the costume's visual and concrete elements can become psychologically and mentally distressing if they do not adhere to the clown-character's needs. Even the colours and prints applied to the costume may affect the performer. For example, one clown named *Mutkalalla* (Bendyly, Figure 6.2.6), has a dance background. She wanted to have a costume that she would find easy to move in. Elements of her earlier costume included a turban and a pair of clogs. I wanted to retain the turban, as she had very long hair which was plaited and then covered with the headgear. I suggested, however, that we change the clogs into tap shoes which would enable her to tap-dance as a way of moving.

Mutkalalla's new costume consisted of a skirt, a shirt, pantaloons, a turban made of African printed fabric with a folded plastic pineapple on top and a pair of red tap-shoes which she enjoyed. After several months of wearing the costume and especially after shortening her long hair, it began to appear as too harsh for her character, especially as the braided hair no longer made it feel softer, thus affecting her whole being, her posture, movements and frame of mind. She began to feel very formal, as if she were a 'bank clerk', even though there were no such visual cues. Trying to understand why,

Figure 6.2.6 Mutkalalla *(Bendyly). Costume design by Merja Väisänen. Courtesy of the Finnish Hospital Clowns. Photograph by Juuso Partti, 2017.*

she began eliminating different parts of her costume to test how the changes affected her. In the end, she came to the conclusion that the plastic pineapple on the turban and the strong geometrical pattern of the African fabric, along with the tap-shoes were too rigid for her clown character. The tap-shoes also caused practical difficulties, as they were slippery when walking through hospital corridors and their metallic components were not permitted in scanning facilities. As she had not worked as a hospital clown for long prior to the new costume it made her consider her clown character's nature anew. She stated that her clown was a soft, girly and doll-like high-school girl. This resulted in a further revision of her costume: she currently wears a softer turban and will soon try a baseball cap. She now wears sneakers, which allow for soft and fast movement. She and her costume are turning into a clown character that represents the high-school girl that she acknowledged the character to be.

Interviews also implied that the clown character, with its inherently anarchic temper might also behave against their own clown character. More experienced clown performers were more equipped to recognize the nature of their clown and were not so prone to impulse. According to one of the interviewed clowns, an expert in physical comedy at the Stockholm Academy of Dramatic Arts, clowns can act against their type rather like a child who plays a princess one moment and a fireman the next.

The Hospital Clown's Costume as a Stage in the Hospital Space

The physical spaces of the hospital environment pose particular challenges to costume, as the clown costume is perceived from both up close and afar. Therefore, the costume requires both features such as bright colours visible from a distance and elements that can be viewed up close such as patterns and buttons. The narrow spaces of patient rooms also affect the elements, shapes and volumes of material suitable for hospital clown costumes. The clown has to be physically able to come close to the hospital bed and to reach the child's gaze and gain consent for the encounter on the child's own terms.

When the clowns meet the child personally, beside their hospital bed, this space is intimate for the child. 'As the hospital clown artist enters the hospital ward and moves closer to the child's bedside to perform, it often seems like they enter the child's private space' (Sextou 2016: 54). This private zone, the bed and the space surrounding it is a sensitive area where people should ask for the child's permission in order to enter. This is also a liminal space between reality and fantasy where magic transpires. Linge (2012) describes this intermediate space as 'a magical safe area', where the child is able to relax in the hospital environment and experience a sense of joy together with the clown.

Hospital Clown's Costume as a Means of Communication

Hospital clowns use both verbal and non-verbal communication to arouse the child's curiosity and to create the magical safe area between the child and the clowns. These verbal and non-verbal expressions are ways of signalling to the child that the 'room is open to all sorts of feelings' (Linge 2008: 33). The types of non-verbal communication include miming, body language, the clown's colourful costume and the red nose along with all kinds of props brought along by the clown (Linge 2008: 33). The costume is an efficient method of non-verbal communication and interaction, supporting the encounter between clown and child.

The costume of a hospital clown is the clown's 'calling card' that invites the child to enter the world of imagination. Thus, the costume affords the clown and child an unvoiced possibility to get to know each other, to build trust between them; the child may just look at the clown and experience all the details that the costume contains and the clown can just wait for the child to open up to the encounter. Additionally, the costume hides the performer's personal identity and she/he appears as an anonymous person to the child with whom the child is able to share things which she/he cannot share with anybody else in the hospital.

The clown costume should communicate to children of all ages and backgrounds. The costume's vibrant colour is especially significant in directing the attention and focus of small children and children with special needs. The visual impulses provided by the costume should not, however. distract the child's attention too much, in order to assist the development of the dialogical encounter between the child and the clown, especially when the clowns work together as pairs, a colourful and visually noisy costume may be too much for children who are sensitive and may be scared of what they will encounter in the hospital. One of the clowns also added that it is important to remember that the child should have time to perceive and look at the clown, before advancing the 'performance'.

Figure 6.2.7 *The clown's costume is a non-verbal societal rule-breaker. Costume design by Merja Väisänen. Courtesy of the Finnish Hospital Clowns Association. Photograph by Juuso Partti, 2017.*

Figure 6.2.8 *The clown's costume may direct the focus of small children. Costume design by Vilma Väisänen. Courtesy of the Finnish Hospital Clowns Association. Photograph by Juuso Partti, 2017.*

Furthermore, the clown persona represents the qualities and characteristics of a non-normative character who presents a societal 'otherness' (McManus 2003) as clowns do stand outside societal norms and thus remain outsiders. Since children in hospital may feel external in that society they can share this feeling of 'otherness' with the clowns. This non-normative and also anarchic quality of the figure of the clown, expressed through their costume affords children and especially teenagers a means to express critical and provocative opinions.

Moreover, the clown's costume is a non-verbal manifestation of societal rule-breaking and this quality allows sceptical teenagers who might perceive clowns as childish, freedom to express their opinions and attitudes. In many cases, even these cynical encounters can turn into positive breaks in the daily routine which can lighten the mood. Therefore, the 'otherness' of the clown in the hospital context has two functions. It creates the intermediate space where fantasy can occur, as mentioned earlier, as well as allowing the child to identify with the clown's position as a social outsider.

The interviews indicated that a clown costume is an important tool in initiating dialogue between the clown and child, especially when working with teenagers. The children do not generally comment on the costumes or the appearance of the clown, as they perceive the clowns to be fairy

Figure 6.2.9 *A clown with a flower hat and a puppet. Design by Merja Väisänen. Courtesy of the Finnish Hospital Clowns Association. Photograph by Juuso Partti, 2017.*

tale figures. Girls, however, tend to comment on the clowns' appearance more than boys and most critical comments are usually made by children between the ages of eight and nine and teenagers. Such comments include: 'that looks horrible. I would not even go to a masquerade in that outfit.'

The costumes also enabled difficult conversations. A straw hat fully decorated with artificial flowers inspired one of the clowns to use the accessory as a medium to embark on the 'birds and the bees' conversation with children (Figure 6.2.9). *Mutkalallaa* (Bendyly), the turban wearer, used her pineapple turban to build empathy with several teenage boys in the spring of 2017, when the so-called 'pineapple haircut' was in fashion.[14]

The Hospital Clown's Costume under Regulations and Social Hierarchies

Even though a hospital clown's costume is a performance costume, it is also a uniform, a garment worn for working in very specific circumstances. The hospital's hygiene and ergonomic requirements dictate some of the clown's costume features: the materials, which must be washed or disinfected each time they are worn, and the lengths of sleeves and trousers in order to prevent the acquisition of bacteria from the floor or table surfaces to clothing. Additionally, each clown's costume should support their way of moving and have enough pockets and space for the props that they carry. Furthermore, the clowns also work in conditions where the temperature varies greatly. The temperature in the children's ward and patients' rooms can be relatively high and transferrence from one ward to another may take place outside the building.

Uniforms play a key role in the delineation of occupational boundaries and in the formation of professional identities in the hospital society indicate a specific status, thus re-inforcing and making the hierarchy within that society visible (Timmons 2011). The clothing worn by different professions differs through the use of different colours and garments themselves. In Finnish healthcare facilities, doctors who are at the top of the hospital hierarchy wear a doctor's coat and the nursing personnel wears a two-part work outfit consisting of shirt and trousers. Staff engaging in specific procedures such as surgery, also use specific protective garments that differ from the clothing worn in other situations. Finnish hospital clowns have always worn a doctor's coat as part of their costume. The doctor's coat worn by the clowns is considered a distinctive mark of their profession which connects them to the hospital personnel and community. As such, the clown doctor's coat can be considered extremely important to the costume, as it facilitates the ways in which the clown doctors assert themselves within the hospital community.

Interviews indicated that the clowns felt a stronger sense of belonging to the hospital community after their costumes were re-designed. Their new costumes, designed with our collaboration, unified the hospital clowns as a specific profession within the broader hospital community. Cohesive visual ideas and a coherent way of making costumes, as well as the harmoniously designed doctors' coats, turned the costumes into a coherent collection which gave the new hospital clown costumes a professional uniform look, making for a well-groomed appearance.

There is also a paradox at work here concerning uniforms and uniformity. The clown's costume is a manifestation of the uniform's function and yet it also acts against these occupational hierarchies and the uniform's tendency to suppress individuality. The costumes of the hospital clowns are a parody of the very status structures within the hospital community. The doctor's coat is well-known as a visible emblem of their higher hierarchical position within the hospital community. When the clown doctors wear such coats it becomes a caricature, useful for hospital staff and patients alike. One clown described how she created jokes with her clown partner by addressing the doctors in the children's ward as their colleagues, sometimes 'writing prescriptions' and 'giving treatments' to the children alongside the actual cures prescribed by hospital personnel. Here, the clown inverts the hierarchy and exceeds the status of the actual doctor. Both children and nurses are amused by the reversal of these hierarchical roles, emphasized by the satirical way in which the clowns deploy their doctor's coats.

Conclusions: Psychological and Social Benefits for Finnish Children's Healthcare

The newly designed costumes described here re-asserted hospital clowns' identification with their costumes and integrated them more successfully into their own profession, differentiating them from other hospital entertainers such as children's theatre and play instructors. The clowns' activities become visible in a more systematic manner within the hospital environment, further improving the sense of community in this workplace. The renewed clown costumes become a sign of professionalism, specialization and identity for the worker-performers. Healthcare facilities are often utilitarian. The hospital clown's colourful and divergent outfits re-arrange the daily scene, bringing cheer to the hospital milieu, a visual signal of the coming entertainment, laughter and joy. One of the clowns commented that 'the way people spontaneously smile at the clowns has been marvellous, as people do not smile that much in hospital'.

Moreover, the process of renewing the costumes also enabled performers to investigate and extend their own clown's characteristics and to recognize the role and the importance of costume in their work, as described earlier. Interestingly at the beginning of the design process, most of the wishes expressed by the clowns were linked to the costumes' functionality, whereas in the feedback interviews they were exceedingly focused on the different psychological and social aspects related to their costumes. It seems that the more the clowns are able to understand the interaction between their clown character and its costume, the easier it becomes for them to work with the clown character's unruly and anarchic nature and the psychologically powerful costume. In addition, all the clowns interviewed were pleased that the revised costumes we designed for them makes their work appear more refined and professional. To them, it is especially valuable that their profession has become established within hospitals and to them their revitalized costumes are a sign of this recognition.

The rejuvenated appearance of Finnish hospital clowns has generated publicity via different social media platforms. This publicity is a straightforward way of conveying information to the general public through the media. It helps to enhance the professional image of hospital clowning and

Figure 6.2.10 *Clowns and their clown characters. Costume design by Tiina Hauta-aho. Courtesy of the Finnish Hospital Clowns Association. Photograph by Juuso Partti, 2017.*

creates awareness of the hospital clowns' valuable work, while adding credibility to the Hospital Clowns Association activities. The impression made by hospital clown costumes within the hospital community and the general public is important. Donors and members financially supporting the association make their decisions based on the image created by hospital clowns' activities.

Finally, this project provides further knowledge for costume designers working with clowns towards developing their own design processes, using more time to develop their ideas in collaboration and actually testing pieces of costume in practice with the clown. Since the clown character is so intimately connected to the performer's self, the design of a costume can be challenging, not only for the designer but for the clown too. As there was a tradition of an ad-hoc approach to costume within the Finnish hospital clown community, the 'outside' perspective of a professional costume designer was challenging as it was also dependent on the clown's own work experience and self-awareness. After wearing their new costumes, many of the clowns gained a new understanding of how integral costume is to their characters and as a result they gained a new interest in working closely with the designer during the creative process.

The 'Hospital Clown Costumes' project developed a critical discourse on costume within the unique frame of hospital clowning and contributed to and advanced the existing knowledge on the agency of performance costume. The information gained through this collaboration has the potential to enrich the future costume design and expand the interaction between costume designer and performer. For vulnerable and sick children, investigating the health and social benefits of hospital clowning deserve our on-going analysis and attention.

Notes

1 This project was funded by the Finnish Culture Foundation, the Costume Design major at Aalto University, the Finnish Hospital Clowns Association and the Finnish textile company Marimekko.

2 The artistic research conducted in this project was developed within the Costume in Focus research group in the frame of the Costume Methodologies Academy of Finland FiDiPro research project, supervised and led by Professor Sofia Pantouvaki (PI).

3 In 1986, Michael Christensen founded the Big Apple Circus Clown Care Unit (CCU) in New York, USA. Concurrently, Karen Ridd created the first Canadian therapeutic clown programme at the Winnipeg Children's Hospital. In 1991, Caroline Simonds who had earlier worked for the CCU, founded the *Le Rire Medicin* organization in France which was the first hospital clown organization in Europe (The Hospital Clown Newsletter 1998, 1999 and 2001).

4 Lilli Sukula-Lindblom brought the hospital clown programme to Finland after studying the hospital clown operations within the CCU (The Finnish Hospital Clowns Association 2018).

5 The main financier of the Finnish Hospital Clowns Association has been RAY (Finland's Slot Machine Association) along with The Finnish Cultural Foundation, The Swedish Cultural Foundation in Finland and The Ministry of Education and Culture. Private citizens along with private sector corporations also take part in funding through membership programmes and individual donations (The Finnish Hospital Clowns Association 2016).

6 EFCHO aims to develop and maintain standards of quality, in order to ensure common qualifications between its member organizations and thus gain acknowledgement for the profession of hospital clowning and its member organizations both within the healthcare practice and in wider communities (The European Federation of Healthcare Clown Organizations 2018).

7 Since the mid-nineteenth century, two clown archetypes have been broadly known in the technical language of the circus as the 'whiteface clowns' and the 'Augustes' and they are based primarily on the type of make-up they wear and their behavioural characteristics (Bouissac 2015: 24). These archetypes are still relevant today.

8 Three bachelor's students (Joona Huotari, Mimosa Kuusimäki and Vilma Väisänen) and one master's student (Tiina Hauta-aho) participated in this project as a part of their studies. The latter wrote her thesis on this project.

9 'os.' is a shortening of the Finnish words 'omaa sukuaan' that refer to one's 'own family name' (maiden name). This clown name is also a playful word game related to the word 'tiukkapipo', which means 'someone who is uptight by nature'.

10 Hospital clowns at Turku University Hospital work in the Pediatric Haematology Outpatient Ward, Pediatric Infection Ward, Pediatric Day Hospital, Pediatric Psychiatry Ward, Pediatric Neurological Day Hospital, Pediatric Asthma & Allergy Outpatient Clinic, Pediatric Emergency Outpatient Clinic and the Pediatric Surgery Outpatient Clinic (Turku University Hospital 2018).

11 The interviews were conducted via telephone conversations. Prior to the interview, each interviewee received their questions by e-mail to familiarize themselves with the questions and enabling them to make notes beforehand. All the interviews were recorded and lasted between half an hour to one hour per person. The interviews proceeded in sequence from theme to theme and the follow-up questions were posed spontaneously to get more information or for possible clarifications.

12 The term 'performance costume' is used here to describe the appearance of the performer as a whole, in the performing arts and in cinema. This appearance consists of clothing, make-up, hairstyles, bodily movements and expressions and it has narrative, symbolic and emotional functions.

13 According to Jacques Lecoq, one of the most influential personalities in modern clowning, 'the little red nose, "the smallest mask in the world" gives the nose a round shape, lights up the eyes with naiveté and makes the face seem bigger, robbing it of all defences. It inspires no fear, which is why children like it' (Lecoq 2002: 116).

14 The term 'pineapple hair cut' refers to a hairstyle where the sides of the head are shaved short and the hair grows longer on the top. It was very popular in Finland in the years 2016–17.

References

Ackroyd, J. (2000), *Literacy Alive!* Drama Projects for Literacy Learning, Literacy Alive Series. London: Hodder & Stoughton Educational.

Bouissac, P. (2015), *The Semiotics of Clowns and Clowning: Rituals of Transgression and the Theory of Laughter*. London and New York: Bloomsbury Academic.

Interviews: Five hospital clowns were interviewed anonymously regarding their user experiences of the renewed costumes on 23–27 February 2018.

Lecoq, J. (2002), *Theatre of Movement and Gesture*. Abingdon: Routledge.
'Le Rire Médecin and Caroline Simonds aka Dr. Giraffe, founder of Le Rire Médecin (Laughter Medicine) Paris, France' (2001), *The Hospital Clown* Newsletter 6 (2): 7–13. Available online: http://www.hospitalclown.com/archives/vol-06/vol-6-1and2/vol6-2_rire-paris.PDF (accessed: 31 March 2019).
Linge, L. (2008), 'Hospital Clowns Working in Pairs: In Synchronized Communication with Ailing Children', *International Journal of Qualitative Studies on Health and Well-being* 3 (1): 12, 27–38. Available online: https://www.tandfonline.com/doi/full/10.1080/17482620701794147 (accessed: 1 April 2019).
Linge, L. (2011), 'Joy without Demands: Hospital Clowns in the World of Ailing Children', *International Journal of Qualitative Studies on Health and Well-being* 6 (1): 1–8. Available online: https://www.tandfonline.com/doi/full/10.3402/qhw.v6i1.5899 (accessed: 2 April 2019).
Linge, L. (2012), 'Magical Attachment: Children in Magical Relations with Hospital Clowns', *International Journal of Qualitative Studies on Health and Well-being* 7 (1): 1–12. Available online: https://www.tandfonline.com/doi/full/10.3402/qhw.v7i0.11862 (accessed: 1 April 2019).
McKinney, J. and S. Palmer (2017), *Scenography Expanded: An Introduction to Contemporary Performance Design*. London/New York: Bloomsbury Methuen Drama.
McManus, D. C. (2003), *No Kidding: Clown as Protagonist in Twentieth-century Theatre*. Cranbury, NJ: Rosemont Publishing & Printing Corp.
'Michael Christensen and the Big Apple Clown Care Unit' (1999), *The Hospital Clown* Newsletter 4 (1): 5–9. Available online: http://www.hospitalclown.com/archives/vol-04/vol-4-1and2/vol4-1_big-apple.pdf (accessed: 1 April 2019).
'Objectives and Activities' (2018), *The European Federation of Healthcare Clown Organizations (EFHCO)*. Available online: http://www.efhco.eu/about/objectives-and-activities (accessed: 2 April 2019).
'Robo's Legacy, Karen Ridd, Clown and Child Life Therapist from Winnipeg Canada' (1998), *The Hospital Clown* Newsletter 3 (2): 3–6. Available online: http://www.hospitalclown.com/archives/vol-03/vol-3-1and2/Vol3-2_robo.PDF (accessed: 1 April 2019).
Sairaalaklovnit ry [*The Finnish Hospital Clowns Association*] (2016), 'Vuosikertomukset' ['Annual Reports']. Available online: http://sairaalaklovnit.fi/vuosikertomukset/(accessed: 2 April 2019).
Sairaalaklovnit ry [*The Finnish Hospital Clowns Association*] (2018), 'Toiminta' ['Activities']. Available online: http://sairaalaklovnit.fi/toiminta/(accessed: 2 April 2019).
Sextou, P. (2016), *Theatre for Children in Hospital: The Gift of Compassion*. Chicago: The University of Chicago Press.
Timmons, E. (2011), 'Uniforms, Status and Professional Boundaries in Hospital', *International Journal of Sociology of Health & Illness* 33 (7): 1035–49. Available online: https://onlinelibrary.wiley.com/doi/abs/10.1111/j.1467-9566.2011.01357.x (accessed: 2 April 2019).
Turku University Hospital (2018). Available online: http://www.vsshp.fi/en/Pages/default.aspx (accessed: 2 April 2019).
van der A, A. P. (2012), 'Becoming Annot: Identity Through Clown', *Platform eJournal* 6 (2): 86–104. Available online: https://www.royalholloway.ac.uk/dramaandtheatre/documents/pdf/platform/062/platformjournal62-becomingannot-identitythroughclown.pdf (accessed: 1 April2019).

6.3 Costume of Conflict

Mateja Fajt

Costume can create its own narration through which relationships between different political actors are revealed. Power is foregrounded in such an analysis. 'Pussy Riot', 'Femen' and the 'SlutWalk' movement are now internationally known for their public actions. They are distinctive due to their selection of specific types of clothing, which I approach here from the perspective of costume. How can we conceptualize these costumes and what meanings are generated within and through costume in such public contexts? Can this type of costume carry conflict by escalating or pacifying it? Is it necessary to define this 'clothing praxis' as a 'costume' or do we by using this term neutralize the political charge of such an expression?

My goal here is to expand the understanding of costume onstage and off, including actions and interventions in public spaces. For this analysis, I use a visual methodology by collecting and analysing not just photography and video from real, lived actions and events, but also the 'echo' that they create and generate in posters, stickers and other ephemera. By using this method to research the cultural, political and ideological elements connected to everyday garments used as costume in public actions, I propose that costume can be involved in an active role within the praxis of everyday life. I use 'praxis' as a concept implying both an engagement and an enactment. Moving beyond the model and level of 'artistic' costume (such as might be seen in theatre, film, television, opera and ballet) I focus here on the field of grassroots politics and everyday life. How does costume mediate and function in conflict-oriented situations? I argue that contemporary social movements make use of clothes as costume as one of their methods. This is not new as 1970s feminism, the Black Power movement and other grassroots activism also used clothing to build their collective identities that were in turn part of their public strategies. The more recent movements challenge us to recognize that costume is not always a product, goal or an end unto itself but can rather be interpreted as a method that evolves, changes and varies depending on the precise social environment and the range of social actors (everyday people) in and with which it appears.

Starting Point

While costume design is an artistic field, costume itself can be present in various situations that occur in various events and settings: when it occurs in the praxis of everyday life, however, it can become a political tool. One of the biggest challenges in this approach is the mainstream schematic framework within which costume is conceptualized. Reducing costume to the status of a quasi-work of art can function as an alienating practice inherent to art itself: the costume's 'author' of the costume becomes an artist, trained within the normative space of artistic educational systems his/her artistic work is judged by experts who contribute added artistic value to the costume, whereas the public is limited to disempowered consumption. Thus, costume often reproduces existing power relations regarding makers and viewers, but costume practices can also question these relations. In this text I use the term 'costume of conflict' to capture contemporary costuming practices that are subversive and political. More precisely, I am interested in the hierarchies embedded in or transmitted through costume and I focus on the type of costume that can create, mediate or take an active role in conflict situations.

Understanding Costume

Since the 1970s post-modern art became more connected with everyday life, but with a precise function and cost: the aestheticization of everyday experience. Artworks became an object of reproduction in times of technological development which led to their 'de-auratisation', meaning that art no longer possessed the authentic and unique nature characteristic of modernism (Debeljak 1999). Much art of the past was kept in elite spaces (although much Medieval and Renaissance art was carried into the street and placed on public view) but we now experience it in all spheres of everyday life, decisively shaped by the late capitalist economic, political and cultural system. As an art form, costume design is thus usually based on the idea of exclusivity within a hierarchical system of institutionalized art that is inherited from older value systems. The costume itself is 'trapped' in these hierarchies of artistic means, meaning and production. The ability to recognize costume outside the usual artistic 'geography' or eco-system, especially in its borderline manifestations, is already an important step towards a more expansive view of costume.

The work of Aoife Monks opens up this perspective when she states, 'costume is a body that can be taken off' (2010: 11). This statement is both inclusive and at the same time neglects some other domains because it focuses on the wearer and not on the environment, hence neglecting context and collective dynamics. Costume inherently carries an action, a change, a metamorphosis that is necessary in order to achieve an un/costumed body. Elements of action come to position costuming itself as a participative praxis. The base of participation is the wearer, who wears the costume in order to participate in an action or event. Another level of participation is when the wearers themselves create costumes. 'Costume of conflict' can also offer a space for active participation: from the perspective of a political action as well as from the perspective of a costume itself.

Participation is not, however, usually seen as the dominant function of costume. The whole spectrum of a costume's functions is usually reduced in a classical way to the embodiment of a character, thus to an identity that communicates with the environment. The artistic costume carries another big function: it creates illusion. This puts the costume in a permanent contradictory position: costume constantly negates or denies itself because it should not be a read as a costume, but should look and function as a form of dress. On the other hand, costume outside the usual artistic geography is dominant: in folk costumes, cosplay or parades there is always the explicit presence of a costume. Here it must look and function as a costume, for example, the representation of a historical, cultural or social body that differs from that within which it is presented. Both types of environments create a consensus around the costume: all participants (wearers or viewers) share a consensus about the interaction that forms the social relationship. The costume is expected 'to take place' in these situations. 'Costume of conflict' often defies this consensus by appearing in unexpected situations. So it functions as a method to break the routine, to disrupt a situation where participants are expected to follow the norm of wearing everyday dress as opposed to costume. As Rachel Hann argues: 'to engage in the act of costuming is to consciously skew or *other* the normative practices of appearance' (2017: 11).

Context of 'Costume of Conflict'

The case studies presented in this chapter are mostly political and expressed in distinct performative ways. A useful term here is 'artivism', introduced by Slovenian theatre theoretician Aldo Milohnić. 'Artivism' combines cases of autonomous movements, as well as artistic movements that are political (Milohnić 2006: 186). These types of actions derive from different protest movements from both the past and present that look for new ways of political action due to ineffectiveness, regulation or normalization of convention. Protest actions often aim to disrupt specific events and emit clearly visible signs of their message. Activists use a range of different tactics, media, art and other cultural and political forms to achieve their goals. Costume is sometimes used to effect different levels of conflict, lowering or heightening it. 'Tactical frivolity' was one of the methods that employed costume in protests in Prague in 2000 against the International Monetary Fund (IMF) and World Bank summit; then activists confronted the police dressed in vivid carnivalesque costumes. The artist, activist and renowned cartoonist Kate Evans noted that the strategy at the time was 'to dress up in outrageous costumes, half Bacchanalian ball-gown, half Rio carnival dancer, and confront the police, unmasked and armed only with feminism and feather dusters' (2003: 290). In a similar manner, clowns from the Clandestine Insurgent Rebel Clown Army, an activist group that uses elements of clowning, tactically dress up wearing traditional clown make-up (usually consisting of a white face and red nose) during highly antagonistic protests and often dispel tensions at such demonstrations (Routledge 2004: 118).

Costume is just one clothing praxis present in these situations. The everyday clothes of people taking part in political actions are very different and depend on the type of action: they exist in relation to the conflict level of the situation. This is particularly the case when police officers are involved. They behave and look as one: they wear uniforms, are depersonalized, armed and on a very explicit level they represent the 'state's personified monopoly on violence' (Scholl 2012: 8). On the other hand, there are groups and individuals who wear a variety of clothes: some look more militant, others less. This creates unpredictable situations that confuse the surveillance forces. Christian Scholl's analysis (2010) of the Clandestine Insurgent Rebel Clown Army and the 'Pink and Silver Block' from the 2000 protest in Prague emphasizes the confusion and subversion they bring: 'Both tactics attempt to confuse the anticipated lines of confrontation during street protests and subvert binary categories such as male-female, violent-non-violent, and fun-activism. By doing so, they confuse and subvert dominant cultural codes' (Scholl 2010: 163).

'Costume of conflict' should not be aestheticized: the criterion is not clothes that so-called 'rebels' wear. It comes from an act, a relation: the costume is in conflict with someone or something, more precisely with the establishment. My focus being Pussy Riot, Femen and SlutWalk, here is a breakdown of the levels of conflict present in these situations from the viewpoint of costume:

1 Level of conflict-orientated situations. The environment is highly charged with a potential conflict. Costume in these situations is part of the confrontation and can be used as a method to achieve a certain goal.
2 Level of disturbance. The environment itself does not have a special conflict or tension, but the costume violates the rules or norms of the social situation. Costume, here, functions as an element of disturbance.
3 The costume itself carries subversion. It is recognized as violent, militant, (sexually) explicit or outrageous and as such it introduces uneasiness, no matter what the situation.
4 Level of the wearer. Conflict here lies in the obstruction of identity. Costume can disguise the wearer's identity, which is already problematic in the eyes of authority, but also breaks the unity of the look/appearance and the self. This is amplified in situations where the participants are not expected to wear costumes.

The last point deals with the concept of an identity that can itself be a reason for conflict. Our everyday clothes can frame the body as a 'putatively foreseeable component of a predictable whole' (Warwick and Cavalaro 2001: 113) through disciplinary mechanisms such as self-control and external management. Costume can deconstruct this predictability by breaking the unity of the wearer's identity. Police forces and protestors perform in two different types of bodies in the course of protests. Even though the faces of the police officers are often covered with helmets they wear signs of identification; this is their official clothing in which they perform their official roles. Protestors, on the other hand are an unpredictable mix of identities that wear various types of clothing and some cover their faces. In the eyes of authority, this way of dressing can be viewed as 'costume', that is as a blurring of identity. This not only happens just physically, but within the concept of identity itself, by embodying a different identity through 'costume'. Hiding identity, or even worse, playing with identity through costume is seen as a dangerous and subversive act.

In 'artivist' actions the artistic aspect is present, but not dominant. It depends on the context: 'When activist art interventions are based on the moment of confrontation, art as such actually disappears, because it will not be judged by the aesthetic qualities it has, but by the effects it produces' (Scholl 2010: 169). This is why it is ineffective to use artistic terms in the context of direct political action. Baz Kershaw, who wrote *The Politics of Performance* (1992) and *The Radical in Performance* ([1999] 2013) explores the relationship between theatre and radical performative praxis and its subversive potential. For him, 'protest is a type of cultural performance that has little or nothing to do with theatre estate and its disciplines' (Kershaw [1999] 2013: 91). Although the use of artistic terms in political actions may be problematic, on the other hand, it may open different ways of reading and entering a sphere that is ideologically charged. Is the power of political action pacified or even disarmed if we interpret it through the parameters of art? Costume does not have a purely artistic genealogy. If we understand costume not exclusively as an artistic object, but can recognize costume practices that occur in the sphere of everyday life (where the act of dressing entails similarities as well as differences via artistic costume) then the term 'costume' is adequate and relevant. Rather than seeking artistic costume in political actions, costume needs to be liberated from artistic exclusivity.

Moreover, performance studies have opened the door to comprehending costume as interdisciplinary and inclusive, where 'any action that is framed, presented, highlighted or displayed is performance' (Schechner 2013: 2). While this offers a great potential for non-dogmatic understanding of costume, it can also work against it by classifying all clothing practices as costume. Hann navigates this dilemma and expands the split between performance as a disciplinary field and performance as an event with a perspective on costume:

> *Costume* with a 'C' and *costume* with a 'c': as a symptom of dressing and as an extra-daily practice. The first feeds an appraisal of how dressing is a socially mitigated construction that, when rehearsed over time, slips into unconscious acts of disciplined appearance. Whereas the second is the method by which individuals alter their appearance in order to demarcate their participation within an artistic or social event. One, exposes how appearance is a product of disciplined conditioning, while the other is concerned with a conscious act of appearance: of 'showing dressing' (2017: 11–12).

Hann also observes: '(t)o engage in the act of costuming is to evoke an explicit theatricality of appearance. Whereas disciplined performativity enacts a structure for the ongoing practice of dressing, costume is always charged through a conscious theatricality whether visible to an observer or not' (Hann 2017: 10).[1] As with protests, violent confrontations and direct actions 'can all be thought of as performances of collective actors geared to a variety of audiences – the media, authorities, counter-movements, the public' (Johnston 2016: 8). 'Costume of conflict' is, therefore, made and worn in distinctive circumstances and with a distinctive purpose, based on an awareness of the situation and the role of clothing.

Costume and Performative Identity

Costume makes a major contribution to embodying identities. If we understand it as a 'body that can be taken off' (Monks 2010), it opens up a broad spectrum of thoughts, wearers and their identities. The concept of performative identity is another key to understanding 'costume of conflict'. Much has been written on costume and identity in the performing arts as well as in ethnography. Ethnographic sources indicate that the feelings of wearers in traditional costume can be similar to those wearing classical artistic costumes; in both cases, the costumes cover or hide the identity of the wearer and express a sense of festivity which gives the wearer a different bodily feeling (Knific 2010).

Even though it might seem clear that in the performing arts we look at actors performing certain characters/identities, things are not so straightforward: as Monks notes 'The actor's body is not singular and stable, but rather multiple and continually shifting in its appearance and possibilities' (2010: 33). Thus, costume cannot be separated from the wearer: 'The borders between the actor and the costume are unclear. The costume is the spectator's means to access the actor's body, and is also a means for the actor to access the world of performance' (Monks 2010: 20). Understanding costume in this way reflects our perception of clothes in everyday life as well 'as part of the subject and as objects for the subject, which are not accommodated within the body and yet cannot be conceived of as totally separate from it' (Warwick and Cavallaro 2001: 44). Ethnologist Pravina Shukla looks at many praxes of costuming and explores the relation between costume and identity. She states that 'costume, like dress, is the clothing of who we are, but that it signals a different self, one other than that expressed through daily dress' (2015: 3). Based on research of Halloween costumes, she concludes that one of the main functions of costume is expressing the wearers' identity: 'far from donning a separate identity, they were communicating a deep sense of themselves' (Shukla 2015: 12). Costume assists the wearer in constructing and the viewer/audience in interpreting, performative identity. As with other forms of costuming, performed identity is also present in 'costume of conflict' where performed actions require a distinct behaviour and mode of operating. Regardless of the costume's appearance, be it ironic, or even trivial looking, standing behind the mode and the message of the action is even more crucial in the environment of political action. For the wearers, costume here is not décor but an underscoring of the message.

'Costume of Conflict': Three Case Studies

The Pussy Riot, Femen and SlutWalk[2] movements are widely known, not least due to their distinct clothing praxes that I interpret here as 'costumes of conflict'. I am interested in the practice, perception, relations and meanings of these costumes rather than the garments themselves, so I look at these cases through the lens of *costuming*: not costume as a noun, but rather as a verb (Monks 2010: 3).

Costume as a Tool: Pussy Riot

The actions of Pussy Riot date back to 2012, when they performed the song 'Punk Prayer' in the Moscow Cathedral of Christ the Saviour and became widely known due to the arrest and trial of three of their members (Figure 6.3.1). Although Pussy Riot are simply defined as a music band in mainstream media, their protest can be considered an 'artivist' action because the group comes from a Russian activist movement background and activist subculture.[3] Wearing short summer dresses, colourful tights and ski masks, they performed a song with uncoordinated choreography and were quickly removed by security. Here, 'costume of conflict' was manifest in a level of disturbance; their image was incompatible with the 'sacred' environment of the cathedral and ski masks, which usually have militant connotations clashed with the playful summer dresses. Wearing masks, thus hiding

Figure 6.3.1 *Pussy Riot in the Moscow Cathedral of Christ the Saviour, 2012. Photo credit: Sergey Ponomarev.*

their individual identities, enabled the participants to act not as individuals, but as a collective and to communicate on a political level. Their 'costume' communicated conflict and playfulness at the same time, but also provided them with anonymity and security. One of their more visible members, Nadezhda Tolokonnikova explains the thought process behind the costumes: they chose the masks because they did not want a focus on their personalities and the colourful dresses were similarly selected: 'We just didn't want to be read as terrorists. We didn't want to scare people; we wanted to bring some fun, so we decided to look like clowns' (Lyon 2016: n.p.). While they problematized an internal Russian political issue, this action launched Pussy Riot as a globally iconic group whose 'costume' way of dressing, began to be copied.A subsequent level related to 'costuming' happened following the Pussy Riot trial. The latter caused an international wave of solidarity actions in which supporters used the group's 'costume-related' imagery and dressed in costumes resembling them (Figure 6.3.2). This can be considered a clear example of 'costume' because it copies the original image (the way the group members were dressed); hence here, the 'original' costume is taken as a reference. This costume functioned as an expression of solidarity and became a political tool, which manifested in various expressions within the public sphere: in illustrations, posters, protests, public interventions and cultural jamming.

This produced different levels of a costume: first, an 'original costume' materialized through clothes worn during the action in the church. A second level is a reference that materialized through the clothes of supporters who imitated the clothes of the original group and used clothing as a medium. A third level is produced on a virtual level (as a poster depicting the costume) where the physical body is no longer required. Here, the costume can be rapidly reproduced and it functions on a visual and virtual level as an image without a corporeal body.

Figure 6.3.2 *Action in support of Pussy Riot, Ljubljana, 2012. Photo credit: Nada Žgank.*

Was Pussy Riot an act of resistance commodified through costume? A costume-based action that originated from do-it-yourself culture became an easily reproduced, trendy rebel costume, eventually reduced to just an image. Another interesting aspect was that the Pussy Riot image was reversed during and after the trial: the group members were no longer costumed and their faces were visible. As their visual representation changed, so did the discourse surrounding them: 'Pussy Riot' became a band of individuals with specific names, stories, history, faces and families. They were transformed from a group into individual persons and from conveying a collective message to expressing individual existence.

Costume and the Body: Femen and SlutWalk

The Femen and SlutWalk movements are connected because they both deal with the relationship between the body and clothes and specifically with the use of nudity. They are involved with the question of moral values, patriarchy and control over women's bodies by using nudity to define their political positions in public events where they intervened with their own bodies.

Femen is an activist group which was established in Ukraine in 2008 and spread across Europe in the following years. By using nudity in their acts of resistance, the group states that women's bodies are constantly used by men; the goal of their actions is to re-appropriate their own bodies when revealed in public spaces (Salem 2013). They became notorious, usually performing topless, with slogans written directly on their skin and flowers in their hair (Figure 6.3.3). Their actions relied on creating a moment of shock: disrupting an event for a short period of time, with revealing

Figure 6.3.3 *Femen action, Brussels, 2013. Photo credit: Georges Gobet/AFP/Getty Images.*

their breasts being the most striking point of their costume. Here, they recall earlier performance, installation, lesbian and queer art and feminist activisms and practices in which the simple baring of the female breasts provokes, shocks and disturbs. Such work was notable in the counterculture and art of the 1960s and 1970s, as well as the club culture of cities such as London (personified by that of the Blitz Club) in the 1980s.

Femen use clothing only as an accessory, while the naked body is the most dominant element of their costumeand invites viewers to turn their attention to just that. In other words, they use nudity as their costume. What kind of bodies are represented in their actions and what kind of images do these actions generate? For Femen's Inna Shevchenko, 'female nudity which is free from the patriarchal system becomes the symbol of women's liberation' (Shevchenko 2013: n.p.). In these new social movements, the body is seen as an ultimate tool of resistance: the bodies of the participants are frequently used as a means of direct political activism (Milohnić 2006). When we have bodies that are naked and fit into a normative image of a woman's body, many questions arise. Barbara Sutton reflects on one of the naked protest actions she witnessed at World Social Forum in 2003:

> On the one hand, women's enacting nakedness on their own terms and for their own political ends may disrupt dominant notions that depict women's bodies as passive, powerless, or as sexual objects for sale. On the other hand, in the context of Western, media-saturated societies, women's naked protests may risk re-inscribing dominant discourses onto women's naked bodies by emphasizing that disrobing is the only means of expression available to women. (Sutton 2007, 145)

The conflict that their costume generates is somehow two-sided. While the Femen costume causes disturbance at certain events since it violates the rules and norms of the situation, it does not surpass the normative image of the wearer. The idea of Femen imagery lies in the assumption that their look mirrors the 'real', 'natural' woman's body that is a naked body decorated with slogans. The corporeality of the performer and their performance both act together, not in conflict. The words on their breasts literally fill the frame (the body) with political content (the slogan). The content might be subversive but the form is static and repetitive. Most of the images seen in Femen's actions, images that include female nudity are also constantly seen in mainstream culture. If slogans were to be erased from their bodies they would not be much different from the ones projected by the mass media. Understanding the image of Femen actions through costume, brings recognition of how we need to understand their whole image (body, paint, flowers) as a costume that is created rather than 'stripped'.

During the Free Amina campaign, Femen launched the so-called 'topless jihad' to support their member Amina Tyler (from Tunis). The costume used in this action followed Femen's usual imagery, topless with slogans, but it also brought into discussion the costume of the 'Other': the male Muslim practitioner. The costume can be analysed in layers: at the bottom, jeans that can be read as an everyday item of dress (greatly tied to the wearer's identity); the torso represents the Femen costume (partly tied to the wearer's identity). While on the top the costume becomes a sign: an improvised beard, a drawn unibrow and a turban represent the Other, somebody that the wearer is not. The costume reproduces two mainstream images layered in one person: the young, slim, white woman mixed with a bearded, turban-wearing image of the Muslim masculine Other. By combining these two images, the costume carries a high level of conflict: the costume itself is controversial and displaying it in a public space (on a street in this case) causes disturbance.

SlutWalk also plays with the concept of morality: while Femen does this by undressing, SlutWalkers do it by dressing. This movement combats the logic that rape victims are to be blamed because they 'asked for it' with their clothes. They organize marches wearing explicitly sexualized clothes that are perceived as indecent and 'slutty'. By wearing bras, shorts, skirts, underwear, stockings, high heels and boots they imitate hetero-normative male-gaze sexual stereotypes while their banners display slogans such as: 'No means no!', 'Still not asking for it!' or 'My clothes are not my consent!' (Figure 6.3.4).

Such hyper-sexualized and hyper-feminine, almost grotesque images of a woman that the participants dress as intentionally challenge the concept of female sexuality. It is a method that takes a negative stereotype, affirms it and by doing so removes the power from the power players (the ones who usually control the meaning) to empower the ones that before were just an object. This costume plays with the image of an individual's intimate and everyday clothing and brings it to the point of hyperrealism where it becomes a costume. Wearing these types of clothes as costume is subversive: demanding legitimacy for these outfits (in the form of a costume) with the aim of such clothing (in the form of everyday dress) gaining as much legitimacy and respect as the SlutWalk costume in another setting. Herein lies the conflict of this costume: how it provokes a crash of morality. Clothes similar to those worn on SlutWalk are restricted to private spaces; thus 'revealing' this in public would cause shame for and the potential degradation of the wearer. Yet, the

Figure 6.3.4 *'Marcha de las Putas', SlutWalk in Bogota, 2014. Photo credit: Eitan Abramovich/AFP/Getty Images.*

accompanying behaviour on the SlutWalk is the opposite of shame, it is vivid, festive and full of pride. As such, it contradicts normative standards of behaviour. Their costume is a constitutive part of this approach and its reading.

Conclusion

Costume itself can be used as a method of political expression, struggle and communication. Using clothes as costume is just one of the methods to challenge costume researchers to think of costume as not only a product, goal or an end unto itself but rather as a method that evolves, changes and varies depending on the social environment in which it appears.

The aforementioned cases are forms of collective action,[4] thus costume can be a collective means of expression in which participants are dressed in a similar mode. By doing so, the wearers not only take part in an action but also in a praxis of costuming. In other words, 'costumes invite others to join in' (Shukla 2015: 12). A clear example of this is the use of costume in the solidarity campaign for Pussy Riot. Costuming is a method as well as a participatory tool. The aim of this tool depends on the collective decision of the participants and results in the disturbance of a social situation for the audience/the viewers/the passers-by. They might not expect a costumed action to happen and/or the 'costumes' are not in line with the dominant norm. Discomfort and even repression occur: 'confusion and subversion are a way to disrupt the reproduction of these ruling relations by appropriating dominant symbols and discourses in order to transport a counter-hegemonic message' (Scholl 2010: 164).

The aim of this contribution is not to invent new definitions or force certain concepts, but to open a space for discussion. The examples presented here are part of a costume praxis; however what is more important is that they invite us to reconsider and re-define costume and how such features can be included and deployed. The registers of thought regarding costume should be progressive and 'costume of conflict' is pertinent and apposite to such an approach.

Notes

1. In his novel, *I Served the King of England*, Bohumil Hrabal describes how his character Jan comes to think of his clothing as a costume: 'And I became a waiter once more and put on my tuxedo, but it was different from the other times I had put it on – it felt more like a costume now' (2004: 134).
2. I do recognize that these cases are characterized by two things that I will not delve into further: geopolitics and gender. Two groups (Pussy Riot and Femen) started their activity in Eastern Europe; in a way their activity can be understood as a micro manifestation of broader East–West relations. Like SlutWalk, most of their members or participants are cis women (women identifying as women that is) or from a queer background, but who almost always act from a female-identifying position.
3. Some members of Pussy Riot came from the activist group Voina, known for explicit and direct artivist actions that are politically motivated and articulated.
4. Femen actions, however, are sometimes performed by a single person.

References

Debeljak, A. (1999), *Na ruševinah modernosti.*Ljubljana: Znanstveno in publicistično središče.

Evans, Kate (2003), 'It's Got To Be Silver and Pink: On the Road with Tactical Frivolity', in Notes from Nowhere (eds), *We Are Everywhere: the Irresistible Rise of Global Anticapitalism*, 290–5, London; New York: Verso. Available online: https://artactivism.gn.apc.org/allpdfs/290-Tactical%20Frivolity.pdf (accessed: 12 March 2019).

Hann, R. (2017), 'Debating Critical Costume: Negotiating Ideologies of Appearance, Performance and Disciplinarity', *Studies in Theatre and Performance* 39:1,21–37, Available online: https://www.tandfonline.com/doi/full/10.1080/14682761.2017.1333831 (accessed: 7 April 2019).

Hrabal, B. (2004), *Stregel sem angleškemu kralju*. Ljubljana: Delo.

Johnston, H. (2016), *Culture, Social Movements and Protest*. Oxford: Routledge.

Kershaw, B. (1992), *The Politics of Performance: Radical Theatre as Cultural Intervention*. London: Routledge.

Kershaw, B. ([1999] 2013), *The Radical Performance: Between Brecht and Baudrillard*. London: Routledge.

Knific, B. (2010), 'Šele v narodni noši se počutim, da sem res doma in v svoji koži', in B. Knific (ed.), *V besede in fotografije ujeti izrazi pripadnostnega kostumiranja*, 9–74.Ljubljana: Javni sklad Repiblike Slovenije za kulturne dejavnosti.

Lyon, J. (2016), 'Pussy Riot: Nadya Tolokonnikova talks Fashion and Identity Politics'. *V Magazine*, 20 September. Available online:https://vmagazine.com/article/pussy-riot-nadya-tolokonnikova-talks-fashion-identity-politics/(accessed: 6 April 2019).

Milohnić, A. (2006), 'Artivizem', in B. Kunst and P. Pogorevc (eds), *Sodobne scenske umetnosti*, 184–207. Ljubljana: Maska.

Monks, A. (2010), *The Actor in Costume*. New York; Basingstoke: Palgrave Macmillan.

Routledge, P. (2004), 'Reflections on the G8 Protests: An Interview with General Unrest of the Clandestine Insurgent Rebel Clown Army (CIRCA)',*ACME: An International Journal for Critical Geographies* 3 (2): 112–20. Available online: https://www.acme-journal.org/index.php/acme/article/view/720/582 (accessed: 7 April 2019).

Salem, S. M. (2013), 'Femen's Neocolonial Feminism: When Nudity Becomes a Uniform'. Available online: https://www.academia.edu/6789752/Femens_Neocolonial_Feminism_When_Nudity_Becomes_a_Uniform (accessed: 15 March 2019).

Schechner, R. (2013), *Performance Studies: An introduction* (Third Edition). New York: Routledge.

Scholl, C. (2010), 'Bakunin's Poor Cousins: Engaging Art for Tactical Interventions', *Thamyris/Intersecting* 21: 157–78. Available online: https://www.academia.edu/2355913/Bakunin_s_poor_cousins_Engaging_art_for_tactical_interventions (accessed: 7 April 2019).

Scholl C. (2012), *Two Sides of a Barricade: (Dis)order and Summit Protest in Europe*. New York: SUNY Press.

Shevchenko, I. (2013), 'Sextremism: The New Way for Feminism to Be'. Available online: http://www.huffingtonpost.co.uk/inna-shevchenko/sextremism-the-new-way-for-feminism_b_2634064.html (accessed: 15 March 2019).

Shukla, P. (2015), *Costume: Performing Identities through Dress*. Bloomington: Indiana University Press.

Sutton, B. (2007), 'Naked Protest: Memories of Bodies and Resistance at the World Social Forum', *Journal of International Women's Studies* 8 (3): 139–48.

Warwick, A. and D. Cavallaro (2001), *Fashioning the Frame*. Oxford: Berg.

Snapshots

6.4 From Effect to Affect: The Costumed Body and the Autistic Child

Melissa Trimingham

In this 'snapshot' I take a broad approach to the costumed body, embracing costume, masks and puppets. My analysis is part of a more comprehensive study, the 'Imagining Autism' research project in which I study the haptic effect of costume on the autistic child within immersive theatre environments (Trimingham 2013).[1] There I demonstrated how Mary, on the severe end of the autistic spectrum and largely without speech, empathized with the character of 'Foxy' by donning the heavily padded costume and full head mask, working with its strong haptic affect and imitating the 'Foxy' movements. Here 'effect' changes to 'affect', in other words a cognitive change is brought about, in this case developing empathy for another, an animal. A mask is clearly part of the costumed body, a device that is insistently haptically present (sometimes strongly so, as in the weight of full head masks). It causes us to look and behave in a different physical manner: even at the very basic level of having to turn more deliberately and I suggest more slowly, in order to see others. Arguably, a mask has the capacity to break up the usually 'unthought of' flow of motion into discrete and noticed parts or units. This can be seen whenever a child puts on a mask in 'Imagining Autism': they slow down, they pause, they wait, they listen. Puppets (and both glove and Bunraku style puppets were used in 'Imagining Autism') might also be considered part of the 'costumed body' and this may also be applied to the experience of holding puppets.

I argue here that materiality itself is particularly helpful to the learning of an autistic child. Autism is characterized by the so-called triad of 'impairments' (a difficult and disputed term): differences in communication, social interaction and imagination. Importantly, in the latest diagnostic criteria, *DMS.5* has added sensory differences in processing style to the manual. These differences are relevant if we try to understand why the physical and material aspects of performance, here masks, puppets and costume, work so well with autistic children.

My discussion is framed by an understanding of the body and mind that is deeply holistic, a mind that is 'embodied' not 'embrained' (Damasio 2006: 118) and an ecological understanding of our actions that does not separate our health and well-being from the environment and 'objects' that co-constitute our very being. Children can be *hyper* (over) sensitive to any of the sensory modalities of sight, hearing, smell, taste and touch; or *hypo* (under) sensitive. At worst, their sensitivity can vary in intensity from day-to-day and the modalities themselves can change. One day they may hate to be touched, the next day noise may be unbearable. Another day, they might need intense touch, (such as pressure around their bodies) perhaps because they feel 'bodiless' and distressed; or they may indulge in 'pica', for example eating coal, play-doh or even drinking shampoo. This enables them to experience intense flavours, again offsetting the hypo-sensitivity. It is fair to say that in their world, materiality assumes a greater presence than is usual in neurotypicals. Mostly, the physical world is highly problematic to them but curiously, their odd perceptions of the world have advantages in terms of creativity and imagination: they tend to have highly detailed perception, for example, honing in on minute facets of what they see or experience. This can result in poetry and writing and drawing of extraordinary richness (Roth 2007a, 2007b, 2008; Higashida 2013) or performance art that can deeply affect its audience through somatic empathy.[2]

Remember that costume, masks and puppets are part of this *physical* world but in the immersive theatre environments of 'Imagining Autism', such physical objects seem to offer them less problems than the materiality of the everyday world. Indeed, materiality when harnessed to art and creativity generally seems to be a source of relief, satisfaction and even enjoyment to them. Why?

It seems that the forms of performed materiality with which we are concerned here (costume, masks, puppets), return control of materiality to the child. In a world where materiality is unpredictable, frightening and unpleasant, to control the strong effects of the physical world in however small and/or intense a way might be hugely comforting. For example, an autistic child might be seen to rock obsessively or at a playground, to spin around repeatedly. Perversely, such behaviours actually counter autistic children's sensory perception difficulties, we see them slowing things down, repeating them and making effects bigger and stronger. Perhaps this offsets the highly detailed perception that derails them so often and gives them something they can process more easily by returning control to the child.

How can we turn effect (spinning/rocking/stimming[3]) into *affect*, that is, bringing about a cognitive change? We can do this through the performed object. Masks, costumes and puppets have the similar effect of slowing, repeating or exaggerating elements such as movement, gesture and posture, for example.

I believe that this is connected to the need for autistic children to think in order to learn, as they so often fail to pick up complex social information automatically through play and interactions with others. The world derails them with irrelevant detail. I suggest that autistic children need to be encouraged to stop, learn and mentalize: and materiality in performance enables them to do so. Simon Baron-Cohen remarks:

> One of the manifestations of a basic metarepresentational capacity is a 'theory of mind'. We have reason to believe that autistic children lack such a 'theory'. If this were so, then they would be unable to impute beliefs to others and to predict their behaviour. (Baron-Cohen, Leslie and Frith: 1985: 1)

'Theory of Mind' is the recognition, firstly, that other people have minds different to your own and, secondly, being able to understand that what they might be thinking is different to what you are thinking; thirdly, and crucially, according to Baron-Cohen, the recognition that from about the age of four years, we work out what this might be through inductive reasoning.

I cannot agree with Baron-Cohen that inductive reasoning is the only way that we learn theory of mind. Embodied cognition regards the mind and body as one organ, inseparable in their operation: I do not believe that the mind receives 'messages' from the sensory organs and then uses reason to sort them all out. I believe we are so embedded in the world that the 'sorting-out' takes place at the moment of perception (and begins when we are born) and only patterns we make sense of are perceived. I take the more extreme view that our brain is not only co-dependent on the world outside ourselves in order to think (extended cognition) but that the mind/body is co-constituted by it (this is enacted cognition). We, the mind/body and the outside world, are one 'unit' so far as the working of human cognition is concerned. It's obvious, however, that such a capacity as Baron-Cohen's theory of mind is essential for communicating effectively with other people and interacting socially; it is also essential for recreative imagination (Curry and Ravenscroft: 2002) i.e. being able to 'put yourself in the shoes of another' and indulging in pretend play.

Autistic people have difficulties with all of these things to varying degrees. But I believe that on the whole, this capacity develops unconsciously within us from birth in our interactions with other people and the world, a belief I share with exemplary theorists such as Jean Mandler (1992), Andy Clark (2008) and Shaun Gallagher (2005). If autistic people have problems with theory of mind then this capacity has not fully developed over time, from birth.

Not only do autistic people not pick up 'theory of mind' automatically, but often they miss out on consciously learning it too. They do not engage enough in joint attention or joint action, both of which are essential for learning. I suggest then that their engaging with costume, masks and puppets in a participatory performance enables this conscious learning of 'theory of mind' to take place in a slower, repetitive, 'bigger' and safer place. In this way the effect of materiality becomes affect, materiality becomes a tool to bring about cognitive change in the form of improved empathy, communication and, ultimately, happiness and well-being. This is a big claim, but one I maintain is actively demonstrated in 'Imagining Autism'. Costume has a significant role in testing these ideas.

Notes

1 'Imagining Autism: Drama, Performance and Intermediality as Interventions for Autistic Spectrum Conditions' was an Arts and Humanities Research Council funded project based at the University of Kent (October 2011–March 2014). Investigators were Professor Nicola Shaughnessy (Drama), Dr Melissa Trimingham (Drama), Dr Julie Beadle-Brown (Tizard) and Dr David Wilkinson (Psychology). The three participating schools covered a wide spectrum of ability. The project worked with six to eight participants in each school, aged seven to eleven with a diagnosis of autism. The intervention involved participants in weekly sessions (forty-five minutes) in a portable installation (the 'pod').

2 See for example, Annette Foster's *Membrane* (1998) http://nettypage.com/.

3 'Stimming' is an activity whereby a child (more usually than an adult) shows an unusual interest in an object often carried around with them. For example, a child may carry a leather shoe-lace around and 'twizzle' it continuously.

References

Baron-Cohen, S., A. M. Leslie and U. Frith (1985), 'Does the Autistic Child have a "Theory of Mind"?', *Cognition* 21 (1): 37–46.

Clark, A. (2008), *Supersizing the Mind: Embodiment, Action, Cognitive Extension*. Oxford: Oxford University Press.

Currie, G. and I. Ravenscroft (2002), *Recreative Minds: Imagination in Philosophy and Psychology*. Oxford: Clarenden Press.

Damasio, A. (2006), *Descartes' Error: Emotion, Reason and the Human Brain*. London: Vintage.

Gallagher, S. (2005), *How the Body Shapes the Mind*. Oxford: Oxford University Press.

Higashida, N. (2013), *The Reason I Jump*, trans. K. Yoshida and D. Mitchell. London: Hodder and Stoughton.

Mandler, J. (1992), 'How to Build a Baby: 11: Conceptual Primitives', *Psychology Review* 99 (4): 587–604.

Roth, I. (2007a), 'Imaginative Minds: Concepts, Controversies and Theories' in I. Roth (ed) *Imaginative Minds*, xxi–xxxvi, Proceedings of the British Academy ,147. Oxford: Oxford University Press.

Roth, I. (2007b), 'Autism and the Imaginative Mind' in I. Roth (ed) *Imaginative Minds*, 207–306, Proceedings of the British Academy, 147.Oxford: Oxford University Press.

Roth, I. (2008), 'Imagination and the Awareness of Self in Autistic Spectrum Poets' in M. Osteen (ed) *Autism and Representation*, 145–65. London: Routledge.

Trimingham, M. (2013), 'Touched by Meaning: Haptic Effect in Autism' in N. Shaughnessy (ed.) *Affective Performance and Cognitive Science: Body, Brain and Being*, 229–40. London: Bloomsbury Academic.

6.5 Designing *Tsunami*: Costume Evolution from Documentary to Surrealist

Michiko Kitayama Skinner

Friday 11 March 2011 was one of the most horrific days in Japan's history. The triple disaster of the Tohoku earthquake, tsunami and meltdown at the Fukushima nuclear power plant all happened on the same day, killing 15,896 people and leaving more than 2,000 missing. I was born and raised in Japan and this terrible event was something I could not ignore. My compulsion to tell the story of this tragic day in a theatrical form led me to go to the disaster-struck area of Tohoku in the north-eastern region of Japan near where my mother grew up to interview victims and write, design and produce a docudrama.

Making a documentary is often about reaching out to people who have had extraordinary experiences. One of the most important missions for any documentary is to tell the actual stories of those people. However, the *Tsunami* project took an unexpected turn and in the end the production developed into something far from a 'realistic' style. It was as if you were looking into Dali's surrealistic painting of a clock melting in the desert with its details of hidden insects. The process of creating a documentary in a surrealistic format was a unique and exciting experience. Here, I explain how the people, whose experiences could not be more factual, evolved into 'characters' whom I dressed in asymmetrical, non-realistic costumes.

To begin my theatrical journey, I asked Pulitzer-Prize-winning playwright and my friend Nilo Cruz to work with me. Cruz's works contain the poetic and surrealistic qualities for which I aimed.

Cruz and I travelled to Japan's Iwate Region from 2 May to 11 May 2012, a year after the disaster. In Iwate, we successfully interviewed over twenty local individuals whose occupations included the town's mayor, a journalist, a salesman, a fisherman, a gardener, a monk, a firefighter, an engineer and a traditional Japanese dancer. All of the interviews were audio-recorded. Some were video-recorded. Along the jagged Tohoku coastal line, we saw devastating damage especially in Ozuchi, a small town located deep in a round cove, completely isolated from other communities. As if it were an island within the mainland, Ozuchi's town centre was completely destroyed (80 per cent of its houses were lost) and its mayor was killed, along with 1,300 other victims which represented about 10 per cent of its population. With a new mayor in place, the town was struggling to rebuild and move forward.

The citizens were grappling with how to make their lives safer in the future. We decided to focus on Ozuchi rather than other areas of the region.

The interviews were conducted and transcribed in Japanese and later translated into English. Each interview was filled with personal experiences that had emotional and tense details. Some interviewees had miraculously survived life-threatening situations. Some of them had searched for their loved ones in mountains of debris. After selecting particular interviews, they were dramaturgically sewn together with parts from other survivors. Although based on individual interviews and monologues, the script was written as if all of the interviewees were interweaving and connecting with one another through similar experiences of life and death.

We were profoundly moved by the people of Ozuchi, who were working tirelessly to rebuild the town, pure, fragile, old-soul, but also very strong. The interviewees gradually started to transform into characters of the play. *Tsunami* became a linked patchwork of their emotional testimonies. The *Tsunami* script was completed in the summer of 2013. At this stage, as a scenographer and costume designer, I was still taking in the landscape and people of Ozuchi as they were. I was impressed with how beautiful the ocean was, despite mountains of destruction sitting right behind me on the beach. I was also observing the survivors' faces carefully; people in this region were well known for their atypical light-coloured eyes that were rumoured to resemble the native Japanese *Ainu* tribes.

Despite their small beginnings, many docudramas have accomplished a great deal. Probably the most famous and most successful docudrama is *The Laramie Project* (2000) concerning the brutal 1998 murder of Matthew Shepard, a young gay man in Laramie, Wyoming. Moises Kaufman's Tectonic Theatre Project went to Laramie and interviewed people who had been associated with the event. *The Laramie Project* subsequently became one of the most influential plays of this generation.

It is essential for a docudrama to hold theatrical essence. This is the difference between documentary films, or investigative reporting on television. Theatrical elements and dramatic staging allow audiences to watch the 'unwatchable' and unimaginable as well as gruesome facts and reality. *Tsunami* is written with the voices of actual victims, as with *The Laramie Project*. During the creative process, however, *Tsunami* began to take on a distinctive difference from the latter. This was because of strange experiences that Cruz and I encountered during our visit to the Tohoku region. As we interviewed survivors, many of them spoke to us about how their loved ones were killed or lost. They shared spiritual experiences of how they were communicating with the dead. There was a tour guide whose fiancée was washed away, but she came back vividly in his dreams and spoke to him about their relationship. There was a man who lost his mother, father and brother, talking to us about how he had midnight visitors in his temporary relief housing every night. There was also an inn worker whose dead husband visited her in her bedroom. These people shared their stories as if the victims were still with them and they were having completely normal conversations with the dead. I realized how this story could enable the re-building of traumatic relationships with the deceased. This discovery steered us further away from a journalistic and more toward a dream-like exploratory approach.

After several readings and an extensive workshop, we began the actual production process. The production premiered at the South Miami-Dade Cultural Arts Center in September 2015. This was a new performing arts centre built on the grounds where Hurricane Andrew had ravaged

Figure 6.5.1 Tsunami *(2015), production photograph. South Miami-Dade Cultural Arts Center. Set and costume designer: Michiko Kitayama Skinner. Photograph by: Monica Juarez. Image courtesy of Monica Juarez.*

houses in 1992. It was meaningful for the team to perform the premiere there. Cruz was the director and I served as scenographer and costume designer for the production.

For the style of the production, Cruz and I decided to find inspiration in the techniques and conventions of classical Japanese theatre and in concepts of traditional Japanese clothing design. Meaning is pronounced in particular ways in traditional Japanese Noh Theatre design. From the patterns of the textiles to a small hand prop, there are connotations that not all audience members would necessarily understand. I had watched a Noh production in which a character died and became a ghost. The transformation was made by the actor spinning slowly in a highly stylized way and putting a single leaf on his forehead. That symbolic movement represented the character entering into the world of the dead.

The Noh Theatre, one of the oldest extant theatrical forms in the world, has been continuously performed on the same set design for six hundred years with an enormous *ukiyo-e*-style painted pine tree in the background. This Japanese pine represents 'every' location in the universe. It is an ultimate unit-set. The setting creates a dynamic, but also unified theatrical atmosphere and experience. A traditional Japanese band dressed in kimono plays old-fashioned instruments and sings on stage.

Cruz and I wanted to incorporate some of these types of heightened stylization into our play, especially to tell the stories and dream sequences of the dead and missing. While the play text uses the actual words and phrasing of the real people who lived through this event, dramatic movements and setting were nonfigurative and abstract. I placed a rectangular platform, painted as wet and damaged wood in the centre stage. Above the platform, there was a thin blue fabric drape, which had many wave-like 'tabs' attached. This was used as a projection screen and also as a curtain. Two smaller and taller wooden scaffoldings moved around the stage, sometimes as fishing boats and

Figure 6.5.2 Tsunami *(2015), production photograph of the Burned Body. South Miami-Dade Cultural Arts Center, Set and costume designer: Michiko Kitayama Skinner. Photograph by: Monica Juarez. Image courtesy of Monica Juarez.*

sometimes transforming themselves into morgue shelves for the dead bodies. Large, thin blue fabric pieces were used to create the sea and the Dead Bride's veil. A thicker, textured brown fabric was dragged out of the centre platform to represent the mud that covered destroyed houses.

There were six actors on stage portraying over twenty characters. The intent was never to make the multiracial, international cast into Japanese people; it was about creating a universal language and vision concerning this Japanese event. Each actor wore a costume inspired by traditional Japanese dress to indicate in an abstract way the location and context of the event. By adding costume and/ or props over the basic clothing, they were transformed into different personalities, including the opposite gender.

Japanese clothing has a long and rich history. The typical traditional Japanese clothing or *Wafuku,* such as the kimono, has distinctive looks, textures and colours. Those textures and colours are often unique to each small region and deeply rooted in their own natural resources. Japanese dye techniques are especially impressive. The *Shibori* dye technique is one of the earliest known examples dating from the eighth century. Similar to the Western tie-dye, a different fold, bind, stitch or twist creates different unique patterns of *shibori* for each prefecture. The famous *Aizome*, indigo dyed textiles with white *shibori* patterns resemble Tohoku's calm sea with foamy caps of waves. The Ozuchi community survived thousands of years besides the water, so it was important to create aqueous costume textures. Typical cotton and linen rustic textures or stunning shiny silk textures of Japanese traditional fabrics became an essential part of the show's design, along with the cuts and drapes of the typical kimono. I designed more Japanese-influenced costumes for some survivors who impressed me as 'old souls'. These characters included the 'Fisherman' who was a young man with light-brown bleached hair referring to Japanese pop-culture. Despite his Westernized appearance, he represented a strong attachment to the sea of Ozuchi and the region's famous seaweed fishing. While most of the young population escaped into big cities to seek their fortune and careers, he knew he would stay in Ozuchi. I decided to design him with old-fashioned, baggy, wrapped pants with a textured-silk waist sash inspired by the fishermen in Japanese folklore.

The wrapping style of Japanese kimono is asymmetrical. Symmetrical cuts were emphasized in Western clothing industries, as Western clothing frequently relied on cut rather than drapery and the inherent value of cloth following the Middle Ages. In Japan, people still appreciate things that have gone through long, tedious and mind-numbing building processes. Japanese people believe that the human body itself is not symmetrical. *Fukinsei,* meaning asymmetry and irregularity is one of the signifiers of nature in Zen philosophy. Japanese art also defines the beauty of things as 'imperfect, impermanent, and incomplete'. Withered flowers can hold their own attraction and a lack of Western-style 'balance' (derived from the Greeks and older hieratic traditions) has its own tenderness. This concept inspired me with visions of the tsunami waves hugging the Ozuchi people and their souls.

Also significant for Japanese attire is *Yofuku* or Western clothing. After Japan opened up for trade with the outside world in the 1850s, Western clothing types including the suit, appeared rapidly, particularly within the military, civil and educational sectors. Important characters such as the central storyteller in our docudrama 'Collector', who gathered survivors' stories and testimonies at a temporary rescue facility wore Western-style clothing. This character was inspired by a renowned Tohoku poet, Kenji Miyazawa whose novel, *Night on the Galactic Railroad*, is about two best friends getting on a railroad to travel to the stars. As they make each stop at a different star, it gradually becomes obvious that one of the boys is no longer alive. In the end, the boys must say goodbye to one another, only to revert to the reality that the boy drowned that day. This novel, acclaimed nationwide and from my mother's hometown was a great source of inspiration for the surrealistic nature of our piece. Growing up poor, Miyazawa always wore the same dark wool coat. A portrait of him wandering across a freezing Tohoku field wearing the long dark coat is an iconic image of the indomitable spirit of the Tohoku people. I used the same type of long coat for the 'Collector'.

Hanging from fishing hooks onstage, costume pieces aided our actors in changing from one character to another. A drowned bride returned to her fiancé in a dream wearing a huge, shiny satin dress that resembled waves. The dead, who lie in the morgue burned and charred, were represented by crinkled brown paper. The characters drifted within the fantastical settings of their emotional dreams. Another Japanese aesthetic concept, *Yugen* is difficult to translate and may be amongst the most generally recondite and ineffable Japanese aesthetic ideas. The term is first found in Chinese philosophical texts, where it has the meaning of 'dark' or 'mysterious' (Parkes with Loughnane, 2005/2011). The Chinese character symbol 'Yu (幽)' means ghosts or spirits floating in the air. *Yugen*, to me, represented the Ozuchi people's unbreakable spirit and their efforts to re-establish relationships with the dead and missing. In the end, *Tsunami* was about how you could continue to experience your relationship with somebody who was no longer physically in this world. *Yugen* is not an allusion to another world. It is about this world, this experience (Chase 2014).

Today, Japan is well-known for its high technology and futuristic styles. It is a country of both traditional and ancient customs, as well as the newest inventions and meticulous manufacturing. Many renowned Japanese fashion designers, such as Issey Miyake, Yohji Yamamoto and Rei Kawakubo work with living cultural traditions and transform them into futuristic templates. They use the most advanced technology to create new fibres and fabric textures. But above all, Japan appreciates *Shizen,* the state of no pretence. People in Ozuchi have always known and feared the sea. They knew that nature possessed the power to destroy human lives. Living in such a fragile condition, yet choosing to live in the middle of nature, is the soul of the Ozuchi folk. Reality versus dream, tradition versus modernization, East versus West, *Tsunami* designs aimed to embody the paradoxical dilemma that Japanese society has continually embraced.

References

Chase, C. (2014), 'Yugen (幽玄):Deep Awareness of the Universe' in *Creative by Nature*, posted on 13 December, 2014. Available online: https://creativesystemsthinking.wordpress.com/2014/12/13/yugen-%E5%B9%BD%E7%8E%84-deep-awareness-of-the-universe/ (accessed: 4 March 2019).

Parkes, G. with A. Loughnane (2005/2011), 'Japanese Aesthetics', in *Stanford Encyclopedia of Philosophy* (first published: 12 December 2005; substantive revision: 4 December 2018). Available online: https://plato.stanford.edu/entries/japanese-aesthetics/ (accessed: 4 March 2019).

6.6 The Collaborative Process of Costume Creation: *Travestis* in São Paulo

Fausto Viana

The starting point for this 'snapshot' is the observation of how *travestis* dressed over many years in São Paulo, Brazil. The turning point, however, was the street performance of an inspired Christmas Eve performer. It was 2016 and I was driving my car in the downtown area of Cracolândia, home to many people with substance addiction issues. I saw a group of men standing around a central feminine figure. Although it was dangerous, I stopped to watch her performance.

High heels and a prop on the head holding very long hair, like a contemporary *onkos* (a high head-dress from Greek tragedy) made the figure extremely long and slim. No part of her body was exposed: she was wearing a black leotard of fine lace, large panties and a corset. She had chosen a location where the street light became a stage spot. Behind, was a large brick wall. She was very 'high'. Cocaine? Crack? Hard to say. A radio played music and she danced, playing with her own shadow on the brick wall. Based on her performance, she seemed too experienced to simply be a *travesti* on the sidewalk. I saw the show and left, before her 'pimp' could come and ask for money or something worse.

That woman had put together all the elements that compose a show: costumes, lights, music, choreography, space and even an audience. As a costume designer, I wondered: who dresses these people? Who is behind these street performers? In 2018, I decided to observe *in situ*.

Definition of the Performer and Body Preparation

From the biological point of view, a *travesti* is a man with male genitals. In terms of gender, however, she doesn't recognize herself as a man. *Travestis* are people who embrace external change to re-shape their bodies in order to make them look as feminine as possible. They dress and live their daily lives as people who belong to the female gender. They do not wish to explicitly undergo transgenitalization surgery. Benedetti, a Brazilian anthropologist who has studied the *travesti* community of São Paulo, states that it is not a *sine qua non* condition. Most of the men who are clients of the *travestis* are married men who want to be penetrated by these 'ladies' and who think of them as a woman with a penis, allowing them to disassociate from being gay men, because in their minds they have sex with a woman (Pizani 1995; Rodriques Jr. 1991). Benedetti states that due to the process of body construction and, also, political reasons it is impossible to have a categoric definition of a *travesti*, calling them *travesties* using the feminine article.[1] For him, a *travesti* has the combined wish/project of feeling like a woman. The word *travesti* should not be translated to 'transvestite', i.e. a person who likes to wear feminine dress for fun, eroticism or other reasons. My study relates to *travestis* who are also sex workers and my specific interest is their costume. To me, these *travestis* are street performers.

Life Cycle of *Travestis*

According to the ANTRA (National Association of Travestis and Transsexuals) Report of 2018, *travestis* are expelled from their home at the early age of 13 for reasons including family embarrassment and prejudice. Their school education is very poor: 50 per cent complete elementary school education, of whom 28 per cent go on to high school, while only 0.02 per cent reach university. Exclusion from their families, society and schools results in prostitution: 90 per cent of the community uses sex work as their means of survival (Benevides and Simpson 2018).

After leaving home, she (then a young boy) has very few financial opportunities until hosted by an older *travesti*. This 'new mother' can offer vast possibilities in terms of costume and the change of appearance. Although it is a relation of dependence, the people within these small communities often support each other when no one else is willing to do so.

Within these small households, young boys start using hormones and their young bodies continue to be shaped in the female form. The injection of industrial liquid silicon, used to waterproof bathrooms and inadequate for human use, is used for breast implants.[2] Many go on to have their penis removed, but not the majority.

This manipulation of the external self also assists the *travesti* to define her style, as Benedetti proposes. 'Style will have to detail gesture, voice, speech training, hair shape, make-up, the way she moves, and the way she relates to the other *travestis'* he states (Benedetti 2005: 72). The *travestis* understand that clothes communicate different social attributes (Laver 2012; Benedetti 2005): sex, age and social position. Costume plays an important role as part of her work.

The Wardrobe of the *Travesti*

A *travesti* first encounters feminine costume at home as a boy, cross-dressing using her mother's and sister's garments. In 2005, Benedetti proposed a classification that is still valid for the three types of clothes in a *travesti's* wardrobe: boy (*sic*) clothes (clothes of loose, large cut and neutral colours used when the *travesti* needs to 'hide' her body), long, expensive evening dresses (often embroidered, used in dress competitions with other *travestis*) and working costumes, which are those that interest me here.

In the recent past, thirty years ago, it was very easy to notice a *travesti* in the streets. They looked different, exotic and exaggerated. They overused make-up, were surrounded by a halo of sweet, cheap perfume and used many intense facial and mouth movements in order to attract attention.

In 2005, Benedetti described a *travesti*'s main intention for wearing costumes, as being to show her sensual feminine curves and insinuate female organs. He said that the most typical outfit was a mini-skirt with a very revealing V-shaped blouse and high-heeled shoes. Bras and very small panties were always part of every outfit, and on very cold nights a large, long coat covered the seductive lingerie on the body. Many *travestis* also posed partially naked.

The Costumes on the Street and the Stage of the *Travesti* Performance

In 2018, I conducted *in situ* observations of costumes used in the *travesti* performance. The observation time was from 11.00 pm to 2.00 am. The activity intensifies after 8.00 pm (however, these areas are active in the daytime too); if the space is not occupied by the team pimps, someone else may invade their area. Three different public spaces were chosen to observe the costumes. Santana, a middle-class district in the north zone of São Paulo has included the occupation of two streets by female sex workers and *travestis* since the 1980s. Largo do Arouche is a poor downtown area where female prostitution has been practised since the nineteenth century, male prostitution from the 1950s to 1960s and *travestis* have worked in the area since the 1970s. Avenida Indianópolis, in Moema (south zone) is a wealthy neighbourhood. Pimps and drug dealers dominate these areas and the sex professionals have to pay for their right to a working space there.

All of these areas are connected via a business system. The *travestis* in Avenida Indianópolis were appointed to that area by agents who negotiated their move and subsequently made money from it. The agents trade in people or objects. As Roberto Sposito, the Italian political philosopher suggests: 'It is not in the sense that it is the possession, or not, of things that define the relation between people, but also in the sense that some people are reduced to the state of being things – even if formally they are still people' (Sposito 2016: 23). Prices for sexual intercourse vary from the less-expensive downtown area to the highly valued prices in Moema where one can even engage in a cocaine extravaganza.

I suspected that there could be a difference in the manner that *travestis* dress in the three locations and this assumption proved to be correct. There was a common outfit that appeared in all three areas and which appeared to be something of a male fetish: mini-shorts with simple white blouses. In Santana and in the downtown area, common feminine clothes similar to those worn by everyday women were worn.

There was a wider diversity of costumes in Moema. One, was the very functional *triquini*, mentioned by Benedetti in 2005 and still in use. That costume can be used to quickly flash a breast, the buttocks or even the penis. The *travesti* receives money to flash parts of the body. It is also very useful to try to disguise oneself from the police.

I conducted interviews with those *travestis* who wished to talk. One of my interviewees was Samantha. Her routine performance was to stay at the corner holding a small bag with both hands and wearing a mini polka-dot jump suit, just like an innocent girl. She said she had picked her costume without thinking, but she also added that her clients liked her to look like a little girl. According to her, men in Moema are very demanding: not only about costumes, but also demanding that feet and nails must be well taken care of. During the day, Samantha also works as a prostitute but wearing the combination of shorts and blouse, because men feel attracted to the 'everyday lady'.

Another interviewee was Vanessa, around eighteen-years-old, white and slim. She played the 'full-of-energy lady'. Her hair had three distinct colours and, according to her, the perfect outfit had to reveal how feminine she was. Vanessa used many words from a kind of dialect that many *travestis* use amongst themselves, a mixture of Portuguese and African. She was waiting for her *padê*, in this case a 'stash', a small bag of cocaine, but in the African rituals an offer to an *orixá* (a god or deity). It derives from the Yoruba word *padé*.

I also saw 'glamour-ladies' wearing sparkling sequinned dresses, fishnet tights and bodysuits with lace-up fronts. Padded push-up and half-cup underwired padded, banded bras were a part of performances everywhere.

It is not possible to describe the dressing habits of an entire community here. It can be concluded, however, that the costume of a *travesti* is the result of a lifetime construction that starts with her mother and sister. The *travesti*'s costume is a collaborative process that has elements from the many different people who share her life. The performer doesn't have much of an option: there is no other alternative when prostitution is involved because of the struggle for survival. A *travesti* knows and uses fashion as much as she can, but she also customizes pieces to emphasize certain parts of her body. The space, the street where the *travesti* is performing also determines what she must wear, because that is where the client will approach her. As in many performing arts, costume is the first visual element of connection between the audience and the stage. In this case, the client has expectations that must be fulfilled.

Notes

1 Respect and the guarantee of their political rights are two of the main demands of ANTRA (the National Association of *Travestis* and Transsexuals) which is an organized movement. (See: https://antrabrasil.org/).

2 After some time, these implants will move around the body, normally in the direction of the legs and form tumour-shaped surfaces. Removal is an expensive operation.

References

Benedetti, M. R. (2005), *Toda feita: o corpo e o gênero das travestis*. Rio de Janeiro: Garamond.

Benevides, B. and K. Simpson (2018), 'Mapa dos assassinatos dos travestis e transexuais no Brasil em 2017', *ANTRA* (National Association of Travestis and Transsexuals). Available online: https://antrabrasil.files.wordpress.com/2018/02/relatc3b3rio-mapa-dos-assassinatos-2017-antra.pdf (accessed: 30 March 2019).

Laver, J. (2012), *Costume and Fashion: A Concise History*. London: Thames & Hudson Ltd.

Pizani, M. (1995), *Formas de prazer*. São Paulo: Record.

Rodrigues Jr., O. M. (1991) *Objetos do desejo: das variações sexuais, perversões e desvios*. São Paulo: Iglu Editora.

Sposito, R. (2016), *As pessoas e as coisas*. São Paulo: Rafael Copetti Editor.

Index